NEW National Cur Mathematics

CW00822013

M. J. Tipler
K. M. Vickers

Target Book 5

© M J Tipler and K M Vickers 2000

Original line illustrations © Stanley Thornes (Publishers) Ltd 2000
The right of M J Tipler and K M Vickers to be identified as the authors of this work has
been asserted by them in accordance with the Copyright Designsand Patents Act 1988.

First Published in 2000 by
Stanley Thornes (Publishers) Ltd
Delta Place
27 Bath Road
CHELTENHAM
GL53 7TH

00 01 02 03 04 05/10 9 8 7 6 5 4 3 2 1

A catalogue record of this book is available from the British Library
ISBN 0 7487 3550 X

Illustrated by Hardlines, Charlbury, Oxford

Typeset by Mathematical Composition Setters Limited, Salisbury, Wiltshire

Printed and bound in Spain by Graficas Estella S.A.

Stanley Thornes (Publishers) Ltd

Contents

Preface   iv

Chapter 1   Number   1
Place value, reading and writing numbers   2
Multiplying and dividing by 10, 100
and 1000   2
Addition, subtraction, multiplication and
division   5
Rounding   10
Estimating answers to calculations   11
Directed numbers   13
Order of operations   16
Key points   18
Chapter review   19

Chapter 2   Symmetry   21
Line symmetry   21
Planes of symmetry   25
Rotational symmetry   26
Key points   31
Chapter review   32

Chapter 3
Decimals, Fractions, Percentages   33
Decimal place value   34
Putting decimals in order   34
Rounding decimals to the nearest whole
number   35
Rounding to decimal places   35
Multiplying and dividing by 10, 100
and 1000   36
Equivalent fractions   37
Simplifying fractions   39
Adding and subtracting fractions   40
Fraction and percentage diagrams   44
Changing between decimals, fractions
and percentages   45
Key points   50
Chapter review   51

Chapter 4
Expressions and Formulae   53
Simplifying expressions   54
Expressions with brackets   58
Finding the value of an expression   60
Formulae   62
Key points   66
Chapter review   67

Chapter 5
Calculation using the Calculator   68
Using the calculator to solve problems   68
Order of operations   75
Squares, cubes, square roots and cube roots   75
Fractions on the calculator   76
Solving problems by trial and
improvement   78
Key points   80
Chapter review   80

Chapter 6   Collecting Data   82
Discrete and continuous data   82
Frequency tables   83
Collection sheets   84
Questionnaires   86
Samples   87
Databases   89
Key points   92
Chapter review   92

Chapter 7   Measures   94
Choosing appropriate units   94
Estimating measurements   95
Changing from one metric unit to
another   97
Imperial and metric units   100
Reading scales   102
Speed   105
Key points   108
Chapter review   109

Chapter 8   Equations   110
Function machines   110
Solving 'think of a number' problems   112
Solving equations   114
Equations with brackets   116
Equations with letters on both sides   116
Solving problems using equations   118
Key points   122
Chapter review   123

Chapter 9   Angles   124
Angles   124
Angles made with intersecting lines
(lines that cross)   127
Angles made with parallel lines   129
Key points   138
Chapter review   139

Chapter 10   Special Numbers   140
Special numbers   140
Squares and cubes   144
Square roots and cube roots   145
Other powers   145
Index notation   146
Key points   149
Chapter review   150

Chapter 11   Probability   151
Likelihood   152
Calculating probability   153
Mutually exclusive events   157
Probability of an event not happening   158
Estimating probability   158
Probability scales   160
Expected number   162
Key points   164
Chapter review   165

Chapter 12
Using Decimals, Fractions and Percentages   167
Using decimals   168
Using fractions and percentages   170
VAT, interest, profit, loss, discount,
% increase and % decrease   174
Key points   179
Chapter review   180

Chapter 13
Triangles, Quadrilaterals and Polygons   182
Triangles   182
Quadrilaterals   186
Polygons   190
Key points   194
Chapter review   195

Chapter 14   Patterns   197
Sequences   197
Finding the rule for the nth term   202
Patterns with pictures   203
More patterns   207
Key points   210
Chapter review   210

Chapter 15
Displaying and Analysing Data   212
Bar charts, pictograms, bar-line
graphs   213
Frequency diagrams   218
Frequency polygons   221
Mean, median, mode and range   224
Finding the mean, median, mode and
range from a frequency table   227
Comparing data   228
Key points   232
Chapter review   232

Chapter 16   2-D and 3-D Shapes   235
Drawing 2-D shapes   236
Drawing parallel and perpendicular lines   238
Congruence   240
3-D shapes   241
Nets   243
Isometric drawing   245
Key points   248
Chapter review   249

Chapter 17   Graphs   250
Using coordinates   250
Straight line graphs   253
Graphs of $y = x^2 + a$ 255
Real-life graphs   258
Travel graphs   261
Key points   265
Chapter review   265

Chapter 18   Ratio and Proportion   268
Ratio   268
Proportion   269
Scale drawing   272
Sharing in a given ratio   275
Key points   278
Chapter review   279

Chapter 19   Transformations   280
Reflection   281
Rotation   284
Translation   287
Enlargement   288
Describing transformations   291
Tessellations   292
Key points   295
Chapter review   295

Chapter 20
Pie Charts and Scatter Graphs   297
Reading pie charts   297
Drawing pie charts   300
Scatter graphs   304
Two-way tables   308
Key points   311
Chapter review   311

Chapter 21
Directions, Maps and Bearings   313
Directions   313
Scales on maps   316
Bearings   318
Finding the position of a point using
two bearings   321
Key points   324
Chapter review   325

Chapter 22   Time and Tables   327
Time   327
a.m./p.m. time and 24-hour time   328
Solving time problems   329
Timetables   331
Other tables   333
Key points   338
Chapter review   339

Chapter 23
Perimeter, Area and Volume   340
Perimeter and area   340
Finding areas of squares, rectangles
and triangles   343
Perimeters and areas of composite
shapes   344
Circumference and area of a circle   348
Volume   350
Key points   353
Chapter review   354

Index   355

Preface

Target Books 4 and 5 will give you an excellent preparation for your GCSE examination.

Each chapter begins by telling you what you will learn in the chapter.

The shaded sections give clear explanations and worked examples that are easy to follow.

In this book there are many *Worked exam questions*. These should help you prepare for your GCSE examination. The part which is in **bold** in the answer shows you what you should write down as your answer.

The questions in each exercise begin with easy questions and gradually get harder. Many of these questions are actual exam questions for you to practise.

Throughout each chapter there are *Investigations* and *Tasks*. These are to help you develop skills for 'using and applying mathematics'.

Each chapter has either one or two *Homework/Review* exercises. These have questions similar to the ones you will have done in the previous few pages. Use these to help you review your work as you go along.

Near the end of each chapter there is a list of *Key points*. These tell you what you should know. You could use them as a checklist for your learning.

At the end of each chapter there is a *Chapter review*. You could use this to test yourself. The questions are similar to the questions you might get in your GCSE examination.

If you see ▦ this means you will need a calculator for the exercise.

If you see ✗ this means you are not allowed to use a calculator for the exercise.

We know you will enjoy using this book.

Best wishes for a successful year.

M J Tipler
K M Vickers

1 Number

By the end of this chapter you will be able to:

* give the place value of a number
* read and write numbers
* put numbers in order
* multiply and divide by 10, 100 and 1000
* add, subtract, multiply and divide whole numbers
* round numbers to the nearest 10 or 100 or 1000
* estimate the answers to calculations
* use, put in order, add and subtract directed numbers
* do addition, subtraction, multiplication, division and brackets in the right order.

Getting started ....

A What is my number?

1. It is a two-digit number.
   It can be divided by 4 and 5.
   When I divide it by 9, there is a remainder of 4.

2. It is between 20 and 50.
   It can be divided by 5.
   When I divide it by 6, there is a remainder of 5.

3. It is between 0 and 70.
   When I divide it by 3 or 7 there is no remainder.
   When I divide it by 4 there is a remainder of 2.

4. It is between 0 and 70.
   When I divide it by 3, 5 or 6 there is no remainder.
   When I divide it by 9 there is a remainder of 6.

B

What digit does ★ stand for?

Place value, reading and writing numbers

The **place** of a digit tells you its **value**.
The number 17 650 042 is shown in this place value chart.

Hundreds of millions	Tens of millions	Millions	Hundreds of thousands	Tens of thousands	Thousands	Hundreds	Tens	Ones (units)
	1	7	6	5	0	0	4	2

We read this as seventeen million, six hundred and fifty thousand and forty two.
700 458 is read as seven hundred thousand, four hundred and fifty eight.

Multiplying and dividing by 10, 100 and 1000

To **multiply by 10** move each digit **one place** to the **left**
multiply by 100 move each digit **two places** to the **left**
multiply by 1000 move each digit **three places** to the **left**.

Examples $\qquad$ 37 × 10 = 370 $\qquad$ 8 × 1000 = 8000 $\qquad$ 42 × 100 = 4200

To **divide by 10** move each digit **one place** to the **right**
divide by 100 move each digit **two places** to the **right**
divide by 1000 move each digit **three places** to the **right**.

Examples $\qquad$ 560 ÷ 10 = 56 $\qquad$ 68 000 ÷ 100 = 680 $\qquad$ 72 000 ÷ 1000 = 72

Worked Exam Question

WJEC

(a) How many thousands are there in 7845? (1)
(b) Write in words the number 4002. (1)
(c) Arrange the following numbers in order of size, smallest first. (1)
    23 $\quad$ 147 $\quad$ 98 $\quad$ 4 $\quad$ 245 $\quad$ 987

Always note carefully whether the biggest or smallest is wanted first.

Answer (a) The 7 is in the thousands place.
$\qquad$ So there are 7 thousands.
$\qquad$ The answer is **7**.

The part in **bold** is the way your answer should be written.

(b) There are 4 thousands, no hundreds, no tens and 2 ones.
$\qquad$ We write this as **four thousand and two**.

(c) From smallest to biggest the numbers are
$\qquad$ 4 $\quad$ 23 $\quad$ 98 $\quad$ 147 $\quad$ 245 $\quad$ 987.

Examples   1.   What is the value of 6 in the number 4680?
                2.   The number 4680 is multiplied by 10.
                      What is the value of 6 in the answer?

Answers   1.   The 6 is in the hundreds place.
                      So the value of 6 is **600**.
                2.   4680 × 10 = 46 800.
                      The 6 is now in the thousands place.
                      The value of 6 in 46 800 is **6000**.

> When a number is multiplied by 10, the value of each digit becomes 10 times bigger.

Exercise 1

A   Write these numbers in words.
   1.   532   2. 609   3. 810   4. 912   5. 7620
   6.   8002   7. 2011   8. 5068   9. 50 005   10. 41 700

B   Write these numbers in figures.
   1.   three thousand, one hundred and seven
   2.   five thousand and eighteen
   3.   sixty five thousand and sixty two
   4.   one hundred thousand and fifty seven
   5.   seventy million
   6.   four and a half million

C   Write these numbers in order, biggest first.
   1.   59, 46, 56, 49, 33, 17   2. 8, 52, 19, 27, 43, 34
   3.   163, 136, 106, 103, 306, 603   4. 524, 245, 452, 542, 425
   5.   87, 69, 169, 108, 78, 136   6. 424, 242, 442, 224, 422

D   Work out the answers to these.
   1.   57 × 10   2. 83 × 100   3. 50 × 10   4. 81 × 1000
   5.   600 ÷ 10   6. 4230 ÷ 10   7. 8200 ÷ 100   8. 56 000 ÷ 100
   9.   72 000 ÷ 1000   10. 45 000 ÷ 1000

E   1.   Write the number 508 in words.
        2.   The number 508 is multiplied by 10.
             (a)   Write the answer in figures.
             (b)   Write the answer in words.

F   What is the value of the 8 in these numbers?
   1. 583   2. 284   3. 138   4. 8642
   5. 7831   6. 78 213   7. 80 604   8. 185 723
   9. 148 009   10. 63 824   11. 4682   12. 13 984
   13. 700 008   14. 800 007   15. 586 421   16. 348 275

G 1. What is the value of the 9 in the number 5930?
    2. The number 5930 is multiplied by 10.
       What is the value of the 9 in the answer?
    3. The number 5930 is divided by 10.
       What is the value of the 9 in the answer?

H The table gives the length of four rivers.
    1. Write the names of the four rivers in order
       of length.
       Put the longest river first.
    2. The Severn is added to the list of rivers
       in **1**.
       It is the 2nd longest.
       What can be said about the length of the
       river Severn ?

Shannon	386 km
Tay	188 km
Thames	346 km
Usk	110 km

I

WJEC

(a) Write in figures the number seven thousand two hundred
    and six. (1)
(b) How many hundreds are there in 936? (1)
(c) Write down the largest four-digit number that can be made
    using each of the four figures 4, 8, 3, 6 once only. (1)

J

Paul has five numbered discs.   SEG

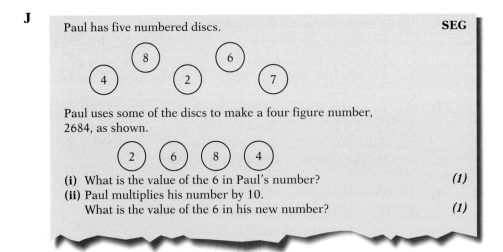

Paul uses some of the discs to make a four figure number,
2684, as shown.

(i) What is the value of the 6 in Paul's number? (1)
(ii) Paul multiplies his number by 10.
    What is the value of the 6 in his new number? (1)

K Write these in figures.

The number which is
  1. 1 less than 600   **2.** 1000 more than 16 842
  3. 1 less than 4000   **4.** 100 more than 2562
  5. 10 less than 70 000 **6.** 100 less than 20 000.

Addition, subtraction, multiplication and division

We often have to use **addition**, **subtraction**, **multiplication** and **division** to solve number problems. When calculators are not allowed, working must be shown.

Worked Exam Questions

SEG

1. 186 pupils at a school use the tuck shop.
   There are 395 pupils in the school.
   Work out how many pupils do not use the tuck shop. *(2)*

Answer We must subtract 186 from 395.
            209 pupils did not use the tuck shop.

$$\begin{array}{r} 3\overset{8}{9}\overset{1}{5} \\ -\ 186 \\ \hline 209 \end{array}$$

> Remember to show all your working.

LONDON

2. There are 560 pupils going on a school trip.
   Each pupil pays £14 to go on the trip.
   Work out the total amount paid by the pupils *(2)*

Answer We must multiply 560 by 14.
            The total amount paid is **£7840**.

$$\begin{array}{r} 560 \\ \times\ _2 14 \\ \hline 2240 \\ 5600 \\ \hline 7840 \end{array}$$

> Don't forget to put the zero here.

> Always check your answer to see if it is reasonable.

WJEC

3. Alison wants to buy as many golf balls as she can for £15. The golf balls cost 70p each.
   (a) How many golf balls can she buy? *(2)*
   (b) How much change should she be given? *(1)*

Answer **(a)** £15 is 1500 p.
                   We must divide 1500 by 70.
                   The answer is 21 with remainder 30.
                   This means she can buy **21** golf balls.
           (b) The remainder is 30.
                   She should be given **30p** change.

$$\begin{array}{r} 21r30 \\ 70\overline{)1500} \\ 140 \\ \hline 100 \\ 70 \\ \hline 30 \end{array}$$

> Change pounds into pence.

Exercise 2

A Work out the answers to these.
1. $868 + 1247$ 2. $8629 - 3058$ 3. 26×132 4. 375×23
5. 584×69 6. $782 \div 23$ 7. $768 \div 32$ 8. $665 \div 19$

B

LONDON

Write down two different pairs of numbers that multiply together to make 24.

(2)

C 26 and 27 are consecutive numbers because 27 is one more than 26.
I add two consecutive numbers together and get 39.
What are the numbers?

D

SEG

Simon makes two long jumps.
His first jump is 285 cm long.
His second jump is 371 cm long.
How much further is Simon's second jump than his first?

(1)

E Sharon and Tim are on holiday in Spain.
1. They buy drinks costing 375 pesetas and 240 pesetas.
   (a) Find the total cost of their drinks.
   (b) They pay for the drinks with a 1000 peseta note.
       How much change should they be given?

2. They stay at a hotel that has a minibus for hire.
   The minibus can hold a maximum of 8 people.
   (a) The minibus was hired 15 times one day
       and was fully loaded on each occasion.
       Find the total number of people who rode
       in the minibus during that day.
   (b) On a different day, the total number of
       people who rode in the minibus was 152.
       The bus was fully loaded each time.
       Find how many times the minibus was
       hired that day.

F

WJEC

Albert buys packets of grass seed to seed his new lawn. The area of his lawn is 98 square metres.
The seed in each packet is enough to cover 8 square metres.
Find the total number of packets of seed that Albert buys.

(2)

G

NEAB

Helen buys a car.
She pays £676 to insure it for the first year.
How much is this per week?
(Use 52 weeks in a year.)
Write down all your working.

(1)

H Cakes cost 35p each.
You have £5 to spend on cakes.
1. How many cakes can you buy?
2. How much change would you get?

I How many 27-seater buses are needed to carry 378 people to a football game?

J A shopkeeper wants to store 500 pens in boxes.
Each box can store 36 pens.
How many boxes can she fill and how many pens will be left over?

K Rob has two £5 notes. He buys some packets of seeds costing 75p each.
1. How many packets of seeds can he buy?
2. How much change should he be given?

L

(a) 693 fans went to a 'Take This' pop concert.
The tickets cost £14 each.
Calculate the total amount paid by the fans. *(2)*

(b) (i) All of these fans travelled on 52-seater coaches.
What is the least number of coaches that could be used? *(2)*
(ii) On the return journey one coach failed to turn up.
How many fans had to be left behind? *(2)*

MEG

'Take This'

£14

ROW 4   Admission   SEAT 27

M

MEG

In a cricket match, England's two scores were 326 runs and 397 runs.
Australia's two scores were 425 runs and 292 runs.
Which team had the higher total score?
How many more runs did they score than the other team? *(4)*

N

MEG

Leroy makes 24 equal monthly payments to repay a debt of £816.
Find the amount of each monthly payment. *(3)*

O

NEAB

Jaimie's grandad said, 'When I was at school there were 12 pennies in 1 shilling and 20 shillings in £1.'
How many pennies were there in £1 when Jaimie's grandad was at school? *(2)*

Task

You will need   a stopwatch or a watch with a second hand

> To multiply a number by 25 it is quicker to multiply it by 100 and then divide by 4.

Time yourself to

1. do the following multiplications by multiplying by 25
2. do the same multiplications by multiplying by 100 and then dividing by 4.

Which way is faster?

86×25 48×25 72×25 123×25 439×25

Investigation

Two brothers, Paul and Leroy, usually save £1 each per week. Paul suggests a different way of saving. He decides to save 1p next week, 2p the week after, 4p the week after that, double again the next week and so on.
Leroy continues to save £1 each week.
Investigate Paul's suggestion.
Compare the total amounts saved by Paul and Leroy after 6 weeks, 12 weeks, 18 weeks, 24 weeks and so on.

Homework/Review 1

A   1. Write the number 1850 in words.
   2. What is the value of the 5 in the number 1850?

B

	MEG
(a) Write the number one thousand and eleven in figures.	(1)
(b) Multiply one thousand and eleven by ten, writing your answer	
(i) in figures	(2)
(ii) in words.	(1)

C 1. Jack had 386 sacks of oranges. Each sack contained 100 oranges.
How many oranges did he have altogether?

2. Joc bought a box of apples with 140 apples in it. She divided them into 10 equal bags.
How many would be in each bag?

D

> Write down the following numbers in order of size, with the smallest number first.
>
>   473,   734,   347,   437,   743
>
> **MEG**
>
> *(2)*

E Mary and Gareth describe the same whole number.

Mary says, 'It is bigger than 4.'
Gareth says, 'It is smaller than 11.'
Write down all possible values of the number.

F

> Make a copy of this.
> Fill in the missing numbers.
>
> (i)   7__ × 100 = __2__0
> (ii)   __0 × 30 = __80__
>
> **NEAB**
>
> *(2)*
> *(2)*

G A packet of sweets costs 28 pence.

Work out the total cost of 48 packets of sweets.

H

> A company sells golf balls in packs of 36.
> How many packs can be filled using 775 golf balls and how many golf balls will be left over?
>
> **WJEC**
>
> *(4)*

I

> **(a)** John replaced the roof tiles on his garage and house.   **WJEC**
> He used 243 tiles on the garage and 678 tiles on the house.
>   (i)   How many tiles did he use altogether?
>   (ii)   To repair his roof John bought 1000 tiles. Fifty tiles were broken while the roof was being repaired.
>   How many unbroken tiles were left over after John repaired his roof?   *(2)*
>
> **(b)** Mary sells records and books in a jumble sale.
>   (i)   She sold 26 books at 6p each.
>   How much money did she receive for the books?
>   (ii)   The money received for the sale of records was 224p.
>   Each record was sold for 8p. How many records were sold?   *(4)*

Rounding

178 to the **nearest ten** is 180.

5624 to the **nearest hundred** is 5600.

42 805 to the **nearest thousand** is 43 000.

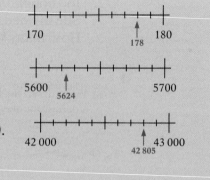

If a number is halfway, we round up.

Examples
125 to the nearest ten is 130.
8450 to the nearest hundred is 8500.
7500 to the nearest thousand is 8000.

Worked Exam Question

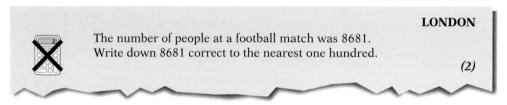

LONDON

The number of people at a football match was 8681.
Write down 8681 correct to the nearest one hundred.

(2)

Answer
We have to give the answer to the nearest hundred.
The answer will be 8600 or 8700.
8681 is closer to 8700.
So 8681 to the nearest hundred is **8700**.

Exercise 3

A Round these numbers.
1. 386 to the nearest 10
2. 4821 to the nearest 100
3. 4724 to the nearest 100
4. 8894 to the nearest 1000
5. 5062 to the nearest 1000
6. 4685 to the nearest 10
7. 7850 to the nearest 100
8. 9500 to the nearest 1000
9. 56 842 to the nearest 100
10. 56 842 to the nearest 1000

B 5682 people went to a football game.
The newspaper said 5700 people had gone to
the game.
To what accuracy has this number been given?

C Max wrote down a 4-digit number.
He rounded it to the nearest 1000 and got 5000.
1. What is the smallest number he could have
written down?
2. What is the biggest number he could have written down?

D   Jasmine rounded the amount she had in her bank account to the nearest hundred pounds and got £1500.
She rounded it to the nearest ten pounds and got £1450.
Write down three possible amounts Jasmine could have in her bank account.

E   19 142 people bought tickets in a raffle.
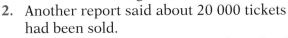
1. A report said about 19 000 tickets had been sold.
   To what accuracy had the number of tickets sold been given?
2. Another report said about 20 000 tickets had been sold.
   To what accuracy had the number of tickets sold been given?

F   The size of a crowd at a cricket match is given as 24 700 to the nearest hundred.
1. What is the smallest number the crowd could be?
2. What is the largest number the crowd could be?

Estimating answers to calculations

To **estimate** an answer we round the numbers so we can do the calculation in our head.

Example   695 + 804
695 is about 700.   804 is about 800   **700 + 800 = 1500**
So 695 + 804 is about 1500.

Example   31 × 59
31 is about 30.   59 is about 60.   **30 × 60 = 1800**
So 31 × 59 is about 1800.

Estimating can be used to check the **reasonableness** of answers to calculations.

Worked Exam Questions

1. A cable is 592 m long.
Pieces of length 32 m are cut from it.
Peter estimates the number of pieces that can be cut from the length of cable.
Write down two numbers he could have used to make his estimate.   *(1)*

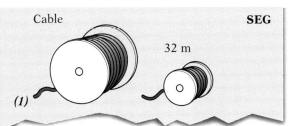

Answer   592 is about 600 m.
32 m is about 30 m.
Two numbers he could have used to make his estimate are **600** and **30**.

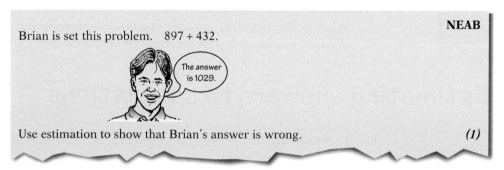

WJEC

2. Obtain an **ESTIMATE** for $\dfrac{314 \times 18}{62}$.   *(2)*

Answer   314 is about 300. 18 is about 20.
62 is about 60.

An estimate for $\dfrac{314 \times 18}{62}$ is **100**.

$\dfrac{300 \times 20}{60} = \dfrac{6000}{60}$

$= 100$

> Multiply the two numbers on the top first.

Exercise 4   **A** Estimate the answers to these calculations.

1. $39 + 41$	**2.** $602 + 809$	**3.** $397 - 132$	**4.** $888 - 406$
5. 98×51	**6.** 48×110	**7.** $897 \div 32$	**8.** 603×38
9. $990 \div 22$	**10.** 496×89	**11.** $808 \div 41$	**12.** 508×33
13. 196×204	**14.** $3980 \div 21$	**15.** $5872 \div 61$	**16.** $4804 \div 81$

B

NEAB

Brian is set this problem. $897 + 432$.

The answer is 1029.

Use estimation to show that Brian's answer is wrong.   *(1)*

C   The total number of boys in a school is 431.
The total number of girls in the same school
is 518.
What simple calculation could you do to show
that the total number of pupils in the school is
greater than 900?

D   There are 48 bottles of cola in a box.
A café sells approximately 2000 bottles of cola each week.
1. Which of these is the most sensible estimate for the number of boxes of
cola sold each week?
        A 4   **B** 40   **C** 400   **D** 50   **E** 5
2. Explain your answer.

E   1. 31×39 is about 1200.
Explain how this estimate was found.
2. Show how you would find an estimate for $2980 \div 23$.
Write down your estimate.

F   A cinema has 32 rows of seats. Each row has 59 seats.
Write down the numbers you could use to get an approximate answer to
32×59.

G

NEAB

Show how you can estimate the value of 97×6.   *(1)*

H

A fairy cake weighs about 20 g.
(a) Estimate the weight of one hundred fairy cakes, in grams. *(1)*
(b) Aimee makes some fairy cakes.
Altogether the fairy cakes weigh 524 g.
Estimate how many fairy cakes she makes. *(1)*

I

A caretaker is setting out a school hall for an assembly. He needs to
seat 591 pupils altogether, and he can get 32 seats in each row.
Estimate how many rows of seats the caretaker needs, and explain how
you worked out this approximate answer. *(4)*

J

John's holiday costs £621.
John has to pay the £621 in 27 equal weekly amounts.
(i) Work out how much he must pay each week.
(ii) Write down an approximate calculation you could use to check
your answer.
(iii) Work out the answer to the approximate calculation. *(5)*

Directed numbers

Directed numbers are positive and negative numbers.
They are sometimes called **integers**.
We use negative numbers to represent quantities less than zero.

Examples   On a very cold day in Edinburgh the temperature was $-6\,°C$.
This is $6\,°C$ below zero.

Bill spent £25 more than he had in his bank account.
His bank balance is $-£25$. This is written as £25.00 DR.

A submarine is at -40 m.
This is 40 m below sea level.

We can show directed numbers on a **number line**.

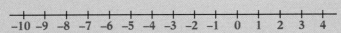

Putting directed numbers in order

$-18\,°C$ is colder than $-14\,°C$.

Example   Put these numbers in order from biggest to smallest.
$-27, 4, -32, -18, -3, -7, 5, 8$

Answer   Numbers greater than zero are bigger than those less than zero.
The first three numbers are 8, 5, 4.
The further below zero we go the smaller the number.
The numbers in order are:
$8, 5, 4, -3, -7, -18, -27, -32$.

Adding and subtracting directed numbers

It is best to use a number line to help you **add and subtract** directed numbers.

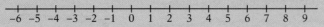

$$4 - 6 = -2$$

$$-3 + 8 = 5$$

$$-2 - 1 = -3$$

$$-4 - (-7) = 3$$

Worked Exam Question

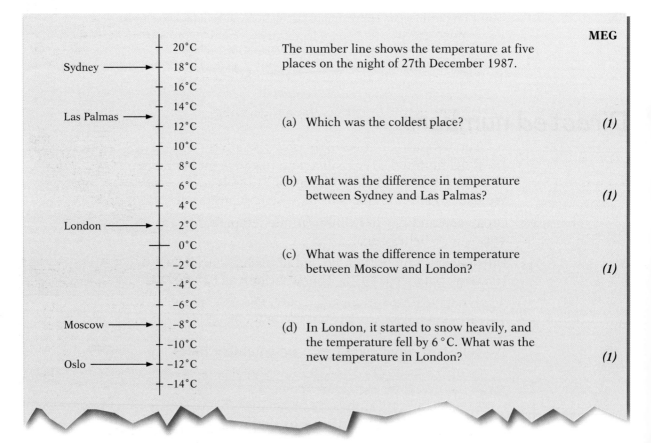

MEG

The number line shows the temperature at five places on the night of 27th December 1987.

(a) Which was the coldest place?   *(1)*

(b) What was the difference in temperature between Sydney and Las Palmas?   *(1)*

(c) What was the difference in temperature between Moscow and London?   *(1)*

(d) In London, it started to snow heavily, and the temperature fell by 6 °C. What was the new temperature in London?   *(1)*

Answer (a) Oslo

(b) Las Palmas is halfway between 12 °C and 14 °C, so it is 13 °C.
Sydney is 18 °C.   18 − 13 = 5
The difference is **5 °C**.

(c) London is 2 °C. Moscow is −8 °C.
The difference is **10 °C**.

(d) 2 °C − 6 °C = −4 °C.
The new temperature is **−4 °C**.

Exercise 5

A Put these temperatures in order from coldest to warmest.
1. –6 °C, –17 °C, 0 °C, 8 °C
2. –13 °C, –2 °C, 4 °C, –8 °C, –5 °C
3. 7 °C, 12 °C, –4 °C, –27 °C, 30 °C
4. –16 °C, –34 °C, 14 °C, –3 °C, 16 °C, –21 °C

B Put these numbers in order from biggest to smallest.
1. –4, –2, 0, 8, –5, 7, 3
2. –26, –16, –31, 8, 31, 14, –19
3. –42, –16, –15, –7, –3, –31
4. 27, –6, 18, –12, 21, –27
5. –15, –34, 8, 0, 6, –6, –2
6. –1, –11, –111, 1, 11, 101, –101

C Find the answers to these.
1. 4 – 8
2. –2 + 7
3. –12 + 8
4. –5 – 7
5. 7 – 12
6. –9 + (–6)
7. –3 + (–1)
8. 7 – (–8)
9. –3 – (–1)
10. –2 – (–4)
11. –1 – (–3)
12. 5 + (–12)

D One morning the temperature went from –3 °C to 8 °C.
1. By how many degrees did the temperature rise?
2. Later in the day the temperature fell by ten degrees from 8 °C. What was the temperature after the fall?

E Sue put yeast in a freezer which was at –17 °C.
How many degrees is this below the storage temperature?

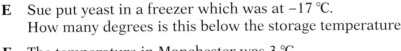

F The temperature in Manchester was 3 °C.
1. The weather forecast said it would fall to –3 °C overnight.
By how many degrees is the temperature expected to fall?
2. The temperature overnight was 2 °C lower than expected.
What did the temperature actually fall to overnight?

G A submarine is at –16 m. It dives to –50 m.
How many metres did it dive?

H This table shows the temperatures in five cities at midday and at midnight.
1. Which city was warmest at midnight?
2. How much colder was Aberdeen than Glasgow at midnight?
3. Which place had the greatest drop in temperature from midday to midnight?
4. Which place had the smallest drop in temperature from midday to midnight?

City	Temp at midday	Temp at midnight
Exeter	4 °C	–1 °C
Coventry	3 °C	–6 °C
Leeds	8 °C	2 °C
Glasgow	6 °C	–4 °C
Aberdeen	5 °C	–7 °C

I In a quiz there are ten questions. Marks are given as follows.

Correct answer	3 marks
Incorrect answer	–2 marks
No answer	0 marks

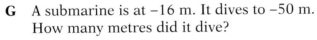

1. Charles answers 5 questions correctly, 3 incorrectly and the other 2 he doesn't answer.
Calculate his total score.
2. Ben got –5. Give an example of how he could have got this score.

Order of operations

The **order** we do operations is:

1. brackets
2. multiplication and division
3. addition and subtraction.

Examples $3 \times (6 + 2) = 3 \times 8$
$= 24$
Do first

$5 \times 2 + 3 \times 4 = 10 + 12$
$= 22$
Do first   Do first

$18 \div (4 + 2) = 18 \div 6$
$= 3$
Do first

Exercise 6

A Work out the answers to these.

1. $(3 + 4) \times 4$
2. $12 \div (6 - 2)$
3. $(3 + 1) \times (5 - 3)$
4. $16 \div (9 - 5)$
5. $(8 - 4) \times 3$
6. $25 \div (12 - 7)$
7. $16 - 3 \times 5$
8. $20 - 5 \times 4$
9. $30 - 5 \times 5$
10. $(10 - 6) \times (14 - 4)$
11. $(2 + 3) \times (10 - 3)$
12. $(8 + 1) \times (12 - 6)$
13. $(20 + 10) \div (12 - 7)$
14. $(30 + 40) \div (14 - 7)$

B Write true or false for each of these.

1. $(4 + 5) + 6 = 4 + (5 + 6)$
2. $4 \times 7 - 4 \times 3 = 4 \times (7 - 3)$
3. $(3 \times 4) + 5 = 3 \times (4 + 5)$
4. $(9 - 5) \times 4 = 9 \times 4 - 5 \times 4$
5. $(8 - 3) \times 4 = 8 - (3 \times 4)$
6. $3 \times 6 + 2 \times 6 = (3 + 2) \times 6$

Puzzle

Put **+**, **−**, **×** or **÷** to make the following true.

You may use brackets.
Some have more than one answer.

Example 4   4   4   4 = 1   can be written as
$(4 \times 4) \div (4 \times 4) = 1$ or $(4 + 4 - 4) \div 4 = 1$.

1. 4   4   4   4 = 16
2. 4   4   4   4 = 8
3. 4   4   4   4 = 256
4. 4   4   4   4 = 60
5. 4   4   4   4 = 48
6. 4   4   4   4 = 4
7. 4   4   4   4 = 0

Homework/Review 2

A

SEG

The summit of Mount Everest is at a height of 29 078 feet.
(a) A climber is at a height of 28 198 feet.
Calculate how far he is below the summit. *(1)*
(b) What is the height of Mount Everest to the nearest ten feet? *(1)*
(c) In a newspaper report the height of Mount Everest is given
as 30 000 feet.
To what accuracy has the height been given? *(1)*

B A report gave the number of people at a concert as 3700 to the nearest
hundred. What is the smallest number of people who could have been at
the concert?

C The total number of children at a cinema is 409.
The total number of adults at the same cinema is 621.
Without adding these two numbers together, write
down a simple calculation you could do to show that
the total number at the cinema is greater than 1000.

D Estimate the answers to these calculations.

1. 89×22 2. 189×42 3. $2832 \div 28$ 4. 604×49

5. $8960 \div 29$ 6. $5869 \div 19$ 7. $\dfrac{114 \times 52}{21}$ 8. $\dfrac{389 \times 59}{29}$

E

WJEC

The following is a weather page from CEEFAX

Weather report for 14th December			
	Daily hours of sunshine	Minimum night-time temperature (°C)	Maximum daytime temperature (°C)
Aberdeen	2.3	−15	−5
Aviemore	0	−18	−7
Belfast	1.3	−1	4
Birmingham	4.1	0	6
Bognor Regis	3.4	2	9
Bournemouth	5.4	4	11
Bristol	1.1	−3	2
Buxton	0	−7	−3
Cardiff	0.8	−2	−1

(a) Which place had the warmest daytime temperature? *(1)*
(b) Which place had the coldest night-time temperature? *(1)*
(c) What is the difference between the minimum night-time temperatures
in Aberdeen and Cardiff? *(1)*
(d) What is the difference between the maximum daytime temperatures
in Bournemouth and Buxton? *(1)*

✔ KEY POINTS

✔ This chart shows **place value**.

Hundreds of millions	Tens of millions	Millions	Hundreds of thousands	Tens of thousands	Thousands	Hundreds	Tens	Ones (units)

✔ To **multiply by 10** move each digit **one place** to the **left**.
To **multiply by 100** move each digit **two places** to the **left**.
To **multiply by 1000** move each digit **three places** to the **left**.
To **divide by 10** move each digit **one place** to the **right**.
To **divide by 100** move each digit **two places** to the **right**.
To **divide by 1000** move each digit **three places** to the **right**.

✔ 156 to the nearest 10 is 160.
2562 to the nearest 100 is 2600.
8164 to the nearest 1000 is 8000.
437 824 to the nearest 10 000 is 440 000.

675 to the nearest 10 is 680.
2650 to the nearest 100 is 2700.
7500 to the nearest 1000 is 8000.
565 000 to the nearest 10 000 is 570 000.

✔ To **estimate an answer**, round each number so that you can do the calculation easily in your head.

Example 692×41 is about 700×40.
$700 \times 40 = 28\,000$.
So 692×41 is about $28\,000$.

✔ We can **add and subtract directed numbers** and **put them in order** using a number line.

Examples
$5 - 9 = -4$

$-6 - (-2) = -4$

✔ The **order in which we do operations** is:
brackets **then**
multiplication and division **then**
addition and subtraction.

Examples
$5 \times (8 - 6) = 5 \times 2$
        $= 10$
Do first

$(40 - 20) \div 5 = 20 \div 5$
            $= 4$
Do first

$8 \times 3 + 20 \div 5 = 24 + 4$
                $= 28$
Do first   **Do first**

◄◄ CHAPTER REVIEW ◄◄ ✖

◄◄
Exercise 1
on page 3

A

LONDON

(a) Write the number 807 in words. *(1)*
(b) Write the number one hundred thousand and fifty seven in figures. *(1)*
(c) Write these numbers in order. Start with the smallest number.
    5342, 2104, 483, 2901, 712 *(2)*

◄◄
Exercise 1
on page 3

B

WJEC

(a) What is the value of the 4 in the number 3648? *(1)*
(b) The number 2539 is multiplied by 10. What is the value of the 5 in the answer? *(1)*
(c) The number 687 is divided by 10. What is the value of the 6 in the answer? *(1)*

◄◄
Exercises 2 and 4
on pages 6 and 12

C

WJEC

(a) Mary and John carry out some work on their house.
They buy a new bathroom suite costing £496, and pay £284 to have the suite fitted and the bathroom tiled.
  (i) John tells Mary that the total cost of buying and fitting the suite, and tiling the bathroom is £850.
Without adding these actual costs, write down a **simple** calculation which will show that John is wrong.
  (ii) Find the actual cost of buying and fitting the suite and tiling the bathroom.
  (iii) John and Mary have saved £950 to buy and fit a new bathroom suite and to tile the bathroom. How much money is left over? *(3)*
(b) (i) John buys 8 tins of paint to paint the outside walls of the house.
Each tin costs £14.
Find the total cost of the paint.
  (ii) Mary buys 7 identical garden pots for £91.
Find the cost of each pot. *(4)*

◄◄
Exercise 2
on page 6

D

WJEC

Kay and Tansy are tour guides at a famous castle. They share the work equally and each of them takes at most 28 people at a time on a tour of the castle. One day 952 people want to see the castle. Find the least number of tours each guide must lead on that day. *(3)*

◄◄
Exercise 2
on page 6

E

NEAB

A gardener buys 375 trays of plants.
There are 54 plants in a tray.
How many plants is this altogether? *(3)*

◀◀
Exercise 4
on page 12

F Bottles of mineral water cost 39p each.
Estimate the cost of 114 bottles.
Show how you obtained your estimate.

◀◀
Exercise 4
on page 12

G Showing all your working, **estimate** the value of $\dfrac{38 \times 211}{78}$.

◀◀
Exercises 2, 3
and 5 on pages
6, 10 and 15

H

SEG

The height of Mount Ararat is 16 805 feet.
The height of Mont Blanc is 15 771 feet.
(a) (i)   How much higher is Mount Ararat than Mont Blanc? *(1)*
     (ii) Write the height of Mont Blanc to the nearest thousand feet. *(1)*
     (iii) Mount Ararat is 5 times as high as Snowdon.
           What is the height of Snowdon? *(2)*

The table shows the temperature at certain places on the mountains.

	Temperature at top	Temperature at bottom
Mount Ararat	−25˚C	12˚C
Mont Blanc	−18˚C	12˚C

(b) (i)   How much warmer is the temperature at the top of Mont Blanc than
           at the top of Mount Ararat? *(1)*
     (ii) What is the difference in temperature between the top and the
           bottom of Mont Blanc? *(1)*

◀◀
Exercise 6
on page 16

I Work out the answers to these.

1. $(4 + 6) \times 7$ 2. $(12 + 8) \div 4$ 3. $3 \times 2 + 4 \times 5$
4. $8 \times (3 + 2)$ 5. $40 \div (12 - 4)$ 6. $(5 + 3) \times (15 - 9)$

◀◀
Exercise 5
on page 15

J

MEG

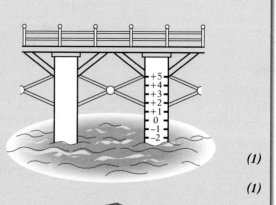

One of the supports on a pier is
marked off in feet.
It is used to measure the water level
above or below the zero mark.
During one Saturday, the reading was
taken every 4 hours and the results
were:
    −2, +1, +5, 0, −1, −4.
(a) How many feet are there
    between the highest and lowest
    of these readings? *(1)*
(b) Write the readings in ascending
    order with the lowest first. *(1)*

2 Symmetry

By the end of this chapter you will be able to:

- recognise and draw lines of symmetry on a 2-D shape
- complete a 2-D shape so that it is symmetrical
- recognise and draw planes of symmetry on a 3-D shape
- decide whether a shape has rotational symmetry
- know the order of rotational symmetry of a shape
- complete a design so that it has rotational symmetry.

Getting started..

You will need

some copies of this square.

1. Shade 10 squares to make a symmetrical pattern.
    Do this in as many ways as possible.
2. Shade 18 squares to make a symmetrical pattern.
    Do this in as many ways as possible.
3. Design a symmetrical tiling pattern for a bathroom or kitchen using grid paper.

Line symmetry

If we folded this 2-D picture in half along the dashed line, one half would fit exactly on top of the other.

The dashed line is called a **line of symmetry** or **axis of symmetry** or **mirror line**.

Some shapes have more than 1 line of symmetry.

Examples

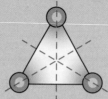

two lines of symmetry

three lines of symmetry

six lines of symmetry

A shape has **line symmetry** if it has one or more lines of symmetry.

Worked Exam Question

LONDON

Draw in all the lines of symmetry on each of the following flags.

You may use tracing paper or a mirror to help.

(4)

Answer

We usually use a dashed line to show a line of symmetry.

Exercise 1   **A**   Use a copy of this.
Draw all the lines of symmetry on each diagram.

1.

2.

3.

4.

5.

6.

B   How many lines of symmetry has the quadrilateral PQRS?

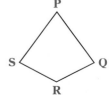

C A square piece of paper is folded in half and then folded in half again. A shape is cut out through all four sections of the paper, as shown.

The piece of paper is opened out.

Use a copy of this.
1. Draw on it the two pieces that have been cut out.
2. On your diagram, draw any lines of symmetry.

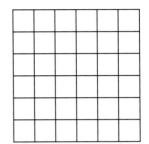

D Which of the following designs have line symmetry?

A

B

C

D

E

Worked Exam Question

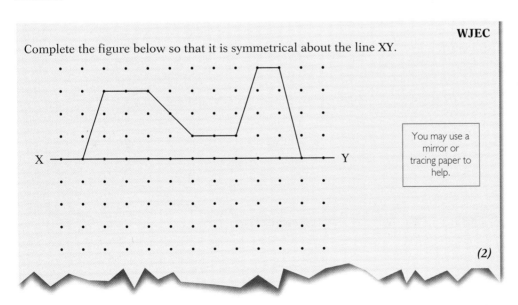

WJEC

Complete the figure below so that it is symmetrical about the line XY.

You may use a mirror or tracing paper to help.

(2)

Answer

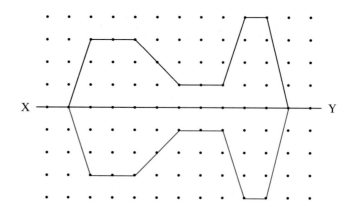

You should be able to fold along XY and one half will fit exactly onto the other half.

Exercise 2   **A**   Use a copy of this.
Complete the figures below so that you get a figure which is symmetrical about the line PQ.

1.

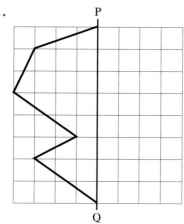

2.

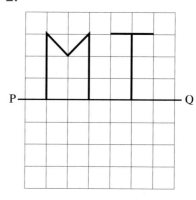

B   Use a copy of this.

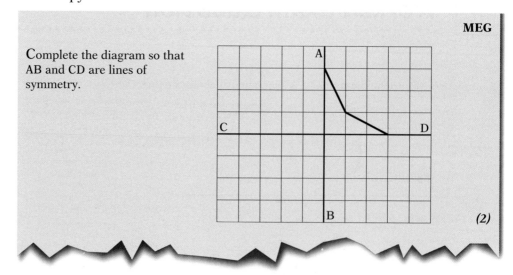

MEG

Complete the diagram so that AB and CD are lines of symmetry.

(2)

Investigation

You will need   some copies of a 3 × 3 grid
                    some copies of a 4 × 4 grid

A   Rory made this symmetrical pattern by shading some
squares on this grid.
It has 2 lines of symmetry.

1. Make a pattern with just **1** line of symmetry by
   shading some of the squares of a 3 × 3 grid.
   How many different ways can you do this?
2. How many patterns can you make which have 2 lines of symmetry?
3. How many patterns can you make which have 4 lines of symmetry?

B   Repeat **A1**, **2** and **3** with a 4 × 4 grid.

Planes of symmetry

This 3-D shape is symmetrical.
The shaded part is called a **plane of symmetry**.
A **plane of symmetry** divides a 3-D shape into
two identical parts. It is parallel to two sides
of the shape.

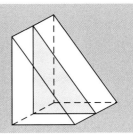

Worked Exam Question

The diagram represents a
prism.
Draw in one plane of symmetry
of the prism on the diagram.

(2)

Answer   There are two possible answers.

Draw the plane
parallel to the sides.

It is best to **shade**
the plane of
symmetry.

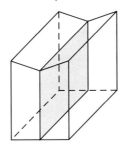 **or**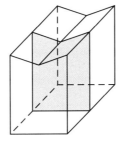

Exercise 3   **A** Which of these 3-D shapes have
   1. one plane of symmetry
   2. more than one plane of symmetry?

A

B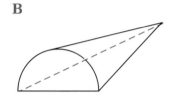

C

D

E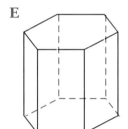

F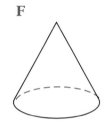

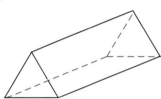

B Use a copy of these shapes.
Draw one plane of symmetry on each diagram.

1.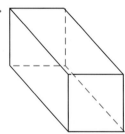

2.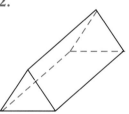

3.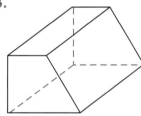

C Use a copy of the 3-D shapes **B**, **C** and **E** in **part A**.
Draw one plane of symmetry on each diagram.

Rotational symmetry

This shape has **rotational symmetry**.

A shape has rotational symmetry if it looks the same in more than one position during a full turn.

The number of times it looks the same during a complete turn is called the **order of rotational symmetry**.

Examples

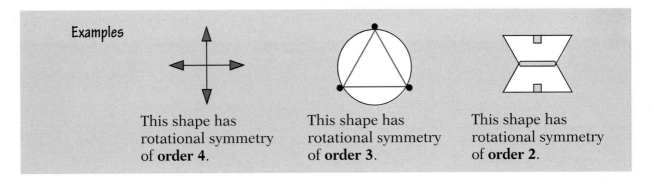

This shape has rotational symmetry of **order 4**.

This shape has rotational symmetry of **order 3**.

This shape has rotational symmetry of **order 2**.

Exercise 4   **A**   Use a copy of this.

LONDON

Draw a circle around each of the shapes that has rotational symmetry.

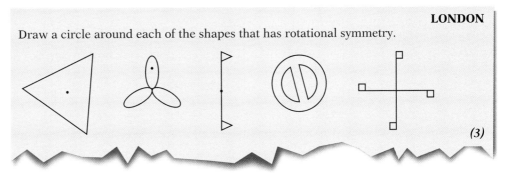

(3)

B   Write down the order of rotational symmetry of the shapes below.

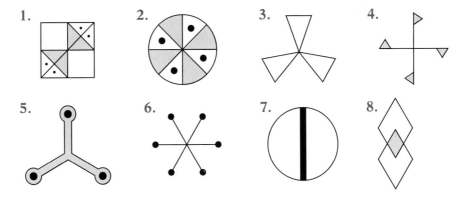

1.   2.   3.   4.

5.   6.   7.   8.

C

SEG

The diagrams P, Q, R and S are drawn accurately.

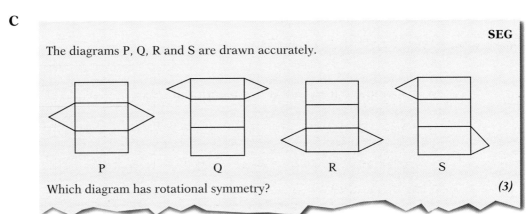

P   Q   R   S

Which diagram has rotational symmetry?   *(3)*

To finish a design so that it has **rotational symmetry**, you may need to use tracing paper.

Example   This shows part of a bathroom tile design. Complete the design so that it has rotational symmetry.

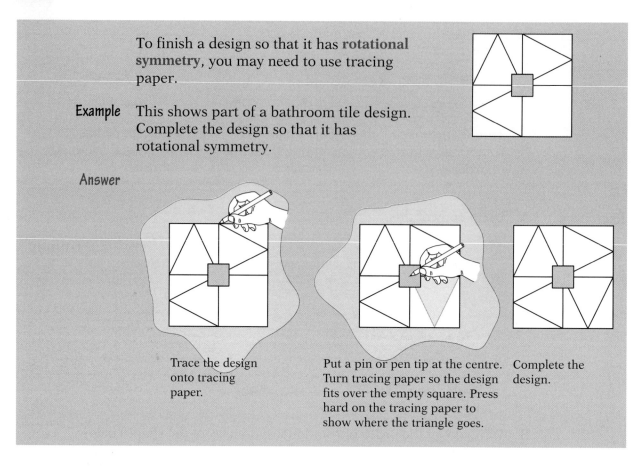

Answer

Trace the design onto tracing paper.

Put a pin or pen tip at the centre. Turn tracing paper so the design fits over the empty square. Press hard on the tracing paper to show where the triangle goes.

Complete the design.

Exercise 5   **A**   Jan started this design for the cover of a book.
Use a copy of it.
Complete the design so it has rotational symmetry.

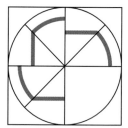

B   A bedspread is made using the following shapes.

Use a copy of this design.
Complete it so that it has rotational symmetry.

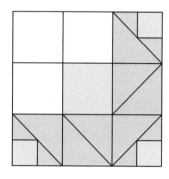

C   The diagram shows two letter Ts.
Copy this diagram onto grid paper.
Draw two more letter Ts so the complete
diagram has rotational symmetry of
order 4.

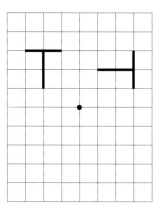

D   1.   This cross stitch pattern has rotational
symmetry.
Write down the order of rotational
symmetry.

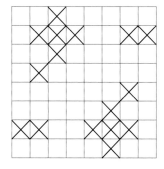

2.   A different cross stitch pattern is to be
drawn.
It is to have rotational symmetry of
order 4.
Jill started this cross stitch pattern.
Use a copy of it.
Complete the pattern.

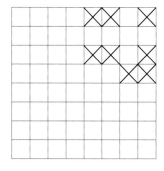

 # Homework/Review

A   Use a copy of these.

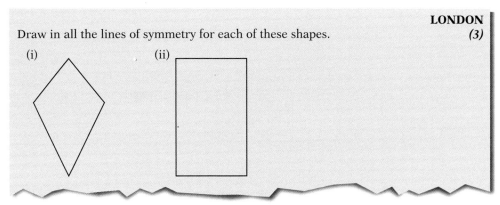

LONDON

Draw in all the lines of symmetry for each of these shapes.   *(3)*

(i)   (ii)

B The diagram shows a pentagon.

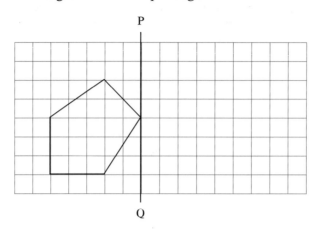

   1. How many lines of symmetry has this pentagon?
   2. Use a copy of the diagram.

   Complete the shape so that it is symmetrical about the line PQ.

C Use a copy of these shapes.
   Draw one plane of symmetry on each diagram.

   1.   2.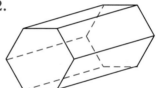

D Brian is making a blank crossword.
   The axes marked x and y are to be
   its two lines of symmetry.
   Use a copy of this.
   Complete the crossword blank by
   shading in the correct squares.

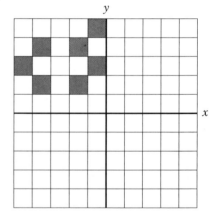

E

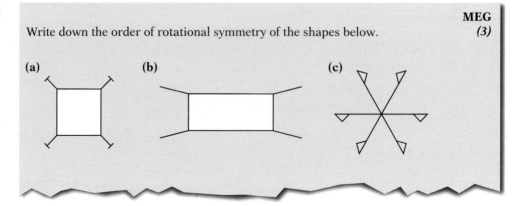

   MEG
   (3)

   Write down the order of rotational symmetry of the shapes below.

   (a)   (b)   (c)

F

SEG

The diagram shows two triangles.

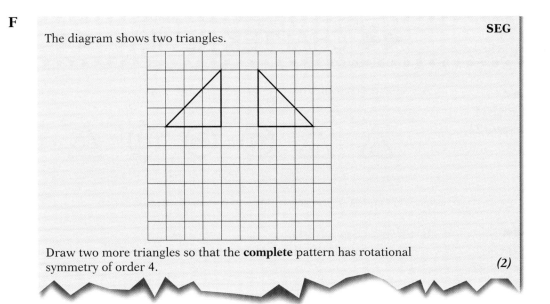

Draw two more triangles so that the **complete** pattern has rotational symmetry of order 4.

(2)

✔ KEY POINTS

✔ If we fold a shape along a **line of symmetry** one half will fit exactly on top of the other half.

✔ A **line of symmetry** is sometimes called a **mirror line** or **axis of symmetry**.

✔ Some shapes have more than one line of symmetry.

Examples

2 lines of symmetry   6 lines of symmetry   3 lines of symmetry

✔ A 3-D shape has a **plane of symmetry** if the plane divides the shape into two identical parts.

Example

✔ A shape has **rotational symmetry** if it looks the same in more than one position as it is turned a complete turn.

✔ The number of times a shape looks the same in one complete turn is called the **order of rotational symmetry**.

Example This shape looks the same in three positions as it is turned. It has rotational symmetry of order 3.

✔ We use **tracing paper** to complete a pattern so that it has a given order of rotational symmetry.

◀◀ CHAPTER REVIEW ◀◀

◀◀
Exercise 1
on page 22

A Use a copy of this.

LONDON

Draw a circle around each of the signs which has line symmetry. *(2)*

◀◀
Exercise 1
on page 22

B Use a copy of this.
Draw on all the lines of symmetry.

◀◀
Exercise 2
on page 24

C Use a copy of this.

WJEC

Complete the shape so that it is symmetrical about the line AB.

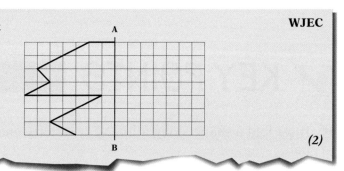

(2)

◀◀
Exercise 3
on page 26

D Use a copy of this.
Draw a plane of symmetry on this diagram.

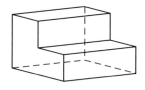

◀◀
Exercise 4
on page 27

E

MEG

Write down the order of rotational symmetry of the following shapes.

(a) **(b)** **(c)** **(d)**

(4)

◀◀
Exercise 5
on page 28

F Use a copy of this.

LONDON

(a) The crossword puzzle below has rotational symmetry. Write down the order of rotational symmetry. *(1)*

(b) A different crossword pattern is to be drawn. It will have rotational symmetry of order 4. The crossword pattern has been started. Complete the crossword pattern. *(3)*

3 Decimals, Fractions, Percentages

By the end of this chapter you will be able to:

- give the place value of a digit in a decimal number
- put decimals in order
- round decimals to the nearest whole number
- round decimals to a given number of decimal places
- multiply and divide by 10, 100 and 1000
- write equivalent fractions
- simplify fractions
- add and subtract fractions
- write down the fraction or percentage of a diagram that is shaded
- change fractions into decimals or percentages
- change decimals into fractions or percentages
- change percentages into fractions or decimals.

Getting started ....

Try these brain teasers.

1. If six potatoes have a mass of one pound, how many potatoes can you put into an empty paper bag which will only hold two and a half pounds without bursting?

2. Two of the nearest stars to Earth are Sirius, 8.7 light-years away, and Wolf, 7.7 light-years away.
    Which is the closest star to Earth?

3. The average Inuit eats 12 walruses in a lifetime. One walrus is equivalent to two and a half seals.
    How many seals would an Inuit eat if walruses were not available?

Decimal place value

This chart shows **place value**.

Thousands	Hundreds	Tens	Ones	•	Tenths	Hundredths	Thousandths
		2	5	•	3	0	7

In the number 25.307   the 2 is 2 tens
                        the 5 is 5 ones
                        the 3 is 3 tenths
                        the 0 is 0 hundredths
                        the 7 is 7 thousandths.

Example   What is the value of the 6 in 304.564?

Answer   The 6 is in the hundredths place.
              The value of the 6 is 6 hundredths or $\frac{6}{100}$.

Exercise 1   **A**   What is the value of the 9 in these numbers?
                       1. 609.32   **2.** 586.394   **3.** 734.629   **4.** 50.93
                       5. 82.913   **6.** 403.009   **7.** 386.09   **8.** 5926.3

                  B   What is the value of the 3 in each of the numbers in **A**?

                  C   Write each of these with a decimal point so that the value of the 4 is
                          4 hundredths.
                       1. 86349   **2.** 93247   **3.** 9864   **4.** 546
                       5. 7841   **6.** 234   **7.** 84   **8.** 4

Putting decimals in order

To put **decimals in order** we write them all with the same number of
digits after the decimal point.
We do this by adding zeros.

Example   Put these numbers in order from biggest to smallest.
                  4.2   4.25   4.02   4.265

Answer   Rewrite all the numbers with 3 digits after the decimal point.
                  4.200   4.250   4.020   4.265
              All the numbers have 4 ones.
              The numbers after the decimal point, in order, are
                  265   250   200   020
              The numbers in order are:
                  4.265   4.25   4.2   4.02

Exercise 2   **A**   Put these in order from smallest to largest.
                       1. £5.65, £5.05, £5.56, £5.50, £5.60
                       2. 7.32 cm, 7.23 cm, 7.02 cm, 7.236 cm, 7.632 cm
                       3. 14.68 kg, 14.068 kg, 14.6 kg, 14.06 kg, 14.8 kg

B This table shows the height that 6 boys jumped.

Sam	Troy	Adam	Chris	Tom	Arvind
1.46 m	1.48 m	1.37 m	1.385 m	1.426 m	1.409 m

Put these heights in order from biggest to smallest.

C Put these numbers in order from smallest to largest.
1. 7.038, 7.8, 7.03, 7.08, 7.803, 7.308
2. 6.4, 6.41, 6.041, 6.104, 6.59, 6.309
3. 15.6, 14.985, 15.85, 17.5, 15.085, 15.06
4. 2.004, 2.008, 2.04, 2.4, 2.8, 2.08, 2.41
5. 0.63, 0.306, 0.603, 0.681, 0.36, 0.6, 0.3
6. 0.987, 0.989, 0.896, 0.996, 0.889, 0.799

Rounding decimals to the nearest whole number

8.67 is closer to 9 than to 8.
8.67 to the nearest whole number is 9.

462.5 is halfway between 462 and 463.
462.5 to the nearest whole number is 463.

5.09 is closer to 5 than to 6.
5.09 to the nearest whole number is 5.

Exercise 3 **A** Round these to the nearest whole number.
1. £8.94   2. 11.68 cm   3. 52.07 m   4. 32.405 km
5. 18.73ℓ   6. 116.209 kg   7. 835.5 g   8. 429.84 m

B Round these to the nearest whole number.
1. 5.04   2. 12.7   3. 18.92   4. 116.84
5. 153.09   6. 128.55   7. 559.64

Rounding to decimal places

To round to a given number of decimal places follow these steps.

Step 1 Look at the first number you want to delete.
Step 2 If this number is 5 or more, increase the number before it by 1.
If this number is less than 5, leave the number before it as it is.

Example Round 8.623 to one decimal place.

Answer The first number to be deleted is 2.
It is less than 5, so leave 6 as 6.

8.6|23

↑
**First number
to be deleted**

8.623 = 8.6 to one decimal place.

Example Round 14.987 to two decimal places.

Answer The first number to be deleted is 7.
It is five or more, so 8 becomes 9.
14.987 = 14.99 to two decimal places.

14.98|7

↑
**First number
to be deleted**

Exercise 4   **A**   Round these numbers to one decimal place.

1. 5.23	**2.** 8.64	**3.** 9.27	**4.** 13.682
5. 11.85	**6.** 0.463	**7.** 124.89	**8.** 146.55
9. 0.56	**10.** 86.084	**11.** 530.093	

   B   Round these numbers to two decimal places.

1. 8.614	**2.** 13.786	**3.** 24.573	**4.** 126.419
5. 0.856	**6.** 0.043	**7.** 0.635	**8.** 14.7258
9. 126.0329	**10.** 44.008	**11.** 13.0038	

Multiplying and dividing by 10, 100 and 1000

When we **multiply a decimal by 10 or 100 or 1000** we move each digit **one place** to the **left** for **each zero** in 10, 100 or 1000.

Examples $8.327 \times 10 = 83.27$ There is one zero in 10, so each digit has been moved one place to the left.

$0.504 \times 100 = 50.4$ There are two zeros in 100, so each digit has been moved two places to the left.

$1.86 \times 1000 = 1860$ There are three zeros in 1000, so each digit has been moved three places to the left.

When we **divide a decimal by 10, 100 or 1000** we move each digit **one place** to the **right** for **each zero** in 10, 100 or 1000.

Examples $96.2 \div 10 = 9.62$ There is one zero in 10, so each digit has been moved one place to the right.

$56 \div 1000 = 0.056$ There are three zeros in 1000, so each digit has been moved three places to the right.

We put a zero in front so the decimal point doesn't get lost.   This zero is a place filler.

Exercise 5   **A**   Find the answers to these.

1. 4.2×10	**2.** 5.6×100	**3.** $13.7 \div 10$
4. 142.4×1000	**5.** 0.86×100	**6.** $53.7 \div 100$
7. $904 \div 1000$	**8.** $0.6 \div 10$	**9.** 0.863×100
10. 0.0052×1000	**11.** $8962 \div 1000$	**12.** $52 \div 1000$

   B   Martha used 1.69 m of lace for a dress.
   1. How much lace would she use for 100 dresses?
   2. How much lace would she use for 1000 dresses?

   C   Christine had the number 0.008 66 on her calculator display.
   What number must she multiply 0.008 66 by to make the display read 8.66?

Investigation

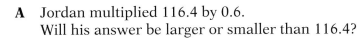

You will need   a calculator

1. $58.6 \div 0.2$ $58.6 \div 0.4$ $58.6 \div 0.1$
   Do these divisions on the calculator.
   Is the answer each time bigger or smaller than 58.6?

2. 58.6×0.2 58.6×0.4 58.6×0.1
   Do these multiplications on the calculator.
   Is the answer each time bigger or smaller than 58.6?

3.   **0.2**, **0.4** and **0.1** all lie between 0 and 1.

   Write down 3 more numbers that lie between 0 and 1.
   (a)   Divide 64 by each of these numbers.
        Is the answer each time bigger or smaller than 64?
   (b)   Multiply 85.2 by each of these numbers.
        Is the answer each time bigger or smaller than 85.2?

Copy these sentences and fill in the gap with **bigger** or **smaller**.

(a)   *When we **divide** a number, N, by a number that lies between 0 and 1, the answer will always be .... than N.*
(b)   *When we **multiply** a number, N, by a number that lies between 0 and 1, the answer will always be .... than N.*

Exercise 6

A   Jordan multiplied 116.4 by 0.6.
Will his answer be larger or smaller than 116.4?

B   Belinda did this calculation: $\dfrac{803.6}{0.7}$

Which of these answers will she get?
A   803.6   B   114.8   C   1148   D   11.48

C   Robert did this calculation: 0.82×0.14
Which of these answers will he get?
A   821.4   B   114.8   C   82.14   D   0.1148

D   Helen divided 0.84 by 0.02.
Will her answer be larger or smaller than 0.84?

Equivalent fractions

$\frac{5}{10}$ means 5 out of 10 $\frac{5}{10}$ also means $5 \div 10$.
The top number is called the **numerator**.
The bottom number is called the **denominator**.

$$\frac{5}{10} = \frac{4}{8} = \frac{3}{6} = \frac{2}{4} = \frac{1}{2}$$

$\frac{5}{10}, \frac{4}{8}, \frac{3}{6}, \frac{2}{4},$ and $\frac{1}{2}$ are called **equivalent fractions** because they are equal.

To make equivalent fractions we multiply both the numerator and the denominator by the same number.

Example

$$\overset{\times 2}{\frac{4}{5} = \frac{8}{10}} \qquad \overset{\times 3}{\frac{4}{5} = \frac{12}{15}} \qquad \overset{\times 4}{\frac{4}{5} = \frac{16}{20}}$$
$$\underset{\times 2}{} \qquad \underset{\times 3}{} \qquad \underset{\times 4}{}$$

$$\frac{4}{5} = \frac{8}{10} = \frac{12}{15} = \frac{16}{20} \longleftarrow \text{ The numerators are all multiples of 4.}$$
$$\longleftarrow \text{ The denominators are all multiples of 5.}$$

Worked Exam Question

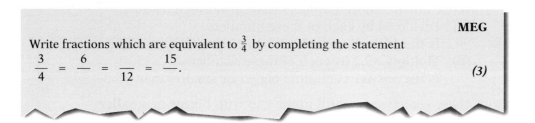

MEG

Write fractions which are equivalent to $\frac{3}{4}$ by completing the statement
$$\frac{3}{4} = \frac{6}{} = \frac{}{12} = \frac{15}{}.$$

(3)

Answer

We make equivalent fractions by multiplying top and bottom by the same number.

$$\overset{\times 2}{\frac{3}{4} = \frac{6}{8}} \qquad \overset{\times 3}{\frac{3}{4} = \frac{9}{12}} \qquad \overset{\times 5}{\frac{3}{4} = \frac{15}{20}}$$
$$\underset{\times 2}{} \qquad \underset{\times 3}{} \qquad \underset{\times 5}{}$$

So the completed statement is
$$\frac{3}{4} = \frac{6}{8} = \frac{9}{12} = \frac{15}{20}.$$

Exercise 7

A Write equivalent fractions by completing each statement.

1. $\dfrac{3}{10} = \dfrac{}{20} = \dfrac{9}{}$

2. $\dfrac{2}{3} = \dfrac{}{6} = \dfrac{6}{} = \dfrac{}{12}$

3. $\dfrac{1}{5} = \dfrac{}{10} = \dfrac{3}{} = \dfrac{4}{}$

4. $\dfrac{1}{4} = \dfrac{2}{} = \dfrac{3}{} = \dfrac{}{16}$

5. $\dfrac{7}{8} = \dfrac{14}{} = \dfrac{}{24} = \dfrac{}{32}$

6. $\dfrac{5}{6} = \dfrac{}{12} = \dfrac{}{18} = \dfrac{}{24}$

7. $\dfrac{2}{7} = \dfrac{4}{} = \dfrac{6}{} = \dfrac{8}{}$

8. $\dfrac{3}{8} = \dfrac{}{16} = \dfrac{}{24} = \dfrac{12}{}$

9. $\dfrac{5}{9} = \dfrac{}{18} = \dfrac{}{27} = \dfrac{20}{}$

10. $\dfrac{9}{10} = \dfrac{}{20} = \dfrac{27}{} = \dfrac{}{40}$

11. $\dfrac{3}{11} = \dfrac{}{22} = \dfrac{}{33} = \dfrac{}{44}$

12. $\dfrac{5}{12} = \dfrac{10}{} = \dfrac{15}{} = \dfrac{}{48}$

B Write down 3 fractions which are equivalent to each of these.
1. $\frac{1}{3}$ 2. $\frac{2}{5}$ 3. $\frac{5}{7}$ 4. $\frac{4}{9}$

C 1. Copy this. Fill in the blanks to make a set of equivalent fractions.

$$\frac{5}{8} = \frac{10}{16} = \frac{}{24} = \frac{20}{} = \frac{}{40}$$

2. What goes in the gap?
The numbers in the numerators of the fractions in part 1 are all
.... *of 5.*

Investigation

$$\frac{1}{2} = \frac{2}{4} = \frac{3}{6} = \frac{4}{8} = \frac{5}{10} = \frac{6}{12} = \ldots$$

The numerators are the multiples of **1**.
The denominators are the multiples of **2**.

1. When we write a set of equivalent fractions are the numerators always multiples of the first numerator?
    Are the denominators always multiples of the first denominator?
    Test by writing sets of equivalent fractions for these.

    $$\frac{2}{3} \quad \frac{3}{4} \quad \frac{1}{8} \quad \frac{3}{7} \quad \frac{4}{9} \quad \frac{6}{7} \quad \frac{9}{10}$$

2. For each set of equivalent fractions you have written, **subtract** the numerator from the denominator for each fraction. Is there a pattern?

3. Test to see if there is a pattern when you **add** the numerator and denominator of each fraction in a set.

    Write some sentences about what you find out.

Simplifying fractions

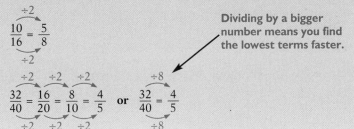

To **simplify a fraction** or give it in its **lowest terms**, divide the numerator and the denominator by the same number. Do this until you cannot divide any further.

Example
$$\frac{10}{16} = \frac{5}{8}$$
($\div 2$)

Dividing by a bigger number means you find the lowest terms faster.

Example
$$\frac{32}{40} = \frac{16}{20} = \frac{8}{10} = \frac{4}{5} \quad \text{or} \quad \frac{32}{40} = \frac{4}{5}$$
($\div 2$, $\div 2$, $\div 2$) ($\div 8$)

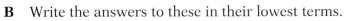

Exercise 8

A Write these fractions in their lowest terms.
1. $\frac{6}{12}$ 2. $\frac{4}{12}$ 3. $\frac{5}{15}$ 4. $\frac{10}{15}$ 5. $\frac{18}{20}$ 6. $\frac{8}{24}$ 7. $\frac{15}{35}$
8. $\frac{20}{30}$ 9. $\frac{25}{40}$ 10. $\frac{9}{12}$ 11. $\frac{40}{100}$ 12. $\frac{18}{45}$ 13. $\frac{80}{100}$ 14. $\frac{18}{54}$

B Write the answers to these in their lowest terms.
1. Richard has 18 grandchildren.
    15 of them are girls.
    What fraction are girls?
2. Ralph has 27 nephews.
    21 of them are married.
    What fraction is married?
3. Anita has 36 cousins.
    24 of them are male.
    What fraction is male?
4. Mindu has 15 brothers and sisters.
    9 of them are sisters?
    What fraction are sisters?

Puzzle

I am equivalent to three quarters.
My numerator is a number between 20 and 30.
My denominator is a number between 30 and 40.
My numerator is a multiple of 4.
What fraction am I?

Adding and subtracting fractions

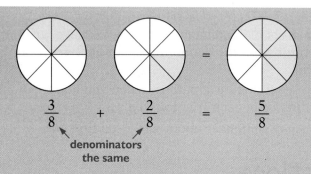

$$\frac{3}{8} \quad + \quad \frac{2}{8} \quad = \quad \frac{5}{8}$$

denominators
the same

If fractions have the **same denominators** we **add** them together by adding the numerators (top lines) and leaving the denominator the same.

Examples $\frac{1}{5} + \frac{2}{5} = \frac{3}{5}$ $\qquad$ $\frac{5}{12} + \frac{2}{12} = \frac{7}{12}$ $\qquad$ $\frac{3}{9} + \frac{4}{9} = \frac{7}{9}$

We **subtract** by subtracting the numerators.

Examples $\frac{4}{5} - \frac{1}{5} = \frac{3}{5}$ $\qquad$ $\frac{6}{7} - \frac{4}{7} = \frac{2}{7}$ $\qquad$ $\frac{7}{9} - \frac{2}{9} = \frac{5}{9}$

Always reduce the answer to its lowest terms.

Examples $\frac{1}{8} + \frac{3}{8} = \frac{4}{8}$ $\qquad$ $\frac{11}{12} - \frac{1}{12} = \frac{10}{12}$ $\qquad$ $\frac{4}{9} + \frac{2}{9} = \frac{6}{9}$
$\qquad\qquad\quad = \frac{1}{2}$ $\qquad\qquad\qquad\quad = \frac{5}{6}$ $\qquad\qquad\qquad\quad = \frac{2}{3}$

Exercise 9

A Find the answers to these.

1. $\frac{1}{3} + \frac{1}{3}$ $\qquad$ 2. $\frac{1}{4} + \frac{1}{4}$ $\qquad$ 3. $\frac{1}{8} + \frac{2}{8}$ $\qquad$ 4. $\frac{2}{5} + \frac{2}{5}$ $\qquad$ 5. $\frac{3}{8} + \frac{4}{8}$

6. $\frac{3}{10} + \frac{2}{10}$ $\qquad$ 7. $\frac{5}{8} - \frac{3}{8}$ $\qquad$ 8. $\frac{9}{12} - \frac{3}{12}$ $\qquad$ 9. $\frac{11}{20} + \frac{3}{20}$ $\qquad$ 10. $\frac{14}{15} - \frac{4}{15}$

11. $\frac{17}{18} - \frac{5}{18}$ $\qquad$ 12. $\frac{3}{20} + \frac{7}{20}$ $\qquad$ 13. $\frac{20}{24} - \frac{6}{24}$ $\qquad$ 14. $\frac{3}{4} + \frac{1}{4}$ $\qquad$ 15. $\frac{5}{8} + \frac{3}{8}$

B 1. $\frac{1}{8}$ of the pupils at Jake's school walked to school. $\frac{3}{8}$ of them came to school by bus.
   What fraction either walked or came by bus?

2. Enid had $\frac{5}{12}$ of a metre of ribbon.
   She used $\frac{3}{12}$ of a metre.
   What fraction of a metre does she have left?

To **add fractions** which do **not** have the same denominator, follow these steps.

Step 1   Write out a set of equivalent fractions for both fractions.
          Example $\frac{2}{3} + \frac{1}{4}$ $\frac{2}{3} = \frac{4}{6} = \frac{6}{9} = \frac{8}{12}$

          $\frac{1}{4} = \frac{2}{8} = \frac{3}{12} = \frac{4}{16}$

Step 2   Find a fraction in each set $\frac{2}{3} = \frac{4}{6} = \frac{6}{9} = \frac{8}{12}$
          that has the *same* denominator. $\frac{1}{4} = \frac{2}{8} = \frac{3}{12} = \frac{4}{16}$

Step 3   Add the fractions you found in **Step 2**.
          $\frac{2}{3} + \frac{1}{4} = \frac{8}{12} + \frac{3}{12}$

          $= \frac{11}{12}$ **Same denominator so we can add the numerators.**

Examples   **1.** $\frac{1}{5} + \frac{2}{3} = \frac{3}{15} + \frac{10}{15}$ $\frac{1}{5} = \frac{2}{10} = \frac{3}{15} = \frac{4}{20}$

         $= \frac{13}{15}$ $\frac{2}{3} = \frac{4}{6} = \frac{6}{9} = \frac{8}{12} = \frac{10}{15}$

         2. $\frac{3}{8} + \frac{1}{2} = \frac{3}{8} + \frac{4}{8}$ $\frac{3}{8} = \frac{6}{16} = \frac{9}{24}$

         $= \frac{7}{8}$ $\frac{1}{2} = \frac{2}{4} = \frac{3}{6} = \frac{4}{8}$

We **subtract** in a similar way.

Example $\frac{7}{8} - \frac{2}{3} = \frac{21}{24} - \frac{16}{24}$ $\frac{7}{8} = \frac{14}{16} = \frac{21}{24} = \frac{28}{32}$

         $= \frac{5}{24}$ $\frac{2}{3} = \frac{4}{6} = \frac{6}{9} = \frac{8}{12} = \frac{10}{15} = \frac{12}{18} = \frac{14}{21} = \frac{16}{24}$

         Same denominators so we can subtract the numerator.

Exercise 10   **A**   Find the answer to these.

1. $\frac{1}{4} + \frac{1}{3}$ 2. $\frac{3}{8} + \frac{1}{4}$ 3. $\frac{1}{2} + \frac{2}{5}$ 4. $\frac{3}{7} + \frac{5}{14}$

5. $\frac{2}{5} + \frac{1}{3}$ 6. $\frac{7}{8} - \frac{1}{4}$ 7. $\frac{4}{5} - \frac{1}{2}$ 8. $\frac{11}{12} - \frac{3}{4}$

9. $\frac{1}{12} + \frac{2}{3}$ 10. $\frac{5}{6} - \frac{1}{3}$ 11. $\frac{9}{10} - \frac{2}{5}$ 12. $\frac{3}{10} + \frac{1}{2}$

13. $\frac{7}{10} - \frac{3}{5}$ 14. $\frac{5}{12} + \frac{1}{4}$ 15. $\frac{2}{3} - \frac{1}{4}$ 16. $\frac{7}{8} - \frac{3}{4}$

B   Janice gave $\frac{1}{3}$ of her apples to one friend and $\frac{2}{5}$ of them to another friend.
    1. What fraction did she give away altogether?
    2. What fraction did she have left?

C   Ray had a length of wood $\frac{3}{4}$ m long.
    He cut $\frac{1}{5}$ m off this.
    What fraction of a metre was left?

A fraction with a whole number in front of it is called a **mixed number**.

Examples $1\frac{3}{4}$, $8\frac{1}{3}$, $16\frac{1}{4}$, $2\frac{1}{8}$, $3\frac{4}{5}$ are all mixed numbers.

To **add or subtract mixed numbers** follow these steps.
Step 1   Add or subtract the whole numbers.
Step 2   Add or subtract the fractions.
Step 3   Add the answers to **Step 1** and **Step 2**.

Example $3\frac{1}{8} + 1\frac{3}{4}$

Answer **Step 1** $3 + 1 = 4$

Step 2 $\frac{1}{8} + \frac{3}{4} = \frac{1}{8} + \frac{6}{8}$ $\frac{1}{8} = \frac{2}{16} = \frac{3}{24}$

$= \frac{7}{8}$ $\frac{3}{4} = \frac{6}{8}$

Step 3 $4 + \frac{7}{8} = 4\frac{7}{8}$

Example $4\frac{2}{3} - 3\frac{1}{4}$

Answer **Step 1** $4 - 3 = 1$

Step 2 $\frac{2}{3} - \frac{1}{4} = \frac{8}{12} - \frac{3}{12}$ $\frac{2}{3} = \frac{4}{6} = \frac{6}{9} = \frac{8}{12}$

$= \frac{5}{12}$ $\frac{1}{4} = \frac{2}{8} = \frac{3}{12} = \frac{4}{16}$

Step 3 $1 + \frac{5}{12} = 1\frac{5}{12}$

Exercise 11

Find the answer to these.

1. $3\frac{3}{8} + 1\frac{1}{8}$
2. $2\frac{1}{4} + 1\frac{1}{4}$
3. $5\frac{7}{8} - 3\frac{5}{8}$
4. $6\frac{4}{5} - 1\frac{1}{5}$

5. $4\frac{3}{8} + 1\frac{1}{4}$
6. $2\frac{1}{4} + 3\frac{1}{3}$
7. $3\frac{9}{10} - 1\frac{1}{5}$
8. $4\frac{7}{8} - 2\frac{3}{4}$

9. $1\frac{1}{12} + 2\frac{2}{3}$
10. $5\frac{4}{5} - 3\frac{1}{4}$
11. $6\frac{1}{3} - 5\frac{1}{4}$
12. $1\frac{1}{5} + 2\frac{1}{2}$

13. $5\frac{5}{6} - 2\frac{1}{3}$
14. $2\frac{1}{2} + 3\frac{2}{5}$
15. $4\frac{11}{12} - 1\frac{3}{4}$
16. $5\frac{1}{3} + 3\frac{1}{2}$

17. $8\frac{3}{4} + \frac{1}{5}$
18. $4\frac{11}{12} - \frac{2}{3}$
19. $7\frac{3}{4} - 2\frac{2}{5}$
20. $8\frac{3}{4} + 2\frac{1}{10}$

A fraction with the numerator bigger than the denominator is called an **improper fraction**.

Example $\frac{13}{8}$ is an improper fraction.

To change an improper fraction into a mixed number:

1. Divide the denominator into the numerator. $\frac{13}{8} = 1$ **with 5 left over**
2. Put the remainder over the denominator. $= 1\frac{5}{8}$

Sometimes the answer to an addition is an improper fraction.

Example $\frac{3}{4} + \frac{7}{8} = \frac{6}{8} + \frac{7}{8}$ $\frac{3}{4} = \frac{6}{8} = \frac{9}{12}$

$= \frac{13}{8}$ $\frac{7}{8} = \frac{14}{16}$

$= 1\frac{5}{8}$

Example $1\frac{2}{3} + \frac{3}{4} = 1 + \frac{8}{12} + \frac{9}{12}$ $\frac{2}{3} = \frac{4}{6} = \frac{6}{9} = \frac{8}{12}$

$= 1 + \frac{17}{12}$ $\frac{3}{4} = \frac{6}{8} = \frac{9}{12}$

$= 1 + 1\frac{5}{12}$

$= 2\frac{5}{12}$

Exercise 12

Find the answers to these. Give your answers as mixed numbers.

1. $\frac{3}{4} + \frac{1}{2}$
2. $\frac{3}{4} + \frac{5}{8}$
3. $\frac{2}{3} + \frac{5}{6}$
4. $\frac{3}{4} + \frac{5}{6}$

5. $\frac{3}{8} + \frac{3}{4}$
6. $\frac{4}{5} + \frac{7}{10}$
7. $\frac{3}{4} + \frac{5}{12}$
8. $\frac{4}{15} + \frac{4}{5}$

9. $1\frac{2}{3} + 1\frac{5}{6}$
10. $2\frac{3}{4} + 1\frac{2}{3}$
11. $1\frac{4}{5} + 3\frac{3}{10}$
12. $3\frac{6}{7} + 1\frac{3}{14}$

13. $1\frac{3}{5} + 2\frac{7}{10}$
14. $3\frac{1}{2} + 2\frac{4}{5}$
15. $1\frac{3}{4} + \frac{7}{8}$
16. $1\frac{5}{6} + \frac{2}{3}$

Homework/Review 1

A   What is the value of the 7 in these numbers?
1. 507.63   2. 248.731   3. 42.017   4. 38.379

B   Put these numbers in order from largest to smallest.
1.03,   1.3,   1.038,   1.4,   1.438,   1.34,   1.083

C   1. Rita weighs 48.271 kg. Round her weight to the nearest kg.
2. A room is 4.685 m long. Round this length to two decimal places.

D   Round these numbers to one decimal place.
1. 5.632   2. 72.879   3. 560.083   4. 415.392

E   Find the answers to these.
1. 83.4×10 2. $86.25 \div 100$ 3. 96.7×1000 4. $58 \div 100$
5. $7 \div 10$ 6. 0.63×100 7. 0.04×1000 8. $25 \div 1000$

F   Jade divided 20.04 by 0.24.
Which of these answers did she get?
A   4.8096   B   2004   C   83.5   D   20.04

G   Which of the answers in **F** would Jade get if she multiplied 20.04 by 0.24?

H   Copy and finish this set of equivalent fractions.
1. $\frac{1}{6} = \frac{}{12} = \frac{3}{} = \frac{4}{}$ 2. $\frac{3}{10} = \frac{6}{} = \frac{9}{} = \frac{}{40}$
3. $\frac{4}{5} = \frac{}{10} = \frac{12}{} = \frac{16}{}$ 4. $\frac{4}{7} = \frac{8}{} = \frac{}{21} = \frac{16}{}$

I   What goes in the gap?
In **H** number **1.**, the numbers in the denominators are all .... of 6.

J   Give these fractions in their lowest terms.
1. $\frac{10}{16}$ 2. $\frac{9}{18}$ 3. $\frac{14}{16}$ 4. $\frac{14}{21}$ 5. $\frac{8}{18}$ 6. $\frac{14}{20}$ 7. $\frac{10}{15}$ 8. $\frac{12}{16}$

K   Write the answer to this in its lowest terms.
Ben's watch cost £27. Ben paid £18 of this.

What fraction of the cost did Ben pay?

L   Find the answer to these.
1. $\frac{5}{12} + \frac{4}{12}$ 2. $\frac{3}{5} + \frac{1}{5}$ 3. $\frac{7}{20} + \frac{3}{20}$ 4. $\frac{11}{12} - \frac{8}{12}$
5. $\frac{2}{5} + \frac{3}{5}$ 6. $\frac{3}{5} + \frac{1}{3}$ 7. $\frac{3}{4} - \frac{5}{8}$ 8. $\frac{7}{8} - \frac{1}{2}$
9. $\frac{7}{8} + \frac{3}{4}$ 10. $3\frac{7}{10} - 1\frac{3}{5}$ 11. $1\frac{2}{3} + 2\frac{5}{6}$ 12. $3\frac{5}{6} - 2\frac{3}{4}$

M   1. Witek was making a design for art.
$\frac{3}{4}$ of the paper was painted black and $\frac{3}{16}$ was painted red. What fraction
was painted either black or red?
2. Simon bought $\frac{7}{8}$ kg of cheese.
He used $\frac{3}{4}$ of a kilogram.
What fraction of a kilogram did he have left?

Fraction and percentage diagrams

Worked Exam Questions

MEG

1. Estimate what percentage of this stick is black.

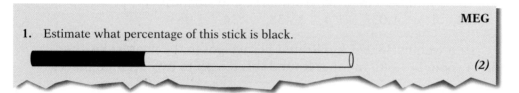

(2)

Answer   Imagine the stick cut into 10 equal parts.

About three and a half parts out of ten are black.
This is **about 35%**.

2. What fraction of the square ABCD is shaded?

WJEC

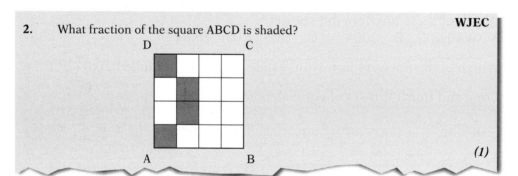

(1)

Answer   4 out of 16 squares are shaded. This is $\frac{4}{16}$.

To reduce $\frac{4}{16}$ to its lowest terms divide top and
bottom by the same number.

So $\frac{1}{4}$ of the square ABCD is shaded.

$$\frac{4}{16} = \frac{1}{4}$$
($\div 4$)

Exercise 13   **A**

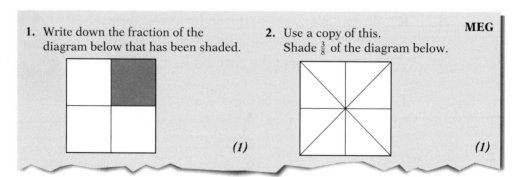

1. Write down the fraction of the
diagram below that has been shaded.

(1)

2. Use a copy of this.
Shade $\frac{3}{8}$ of the diagram below.

MEG

(1)

B   **1.** Is this statement true or false? Explain why.

$\frac{3}{5}$ of the diagram is shaded.

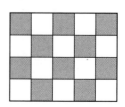

2. Use a copy of this.
   (a) Shade $\frac{2}{5}$ of this diagram.
   (b) What percentage have you shaded?

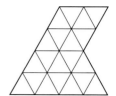

C

Here is a diagram of a chessboard.
It is made up of black and white squares.
What fraction of the chessboard is white?

NEAB

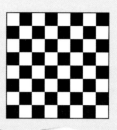

(1)

D 1. What fraction of the whole shape is shaded?

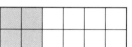

2. Use a copy of this diagram.
   Shade $\frac{2}{5}$ of this shape.

3. Use another copy of the diagram.
   in **2**. Shade 0.3 of the diagram.

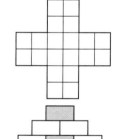

E 1. What fraction of the diagram is shaded?
     2. What percentage of the diagram is shaded?
     3. What decimal fraction of the diagram is shaded?

F Use a copy of this.
   1. Mark with an X a point
      approximately $\frac{2}{3}$ of the way
      along the line from Q.   Q ————————————————
   2. Mark with an X a point
      approximately 75% of the way   R ————————————————
      along the line from R.
   3. Mark with an X a point
      approximately $\frac{1}{4}$ of the way   S ————————————————
      along the line from S.
   4. Estimate what fraction of the way   T ————X————————————
      from T, the point X is on this line.

Changing between decimals, fractions and percentages

Here are some **common conversions** you should learn.

$\frac{1}{2} = 0.5 = 50\%$ $\frac{1}{4} = 0.25 = 25\%$

$\frac{3}{4} = 0.75 = 75\%$ $\frac{1}{10} = 0.1 = 10\%$

$\frac{1}{8} = 0.125 = 12\frac{1}{2}\%$

Decimals to fractions

Write the decimal as tenths, hundredths or thousandths and then reduce the fraction to its lowest terms.

This place value chart helps us to write decimals as fractions.

Tens	Ones		Tenths	Hundredths	Thousandths
	0	•	6		

Always reduce fractions to their lowest terms.

Examples

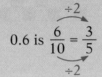

$$0.6 \text{ is } \frac{6}{10} = \frac{3}{5} \quad (\div 2)$$

$$0.25 \text{ is } \frac{25}{100} = \frac{1}{4} \quad (\div 25)$$

$$0.85 \text{ is } \frac{85}{100} = \frac{17}{20} \quad (\div 5)$$

Exercise 14

Write these as fractions in their lowest terms.
1. 0.7   2. 0.3   3. 0.1   4. 0.2   5. 0.75   6. 0.4
7. 0.6   8. 0.5   9. 0.25   10. 0.95   11. 0.125

Fractions to decimals

If the fraction has 10 or 100 as the denominator we can write the decimal straight down.

Examples $\frac{4}{10} = 0.4$ $\frac{83}{100} = 0.83$ $\frac{4}{5} = \frac{8}{10}$ $\frac{16}{25} = \frac{64}{100}$
$= 0.8$ $= 0.64$

If the denominator is not 10 or 100, we divide the numerator by the denominator.

Example $\frac{1}{8}$ means $1 \div 8$.
$1 \div 8 = 0.125$

$$\begin{array}{r} 0.125 \\ 8)\overline{1.000} \\ \underline{8} \\ 20 \\ \underline{16} \\ 40 \end{array}$$

Exercise 15

Write these as decimals.
1. $\frac{3}{10}$ 2. $\frac{7}{10}$ 3. $\frac{1}{10}$ 4. $\frac{1}{4}$ 5. $\frac{2}{5}$ 6. $\frac{33}{100}$
7. $\frac{3}{8}$ 8. $\frac{5}{8}$ 9. $\frac{9}{20}$ 10. $\frac{7}{25}$ 11. $\frac{9}{50}$ 12. $\frac{6}{25}$

Percentages to decimals

Divide the percentage by 100.
$$45\% = \frac{45}{100} \qquad 0.69 = \frac{69}{100} \qquad 40\% = \frac{40}{100}$$
$$= 0.45 \qquad\qquad = 0.69 \qquad\qquad = 0.4$$

Exercise 16

Write these as decimals.
1. 59%   2. 63%   3. 75%   4. 82%   5. 78%   6. 31%
7. 28%   8. 16%   9. 90%   10. 60%   11. 20%

Decimals to percentages

Multiply the decimal by 100%.

Examples $0.7 \times 100\% = 70\%$ $0.04 \times 100\% = 4\%$ $0.125 \times 100\% = 12.5\%$

Exercise 17   Write these as percentages.

1. 0.5   2. 0.8   3. 0.2   4. 0.1   5. 0.81   6. 0.72
7. 0.94   8. 0.63   9. 0.05   10. 0.06   11. 0.335   12. 0.455

Percentages to fractions

Write the percentage as a fraction with 100 as the denominator.
Reduce it to its lowest terms.

Examples $30\% = \frac{30}{100}$ $65\% = \frac{65}{100}$
$ = \frac{3}{10}$ $ = \frac{13}{20}$

Exercise 18   Write these as fractions in their lowest terms.

1. 57%   2. 60%   3. 40%   4. 33%   5. 20%   6. 23%
7. 85%   8. 91%   9. 17%   10. 30%   11. 35%   12. 81%

Fractions to percentages

Write the fraction as a decimal and then multiply by 100%. Or change
the denominator of the fraction into 100.

Examples $\frac{3}{8} = 3 \div 8$ $\overset{\times 5}{\frac{7}{20}} = \underset{\times 5}{\frac{35}{100}}$
$\phantom{\frac{3}{8}} = 0.375$

$0.375 \times 100\% = 37.5\%$ $= 35\%.$

Exercise 19   Write these as percentages.

1. $\frac{3}{4}$ 2. $\frac{7}{10}$ 3. $\frac{1}{10}$ 4. $\frac{9}{10}$ 5. $\frac{2}{5}$ 6. $\frac{4}{25}$
7. $\frac{81}{100}$ 8. $\frac{1}{5}$ 9. $\frac{8}{50}$ 10. $\frac{9}{20}$ 11. $\frac{1}{8}$ 12. $\frac{5}{8}$

Worked Exam Question

· ·

WJEC

(i)   Write $\frac{1}{4}$ as a decimal.
(ii) Write 0.2 as a fraction.
(iii) Write 30% as a decimal.
(iv) Write $\frac{1}{4}$, 0.2 and 30% in order of size, starting with the smallest.   *(4)*

Answer   (i) $\frac{1}{4} =$ **0.25**.   (ii) 0.2 is $\frac{2}{10} = \frac{1}{5}$.   (iii) 30% = 30 ÷ 100 = **30**.

(iv) Make them all decimals $\frac{1}{4} = 0.25$,   30% = 0.3
Write them all with the same number of digits after the decimal point.
0.25   0.20   0.30.
In order these are 0.20, 0.25 and 0.30. So the order is **0.2**, $\frac{1}{4}$, **30%**.

> To put decimals in order write them with the same number of digits after the decimal point.

Exercise 20

A Make a copy of this table.
Fill it in. The first one is done.

Fraction	Decimal	Percentage
$\frac{1}{2}$	0.5	50%
$\frac{2}{5}$		
		25%
	0.75	
	0.7	
$\frac{1}{8}$		

B $\frac{4}{5}$ of pupils at a school were away with the flu.
   1. Change $\frac{4}{5}$ to a decimal.
   2. Change $\frac{4}{5}$ to a percentage.
   3. Work out what percentage of the school were **not** away with the flu.

C

		MEG
(a)	Work out $\frac{1}{4} + \frac{3}{8}$.	*(2)*
(b)	Write $\frac{1}{4}$ as a percentage.	*(1)*
(c)	Change $\frac{3}{8}$ to a decimal.	*(1)*

D Here is a list of fractions, decimals and percentages.
   0.65, $\frac{1}{2}$,   60%,   25%,   0.3, $\frac{3}{8}$
   Rewrite the list in order of size, starting with the smallest.

Descending
means from
biggest to
smallest.

E List the following in descending order.
   $\frac{1}{4}$,   0.15,   33%,   0.3

F $\frac{3}{8}$ of all animals in an area were cattle.
   1. Change $\frac{3}{8}$ to a decimal.
   2. Write your answer to part **1.** correct to two decimal places.
   3. What percentage of animals in the area were **not** cattle?
   4. List these in ascending order.
      $\frac{4}{5}$, $\frac{1}{2}$,   75%,   0.83,   0.875

Ascending
means from
smallest to
biggest.

G Use a copy of this.
   The point 2.5 has been marked on the number line below.

   Mark the following numbers in the same way.
   1. −1.6   **2.** 2.8   **3.** $1\frac{2}{3}$ **4.** $-1\frac{3}{4}$

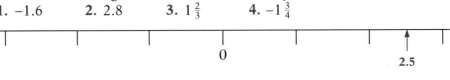

Homework/Review 2

A

Estimate what fraction of the cake this is.

MEG

(2)

B What fraction of these shapes has been shaded?

1. 2. 3.

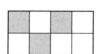  

C What percentage of the shape in **B** part **2.** has been shaded?

D Use a copy of this.
Shade the fraction or percentage written beside each diagram.

1. 2. 3.

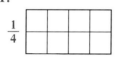 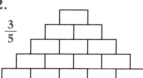 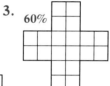

E Use a copy of this. Fill it in.

Fraction	Decimal	Percentage	Fraction	Decimal	Percentage
$\frac{1}{2}$				0.8	
	0.25				30%
		75%	$\frac{3}{8}$		
	0.1			0.39	

F 1. Write $\frac{3}{4}$ as a decimal.
   2. Write 0.8 as a fraction.
   3. Write 70% as a decimal.
   4. Write $\frac{3}{4}$, 0.8 and 70% in order of size, starting with the smallest.

G Use a copy of this number line. Mark these numbers on it.
   1. −1.8   **2.** $1\frac{3}{5}$ **3.** $-2\frac{7}{8}$

2.5

0

H Rewrite this list in order of size, starting with the smallest first.
   66%, $\frac{1}{2}$, 0.6,   24%,   0.3, $\frac{3}{8}$

☑ KEY POINTS

☑ This chart gives **decimal place value**.

thousands	hundreds	tens	ones •	tenths	hundredths	thousandths

☑ To put **decimals in order**, write them all with the same number of digits after the decimal point.

☑ To **round a decimal to the nearest whole number**, decide which whole number the decimal is closest to.

☑ To **round to decimal places**: Look at the first digit to be deleted.
If this digit is 5 or more, make the digit before this one more.
If this digit is less than 5, leave the digit before this as it is.

    Examples   5.37 to 1 decimal place is 5.4.   84.823 to 2 decimal places is 84.82.

☑ To **multiply by 10 or 100 or 1000** move each digit **one place** to the **left** for each zero.

☑ To **divide by 10 or 100 or 1000** move each digit **one place** to the **right** for each zero.

☑ $\frac{3}{5}$ means 3 out of 5 or $3 \div 5$. $\frac{3}{5}$ ← numerator / denominator

☑ **Equivalent fractions** are found by either multiplying or dividing both the numerator and denominator by the same number.

    Examples $\overset{\times 2 \quad \times 2}{\frac{3}{4} = \frac{6}{8} = \frac{12}{16}}$ $\overset{\div 3 \quad \div 2}{\frac{18}{24} = \frac{6}{8} = \frac{3}{4}}$

☑ To give a fraction in its **simplest form** or **lowest terms**, divide the numerator and denominator by the same number until you can't divide any more.

☑ To **add or subtract fractions with the *same* denominator**, add or subtract the numerators.

    Examples $\frac{3}{5} + \frac{1}{5} = \frac{4}{5}$ $\frac{3}{8} - \frac{2}{8} = \frac{1}{8}$

☑ To **add or subtract fractions which do *not* have the same denominator** do as follows.

    1. Write out a set of equivalent fractions for each fraction.
    2. Find a fraction in each set that has the same denominator.
    3. Add the fractions you found in **2**.

    Example $\frac{1}{4} + \frac{1}{3} = \frac{3}{12} + \frac{4}{12}$ $\frac{1}{4} = \frac{2}{8} = \frac{3}{12} = \frac{4}{16}$

                   $= \frac{7}{12}$ $\frac{1}{3} = \frac{2}{6} = \frac{3}{9} = \frac{4}{12}$

☑ To **add and subtract mixed numbers** add or subtract the whole numbers first.

☑ To change a:

| decimal to a fraction – | write as tenths, hundredths or thousandths and then reduce to its lowest terms. | $0.4 = \frac{4}{10}$ $= \frac{2}{5}$ |
| fraction to a decimal – | divide the numerator by the denominator. | $\frac{1}{4} = 1 \div 4$ $= 0.25$ |

percentage to a decimal –	**divide by 100%**	$85\% = 85 \div 100$
		$= 0.85$
decimal to a percentage –	**multiply by 100%**	$0.65 = 0.65 \times 100\%$
		$= 65\%$
percentage to a fraction –	**write as a fraction with 100 as the denominator and reduce to its lowest terms.**	$40\% = \frac{40}{100}$
		$= \frac{2}{5}$
fraction to a percentage –	**write as a decimal and then multiply by 100%.**	$\frac{3}{5} = 0.6 \times 100\%$
		$= 60\%$

 ◀◀ CHAPTER REVIEW ◀◀

 ◀◀
Exercise 1
on page 34

A What is the value of the 6 in these numbers?
1. 842.631   2. 582.036   3. 52.064   4. 82.006

◀◀
Exercises 2, 3
and 4 on pages
34, 35 and 36

B This table shows the mass of 5 cats.
1. Put these masses in order, heaviest first.

Gizmo	Bart	Monty	Simba	Ug
2.64 kg	2.751 kg	2.75 kg	1.984 kg	2.704 kg

2. Round Gizmo's weight to the nearest whole number.
3. Round Bart's weight to one decimal place.
4. Round Ug's weight to two decimal places.

◀◀
Exercise 5
on page 36

C Lance had the number 0.004 21 on his calculator display.
1. What number must he multiply it by to make the display read 4.21?
2. What number must he divide it by to make the display read 0.000 421?

◀◀
Exercise 7
on page 38

D Use a copy of this.

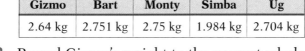

Fill in the blanks in this set of equivalent fractions.

$$\frac{3}{4} = \frac{6}{8} = \frac{}{12} = \frac{12}{} = \frac{}{20}$$

MEG

(2)

◀◀
Exercise 8
on page 39

E Write these in their lowest terms.

1. $\frac{5}{10}$ 2. $\frac{14}{20}$ 3. $\frac{16}{20}$ 4. $\frac{21}{35}$ 5. $\frac{24}{36}$

◀◀
Exercises 10, 11
and 12 on pages
41 and 42

F Find the answers to these.

1. $\frac{1}{4} + \frac{3}{5}$ 2. $1\frac{3}{8} + \frac{3}{4}$ 3. $\frac{9}{10} - \frac{2}{5}$ 4. $3\frac{3}{4} - 1\frac{3}{8}$

Exercise 10
on page 41

G

NEAB

One day at St. George's Comprehensive,
$\frac{1}{2}$ of the pupils walked to school,
$\frac{2}{5}$ of the pupils came to school by bus,
the remaining 68 pupils came by car.

(a) Work out $\frac{1}{2} + \frac{2}{5}$. *(2)*
(b) What fraction of the pupils came by car? *(1)*

Exercise 13
on page 44

H Use a copy of this.

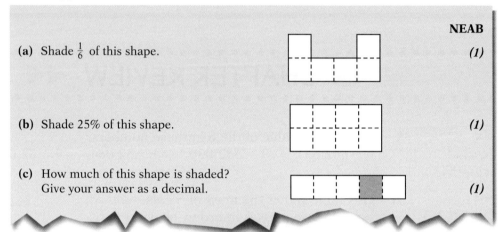

NEAB

(a) Shade $\frac{1}{6}$ of this shape. *(1)*

(b) Shade 25% of this shape. *(1)*

(c) How much of this shape is shaded?
Give your answer as a decimal. *(1)*

Exercise 20
on page 48

I Make a copy of this table.
Fill it in.

Fraction	Decimal	Percentage
$\frac{3}{4}$		
	0.125	
		80%

Exercises 4 and
20 on pages 36
and 48

J About $\frac{5}{8}$ of a class finished their Maths homework.
1. Change $\frac{5}{8}$ to a decimal.
2. Write your answer to part 1. correct to two decimal places.
3. Work out what percentage of the class did **not** finish their Maths homework.

Exercise 20
on page 48

K

WJEC

Showing all your working, find which of the quantities 0.4,
33% and $\frac{3}{8}$ is (i) the smallest, (ii) the largest. *(3)*

Exercise 20
on page 48

L

MEG

Change $\frac{9}{25}$ to a percentage. *(2)*

4 Expressions and Formulae

By the end of this chapter you will be able to:

- write and simplify expressions
- work out the value of an expression
- use a formula given in words or symbols.

Getting started ....

1. The letters *A*, *B*, *C*, *D* and *E* stand for whole numbers.
   The red numbers show the sum of each row and column.
   E = 3

E	E	D	C	14
C	B	C	A	21
B	B	D	A	15
C	A	E	D	16
19	**16**	**13**	**18**	

   Use a copy of this.
   Starting with the letter given, work out what each of the other letters stands for.

3	3			14
				21
				15
		3		16
19	**16**	**13**	**18**	

2. The letters *P*, *Q*, *R*, *S* and *T* stand for whole numbers.
   The red numbers show the sum of each row and column.
   T = 4

T	R	Q	P	15
T	Q	S	P	14
R	P	Q	T	15
Q	P	S	R	16
16	**14**	**14**	**16**	

   Use a copy of this.
   Starting with the letter given, work out what each of the other letters stands for.

4				15
4				14
			4	15
				16
16	**14**	**14**	**16**	

Simplifying expressions

$n - 3$ $2x + 4y$ $6a + 4 - 3a + 2$ are all expressions.

The letters n, x, y and a stand for numbers.

$7a + 2b + 5c$

7a, 2b and 5c are called terms.

Remember: We write $1x$ as x and $1n$ as n.

Adding and subtracting

$2x + 4y + 5x + y$

like terms   like terms

We can simplify an expression by adding or subtracting like terms

Examples $2x + 4y + 5x + y = 2x + 5x + 4y + y$ Write like terms next to each other.
$$= 7x + 5y$$

$$5a + 3b - 2a - 4b = 5a - 2a + 3b - 4b$$ Note: $3 - 4 = -1$ so
$$= 3a - b$$ $3b - 4b = -b$

$$4x + 3 - 2x + 7 = 4x - 2x + 3 + 7$$
$$= 2x + 10$$

Exercise 1   Simplify these expressions.
1. $2x + 4x$
2. $7y + 3y$
3. $2n + 5n$
4. $2p + 3p + 4p$
5. $a + a + 2a + 5a$
6. $13m - 5m$
7. $8x + 3x - 2x$
8. $12y + 3y - 2y$
9. $5x + 2x + 3y + 2y$
10. $15n - 6n + 5m + 2m$
11. $8y - 3y + 10w - 5w$
12. $6x + 3y - 2x - y$
13. $20p + 10q - 16p - 7q$
14. $2a + 3b - 4a$
15. $3p + 5q - 5p - 4q$
16. $8x + 3 + 4x + 2$
17. $9y + 7 - 5y - 10$
18. $8p + 4 - 5p - 2$
19. $8x + 5 - 12x - 4$
20. $12w + 2 - 5w - 3$
21. $10x + 8y - 5x - 10y$

Multiplying

We write $3 \times a$ as $3a$
$a \times b$ as ab
$4 \times a \times b$ as $4ab$
$x \times y \times 2$ as $2xy$.   Note: We write the number first.

Examples $2 \times 2a = 2 \times 2 \times a$ $p \times 2 \times 7 = 2 \times 7 \times p$ $3a \times 4b = 3 \times a \times 4 \times b$
$$= 4a$$ $$= 14p$$ $$= 3 \times 4 \times a \times b$$
$$= 12ab$$

Exercise 2   Simplify these expressions.

1. $s \times t$ 2. $x \times y$ 3. $4 \times p \times q$
4. $3 \times c \times d$ 5. $m \times 3 \times n$ 6. $x \times y \times 5$
7. $p \times q \times 9$ 8. $5 \times x$ 9. $7 \times y$
10. $3 \times 2x$ 11. $5 \times 6y$ 12. $2 \times 4p$
13. $5 \times 3n$ 14. $7 \times 6m$ 15. $4x \times 3$
16. $7x \times 2$ 17. $2a \times 3b$ 18. $4p \times 5q$
19. $4p \times 3q$ 20. $8b \times 4c$ 21. $9x \times 7y$
22. $3w \times 7x$ 23. $9p \times 3q$ 24. $3a \times 5b$

We write $a \times a$ as a^2
$p \times p \times p$ as p^3
$m \times m \times m \times m \times m$ as m^5.

Examples $4 \times a \times a = 4a^2$ $3a \times 4a = 3 \times a \times 4 \times a$ $5 \times y \times x \times x = 5 \times y \times x^2$
$= 3 \times 4 \times a \times a$ $= 5x^2 y$
$= 12 \times a^2$
$= 12a^2$

We usually put letters
in alphabetical order
in the answer.

Exercise 3   Simplify these expressions.

1. $5 \times a \times a$ 2. $6 \times x \times x \times x$ 3. $5 \times p \times p \times p \times p$
4. $3 \times y \times y$ 5. $12 \times x \times x \times x \times x$ 6. $2a \times 3a$
7. $4x \times 2x$ 8. $6b \times 4b$ 9. $2m \times 7m$
10. $5n \times 3n$ 11. $4t \times 5t$ 12. $6p \times 7p$
13. $9x \times 5x$ 14. $5 \times d \times d \times e$ 15. $3 \times n \times m \times m \times m$
16. $4 \times x \times x \times x \times y$ 17. $4 \times a \times a \times b$ 18. $6 \times x \times x \times y \times y$
19. $7 \times x \times y \times y$ 20. $x \times x \times 3 \times y$ 21. $12 \times x \times x \times x \times y \times y$

Worked Exam Questions

MEG

1. **(a)** Maria takes 20 minutes to walk 1 mile.
   How many minutes does she take to walk
   (i) 4 miles,   *(1)*
   (ii) n miles?   *(2)*

   (b) An isosceles triangle has sides of length a, b and b.
   Write down an expression for the perimeter of the
   triangle in terms of a and b.   *(2)*

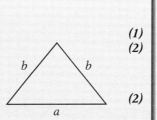

Remember that
the perimeter is
the distance
around the
outside.

Answer   (a)   (i) $4 \times 20 = 80$
She takes **80** minutes.
(ii) $20 \times n = 20n$
She takes **20n** minutes.

(b)   The perimeter is the distance around the outside.
Perimeter $= a + b + b$
$= a + 2b$

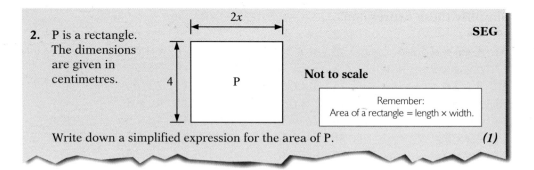

2. P is a rectangle. The dimensions are given in centimetres.

2x

4

P

SEG

Not to scale

Remember:
Area of a rectangle = length × width.

Write down a simplified expression for the area of P. **(1)**

Answer Area = length × width
$$= 2x \times 4$$
$$= 2 \times x \times 4$$
$$= 2 \times 4 \times x$$
$$= 8x \text{ cm}^2$$

Remember to write the number first in the answer.

Exercise 4 **A**

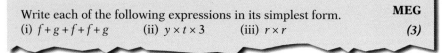

Write each of the following expressions in its simplest form. **MEG**
(i) $f + g + f + f + g$ (ii) $y \times t \times 3$ (iii) $r \times r$ **(3)**

B **1.** Helen bought a stereo.
She paid £x deposit and 12 monthly instalments of £y each.
Write down an expression for the total amount that Helen pays.

2. Ana bought a bike.
She paid £n deposit and 14 monthly instalments of £m each.
Write down an expression for the total amount that Ana paid.

C **1.** A ribbon is 4 metres long.
t metres is cut off the ribbon. How much is left?

2. A piece of wood is x feet long.
y feet is cut off the length. How much is left?

D

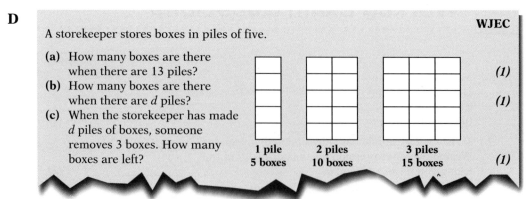

WJEC

A storekeeper stores boxes in piles of five.

(a) How many boxes are there when there are 13 piles? **(1)**

(b) How many boxes are there when there are d piles? **(1)**

(c) When the storekeeper has made d piles of boxes, someone removes 3 boxes. How many boxes are left? **(1)**

1 pile
5 boxes

2 piles
10 boxes

3 piles
15 boxes

E Brendon collects model cars. Each costs £12.

1. Write an expression for the cost of n cars.

2. A box to keep the cars in costs £24.
Write an expression for the cost of the box and n cars.

3. Brendon buys the box and n cars.
He then sells one car for £8.
Write an expression for the amount he has spent in total, after selling the car.

F 1. Max is paid £*y* per hour for working on a
Saturday.
Last weekend he worked 7 hours on Saturday.
How much was he paid for the 7 hours?

2. Max is paid twice as much if he works on
Sunday.
Last weekend he worked 8 hours on Sunday.
How much was he paid for his work on Sunday?

3. How much was Max paid altogether last
weekend?
Give your answer in its simplest form.

G Write an expression for the perimeter of these shapes.
Simplify the expression as much as possible.
Note: The perimeter is the distance right around the outside.

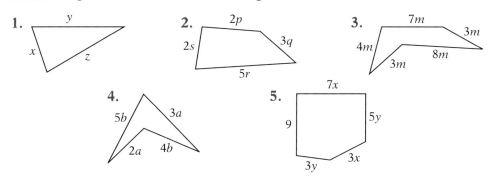

H Write an expression for the area of these rectangles.
Simplify the expression as much as possible.
Note: Area of a rectangle = length × width.

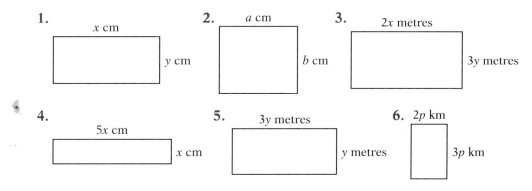

I A park is *x* metres long and *y* metres wide.
Write down an expression, in terms of *x* and *y* for:
1. the perimeter of the park
2. the area of the park.

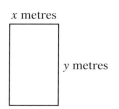

Expressions with brackets

$5(x + 2)$ is the same as $5 \times (x + 2)$.
$5 \times (x + 2) = 5 \times x + 5 \times 2$.
$\qquad\qquad\;\; = 5x + 10$.

To write an **expression without brackets** we multiply each term inside the bracket by the number outside.

Examples

$4(y + 5) = 4 \times y + 4 \times 5$
$\qquad\qquad = 4y + 20$

$7(2x + 3) = 7 \times 2x + 7 \times 3$
$\qquad\qquad = 14x + 21$

$3(p - 6) = 3 \times p - 3 \times 6$
$\qquad\qquad = 3p - 18$

$5(w - 4x) = 5 \times w - 5 \times 4x$
$\qquad\qquad = 5w - 20x$

Exercise 5   Write these expressions without brackets.
1. $5(x + 2)$
2. $4(y + 3)$
3. $2(b + 5)$
4. $6(d - 3)$
5. $5(w - 2)$
6. $4(x + 7)$
7. $3(x - 10)$
8. $7(x - 3)$
9. $2(2x + 3)$
10. $3(2y + 4)$
11. $4(2b - 3)$
12. $5(3y - 4)$
13. $2(2x + y)$
14. $3(2a - b)$
15. $2(2x - 3z)$
16. $4(2a + 2b)$
17. $5(3x - 4y)$
18. $3(2y - 4z)$

Example   Simplify $3a + 2(2a - 3b)$.
Answer   To simplify, rewrite the expression without brackets.
$3a + 2(2a - 3b) = 3a + 2 \times 2a - 2 \times 3b$ **Multiply out the bracket first.**
$\qquad\qquad\qquad = 3a + 4a - 6b$ **Add or subtract like terms.**
$\qquad\qquad\qquad = 7a - 6b$

Example   Simplify $9x + 3(2x - 3y)$.
Answer $9x + 3(2x - 3y) = 9x + 3 \times 2x - 3 \times 3y$
$\qquad\qquad\qquad = 9x + 6x - 9y$
$\qquad\qquad\qquad = 15x - 9y$

Exercise 6   **A**   Simplify these.
1. $x + 2(x + 1)$
2. $5 + 2(x + 3)$
3. $y + 2(y - 1)$
4. $13 + 4(x - 2)$
5. $2y + 3(y + 2)$
6. $4x + 3(x - 2)$
7. $3b + 2(b + 1)$
8. $5a + 2(a - 3)$
9. $20 + 5(x - 3)$
10. $x + 2(x + y)$
11. $a + 3(a + b)$
12. $y + 2(2y + 1)$
13. $2b + 3(b - 1)$
14. $8 + 6(b - 2)$
15. $10 + 5(x - 3)$
16. $3x + 2(2x - 3y)$
17. $4y + 3(2y - 4z)$
18. $4b + 2(2a - b)$
19. $5y + 3(2x - y)$
20. $8q + 3(3p - 4q)$
21. $7b + 4(3a - 2b)$

B

MEG

Multiply out the following expression by removing the brackets.
$3(2t + 5)$
(2)

Worked Exam Question

• •

A coach has x passengers upstairs and y passengers downstairs.

LONDON

(a) Write down an expression, in terms of x and y, for the total number of passengers on the coach.

Tickets for the journey on the coach cost £5 each.

(b) Write down an expression, in terms of x and y, for the total amount of money paid by the passengers on the coach.

(1)

(1)

> An expression in terms of x and y means the expression must have x and y in it.

Answer (a) The total number of passengers is $x + y$.

(b) Each passenger pays £5.

The total paid, in pounds, is $5 \times (x + y) = 5 \times x + 5 \times y$

$$= 5x + 5y$$

$5x + 5y$ pounds is paid in total.

> The $(x + y)$ must be put in a bracket because *all* of it is multiplied by £5.

Exercise 7

A A knife costs n pence. A fork costs $(n + 3)$ pence.
  1. Write an expression, in terms of n, for the cost of 8 knives.
  2. Write an expression, in terms of n, for the cost of 8 forks.
  3. Write an expression, in terms of n, for the cost of 8 knives and 8 forks. Simplify your expression as much as possible.

B There were a children in the junior tennis club and b children in the senior tennis club.
  1. Write down an expression, in terms of a and b, for the total number of children in the tennis club.
  2. Each child paid a fee of £10.
      Write an expression, in terms of a and b, for the total amount of money paid by children in the tennis club.

C Bob had £$2x$. Zenta had £3 more than Bob.
  1. Write an expression, in terms of x, for the amount of money Zenta had.
  2. Bob and Zenta spent all of their money on a raffle ticket.
      They won three times the amount they had spent.
      Write an expression for the total amount they won.
      Simplify your expression as much as possible.

D The width of a rectangle is $2x + 3$ centimetres.
      The length is twice as long as the width.
  1. Write an expression, in terms of x, for the length of the rectangle.
  2. Write an expression, in terms of x, for the perimeter of the rectangle.
      Simplify your expression as much as possible.

Finding the value of an expression

Example   Given that $a = 5$, $b = 8$ and $c = 19$, find the value of

1. $3a$ 2. $b + 3c$ 3. a^3 4. $\dfrac{c}{a}$ 5. $3(a + b)$

Answer
1. $3a = 3 \times a$
   $= 3 \times 5$
   $= 15$

2. $b + 3c = b + 3 \times c$
   $= 8 + 3 \times 19$
   $= 8 + 57$
   $= 65$

3. $a^3 = a \times a \times a$
   $= 5 \times 5 \times 5$
   $= 125$

4. $\dfrac{c}{a} = \dfrac{19}{5}$
   $= 3 \cdot 8$

5. $3(a + b) = 3 \times a + 3 \times b$
   $= 3 \times 5 + 3 \times 8$
   $= 15 + 24$
   $= 39$

> Remember to do the multiplication first.

Putting negative numbers into expressions

We sometimes have to **multiply with negative numbers**.
The rules are

1. **positive × negative = negative**	**Example** $4 \times -3 = -12$
2. **negative × positive = negative**	**Example** $-5 \times 2 = -10$
3. **negative × negative = positive**	**Example** $-3 \times -7 = 21$

Example   Find the value of $2x + 3y$ when $x = -1$ and $y = 3$.

Answer $2x + 3y = 2 \times x + 3 \times y$
$= 2 \times -1 + 3 \times 3$
$= -2 + 9$
$= 7$

Note: $2 \times -1 = -2$

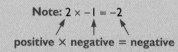

positive × negative = negative

Note: You could use a number line to help.

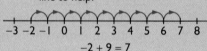

$-2 + 9 = 7$

Exercise 8

A Given that $x = 4$, $y = 3$, $z = 15$ find the value of
1. $4y$ 2. $3x$ 3. $2z$ 4. $3x + y$ 5. $4x + y$
6. $z - x$ 7. $z - 2y$ 8. $3x + 2y$ 9. $2z - 3x$ 10. x^2
11. y^3 12. $4(x + y)$ 13. $3(x - y)$ 14. $\dfrac{z}{y}$ 15. $\dfrac{z}{x}$

B Find the value of the following when $a = -1$ and $b = 2$.
1. $2b$ 2. $3a$ 3. $2a + b$ 4. $3a + b$ 5. $4a - b$
6. $5a - 2b$ 7. $2a + 10b$ 8. b^3 9. $a + b^2$ 10. $2b - 2a$

C Find the value of the following when $x = 2.5$, $y = 6$, $z = -3$.
1. $3y$ 2. y^2 3. $y - x$ 4. $2x$ 5. $2x + y$
6. $2z$ 7. $y + z$ 8. $z + 2y$ 9. $z - 2y$ 10. $z + x$
11. $10 - 2z$ 12. $y - z$ 13. $2y - 2z$ 14. $4x - 2z$ 15. $y - 3z$

Homework/Review 1

A **What do you call a robber wearing four balaclavas?**

$$\overline{6xy}\ \overline{15x}\ \overline{28x}\ \overline{3xy}\ \overline{3x^2y^3}\ \overline{2x+y}\ \overline{15x}\ \overline{7x+3}\ ,\qquad \overline{3x^2y^3}\ \overset{\mathbf{E}}{\overline{11x}}$$

$$\overline{5x+2}\ \overline{6xy}\ \overline{15x}\ \overline{3xy}\qquad \overline{3x^2y^3}\ \overset{\mathbf{E}}{\overline{11x}}\ \overline{6xy}\ \overline{24x^2}\qquad \overline{28x}\ \overline{xy}\ \overline{10x}$$

Use a copy of this box.
Simplify these expressions.

E $5x + 6x = 11x$ **U** $15x - 6x + x$ **I** $7x + 2y - 5x - y$
C $9x + 3 - 4x - 1$ **G** $11x + 10 - 4x - 7$ **O** $x \times y$
T $x \times y \times 3$ **Y** $4 \times 7x$ **N** $5x \times 3$
A $3x \times 2y$ **R** $4x \times 6x$ **H** $3 \times x \times x \times y \times y \times y$

B

The letter **s** represents the area of the square.
The letter **t** represents the area of the triangle.
So the area of this shape is **s + t**.

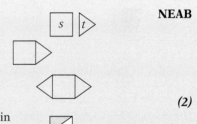

NEAB

(a) Write down an expression for the area of this
shape.
Give your answer in its simplest form. *(2)*
(b) Write down an expression for the shaded area in
this diagram. *(1)*

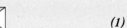

C Write these without brackets. Simplify if possible.
1. $3(x + 2)$ 2. $4(2x - 3)$ 3. $3(2y + 3z)$
4. $4x + 3(2x + 2)$ 5. $7a + 2(3a - 4)$ 6. $8y + 3(2x - 4y)$

D

WJEC

Richard takes t minutes to cycle to school.

(a) It takes him twice as long to walk to school. Write down, in terms of t,
how long it takes him to walk to school. *(1)*
(b) One week he walks to school on 5 days. Write down, in terms of t, the
total time he spends walking to school that week. *(1)*
(c) When Richard goes to school by bus, it takes him 15 minutes longer than
when he cycles. Write down, in terms of t, how long it takes him to go to
school by bus. *(1)*
(d) In another week, Richard cycles to school on 3 days and goes by bus on
2 days. Write down, in terms of t, the total time he spends travelling to
school that week. Simplify your answer as far as possible. *(3)*

E Find the value of the following when $a = -2$, $b = 4$ and $c = 7$.
1. $b + 2c$ 2. b^3 3. $3(c - b)$ 4. $2a + 3b$

Formulae

A **formula** is a rule. Sometimes it is written in words.

Worked Exam Question

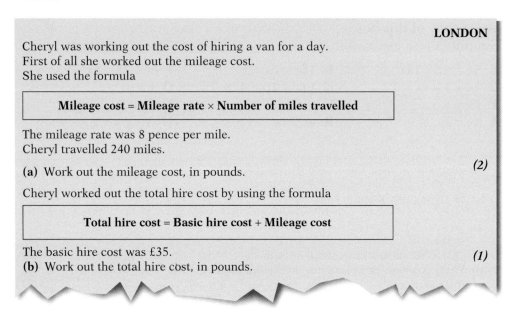

Cheryl was working out the cost of hiring a van for a day.
First of all she worked out the mileage cost.
She used the formula

LONDON

> **Mileage cost = Mileage rate × Number of miles travelled**

The mileage rate was 8 pence per mile.
Cheryl travelled 240 miles.

(a) Work out the mileage cost, in pounds.

(2)

Cheryl worked out the total hire cost by using the formula

> **Total hire cost = Basic hire cost + Mileage cost**

The basic hire cost was £35.
(b) Work out the total hire cost, in pounds.

(1)

Answer   (a)   Mileage cost = Mileage rate × Number of miles travelled
     = 8 × 240
     = 1920 pence
    1920 pence is **£19.20**.

   (b)   Total hire cost = Basic hire cost + Mileage cost
     = £35 + £19.20
     = **£54.20**

Exercise 9

A   This is how to cook a chicken.

Bake for 40 minutes per kilogram plus 15 minutes extra.

1. How long will it take to cook a chicken that weighs 1.5 kg?
2. A chicken which weighs 1.5 kg is put in the oven at 4 p.m.
   At what time will it be cooked?

B

LONDON

The number of teachers needed on a trip is found by using this formula:

> Number of teachers on the trip equals
> 'the number of pupils divided by 25 and rounded down to the next
> whole number'.

560 pupils are going on the trip.
How many teachers are needed?

(3)

C   The following formula can be used to find the cost, in pounds, of servicing a dishwasher.

Cost = 45 + 30 × number of hours worked

Calculate the cost of servicing a dishwasher when the work took
1. 2 hours   **2.** 3 hours   **3.** half an hour   **4.** $2\frac{1}{2}$ hours.

D   The cost, in pounds, to hire a ladder for a certain number of days is worked out using the rule

multiply the number of days by 3 and add 12

How much does it cost to hire a ladder for
1. 2 days   **2.** 5 days   **3.** 4 weeks   **4.** $3\frac{1}{2}$ days?

E   The area of a trapezium can be found using this formula.

$$\text{Area} = \left(\frac{\text{length of } x + \text{length of } y}{2}\right) \times \text{height}$$

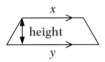

Find the area of trapezia with these values for x, y and height.
1. $x = 3$, $y = 5$, height = 2   **2.** $x = 4$, $y = 6$, height = 3
3. $x = 2.5$, $y = 3.5$, height = 4   **4.** $x = 3$, $y = 2$, height = 4
5. $x = 5.5$, $y = 6.5$, height = 3.5   **6.** $x = 4$, $y = 3$, height = 2.5

Sometimes formulae are written in **symbols**.

Example   The formula for converting temperature in °C into K (degrees Kelvin) is $K = C + 273$. K is the temperature in Kelvin. C is the temperature in °C. Convert −8 °C into degrees Kelvin.

Answer $K = C + 273$
           $= -8 + 273$
           $= 265$
           −8 °C is 265 K.

Exercise 10

A   Use the formula in the example above to convert these temperatures to degrees Kelvin.
1. 4 °C   **2.** 10 °C   **3.** 50 °C   **4.** 29 °C
5. −1 °C   **6.** −9 °C   **7.** −6 °C   **8.** −10 °C

B   The cost, C, in pence, of having n pages printed is

$$C = 10n + 30.$$

Work out the cost to have these numbers of pages printed.
1. 5   **2.** 29   **3.** 360   **4.** 1424

C   Speed is given by the formula $V = at$, where V is the speed, a is the acceleration and t is the time.
Find V when
1. $a = 3$, $t = 8$ **2.** $a = 2.5$, $t = 3$ **3.** $a = 9.8$, $t = 3.5$.

D Use the formula $s = 3a + 24$ to work out s when

1. $a = 5$ 2. $a = 4.2$ 3. $a = -6$ 4. $a = -2$
5. $a = 0.5$ 6. $a = 0.3$ 7. $a = \frac{2}{3}$ 8. $a = \frac{1}{4}$.

E

MEG

P and k are connected by the formula $P = 20 + 4k$.
Find the value of P when (i) $k = 2$,   (ii) $k = -3$.

(2)

Worked Exam Question

LONDON

Write, in symbols, the rule
'To find y, multiply k by 3 and then subtract 1.'

(3)

Answer   We want to find y, so the rule will begin '$y=$ '.
We write 'multiply k by 3 and then subtract 1' as $3k - 1$.
So the rule is $y = 3k - 1$.

Exercise 11   **A**   An approximate rule to change degrees Fahrenheit (F) into degrees
Celsius (C) is

**Subtract 30 from the Fahrenheit temperature and then divide the
answer by 2**.

1. Write this rule as a formula for C in terms of F.
2. Use your formula to find
    (a) C when $F = 130°$.   **(b)** C when $F = 60°$.

B   The length of each side of a regular hexagon is x centimetres.
Write down a formula for the perimeter, P, of the regular hexagon.
Give your answer as simply as possible.

C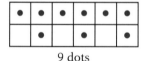

3 dots   6 dots   9 dots

d is the number of squares with dots
e is the number of empty squares

1. Write a formula that links d and e.
2. Use the formula to work out the number of black dots there will be
    when there are 50 empty squares.

D   A rule for finding the cost, in pounds, to hire a car is

Multiply the number of miles travelled, m, by 0.6 and add 20.

1. Write this rule as a formula for C, the cost, in terms of m, the number
    of miles travelled.
2. Use your formula to find the cost of hiring a car to travel
    100 miles.

Homework/Review 2

A Peter has a weekend job. His wages are worked out using this rule.

> **Wages in pounds** = number of hours worked × **6**.

How much will he get for working
1. 5 hours   2. 7 hours   3. $5\frac{1}{2}$ hours   4. $6\frac{1}{2}$ hours?

B

The following formula can be used to find the area, in square centimetres, of the figure shown.

WJEC

> **Area = 36 + 3 × height**

Calculate the area when the height is 4 cm.

(2)

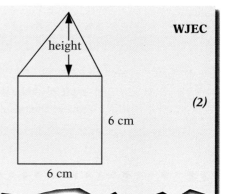

C

MEG

shape X   shape Y

(a) What goes in the gaps?
Shape X has 8 dots on its perimeter and 1 dot inside it.
Shape Y has ____ dots on its perimeter and ____ dots inside it.

(2)

The formula $A = \dfrac{P}{2} + N - 1$

gives the area (A) of any shape with straight edges,
where P is the number of dots on the perimeter of the shape
and N is the number of dots inside it.

Using this formula, the area of shape X is $\frac{8}{2} + 1 - 1 = 4$ cm².

(b) Use the formula to find the area of shape Y.

(c) Use a copy of this.
Draw another shape, different from shapes X
and Y, on the grid.
Use the formula to find its area.
You must show your working.

(2)

(3)

D Given $s = 5a + 10$ find the value of s when
1. $a = 2$ 2. $a = -4$ 3. $a = 5.6$ 4. $a = \frac{3}{5}$.

E The cost, in pounds, to have a refrigerator serviced is

> **Multiply the number of hours taken to service by 25 and add 40.**

Write the rule as a formula to find the cost C when it takes n hours to service.

Puzzles

1. * between two numbers means

   double the first number
   halve the second number
   add the results together.

   Example   double halve

   $2 * 6 = 4 + 3$
   $= 7$

   Find the value of these.

   (a) $3 * 8$ (b) $4 * 6$ (c) $10 * 2$ (d) $2 * 3$ (e) $5 * 5$

2. $\triangle$ between two numbers means

   multiply the two numbers together
   divide the result by 2.

   Find the value of these.

   (a) $3 \triangle 6$ (b) $5 \triangle 4$ (c) $9 \triangle 3$ (d) $2.5 \triangle 4$ (e) $8.5 \triangle 6$

☑ KEY POINTS

☑ $x + 8$ $y - 4$ $2n - 4$ $\dfrac{3m}{4}$ are examples of **expressions**.

 x, y, n and m stand for numbers.

☑ We can simplify expressions by **adding and subtracting like terms**.

 Example $7x + 4y - 5x + y = 7x - 5x + 4y + y$
 $= 2x + 5y$
 like terms   like terms

☑ $3 \times a = 3a$ $a \times a = a^2$ $3 \times 4 \times a \times b = 12ab$

☑ Some expressions are written with **brackets**.
 We can remove these by multiplying all the terms inside the brackets by the number outside.

 Example $2(2x - 3y) = 2 \times 2x - 2 \times 3y$
 $= 4x - 6y$

☑ We can work out the **value of an expression** if we are told what numbers the letters stand for.

 Example If $a = -1$ and $b = 4$ then $3a + 2b$ $= 3 \times a + 2 \times b$
 $= 3 \times -1 + 2 \times 4$
 $= -3 + 8$
 $= 5$

☑ **Formulae** or rules may written in words or symbols.

 Example The cost, C pounds, to hire a video recorder is given by

   Cost = 15 + 3 times the number of days hired.

   or $C = 15 + 3n$ where n is the number of days hired.

◄◄ CHAPTER REVIEW ◄◄

◄◄
Exercises 1, 2
and 3 on pages
54 and 55

A Simplify these.
1. $8a + 7b - 3a - 4b$ 2. $9n + 7 - 5n - 3$ 3. $7 \times 3n$
4. $3y \times 4y$ 5. $3(4x - 2y)$ 6. $p + 3(p - q)$

◄◄
Exercise 4
on page 56

B

WJEC

David makes a certain type of shirt with 8 buttons on each shirt.
In one week, David makes x of these shirts.
(a) Write down, in terms of x, the total number of buttons on these x shirts.   *(1)*
(b) David also makes blouses. Each week he makes twice as many blouses as
shirts. Write down, in terms of x, the total number of blouses that he
makes in a week.   *(1)*
(c) Each blouse has 6 buttons. Write down, in terms of x, the total number of
buttons on the blouses that he makes each week.   *(1)*
(d) Write down, in terms of x, the total number of buttons on the shirts and
blouses that he makes each week. Simplify your answer as far as possible.   *(2)*

◄◄
Exercise 8
on page 60

C Given that $a = -2$, $b = 3$ and $c = 4$ find the value of
1. $3b - c$ 2. $\frac{6b}{c}$ 3. $2a + b$ 4. $5a - b$ 5. b^3 6. $4(2c - b)$

◄◄
Exercises 1
and 10 on pages
54 and 63

D

SEG

(a) Simplify the algebraic expression $6x + 7 - 2x + 4$ *(2)*
(b) Using the formula $a = 5b - \frac{c}{4}$,
find the value of a when $b = 12$ and $c = 24$.   *(3)*

◄◄
Exercise 9 on
page 62

E

LONDON

Natasha uses this formula to work out her Total pay.
   Total pay = Rate per hour × Number of hours + Bonus
Her Rate per hour is £3.50.
She works for 35 hours
She has a Bonus of £5.50.
Work out her Total pay.   *(2)*

◄◄
Exercise 11
on page 64

F

SEG

The cost, in pounds, of hiring a drill for a number of days is worked out using
the rule:
   Multiply the number of days by 5 and add 15.
(a) How much does it cost to hire the drill for 3 days?   *(1)*
(b) Write the rule as a formula to find the cost, C, when the drill is hired
for n days.   *(2)*

5 Calculation using the Calculator

By the end of this chapter you will be able to:

- use the calculator to solve problems involving the four operations
- use the calculator to find squares, cubes, square roots and cube roots
- use the calculator to solve trial and improvement problems.

Getting started ....

Solve these problems using your calculator.

1. A two digit number is multiplied by itself.
   The answer is between 4700 and 4800.
   What is the two digit number?

2. The sum of three numbers is 19.
   When the three numbers are multiplied together the answer is 240.
   What are the three numbers?

3. Consecutive numbers come one after the other.
   17 and 18 are consecutive numbers.
   Two consecutive numbers are multiplied together.
   The answer is 650.
   What are the two consecutive numbers?

4. Three consecutive numbers are multiplied together.
   The answer is 990.
   What are the three consecutive numbers?

Using the calculator to solve problems

Worked Exam Questions

1. A teacher is organising a trip to Pleasureland. There are 560 pupils going on the trip. The pupils will go by coach.
   Each coach can carry 52 pupils.
   Work out how many coaches are needed.

   LONDON

   (3)

Answer We must divide 560 by 52.
$560 \div 52 = 10.769\,230\,77$
This means 10 and a bit coaches are needed.
We can't hire a bit of a coach. We must round up.
So **11** coaches are needed.

Think carefully about whether to round up or down.

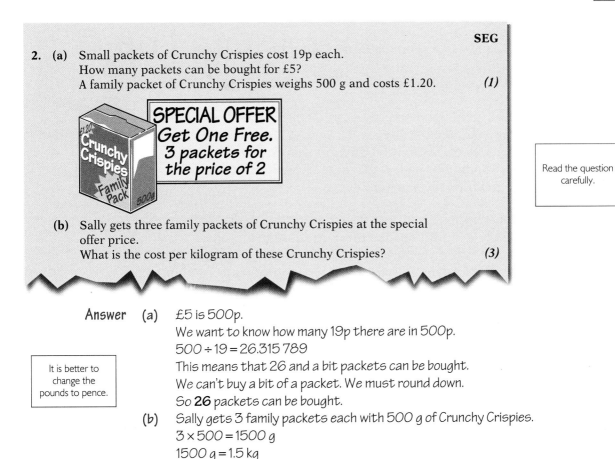

SEG

2. (a) Small packets of Crunchy Crispies cost 19p each.
How many packets can be bought for £5?
A family packet of Crunchy Crispies weighs 500 g and costs £1.20.   *(1)*

SPECIAL OFFER
Get One Free.
3 packets for
the price of 2

Read the question
carefully.

(b) Sally gets three family packets of Crunchy Crispies at the special
offer price.
What is the cost per kilogram of these Crunchy Crispies?   *(3)*

Answer **(a)** *£5 is 500p.*
We want to know how many 19p there are in 500p.
500 ÷ 19 = 26.315 789
This means that 26 and a bit packets can be bought.
We can't buy a bit of a packet. We must round down.
*So **26** packets can be bought.*

It is better to
change the
pounds to pence.

(b) *Sally gets 3 family packets each with 500 g of Crunchy Crispies.*
3 × 500 = 1500 g
1500 g = 1.5 kg
Sally gets the 3 packets for the price of 2.
So the 3 packets cost 2 × £1.20 = £2.40.
The cost per kilogram is found by dividing £2.40 by 1.5.
2.40 ÷ 1.5 = 1.6
*So the cost per kilogram is **£1.60**.*

Remember
1 kg = 1000 g.

Exercise 1   **A 1.** How many 53-seater coaches are needed to carry 395 people to a
football game?

2. Alan organises a coach trip for 260 people.
If each coach holds 48 people, how many coaches will be needed?

B

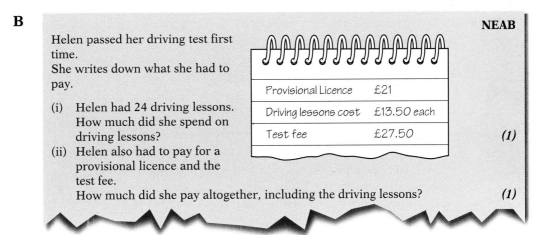

NEAB

Helen passed her driving test first
time.
She writes down what she had to
pay.

Provisional Licence   £21

Driving lessons cost   £13.50 each

Test fee   £27.50

(i) Helen had 24 driving lessons.
How much did she spend on
driving lessons?   *(1)*

(ii) Helen also had to pay for a
provisional licence and the
test fee.
How much did she pay altogether, including the driving lessons?   *(1)*

C   Jake buys a television.
He pays £175 deposit and 12 monthly instalments of £31.72.
Work out the total amount that Jake pays.

D   In a shop, Sam spends £1.42 on milk, £3.14 on tea and £0.68 on sugar.
1.   Calculate the total amount that Sam spends.
2.   Sam pays with a £10 note. How much change should he be given?

E   George has a sausage stall.
He puts 8 mℓ of sauce on each sausage he sells.
Each bottle of sauce holds 256 mℓ.
1.   How many sausages can have sauce from one bottle?
2.   George buys the bottles of sauce in boxes of 48 bottles.
One full bottle weighs 285 g.
The box weighs 1250 g.
What is the total weight of a box full of sauce bottles?

F

NEAB

Chocolate bars cost 23p each.
    (a)   How many chocolate bars can be bought for £5?   *(2)*
    (b)   How much change will there be?   *(2)*

G   The Langham family went into a café.
This table shows what they ordered.
1.   How much did this cost altogether?
2.   Mrs Langham paid the bill with a £10 note.
How much change did she get?

| Three cans of cola at 63p each |
| Two cups of coffee at 64p each |
| Five cakes at 42p each |

H   The thickness of 200 pages of a book is 2.86 cm.
1.   Find the thickness, in cm, of one page.
2.   Calculate the thickness of 380 pages of the same book.

I

LONDON

Tickets for a football match cost £4.70 each.
(a)   How much will 100 tickets cost?   *(2)*

Children can buy tickets at half price.
Mr and Mrs Smith and their two children buy tickets.
(b)   Work out the total cost of the tickets.   *(3)*

J   The diagram shows a fence with fencing rails which are 3.8 m long.
How many rails are needed for a fence 200 m long?

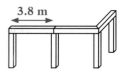

3.8 m

K Mr and Mrs Douglas take their children to the art gallery.
The admission cost for them all was £3.30.
How many children did they take?

<table>
<tr><td colspan="2" align="center">**ART GALLERY**</td></tr>
<tr><td>Adult</td><td>90p</td></tr>
<tr><td>Child</td><td>50p</td></tr>
</table>

L   **NEAB**

The table shows the cost of hiring a ladder.

Cost for the first day	Extra cost per day for each additional day
£13.75	£2.25

(i) What is the cost of hiring the ladder for 3 days?   *(2)*
(ii) A family hires the ladder.
      The total cost of hiring the ladder was £25.
      How many days did the family hire it for?   *(3)*

M A piece of ribbon is 420 centimetres in length.
It is to be cut into pieces which are 16 cm long.
Calculate
1. how many 16 cm pieces can be cut from the ribbon
2. the length of the small piece of ribbon that is left over.

N Murray saved £580 for his holiday in Greece. How many drachma would he get if the exchange rate was 358 drachma to the pound?

O   **MEG**

You buy 31 stamps at 19p each.
(a) Work out the total cost of the stamps in pence.   *(1)*
(b) Check that your answer is sensible by giving an approximate
        calculation.   *(1)*

P   **LONDON**

John is going to Spain on holiday.
He changes £190 to Spanish pesetas.
£1 = 183 pesetas.
Work out how many pesetas John gets.   *(2)*

Q

These notices were seen on two shop windows.
At which shop was the price of one apple cheaper?
By how much?

R   The size and selling price of small
and medium mouthwash is shown.

Which size mouthwash gives better
value for money?

Small size
144ml
£1.00

Medium size
270ml
£1.80

S

NEAB

A road 750 metres long is to be resurfaced.
(a) *Workalot* say they can resurface it in
    23 days.
    How many metres is this each day?
    Give your answer to the nearest metre.   *(3)*
(b) *Roadfill* say they can resurface 40 metres
    of the road each day.
    How many days will it take them to do
    the job?   *(2)*

T

MEG

Tom went on a day trip to France.
(a) On the ferry he changed £120 into francs.
     The exchange rate was £1 = 7.80 francs.
     How many francs did he get for his £120?   *(2)*
(b) On his return he had 200 francs left.
     He changed them back into pounds at the rate of £1 = 9.30 francs.
     How much did he get to the nearest penny?   *(3)*

Investigation

		Example
Step 1	Choose a number between 100 and 999.	**126**
Step 2	Multiply it by 11.	$126 \times 11 = 1386$
Step 3	Multiply the answer to **step 2** by 91.	$1386 \times 91 = 126126$

The answer is the number you chose, repeated to
make a 6-digit number.
Does this work for these numbers?

187   200   586   732   964

Does it work for all numbers between 100 and 999?

Investigation

Reversing digits

MEG

(a) **(i)** Follow the instructions:

Write down any two-digit number.   e.g.   46

Write down the number that has your
two digits reversed.   e.g.   64

Add your two numbers.   e.g.   46
+64
110

Repeat the process for three other two-digit numbers.   *(2)*

(ii) What do you notice about all your answers?   *(1)*

(iii) Test the correctness of your observation.   *(1)*

(b) **(i)** Follow the instructions:

Write down any three-digit number.   e.g.   157

Write down the number that has your
three digits reversed.   e.g.   751

Subtract the smaller of your two numbers
from the larger.   e.g.   751
−157
594

Repeat the process for three other three-digit numbers.   *(2)*

(ii) What *three* things do you notice about all your answers?   *(3)*

(iii) Test the correctness of your observations.   *(1)*

Puzzle

Use a copy of this crossnumber.
Fill it in using the clues.

Across

1. Total number of days in 1999, 2000, 2001 and 2002.
4. Half of 1460.
5. Multiply 1404 by 5 and then add 3.
6. Double 43.1. Multiply the answer by 25.
9. Quarter of 744.
11. Double 1011 then subtract 20.
12. 16 squared subtract 2.
13. 360 divided by 2.5.
15. 153.8 × 50.
16. One third of 6675.

Down

1. Three times the sum of 16 and 18.
2. The product of 25 and 27.
3. The first multiple of 5 that is bigger than 100.
4. Number of days in 2 non leap years.
7. 899 × 25
8. Five times the difference between 20 000 and 1862.
10. Thirty three more than the days in 17 years (4 of them are leap years).
14. 6 times the number of days in a week.

Homework/Review 1

A

> Petrol costs 62p per litre.
> Work out the cost of 12 litres. (Answer in pounds.)
>
> **LONDON**
> *(2)*

B

> Tickets for a concert cost £3 each. Ramana has £17.
> Work out the greatest number of tickets that Ramana can buy.
>
> **LONDON**
> *(2)*

C

> Apples cost 99p per kilogram.
> Work out the total cost of 3.65 kg of apples. (Answer in pounds.)
>
> **LONDON**
> *(3)*

D

> Samir is baking apple pies and gooseberry pies.
> He uses 1.25 kg of flour in the apple pies.
> He uses 0.92 kg of flour in the gooseberry pies.
> How much flour will he have left from a 3 kg bag of flour?
>
> **SEG**
> *(2)*

E

> 56 and 57 are consecutive numbers as 57 is one more than 56.
> **(a)** Write down any two consecutive numbers between 20 and 30.
> **(b)** I add two consecutive numbers and get the answer 35.
> What are the numbers?
>
> **NEAB**
> *(1)*
> *(2)*

F

> **(a)** Work out the cost of 5 Breakfasts.
>
> Dara buys some cups of tea.
> **(b)** Work out the greatest number of
> cups of tea she can buy with £5.
>
> **LONDON**
> *(2)*
> *(2)*
>
> **Sam's Cafe**
>
> | | |
> |---|---|
> | Cup of Tea | 80p |
> | Cup of Coffee | 90p |
> | Breakfast | £2.95 |
> | Today's Special | £4 |

G

> Leroy weighed 300 sheets of paper, and found
> that the total weight was 1350 grams.
> **(a)** Find the weight of one sheet of paper.
>
> The height of the stack of paper is 27 millimetres.
> **(b)** Work out the thickness of one sheet of
> paper.
> **(c)** Find the height of a stack of paper
> containing 472 sheets.
>
> **MEG**
> *(2)*
> *(2)*
> *(2)*

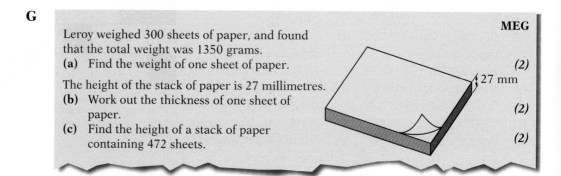

Order of operations

Most calculators do **operations in the correct order**.

Example $5 \times 3 - 2 \times 4$
The multiplication must be done before the subtraction.
Without the calculator we would work this out as follows.

$$5 \times 3 - 2 \times 4 = 15 - 8$$
$$= 7$$

do first   do first

Using the calculator key the numbers in order.
Note: Do not press the $=$ until the end.

| 5 | × | 3 | − | 2 | × | 4 | = |

The calculator will give the correct answer.
Note: Some calculators have **EXE** instead of $=$.

Exercise 2   **A**   Use your calculator to find the answers to these.

1. $5 + 2 \times 3$
2. $6.8 + 4 \times 1.4$
3. $3 \times 2 + 6 \times 8$
4. $5.4 \times 3 - 1.2$
5. $6.4 \times 2.1 - 1.2 \times 3$
6. $5.4 \div 3 + 2 \times 4$
7. $8.8 \div 2 - 4.8 \div 1.2$
8. $1 \div 4 + 1 \div 2$
9. $5.6 \times 3 - 12.4 \div 3.1$
10. $8 \times 1.6 - 4.8 \div 2.4$
11. $\dfrac{18.6}{3} + 6.3$
12. $17.3 - 8.6 \times 2 \div 5$

B   Copy these. Insert a $+$, $-$, $\times$ or $\div$ to make them true.
1. $3 \_\_\_ 4 \_\_\_ 2 = 11$
2. $5 \_\_\_ 12 \_\_\_ 3 = 1$
3. $(3.6 - 1.2) \_\_\_ 2 = 4.8$
4. $5.6 \_\_\_ 2 \_\_\_ 3.9 \_\_\_ 3 = 1.5$

Squares, cubes, square roots and cube roots

Find out how to do these using your calculator.
* **square** a number, for example 4.2^2
* **cube** a number, for example 7^3
* take the **square root** of a number, for example $\sqrt{85}$
* take the **cube root** of a number, for example $\sqrt[3]{72}$

Example   Use your calculator to find the values of these.

1. $2.3^2 + \sqrt{2.8}$
2. $\dfrac{2.4 \times 3.6}{4.6 - 1.8}$ to 1 decimal place
3. $1.2^3 + \sqrt[3]{22.5}$

Answer   1. Possible keying sequences are:

| 2.3 | shift | x^2 | + | 2.8 | √ | = | **6.9633201**

or

| 2.3 | x^2 | + | √ | 2.8 | = | **6.963320053**

Sometimes you have to decide what to round to. Always say what you have rounded to.

We must round the answer.
The answer is **6.96** to 2 decimal places.
The answer is **7.0** to 1 decimal place.

2. We must calculate the bottom line first
   $4.6 - 1.8 = 2.8$

   $$\frac{2.4 \times 3.6}{4.6 - 1.8} = \frac{2.4 \times 3.6}{2.8}$$

   $$= 3.1 \text{ to 1 decimal place.}$$

3. Possible keying sequences are:

   or

   | 1.2 | y^x | 3 | + | shift | $\sqrt[3]{}$ | 22.5 | = |

Exercise 3

A Use your calculator to find the answers to these.

1. 0.6×4.3
2. 5.6×0.2
3. 0.8×2.5
4. $\sqrt{169}$

5. $8^2 - 5^2$
6. $\dfrac{0.7 \times 0.4}{2}$
7. $\dfrac{18 \times 48}{24}$
8. $\dfrac{78 \times 14}{112 - 86}$

9. $\dfrac{90 \times 18}{78 - 42}$
10. $\dfrac{18 - 5.6}{3.1}$
11. $\dfrac{3.6 - 1.2}{2 - 0.8}$

B Use your calculator to find the answers to these.
Give your answer correct to 1 decimal place.

1. 0.27×1.38
2. $\dfrac{5.6}{1.3^2}$
3. $\dfrac{8.7 - 3.2}{4.6}$
4. $\dfrac{4.6 - 0.86}{4.7}$

5. $\dfrac{6.3 \times 1.2}{5.1}$
6. $\dfrac{4.3 \times 1.7^3}{5.9}$
7. $2.13^2 + \sqrt[3]{4.72}$
8. $8.16^2 - 3.18$

9. $\sqrt{5.32} - 1.25$
10. $\sqrt[3]{5.75} + 2.31^2$
11. $\dfrac{0.5 + 1.07}{2.6 + 1.1}$
12. $\dfrac{2.9 \times 0.59}{3.6 - 1.4}$

C (a) Work out $\dfrac{8.1 \times 9.7}{7.2 - 2.9}$.
       Write down your full calculator display.
   (b) Use estimation to check your answer.
        Show each step of your working.

Fractions on the calculator

Example Find the answer to $\frac{1}{4} + \frac{2}{3}$ as a decimal.

Key as | 1 | ÷ | 4 | + | 2 | ÷ | 3 | = | to give 0.9 to 1 d.p.

Exercise 4

A Find the answer to these as a decimal correct to 2 decimal places.

1. $\frac{1}{4} + \frac{1}{18}$
2. $\frac{1}{24} + \frac{1}{32}$
3. $\frac{1}{27} + \frac{1}{53}$
4. $\frac{3}{25} + \frac{7}{29}$

5. $\frac{8}{17} + \frac{9}{16}$
6. $\frac{14}{29} + \frac{3}{52}$
7. $\frac{48}{86} + \frac{59}{99}$
8. $\frac{4}{17} + \frac{1}{57}$

B Tina wanted to find the answer to $\frac{1}{28} + \frac{1}{52}$.
She keyed

| 1 | ÷ | 28 | + | 52 | = |

1. Will she get the correct answer?
2. Use your calculator to calculate $\frac{1}{28} + \frac{1}{52}$.
   Give your answer to 3 decimal places.

Puzzle

Use a copy of this crossnumber.
Fill it in.

Across

1. 1.23×2.6

5. $\dfrac{7200}{100}$

7. $68.3 - 7.1$

8. $\dfrac{14.8}{0.2}$

9. $274.6 + 235.8$

11. $400 \times \sqrt{0.04}$

12. 4.8452 to 3 d.p.

14. $6.8 + 3.4 \times 7$

16. $1.3 \times 1.4 + 4.26$

18. $6.2 \times 5.4 - 4 \times 6.07$

20. 2.99 to 1 d.p.

21. $1349 \div 19$

23. $5.1 - \dfrac{2.4}{0.6}$

24. $3.023 \times \sqrt{100}$

25. $\dfrac{4.2 \times 2^3}{0.1}$

Down

1. 3.47 to 1 d.p.

2. $183.568 - 23.259$

3. $\dfrac{367.012}{2^2}$ to 1 d.p.

4. $3.4 + 5.043$

6. $1350 \div \sqrt[3]{125}$

10. $252 \div 18$

13. $\dfrac{232 + 18}{7.6 - 2.6}$

15. $146.98 - 84.25$

16. 6.7281 to 2 d.p.

17. $\dfrac{0.0812 \times 50 \times 4}{2}$

19. $\dfrac{10.35}{4.5}$

22. $\dfrac{680 + 20}{70}$

Investigation

A $40 \times 50 = 2000$

Do *not* use the calculator to answer these.

1. Do you think 41×49 will be bigger or smaller than 40×50?

Note: $40 + 1 \longrightarrow 41 \times 49 \longleftarrow 50 - 1$

2. Do you think 39×51 will be bigger or smaller than 40×50?

Note: $40 - 1 \longrightarrow 39 \times 51 \longleftarrow 50 + 1$

Now use your calculator to find the answers.
Were you right? What is the difference between the answers to 41×49 and 39×51?

B $50 \times 60 = 3000$
Is 51×59 bigger or smaller than 50×60?
Is 49×61 bigger or smaller than 50×60?
Use your calculator to check.
What is the difference between the answers to 51×59 and 49×61?

C $30 \times 40 = 1200$
What is the difference between the answers to 31×39 and 29×41?
Is the difference always the same when we do this?
Check for these.
$80 \times 90 \qquad 70 \times 80 \qquad 60 \times 70$

Solving problems by trial and improvement

We can solve problems using **trial and improvement**.

Example   The length of a rectangle is 2 cm longer than the width.
The area of the rectangle is 28 cm².
Use trial and improvement to find the length and width to the nearest millimetre.

Answer   Area of a rectangle = length × width
Choose a number for the width, add 2 to it to get the length
and multiply these together to find the area.

Choose   width = 5 cm   length = 7 cm   Area = 5 × 7
= 35 cm²   **too big**

Choose   width = 4 cm   length = 6 cm   Area = 4 × 6
= 24 cm²   **too small**

Choose   width = 4.5 cm   length = 6.5 cm   Area = 4.5 × 6.5
= 29.25 cm²   **too big**

Choose   width = 4.3 cm   length = 6.3 cm   Area = 4.3 × 6.3
= 27.09 cm²   **too small**

Choose   width = 4.4 cm   length = 6.4 cm   Area = 4.4 × 6.4
= 28.16 cm²   **too big**

The exact width lies somewhere between 4.3 cm and 4.4 cm.   4.4 cm is closer than 4.3 cm because 28.16 is closer than 27.09 is to 28.
So width = 4.4 cm and length = 6.4 cm to the nearest millimetre.

Exercise 5

A   The length of a rectangle is 2 cm longer than the width.
The area of the rectangle is 30 cm².
Use trial and improvement to find the length and width to the nearest millimetre.

B   Use trial and improvement to find the length and width of these rectangles to the nearest millimetre.
1.   length 3 cm longer than width and area = 42 cm²
2.   length 2.5 cm longer than width and area = 35 cm²

C   The length of Jane's pool is 4 m longer than the width.
The area of the pool is 340 m².
Use trial and improvement to find the length and width of the pool to the nearest tenth of a metre.

D   The length of a field is 50 m longer than the width.
The area of the field is 5050 m².
Use trial and improvement to find the length and width of the field to the nearest 10 cm (0.1 of a metre).

Example   Peter wanted to find $\sqrt{1.8}$.
His calculator did not have a $\boxed{\sqrt{}}$.

Using **trial and improvement**, find $\sqrt{1.8}$ to 2 decimal places.

Answer
Try	1.4	$1.4 \times 1.4 = 1.96$	too big
Try	1.3	$1.3 \times 1.3 = 1.69$	too small
Try	1.35	$1.35 \times 1.35 = 1.8225$	too big
Try	1.34	$1.34 \times 1.34 = 1.7956$	too small

The answer lies between 1.34 and 1.35. 1.34 is closer because 1.7956 is closer than 1.8225 is to 1.8.
So $\sqrt{1.8} = 1.34$ to 2 decimal places.

Exercise 6   Using trial and improvement, find the answers to these to 2 decimal places.

1. $\sqrt{2.4}$ 2. $\sqrt{4.3}$ 3. $\sqrt{6.1}$ 4. $\sqrt{2.7}$ 5. $\sqrt{8.4}$
6. $\sqrt{10.3}$ 7. $\sqrt{16.5}$ 8. $\sqrt{22}$ 9. $\sqrt{41}$

 # Homework/Review 2

A **What gets wetter the more it dries?**
Use a copy of this box.

				E	
22		56	0.16	65	3.76	45

Use your calculator to find the value of these.

E 0.8×4.7 **A** $\sqrt{484}$ **W** $9^2 - 4^2$

O $\dfrac{0.6 \times 0.8}{3}$ **L** $\dfrac{20 \times 72}{32}$ **T** $\dfrac{16 \times 77}{58 - 36}$

B Using your calculator find the answers to these, giving your answer correct to 1 decimal place.

1. 0.68×4.23 2. $\dfrac{8.9}{2.4}$ 3. $\dfrac{4.7 - 3.2}{2.1}$

4. $\dfrac{5.8 - 0.96}{5.2}$ 5. $\dfrac{4.2 \times 1.4}{3.2}$ 6. $\dfrac{5.7 \times 9.6}{2.3}$

7. $4.13^2 + 5.72$ 8. $13.46^2 - 5.26$ 9. $\sqrt{8.62} - 1.32^3$

10. $\sqrt[3]{6.72} + 4.13$ 11. $\dfrac{0.8 + 3.64}{2.6 - 0.82}$ 12. $\dfrac{4.1 \times 0.68}{4.7 - 3.8}$

C In which order will the calculator do the operations in this calculation?
$5 \times 6 - 3 \times 2 + 4$

D Find the answer to these as a decimal rounded to 2 decimal places.
1. $\frac{1}{32} + \frac{1}{53}$ 2. $\frac{1}{46} + \frac{1}{18}$ 3. $\frac{3}{25} + \frac{5}{27}$

E   Using trial and improvement find the answers to these, giving your answer to 2 decimal places.
1. $\sqrt{5}$ 2. $\sqrt{4.3}$ 3. $\sqrt{18}$ 4. $\sqrt{84}$

F   The length of a rectangle is 4 cm longer than the width.
The area of the rectangle is 50 cm^2.
Use trial and improvement to find the length and width to the nearest millimetre (nearest 0.1 cm).

G

NEAB

(a)   Work out $\dfrac{4.7 \times 20.1}{5.6 - 1.8}$
Write down your full calculator display.   (1)
(b)   Use estimation to check your answer.
Show each step of your working.   (2)

✔ KEY POINTS

✔ We can use the **calculator** to solve problems.

✔ We can use the calculator to find **squares**, **cubes**, **square roots** and **cube roots**.

✔ Most calculators **do operations in the correct order** if the numbers are keyed in as the calculation is written.

   Example $5 + 6 \times 4 - 3$ is keyed as

   $\boxed{5}\ \boxed{+}\ \boxed{6}\ \boxed{\times}\ \boxed{4}\ \boxed{-}\ \boxed{3}\ \boxed{=}$

   The calculator will do the multiplication before the addition and subtraction.

✔ We can use **trial and improvement** to solve problems.

◄◄ CHAPTER REVIEW ◄◄

◄◄
Exercise 1
on page 69

A

SEG

A coach will seat 46 pupils.
(i)   How many coaches are needed to take 197 pupils on a trip?   (2)
(ii) The 197 pupils pay £2.60 each to cover the cost of the coaches.
How much does it cost to hire each coach?   (3)

◄◄
Exercise 1
on page 69

B

WJEC

Sali and Marc are decorating their house.
(a) They buy two tins of paint. One tin costs £8.98 and the other costs £9.87.
(i)   Find the total cost of the paint.
(ii) They pay for the paint using a £20 note. How much change should they be given?   (2)
(b) Marc buys 18 packets of patterned tiles.
(i)   Each packet contains 6 tiles.
How many tiles does Marc buy?
(ii) Marc paid £234 for the tiles.
What is the cost of one packet of tiles?   (4)

◀◀
Exercise 1
on page 69

C

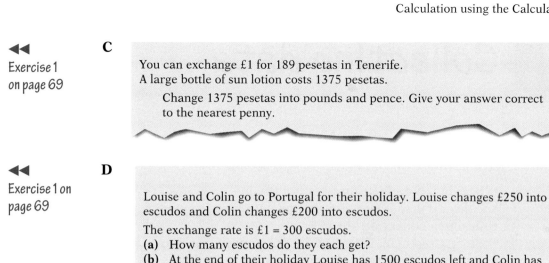

LONDON

You can exchange £1 for 189 pesetas in Tenerife.
A large bottle of sun lotion costs 1375 pesetas.

Change 1375 pesetas into pounds and pence. Give your answer correct
to the nearest penny. *(3)*

◀◀
Exercise 1 on
page 69

D

WJEC

Louise and Colin go to Portugal for their holiday. Louise changes £250 into
escudos and Colin changes £200 into escudos.

The exchange rate is £1 = 300 escudos.
(a) How many escudos do they each get? *(2)*
(b) At the end of their holiday Louise has 1500 escudos left and Colin has
1100 escudos left.
They put their escudos together and go to the bank to change them into
pounds.
The bank changes escudos into pounds at the rate of 325 escudos = £1.
How many pounds do they get? *(2)*

◀◀
Exercise 1
on page 69

E

SEG

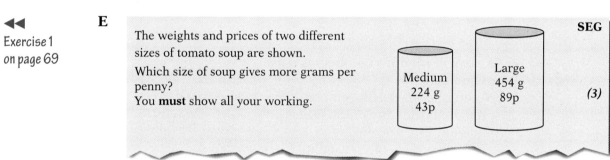

The weights and prices of two different
sizes of tomato soup are shown.

Which size of soup gives more grams per
penny?
You **must** show all your working.

Medium
224 g
43p

Large
454 g
89p

(3)

◀◀
Exercise 2
on page 75

F Use your calculator to work these out.

1. 0.6×0.25 2. $\dfrac{0.8 \times 1.4^3}{1.12}$ 3. $9^2 - 7^2$ 4. $\dfrac{5.8 \times 6}{5.6 - 2.6}$

◀◀
Exercise 2
on page 75

G

LONDON

Use a calculator to work out

$$15.2 \times \sqrt{10.24} - 3.62$$ *(3)*

◀◀
Exercise 5
on page 78

H The length of a rectangle is 2 cm longer than the width.
The area of the rectangle is 32 cm².
Use trial and improvement to find the length and the width to the nearest
millimetre.

◀◀
Exercise 6
on page 79

I Use trial and improvement to find $\sqrt{18.4}$ correct to 2 decimal places.

6 Collecting data

By the end of this chapter you will be able to:

- decide if data is discrete or continuous
- collect discrete and continuous data on a frequency table
- design a collection sheet
- design and criticise questions for a questionnaire
- recognise a random sample and a biased sample
- read information from a database.

Getting started ....

A table of random numbers is a list of numbers.
No number in this list can be predicted from any of the other numbers.
These tables are often used in statistics.
What for?
Investigate to see whether your calculator can produce random numbers.
If it can, use it to produce a list of 20 random numbers.

Table of Random Numbers					
2907	7261	7111	6105	8189	1024
2759	9598	1295	3523	8633	1282
6770	2309	8940	8495	5214	8956
1004	2394	1931	3787	0668	0283
4533	0996	3576	3201	1741	6840
3468	2125	2739	1437	7105	0205
3223	5926	7235	6515	6858	5106
6259	9214	5168	6623	4845	7707
4189	7661	3694	2428	0772	9934

Discrete and continuous data

Discrete data is data which can only have certain values.
Continuous data is data which can have any value within a certain range.

Discrete data is often found by counting.

Example The number of babies born last July at hospitals.

Continuous data is found by measuring.

Example The lengths of the babies born last July.

Exercise 1   Which of the following are discrete data and which are continuous data?
1. The number of leaves on trees.
2 The masses of cows.
3. The number of posters on classroom walls.
4. The volume of water in tanks.
5. The areas of school staff rooms.
6. The number of staff at schools.
7. The quantity of oil in cars.
8. The length of school bikesheds.

Frequency tables

We can collect data on **tally charts** or **frequency tables**.

Example   This table shows the number of
pupils who wear glasses in each
year group.
This is **discrete** data.

IIHI is 5.

Year group	Tally	Frequency
Year 7	IHI IHI IHI I	16
Year 8	IHI IHI IHI IHI IIII	24
Year 9	IHI IHI IHI IHI IHI I	26
Year 10	IHI IHI IHI IHI IHI III	28

Sometimes discrete and continuous data are grouped into **equal class intervals**.

Examples

We usually have about 5 or 6 equal class intervals.

Number of coins in purse	Tally	Frequency
0–4	IHI III	8
5–9	IHI IHI IHI I	16
10–14	IHI IHI IHI III	18
15–19	IHI IHI IIII	14
20–24	II	2

↑ Equal class intervals

This is **grouped discrete data.**

Weight of suitcases(kg)	Tally	Frequency
15–	IHI I	6
20–	IHI IHI IHI IHI II	22
25–	IHI IHI IHI IHI IHI	25
30–	IHI IHI IHI IHI III	23
35–	IHI III	8

↑ Equal class intervals

This is **grouped continuous data.**

Exercise 2   **A**   The number of people who used the photocopier each hour is given in this list.

4 3 0 4 2 0 1 3 4 5

2 4 5 5 3 4 5 2 1 3

1. Use a copy of this frequency table.
   Fill it in.
2. What was the most common number
   of people to use the photocopier in
   an hour?

Number of people	Tally	Frequency
0		
1		
2		
3		
4		
5		

B   The scores (out of 25) achieved by 20 people in a
quiz were

16   19   17   7   12   9   15   22   24   10

13   8   15   19   23   14   25   5   23   13

Use a copy of the frequency table below.
Fill it in.

Score	Tally	Frequency
1–5		
6–10		
11–15		
16–20		
21–25		

C   On a market stall the price of an apple depends on the mass.
The masses of 20 apples on the stall were recorded
to the nearest gram.

129   121   185   114   171   207   178   100

93   157   235   193   107   164   181   101

120   150   174   233   116   201   167   197

Fruit Stall

Use a copy of the frequency table below.
Fill it in.

Mass (g)	Tally	Frequency
$90 \leq g < 140$		
$140 \leq g < 190$		
$190 \leq g < 240$		

Collection sheets

The design of a **collection sheet** depends on the data being collected.
Collection sheets are sometimes called **observation sheets** or **tally sheets**
or **data sheets**.

Examples

Make of car	Tally	Frequency
Ford		
Mazda		
BMW		
Volvo		
Toyota		
Mitsubishi		
Mercedes		
Rover		

This collection sheet was used to find the
make of car owned by people in a village.

Name	Tally	Number
Ruth B		
Tom C		
Zenta D		
Shana E		
Bryn E		
Huw F		
Anna F		

This collection sheet was used to count
the number of times students ran round
a track.

Worked Exam Question

LONDON

Karl's and Eleanor's school is near a busy main road.
They decide to carry out a survey of the different types of vehicles that
travel on the main road.
Design a suitable data sheet so that they can collect their data easily. *(3)*

> A data sheet is
> another name for a
> collection sheet.

Answer

Type of vehicle	Tally	Frequency
Car		
Lorry		
Van		
Motor bike		
Cycle		
Coach/bus		

You could put
'Number' or
'How many' here

Exercise 3

A Kelly decides to find out which brand of dish
washing liquid people prefer.
She carries out a survey at a supermarket.
The supermarket sells **Persil**, **Suncare**, **Advance**
and **Tesco**.
Devise a table on which Kelly can record her
results.

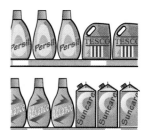

B Ravinda has to ask 50 people how old they are in years.
Design a sheet that she could use to record the answers.
Remember to have about 5 class intervals.

C

MEG

You are to carry out a survey on the number of hours of television
watched last Sunday by collecting data from a sample of girls and boys of
different ages.
Design an observation sheet to help you to do this. *(4)*

D

NEAB

Jane does a survey about vehicles passing her school.
She wants to know about the types of vehicles and their colours.
Design a suitable observation sheet to record this information.
Fill in your observation sheet as if you had carried out this survey.
You should invent suitable data for 25 vehicles. *(4)*

E Think about a survey that you could do.
1. What is your survey about?
2. Design a collection sheet for your survey.
3. Write down two things you might expect to find out.

Questionnaires

When writing questions for a **questionnaire**:

- word the questions clearly
- write short, simple questions.

Examples   How many hours each week do you exercise?

less than 1 ☐   1 up to 3 ☐
3 up to 5 ☐   5 or more ☐

Tick the type of TV programme you like best.

Drama ☐	Comedy ☐	Documentary ☐
Sport ☐	News ☐	Other ☐

Don't make the question influence the answer.

Example   Do you agree that red meat is bad for you?

Yes ☐   No ☐

> This suggests the correct answer is yes.

Make sure the answers cover all options and are not vague.

Example   How often do you exercise?

seldom ☐   sometimes ☐   often ☐

> These words may mean different things to different people.

Worked Exam Question

MEG

Customers in a supermarket are asked to taste a new brand of cola.
The customers are then asked, 'What do you think of this much improved cola?'
(a) What is wrong with this question?   *(2)*
(b) Write a new version of the question which could give useful information to the makers of the cola.   *(1)*

Answer   (a)   The question influences the answer by saying it is improved.
No choices are provided.

(b)   There are several ways this question could be reworded.
Here are two possible ways.
How do you rate this cola compared to the one you usually drink?
Better ☐   the same ☐   worse ☐

How much do you like this cola?
Love it ☐   Like it lots ☐   Like it ☐   Don't like it ☐   Hate it ☐

Exercise 4   **A**   Choose which of the following questions, A or B, is better for finding the data required.
1. To find out: if people like fruit.
    Question A: Do you like fruit? Yes ☐ No ☐
    Question B: Fruit is really good for you, isn't it?
        Yes ☐ No ☐
2. To find out: how much time people spend in a car each week.
    Question A: How much time do you spend in a car each week?
        Lots ☐ A little ☐ Not much ☐
    Question B: How much time do you spend in a car each week?
        None ☐ 0 up to 1 hr ☐ 1 up to 2 hrs ☐ 2 up to 3 hrs ☐
        3 up to 4 hrs ☐ 4 or more hours ☐

B   Each of these questions is unsuitable for a questionnaire.
    For each, write down one reason why.
    Write a new version of the question.
1. How much TV do you watch? Lots ☐ Not much ☐
2. It is good to read the newspaper every day, isn't it?
    Yes ☐ No ☐
3. What is your favourite subject? Maths ☐ Other ☐
4. Do you like the super new school uniform? Yes ☐ No ☐
5. How old are you?

C   Write 2 questions you might include in a questionnaire to find out about students' leisure time.

D

LONDON

Fred is conducting a survey into television viewing habits.
One of the questions in his survey is
'How much television do you watch?'
His friend Sheila tells him that it is not a very good question.
Write down two ways in which Fred could improve his question.   *(2)*

Samples

When we carry out a survey it is usually not practical to ask every person or collect data from every person.

Example   Liam wanted to know how many pupils at his school played sport on Saturdays.
He could not ask all 860 pupils.
Instead he asked every 5th pupil on the school roll.
This meant every pupil had the same chance of being asked.

This is called a **random sample**.
If Liam had just asked the pupils in his class, this would have been a **biased sample**. The pupils in his class may not be representative of the whole school.

Worked Exam Question

....

WJEC

A dog food survey is carried out by questioning three children aged 8, 9 and 11.
Do you think the results would be useful?
Give **two** reasons for your answer. *(6)*

Answer | No. Children are not a representative sample of the people who buy dog food, and three people is not enough people to be representative of the people who buy dog food.

Exercise 5 | **A** Which group of people would give the **most** representative sample to ask the question given?
Choose from the box.
Give a reason why the other two groups might be biased.
1. Which supermarket do you like best?

A Every 5th person who enters a Tesco supermarket.
B The people at a café.
C Every 10th person on the town's electoral roll.

2. How far do you travel to work?

A Every person at a particular bus stop.
B Every 5th person coming out of Victoria Station.
C Every 10th person walking down the main street.

B Reece carried out a survey. He asked three sets of 50 people, 'Do you think there should be a ban on cutting down trees?'
Here are his results.

Set A Yes 46 No 4   **Set B** Yes 23 No 27   **Set C** Yes 1 No 49

The sets were:
a group of timber workers, a group called 'Save the Trees' and a group coming out of a supermarket.
Which result do you think goes with which set?
Give a reason for your answer.

Databases

A **database** is information which is stored in an organised way either on paper or on a computer.

Example

Name	Age	Year	Maths mark	English mark
Paul	16	11	82	68
Chandra	15	11	86	52
Anna	15	10	74	83
Cameron	14	9	81	73
			78	69

Information in a database can be sorted in several different ways. It can then be obtained very quickly.

Examples

Alphabetical order
Age
Pupils who got over 80 in maths

Worked Exam Question

A travel agent has printed out details of holidays in August.

LONDON

Complex	Hotel	Children's Club	Price 7 nights	Price 14 nights
Alcudia	Bahia	No	£489	£599
Alcudia	Pins	Yes	£299	£399
Alcudia	Siesta	Yes	£309	£379
Picafort	Tonga	No	£379	£569
S'illot	Arcos Playa	No	£249	£369
Sa Coma	Bougauvilla Park	Yes	£304	£389
Calas	Eurocalas	No	£329	£499
Santa Ponsa	Punta del Mar	No	£409	£419
Santa Ponsa	Jadin del Sol	No	£309	£419

Read the questions carefully.

(a) Write down the name of the hotel at complex Picafort. *(1)*
(b) Which hotels have 7-night holidays for under £300? *(2)*
(c) Which hotels have 14-night holidays costing between £320 and £390, and also have a children's club? *(2)*

Answer
(a) Tonga
(b) Pins, Arcos Playa
(c) Siesta, Bougauvilla Park

Exercise 6   **A**

NEAB

Here is information about some books in a library.

Author	Title	Published	Hardback
Cook R.	Fever	1982	Yes
Francis D.	Comeback	1991	Yes
Goddard R.	Closed Circle	1993	No
....	....	....	......
Rendall R.	The Bridesmaid	1989	No
Segal E.	Love Story	1970	No
Steel D.	Heartbeat	1991	No

(a) Stephen King's book 'Christine' was published in hardback in 1983.
    Add this information to the list above. *(3)*
(b) Which of these books was published first? *(1)*
(c) Which hardback book was published in the 1990s? *(1)*

B   This table shows data held about some pupils in Year 11.

No.	Name	Tutor group	Date of birth	Cycle to school	Lunch
1	Edward	114	11.04.84	Yes	Packed
2	Greta	114	06.01.84	Yes	School
3	Boris	115	15.08.84	No	Home
4	Ayesha	113	09.06.84	No	Packed
5	Mark	112	24.09.84	Yes	Packed
6					

1. Write down Greta's tutor group.
2. Write down the names of the pupils who do not cycle to school.
3. Write down the names of all the pupils who cycle to school and have a packed lunch.
4. John's date of birth is 28.09.84. He has a school lunch. He takes the bus to school. His tutor group is 115.
   Write an entry for John.

Homework/Review

• •

A   Is the following data discrete or continuous?
   1. Masses of chickens   2. Number of eggs layed

B   (a) Measure accurately the lengths of these two lines.
     (i) _____
     (ii) _____

(b) The lengths, in centimetres, of eleven other lines are given below.
   7.3,   12.0,   5.0,   6.9,   9.4,   15.6,   4.0,   18.4,   4.4,   10.5,   3.7
Use a copy of the table. Complete it for **all** thirteen lines.

Length of line (x centimetres)	Tally	Frequency
$0 \leq x < 4$		
$4 \leq x < 8$		
$8 \leq x < 12$		
$12 \leq x < 16$		
$16 \leq x < 20$		

C

MEG

During a sponsored event, pupils are to walk a maximum of 40 laps of the school field. A teacher keeps count of the laps every time each pupil passes her.
Design an observation sheet for the teacher to use. The sheet should record completed laps, and should include the pupils' names and numbers.

(4)

D

WJEC

Kurt has to undertake a survey to find out the most popular drink in Wales. He carries out his survey by asking pupils at a school disco to answer this question:

(a) State **one** reason why the design of this question is unsuitable for his survey.

(b) State **two** reasons why his survey is likely to be biased.

> Which is your favourite drink?
> Tick the appropriate box.
> Tea ☐   Coffee ☐   Cola ☐

(1)

(2)

E This is part of a computer database of people who belong to a computer club.

Name	Age	Computer	Printer	E-mail
John	19	Yes	Yes	Yes
Martha	16	Yes	No	No
Huw	21	Yes	Yes	No
Sue	17	Yes	Yes	Yes
Luke	17	Yes	No	No
Misa	18	Yes	No	Yes
Ashley	18	No	No	No

1. Write the name of the person who has a computer and a printer but does not have e-mail.
2. List the people who do not have a printer.
3. Who has e-mail and a computer but no printer?
4. List the people who are 17 or 18 and have e-mail.

Task

A Choose one of the following questions or a different question of your own choice.
Design a collection sheet to collect the data.
Collect the data and write some sentences about what you found out.
• How many people in your class have computers, printers and e-mail?
• How many step-ups can people in your class do in 1 minute?

B Write a questionnaire on one of these. Include at least three questions.
• Food preferences and eating habits.
• Radio listening.
• Clothes choices for various situations.
• Opinions on a current issue in your area.
Choose a random sample.
Give your questionnaire to this sample.
Write a few comments on the results.

✔ KEY POINTS

✔ **Discrete data** can only have certain values. It is usually found by counting.
Example The number of cups in cupboards.

✔ **Continuous data** can have any value within a certain range.
It is found by measuring.
Example The length of hens' beaks.

✔ We can collect data on a **tally chart**.
If a tally chart has a frequency column it is sometimes called a **frequency table**.

✔ When we group data we usually make 5 or 6 **equal class intervals**.

✔ A **collection sheet** can also be called a **data sheet**, an **observation sheet** or a **tally chart**.
We design a collection sheet to suit the data being collected.

✔ When writing questions for **questionnaires**:
  • make them short and simple
  • make sure the question doesn't influence the answer
  • make sure the choice of answers covers all options.

✔ When we collect data or give out a questionnaire, we usually use a **sample** of the population.
The sample should be randomly chosen and every data item should have the same chance of being chosen.
This is called a **random sample**

✔ A **database** is information which is stored in an organised way either on paper or on a computer.

◄◄ CHAPTER REVIEW ◄◄

◄◄
Exercise 3
on page 85

A

LONDON

Rachel and Teri were collecting information on the type of meal bought by students in the school canteen.
Draw a suitable data collection sheet for this information.   *(3)*

◄◄
Exercise 3
on page 85

B Mike did a survey about how his class travelled to school.
These were his conclusions.
  • Most came by bus.
  • Nobody cycled.
  • More girls than boys came by car.
Think about a survey that you could do on a different subject.
  1. What is your survey about?
  2. Design a collection sheet for your survey.
  3. Write down three things you might expect to find out.

◀◀
Exercise 2
on page 83

C Use a copy of this.

NEAB

There are 30 people in a class.
They are asked how many pets they have.
Here are the results.

1 4 7 3 1 0 0 1 3 8
3 5 1 0 2 8 1 4 2 1
7 5 1 0 2 4 1 6 3 5

Complete the frequency table for this data.

Number of pets	Tally	Frequency
0–1		
2–3		
4–5		
6–7		
8–9		

(2)

◀◀
Exercises 4 and 5
on pages 87
and 88

D

WJEC

In a survey, Jason uses the following questionnaire to test the hypothesis 'more boys than girls like sport'.

Which sex are you?   Male ☐ Female ☐

Which **ONE** of these sports do you like best?

Football ☐   Cricket ☐   Netball ☐   Basketball ☐

Hockey ☐   Rugby ☐   None of these ☐

(a) Explain why this questionnaire is not suitable for his survey. *(1)*
(b) One evening he gives the questionnaire to all the people in the local gymnasium. Give **two** reasons why this is unlikely to be a suitable group of people to survey. *(2)*

◀◀
Exercise 6
on page 90

E

MEG

The information below is part of a computer database.

Name	Age	Sex	Home town	Hair colour	Wears glasses
Anne	23	F	Coventry	Fair	No
Bill	25	M	Leeds	Brown	No
David	19	M	Nottingham	Brown	Yes
Gary	22	M	Birmingham	Black	No
Mary	22	F	Hull	Brown	No
Pat	18	F	Kettering	Fair	Yes
Rashid	24	M	Cambridge	Brown	No
Sue	19	F	Leicester	Red	No

(a) What is David's home town? *(1)*
(b) What fraction of this group of people wear glasses? *(2)*
(c) List all the people under 21. *(2)*
(d) List all the males with brown hair. *(2)*

7 Measures

By the end of this chapter you will be able to:

- choose appropriate instruments and units of measurement
- estimate measurements
- convert from one metric unit to another
- convert between metric and Imperial units
- read scales
- use formulae to calculate average speed, distance travelled and time taken.

Getting started ....

1. Measure the distance from the tip of your nose to the end of your outstretched arm. Who in your class is closest to one metre for this measurement?
2. Measure the end of your thumb in inches. Who in your class has a thumb closest to one inch?
3. Measure the length of your foot, in inches. Who in your class has a foot closest to 12 inches (1 foot)?

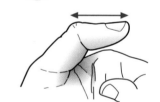

Choosing appropriate units

When we want to measure something we must use appropriate **instruments** and **units**.

Metric units

kilometre (km), metre (m), centimetre (cm), millimetre (mm)
kilogram (kg), gram (g), tonne (t)
litre (ℓ or L), millilitre (mℓ or ml)

Imperial units

mile, yard (yd), foot (ft), inch (in)
pound (lb), ounce (oz)
gallon, pint

Exercise 1   Use a copy of this.
Choose appropriate metric and Imperial units for each.

		Metric	Imperial
1.	The length of a book		
2.	The distance between Paris and London		
3.	The weight of a sack of wheat		
4.	The weight of a toothbrush		
5.	The amount of juice in a large jug		
6.	The length of a tennis court		
7.	The time it takes to have a shower		
8.	The amount of water in a bath		

Estimating measurements

We often **estimate** a measurement.
You should be able to estimate in both metric and Imperial units.

Example   The length of a calculator is about 15 cm or 6 inches.

Worked Exam Question

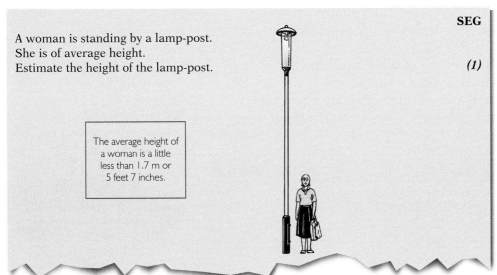

A woman is standing by a lamp-post.
She is of average height.
Estimate the height of the lamp-post.

SEG

(1)

The average height of a woman is a little less than 1.7 m or 5 feet 7 inches.

Answer   The woman is 2 cm tall.
The lamp-post is 6 cm tall.
The lamp-post is three times taller than the woman.
The average height of a woman is a little less than 1.7 m.
So the lamp-post is $3 \times 1.7 =$ **5.1 m**. or **about 5 m**
In Imperial units this is about **16 feet**.

Exercise 2

A This picture shows a whale.
A man of average height is standing by it.
Estimate the height of the man and hence estimate the length of the whale.
Show all your working.

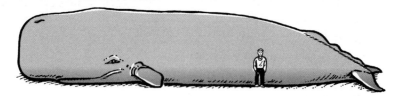

B Use a copy of this.

For each of the following items, place a tick (✓) in the appropriate box to show your estimate for its length.

Item	Length of item		
	0 m to 1 m	1 m to 2.5 m	2.5 m to 5 m
A mountain bike for adults			
A text book			
A full size bed			

WJEC

(3)

C Using metric units, estimate a measurement for these.
1. The height of the back of your chair
2. The weight of an orange
3. The volume of water in a full cup
4. The length of your little finger

D Use a copy of the table below.
Look at the pictures.
Fill in the table with your estimates.

	Metric	Imperial
Weight of bag of apples		
Amount of milk in full carton		
Length of car		
Weight of bag of sweets		
Amount of juice in glass		
Height of little girl		
Weight of butter		
Weight of 16-year-old girl		

E Are these statements sensible?
Write Yes or No.
1. I am 6 m tall.
2. My dog weighs about 100 kg.
3. My window is about 1.6 m long.
4. Yesterday the temperature was 18 °C.
5. My cat has a 2 m tail.
6. I sent a parcel that weighed 1.8 kg.
7. My brother weighs 41 kg.
8. I filled a bucket with 200 ℓ of water.
9. I bought a 2 ℓ carton of juice.
10. My shoes weigh 2 tonnes.
11. An apple weighs about 2000 g.
12. A banana is about 20 cm long.
13. A pizza weighs about 500 g.
14. A cup holds about 25 mℓ.

Changing from one metric unit to another

Learn these **metric conversions**.

Length	Mass (weight)	Capacity (volume)
10 mm = 1 cm	1000 mg = 1 g	1000 mℓ = 1 ℓ
100 cm = 1 m	1000 g = 1 kg	100 cℓ = 1 ℓ
1000 mm = 1 m	1000 kg = 1 tonne	1000 ℓ = 1 cubic metre (m³)
1000 m = 1 km		1 mℓ = 1 cubic centimetre (cm³)

To convert between metric units, you must know how to multiply and divide by 10, 100 and 1000.
This diagram will help you remember how to convert.

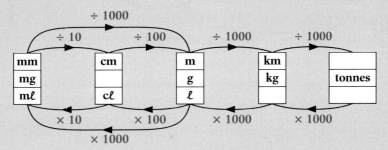

Note: To change from a smaller unit to a larger unit, divide.
To change from a larger unit to a smaller unit, multiply.

Worked Exam Question

MEG
(a) Change 4 kilograms to grams. *(1)*
(b) Change 6000 centimetres to metres. *(1)*

Answer (a) To change kilograms to grams we multiply by 1000.
4 × 1000 = 4000
4 kilograms is **4000 g**.
(b) To change centimetres to metres we divide by 100.
6000 ÷ 100 = 60
6000 centimetres is **60 m**.

Exercise 3   Change

1. 10 cm to mm
2. 5000 m to km
3. 6 ℓ to mℓ
4. 2 g to mg
5. 7000 mℓ to ℓ
6. 7000 mm to cm
7. 200 cm to m
8. 3 km to m
9. 60 m to cm
10. 1.2 ℓ to mℓ
11. 3.4 m to mm
12. 8.1 kg to g
13. 5060 mm to m
14. 7130 mg to g
15. 4 tonnes to kg
16. 0.6 tonnes to kg
17. 500 kg to tonnes
18. 100 cℓ to ℓ
19. 826 m to km
20. 1.08 m to cm
21. 2.1 kg to g
22. 50 cm to m
23. 200 g to kg
24. 350 mℓ to ℓ
25. 5 mℓ to cm³
26. 80 mℓ to cm³
27. 108 cm³ to mℓ
28. 1000 ℓ to m³
29. 3 m³ to ℓ
30. 8500 ℓ to m³.

Worked Exam Question

The diagram shows a can of lemonade.
Each can holds 330 ml of lemonade.

How many cans have to be opened in order
to fill a $2\frac{1}{2}$ litre jug?

NEAB

(3)

Always check to
see if the units
need changing
before you do
the calculation.

Answer   We must change $2\frac{1}{2}$ litres into millilitres.
To do this we multiply by 1000.
$2\frac{1}{2} \times 1000 = 2500$
To find how many cans must be opened, divide 2500 by 330 using the calculator.
The answer is 7.575 7576.
So **8** cans must be opened.

Exercise 4   **A**   A shopkeeper orders one hundred 60 g packets of nuts.
    What is the weight of the order in kilograms?

B   A saucepan holds 4 litres.
How many 250 mℓ cups of water are needed to fill it?

C   Rosalyn has a piece of ribbon 1.9 m long.
How many 12 cm pieces can she cut from it?

D   How many 14 cm high boxes can be stacked on top of
one another in a cupboard 1.8 m high?

E   Janice ran around a 650 m track 11 times.
How far, in kilometres, did she run?

F   Ravinder sent 40 letters which each weighed 58 g.
How many kilograms did she send in total?

Example Write all of these in metres and then put them in order, smallest first.

   2 m   45 cm   105 cm   60 m   3 km   862 cm   5000 mm

Answer   45 cm = 0.45 m   105 cm = 1.05 m   3 km = 3000 m
   862 cm = 8.62 m   5000 mm = 5 m
   From smallest to largest these are:
   0.45 m, 1.05 m, 2 m, 5 m, 8.62 m, 60 m, 3000 m.

Exercise 5

A Write these capacities in mℓ and then put them in order from largest to smallest.

   500 mℓ   2.4 ℓ   0.6 ℓ   860 mℓ   0.85 ℓ

B The distances five pupils lived from school are given.

   4.2 km   850 m   5682 m   1.8 km   4250 m

Put these in order from smallest to largest.

C Write these lengths in km and then put them in order, largest first.

   5280 m   1.2 km   850 m   6.4 km   3820 m

D Write these masses in kilograms and then put them in order, smallest first.

   4.6 kg   4685 g   468 g   4.16 kg   4100 g

 # Homework/Review 1

A

Write down the **metric** unit you would use to measure,
(i)   the length of a person's hand
(ii) the weight of a mouse
(iii) the distance from Manchester to London
(iv) a teaspoon of medicine.

LONDON

(4)

B This is a picture of a building and a woman of average height standing beside it.
   1. Estimate the height of the man.
   2. Use your answer to question **1.** to estimate the length of the building. Show all your working.

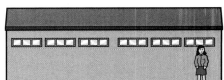

C

Using **metric units**, write down the approximate measurements for

(a) the height of a classroom door,   *(2)*
(b) the weight of an apple,   *(2)*
(c) the volume of liquid in a full cup.   *(2)*

MEG

D Are these statements sensible?
   1. My house is 8 km high.   2. I weigh 65 kg.

E   Where do you find the biggest spider?

														I						
600	0.21		6000	2100	60		0.06	600	21	0.6	210		0.06	6	210	60		0.06	60	2.1

Use a copy of this box.
What goes in the gap?

I	600 cm = __6__ m	O	60 cm = ____mm	E	6000 cm = ____m
L	600 m = ____km	H	2.1 kg = ___g	T	6 ℓ = ____mℓ
N	210 mℓ = ___ℓ	D	2.1 m = ___cm	R	2100 cm = ____m
B	2100 kg = ____tonnes	W	6 cm = ___m		

F   5.08 m of rope is cut from a 6.50 m length.
How much is left?
Give your answer in centimetres.

G   Write all of these masses in kilograms and then put them in order from
biggest to smallest.
0.4 kg   450 g   0.46 kg   468 g   4580 g

Imperial and metric units

You must know these approximate **metric to Imperial conversions.**

Length	Mass	Capacity
8 km = 5 miles	1 kg = 2.2 pounds (lb)	1 litre = 0.2 gallons
1 metre = 39.37 inches	28 g = 1 ounce (oz)	1 litre = 1.75 pints
30.5 cm = 1 foot		4.5 litres = 1 gallon
2.5 cm = 1 inch		

Example   Write

1. 2 metres in inches   2. 4 litres in pints
3. 3 gallons in litres   4. 3 ounces in grams.

Answer
1.   1 metre = 39.37 inches
      2 metres = 2 × 39.37 inches
              = 78.74 inches

2.   1 litre = 1.75 pints
      4 litres = 4 × 1.75 pints
              = 7 pints

3.   1 gallon = 4.5 litres
      3 gallons = 3 × 4.5 litres
              = 13.5 litres

4.   1 ounce = 28 grams
      3 ounces = 3 × 28 grams
              = 84 grams

Worked Exam Question

● ●

MEG

1.   (i)   In Imperial units, 1 ounce is about 28 grams.
          Write 100 grams in ounces.   **(2)**
      (ii)   Write 1 kilogram in pounds (lb).   **(1)**

Answer   (i)   We need to find how many lots of 28 grams (1 ounce) there are in 100 grams.
$$100 \div 28 = 3.571\,428\,6$$
We round this sensibly to 3.6.
So there are about **3.6 ounces** in 100 g.

(ii) 1 kilogram is about **2.2 lb**.

SEG

2.   The distance between two villages is 20 km.
What is the distance between the two villages, in miles?   *(2)*

Answer   8 km = 5 miles
We need to find how many lots of 8 km (5 miles) there are in 20 km.
$20 \div 8 = 2.5$. There are 2.5 lots of 5 miles in 20 km.
So the distance between the two villages is $2.5 \times 5 = $ **12.5 miles**.

> A simple way of converting km to miles is to multiply by 5 and divide by 8

Exercise 6

A
1. Write 10 miles in kilometres.
2. Write 40 km in miles.
3. Write 4 ounces in grams.
4. Write 3 litres in pints.
5. Write 3 kg in pounds.
6. Write 3 feet in centimetres.
7. Write 5 inches in centimetres.
8. Write 140 km in miles.
9. Write 200 grams in ounces.
10. Write 8 pints in litres.
11. Write 10 lb in kilograms.
12. Write 8 cm in inches.
13. Write 90 cm in feet.
14. Write 5 litres in gallons.
15. Write 10 gallons in litres.

B

SEG

The width of a kitchen is $3\frac{1}{2}$ m.
What is the approximate width of the kitchen, in feet?   *(2)*

C   A recipe needed 5 pounds of potatoes and 2 pints of milk.
Rachel had a 3 kilogram bag of potatoes and a litre carton of milk.
Did she have enough potatoes and milk?
Give reasons for your answers.

D   Gary measures the height of a CD rack.
It is 98 cm high.
Estimate the height of the CD rack to the nearest foot.

E
1. Work out the distance, in kilometres, from Exeter to Penzance along this road.
2. Work out the approximate distance, in miles, from the signpost to Penzance.

F   A packet of sugar is shown.
Estimate the weight of the sugar in pounds.

G

NEAB

Nowadays, the 1500 metre race is more common than the mile race.
Which is the longer race?
(5 miles = 8 kilometres)   *(2)*
Show all your working.

H   Work out the approximate weight, in pounds, of 3.65 kg of apples.

Reading scales

To **read a scale** we must work out what each mark stands for.

Example   The difference between 20 and 30 is 10.
There are 5 spaces between 20 and 30.
Each mark stands for $\frac{10}{5} = 2$ L
The pointer is at 26 L

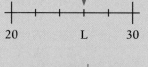

The difference between 4.1 and 4.2 is 0.1.
There are 10 spaces between 4.1 and 4.2.
Each mark stands for $\frac{0.1}{10} = 0.01$ m.
The pointer is at 4.16 m.

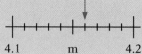

To find what each mark stands for

1. find the difference between any two numbers on the scale
2. count the number of spaces between the two numbers
3. divide the difference between the numbers by the number of spaces.

Worked Exam Question

MEG

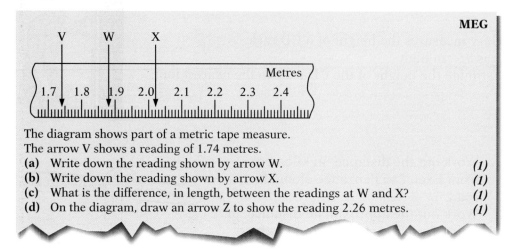

The diagram shows part of a metric tape measure.
The arrow V shows a reading of 1.74 metres.
(a)   Write down the reading shown by arrow W.   *(1)*
(b)   Write down the reading shown by arrow X.   *(1)*
(c)   What is the difference, in length, between the readings at W and X?   *(1)*
(d)   On the diagram, draw an arrow Z to show the reading 2.26 metres.   *(1)*

Answer (a) Each mark stands for $\frac{0.1}{10} = 0.01$ m.
So W reads **1.88 m**.

(b) X reads **2.02 m**.

(c) The difference is $2.02 - 1.88 = $ **0.14 m**.

(d)

| V | W | X | | Z |

Metres

1.7 1.8 1.9 2.0 2.1 2.2 2.3 2.4

Make sure you draw the arrow accurately. Label your arrow clearly.

Exercise 7 **A**

LONDON

The picture shows the scale on the side of a kettle. How many litres of water are needed to fill 5 cups?

(2)

8 1.5 L
7
6
5
4 1.0 L
3
2
Cups Litres

B These kitchen scales measure in kilograms.

1. Write down the weight when the pointer is at A.
2. Write down the weight when the pointer is at B.

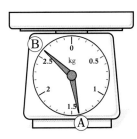

C

LONDON

The diagram shows some potatoes on a set of scales.

(a) Write down the weight of the potatoes.

(1)

Fred buys some apples.
They weigh 3.65 kilograms.
Use a copy of these scales.

(b) Draw a pointer showing 3.65 kilograms on the scales.

(1)

D   Two instruments in a car show speed and temperature.

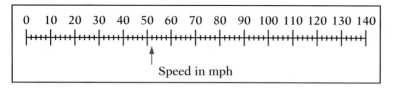
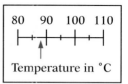

1. What is the speed of the car?
2. What is the temperature?

E   The diagram shows the parking meter for June's car.
1. How much time is left before the arrow reaches zero?
2. Parking costs 20p for 30 minutes. June inserts two 20p coins. How much time would she have left now?
3. If time runs out on the metre an excess charge is £10. A penalty charge is £25. Ray has to pay four excess charges and one penalty charge. He also has to pay £50 for not paying these on time. How much does he have to pay altogether?

F

1. What is the length of the handle?
2. What is the length of the blade?

G

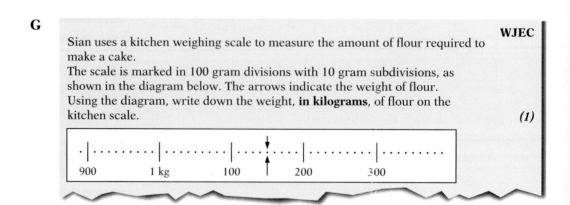

WJEC

Sian uses a kitchen weighing scale to measure the amount of flour required to make a cake.
The scale is marked in 100 gram divisions with 10 gram subdivisions, as shown in the diagram below. The arrows indicate the weight of flour.
Using the diagram, write down the weight, **in kilograms**, of flour on the kitchen scale.

(1)

Speed

Speed is a measure of distance covered in a certain time.
It can be measured in metres per second (m/s) or kilometres per hour (km/h) or miles per hour (mph).
Because speed often changes over a period of time, we usually work out the average speed.
We can work out average speed or time taken or distance travelled using these formulae.

| Learn these formulae. |

$$\text{average speed} = \frac{\text{total distance travelled}}{\text{time taken}}$$

$$\text{time taken} = \frac{\text{total distance travelled}}{\text{average speed}}$$

$$\text{total distance travelled} = \text{average speed} \times \text{time taken}$$

Example John travelled 120 miles in 4 hours.
What was his average speed?

Answer Average speed $= \dfrac{\text{total distance travelled}}{\text{time taken}}$

$$= \frac{120}{4}$$

$$= 30 \text{ miles per hour}$$

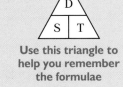

Use this triangle to help you remember the formulae

Example Julie left home at 9 a.m. She travelled 30 km at an average speed of 50 km/h. What time did she arrive?

Answer Time $= \dfrac{\text{total distance travelled}}{\text{average speed}}$

$$= \frac{30}{50}$$

$$= 0.6 \text{ hours}$$

| To find what 0.6 of an hour is you need to multiply 0.6 × 60 minutes. |

0.6 hours is 0.6 × 60 = 36 minutes.
Julie arrived at 9.36 a.m.

Example Amber took 4 hours to travel from Paris to Dijon. She travelled at an average speed of 79 km/hr. How far is it from Paris to Dijon?

Answer Distance travelled = average speed × time taken
$$= 79 \times 4$$
$$= 316 \text{ km}$$

Exercise 8

A
1. Find the average speed if
   (a) 50 km is travelled in 2 hours
   (b) 175.5 miles is travelled in 3 hours.
2. Find the distance Jim travelled if he rode at 10 m/s for
   (a) 20 seconds   (b) 100 seconds   (c) 4 minutes.
3. Find the time taken to travel
   (a) 500 km at 60 km/h   (b) 352 miles at 55 mph.

B A cyclist took 3 hours to travel 60 km.
What was the cyclist's average speed?

C Charlotte walked for $2\frac{1}{2}$ hours at 4 miles per hour.
How far did she walk?

D Andrew drove to Oxford from this signpost at an average speed of 70 km an hour. How long did the journey take?

E Rebecca rode her horse for 2 hours and travelled 12 miles. What was her average speed?

F Eric left Aberdeen at 12.00 noon and travelled 108 km to Edinburgh. The average speed for his journey was 30 km per hour. What time did Eric arrive at Edinburgh?

G Emily ran for 42 minutes and travelled 10 miles. What was her average speed? (Remember to change 42 minutes into hours.)

H Anna rowed for 2 minutes and travelled 240 metres. What was her average speed, in metres per second? (Remember to change the minutes into seconds.)

Task

Estimate your walking speed in metres per second, kilometres per hour and miles per hour.

Mark out 200 m on your playing field.
Time, in seconds, how long it takes you to walk the 200 m.
Work out your actual speed in metres per second.

Change 200 m into kilometres.
Change the time it took you into hours by dividing by 60 and then dividing by 60 again.
Work out your speed in kilometres per hour.

Work out your speed in miles per hour.

Homework/Review 2

A
Sarah is 122 cm tall.   **SEG**
Estimate Sarah's height in feet.
Give your answer to the nearest foot.
                                                            (2)

B Mark had 150 g of cheese.
 1. How many ounces is this?
 2. He ate 100 g of the cheese.
    How many ounces did he have left?

C 1. Write 32 km in miles.
 2. Write 5 kg in pounds.
 3. Write 15 lb in kilograms.
 4. Write 90.1 cm in feet, to the nearest foot.

D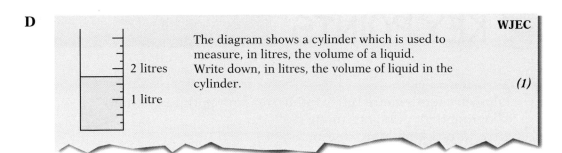

The diagram shows a cylinder which is used to measure, in litres, the volume of a liquid.
Write down, in litres, the volume of liquid in the cylinder.

(1)

WJEC

E 1. The diagram represents a set of scales with a parcel on the scale pan. Write down the weight of the parcel.

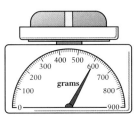

2. The packet on the scales weighs 360 grams.
Use a copy of the diagram.
On the diagram draw the pointer.

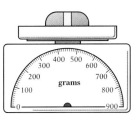

3. The diagram shows another set of scales after a small package has been placed on the pan.
   (a) Write down the weight of the small package.
   (b) Jake posts 30 of these small packages.
       All are the same weight.
       Work out the total weight of the 30 small packages.
   (c) Change your answer in part (b) to kilograms.
   (d) About how many pounds, to the nearest pound, do the 30 small packages weigh?

F 1. Joseph took 4 hours to travel a total distance of 180 km.
What was his average speed?

2. Joseph left Galway at 9.30 a.m. He arrived at Sligo at 11.45 a.m.
   (a) How long had the journey taken him, in hours?
   (b) He travelled at an average speed of 40 mph.
       How far is it from Galway to Sligo?
   (c) Joseph left Sligo at 12.00 noon and travelled 120 miles home at an average speed of 50 mph.
       At what time did he arrive home?

☑ KEY POINTS

☑ **Metric units**
  kilometre (km), metre (m), centimetre (cm), millimetre (mm)
  kilogram (kg), gram (g), tonne (t)
  litre (ℓ or L), millilitre (mℓ or ml)
Imperial units
  mile, yard (yd), foot (ft), inch (in)
  pound (lb), ounce (oz)
  gallon, pint
We measure and estimate using the above units.

☑ You need to know these **conversions**.

Length	Mass	Capacity (volume)
10 mm = 1 cm	1000 mg = 1 g	1000 mℓ = 1 ℓ
100 cm = 1 m	1000 g = 1 kg	100 cℓ = 1 ℓ
1000 mm = 1 m	1000 kg = 1 tonne	1000 ℓ = 1 cubic metre (1 m³)
1000 m = 1 km		1 mℓ = 1 cubic centimetre (1 cm³)

☑ This diagram will help you to **convert** between metric measures.

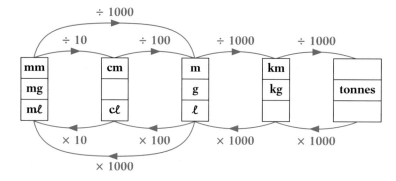

☑ You need to know these approximate **metric and Imperial equivalents**.

Length	Mass	Capacity
8 km = 5 miles	1 kg = 2.2 pounds (lb)	1 litre = 0.2 gallons
1 metre = 39.37 inches	28 g = 1 ounce (oz)	1 litre = 1.75 pints
30.5 cm = 1 foot		4.5 litres = 1 gallon
2.5 cm = 1 inch		

☑ To **read scales** you need to work out what each division stands for.

☑ Learn these **formulae**.

$$\text{average speed} = \frac{\text{total distance travelled}}{\text{time taken}} \qquad \text{time taken} = \frac{\text{total distance travelled}}{\text{average speed}}$$

$$\text{distance travelled} = \text{average speed} \times \text{time taken}$$

◄◄ CHAPTER REVIEW ◄◄

◄◄
*Exercise 2
on page 96*

A   For each of the following items, place a tick (✓) in the appropriate box to show   **WJEC**
your estimate for its weight.

Item	Weight between		
	10 g & 500 g	0.5 kg & 1.5 kg	1.5 kg & 5 kg
a teacup			
a light bulb			
1 litre of water			

(3)

◄◄
*Exercise 4
on page 98*

B

SEG

A bag contains 1.1 kg of chocolate bars.
Each bar weighs 55 g.
How many chocolate bars are in the bag?

(3)

◄◄
*Exercise 5
on page 99*

C   Write these lengths in metres and then put them in order from smallest to
biggest.   50 cm   560 mm   0.52 m   500 cm   0.8 m   5682 mm

◄◄
*Exercise 6
on page 101*

D

WJEC

(a) Darren claims that 6 pounds of potatoes is heavier than 3 kilograms
of sugar.
Is he correct? **You must give a reason for your answer.**   *(2)*
(b) Mary pours three pints of milk into a jug which has a volume of
2 litres.
Will the milk overflow? **You must give a reason for your answer.**   *(2)*

◄◄
*Exercise 7
on page 103*

E

SEG

Hannah buys some Edam.
The amount she buys is shown by the scales.
Estimate the weight of Edam to the nearest hundredth of a kilogram.   *(1)*

◄◄
*Exercise 8 on
page 105*

F

SEG

A coach took 3 hours to complete a journey of 132 miles.
Calculate the average speed of the coach.   *(2)*

◄◄
*Exercise 8
on page 105*

G   A cyclist travelled at an average speed of 25 km/h for 15 km.
How long did it take him? Give your answer in minutes.

Equations

By the end of this chapter you will be able to:

- find input and output from a function machine
- solve 'think of a number' problems
- solve equations including those with brackets and those with letters on both sides
- solve problems by using equations.

Getting started ....

A box containing 9 blocks weighs 56 kg.
A box containing 5 blocks weighs 32 kg.
How heavy is the box?
How heavy is each block?

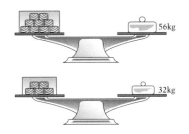

56kg

32kg

Function machines

Remember **Subtracting undoes adding** and **adding undoes subtracting.**
Multiplying undoes dividing and **dividing undoes multiplying.**
Subtracting and adding are **inverse operations**, as are multiplying and dividing.

Worked Exam Question

NEAB

This machine multiplies all numbers by 7 then subtracts 2.

IN → | × 7 | → | – 2 | → OUT

(a) Complete this table

IN	OUT
5	33
2	
7	

(b) 26 comes OUT of the machine. What was put IN?

(2)

(2)

Answer **(a)** To find what comes out we use the machine

IN   OUT

2 → | × 7 | → 14 → | – 2 | → 12

7 → | × 7 | → 49 → | – 2 | → 47

We can now fill in the table.

IN	OUT
5	33
2	12
7	47

(b) To find what went in we work backwards through the machine and do the inverse operations.

4 ← | ÷ 7 | ← 28 ← | + 2 | ← 26   **4** was put in.

Exercise 1

A

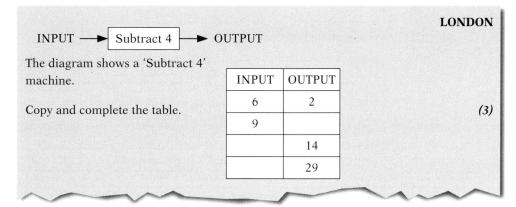

LONDON

INPUT ⟶ Subtract 4 ⟶ OUTPUT

The diagram shows a 'Subtract 4' machine.

Copy and complete the table. *(3)*

INPUT	OUTPUT
6	2
9	
	14
	29

B

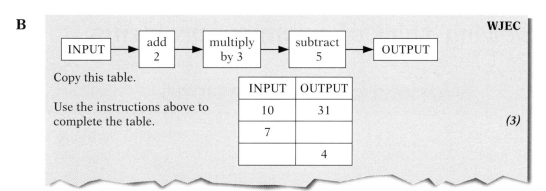

WJEC

INPUT ⟶ add 2 ⟶ multiply by 3 ⟶ subtract 5 ⟶ OUTPUT

Copy this table.

Use the instructions above to complete the table. *(3)*

INPUT	OUTPUT
10	31
7	
	4

C

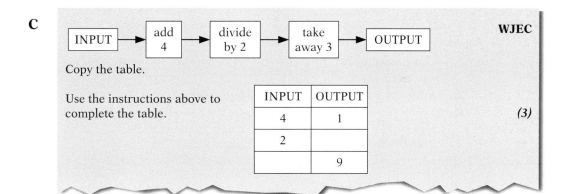

WJEC

INPUT ⟶ add 4 ⟶ divide by 2 ⟶ take away 3 ⟶ OUTPUT

Copy the table.

Use the instructions above to complete the table. *(3)*

INPUT	OUTPUT
4	1
2	
	9

D

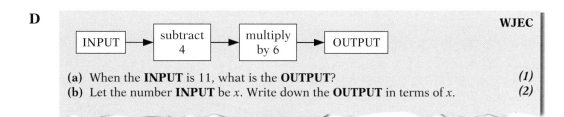

WJEC

INPUT ⟶ subtract 4 ⟶ multiply by 6 ⟶ OUTPUT

(a) When the **INPUT** is 11, what is the **OUTPUT**? *(1)*
(b) Let the number **INPUT** be x. Write down the **OUTPUT** in terms of x. *(2)*

E

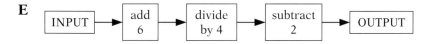

INPUT ⟶ add 6 ⟶ divide by 4 ⟶ subtract 2 ⟶ OUTPUT

1. Find the output if the input is
   (a) 22   (b) 3   (c) −2   (d) 7   (e) n.
2. Find the input if the output is
   (a) 7   (b) 5   (c) 10   (d) 0.125   (e) −0.5.

F

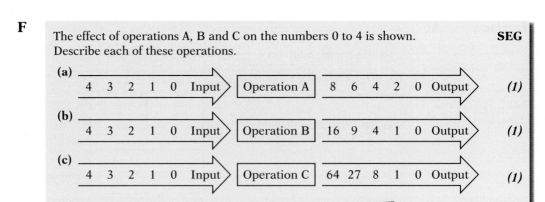

The effect of operations A, B and C on the numbers 0 to 4 is shown.   **SEG**
Describe each of these operations.

(a) 4 3 2 1 0 Input › Operation A │ 8 6 4 2 0 Output ›   *(1)*

(b) 4 3 2 1 0 Input › Operation B │ 16 9 4 1 0 Output ›   *(1)*

(c) 4 3 2 1 0 Input › Operation C │ 64 27 8 1 0 Output ›   *(1)*

Solving 'think of a number' problems

Worked Exam Questions

1.   Lindi thought of a number.   **LONDON**
She multiplied the number by 5.
Her answer was 30
What number did Lindi think of?   *(2)*

Answer   We can use a function machine to find the answer.

Lindi's
number   → │ × 5 │ → answer

Use an 'undoing' machine to find Lindi's number.

6 ← │ ÷ 5 │ ← 30

Lindi's number is **6**.

2.   Denise gives the following instructions.   **WJEC**
        Step 1.   Think of a number.
        Step 2.   Multiply the number by 3.
        Step 3.   Subtract 6 from the answer to step 2.
        Step 4.   Write down your answer to step 3.

(a)   If at step 1 you think of the number 5, what will your answer be
      at step 4?   *(1)*
(b)   At step 1, let the number you think of be n. Write down, in terms
      of n, the answer you get at step 4.   *(1)*

Answer   (a)   Step 1.   5
              Step 2. $5 \times 3 = 15$
              Step 3. $15 - 6 = 9$
              Step 4.   **9**
         (b)   Step 1. n
              Step 2. $n \times 3 = 3n$
              Step 3. $3n - 6$
              Step 4.   **$3n - 6$**

Exercise 2   **A**

LONDON

Maureen thought of a number. She divided this number by 4. She then added 3. Her answer was 9.
What number did Maureen think of?   *(3)*

B

WJEC

(a) When a number is multiplied by 3 and then 7 is added to the result, the answer is 22.
What is the number?   *(2)*

(b) When a number is divided by 8 and then 3 is taken away from the result, the answer is 4.
What is the number?   *(2)*

C   Tina thinks of a number.
She doubles it and then subtracts 3.
1. What is her number when the answer is 27?
2. What is her number when the answer is −1?

D   Zeenat's teacher told the class to, 'think of a number, double it and add 5'.
1. Zeenat thought of the number 35. What was her answer?
2. Ruby's answer was 17. What number did she think of?
3. Emily's answer was 3. What number did she think of?

E   Briony thinks of a number.
She halves it then subtracts 5.
What number is she thinking of if the answer is
1. 3   2. 7   3. −1   4. −3   5. 4?

F   Nick follows these steps.
    Step 1   Think of a number.
    Step 2   Double the number.
    Step 3   Subtract 4 from the answer to Step 2.
    Step 4   Write down your answer to Step 3.
1. What will Nick's answer be at Step 4 if he thinks of the number
    (a) 5   (b) 30   (c) 0.5   (d) 25   (e) −1?
2. What number did he think of if his answer at Step 4 is
    (a) 8   (b) 0   (c) 2   (d) 196   (e) −8?
3. At Step 1, let the number Nick thinks of be n. Write down, in terms of n, the answer he gets at Step 4.

Investigation

Think of a number.
Add 8.
Multiply by 3.
Add the number you first thought of.
Divide the result by 4.
Take away the number you first thought of.

The answer is always 6.
Try and work out why?

Try and make up your own 'think of a number' puzzle that always has the same answer.

Solving equations

There are several ways to **solve an equation.**

1. Look and see method   2. Balance method
3. Function machine method

Look and see method

    Example $20 - n = 5$

           $n = 15$ **We can see by looking that n must equal 15.**

Balance method

    Example $x + 17 = 28$

 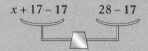 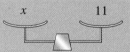

                                     We must subtract 17 from both sides.

We write this as follows
$$x + 17 = 28$$
$$x + 17 - 17 = 28 - 17 \quad \text{subtract 17 from both sides}$$
$$x = 11$$

Function machine method

    Example $x + 23 = 11$
                 $x = -12$

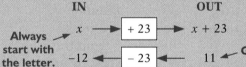

Exercise 3   Solve these using a method of your choice.

   1. $x + 6 = 7$ **2.** $b + 3 = 5$ **3.** $y + 2 = 9$ **4.** $p - 4 = 7$

   5. $w - 3 = 6$ **6.** $x - 3 = 2$ **7.** $n + 2 = 7$ **8.** $t + 4 = 9$

   9. $a + 5 = 10$ **10.** $s - 11 = 16$ **11.** $5 + t = 7$ **12.** $m + 16 = 20$

  13. $x + 6 = 6$ **14.** $p - 5 = 5$ **15.** $a + 16 = 37$ **16.** $n + 24 = 39$

  17. $p + 7 = 2$ **18.** $x + 4 = 1$ **19.** $y + 5 = 2$ **20.** $m + 1 = 0$

  21. $24 - x = 20$ **22.** $16 - n = 12$ **23.** $18 + x = 22$ **24.** $35 - p = 21$

  25. $x - 3 = -2$ **26.** $n - 5 = -3$ **27.** $p - 12 = -9$ **28.** $y - 4 = -2$

  29. $b + 3 = -2$ **30.** $n + 7 = -4$ **31.** $a + 5 = -7$

Example $3x = -18$

Using the balance method

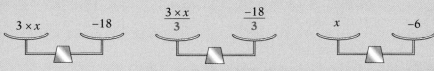

Divide both sides by 3.

We write this as follows
$3x = -18$

$\dfrac{3x}{3} = -\dfrac{18}{3}$ **Divide both sides by 3**

$x = -6$

Exercise 4

Solve these using a method of your choice.

1. $4x = 12$ 2. $5p = 15$ 3. $6y = 24$ 4. $3n = 21$
5. $7b = 42$ 6. $8x = 24$ 7. $9m = 36$ 8. $5x = 25$
9. $8y = 32$ 10. $2a = 9$ 11. $12x = 30$ 12. $2m = -6$
13. $8x = -16$ 14. $4x = -18$ 15. $5y = -22$ 16. $8b = 21$

Example $\dfrac{b}{4} = 3.2$

Using the function machine method

IN   OUT

$b \longrightarrow \boxed{\div 4} \longrightarrow \dfrac{b}{4}$

$12.8 \longleftarrow \boxed{\times 4} \longleftarrow 3.2$

$b = 12.8$

Exercise 5

Solve these using a method of your choice.

1. $\dfrac{x}{3} = 2$ 2. $\dfrac{y}{5} = 4$ 3. $\dfrac{b}{7} = 10$ 4. $\dfrac{m}{6} = 8$ 5. $\dfrac{n}{10} = 3$

6. $\dfrac{t}{4} = 9$ 7. $\dfrac{x}{5} = 7$ 8. $\dfrac{n}{6} = 7$ 9. $\dfrac{c}{9} = 9$ 10. $\dfrac{f}{8} = 6$

Example $4x - 8 = 14$

Using the function machine method

IN   OUT

$x \longrightarrow \boxed{\times 4} \longrightarrow 4x \longrightarrow \boxed{-8} \longrightarrow 4x - 8$

$5.5 \longleftarrow \boxed{\div 4} \longleftarrow 22 \longleftarrow \boxed{+8} \longleftarrow 14$

$x = 5.5 \text{ or } 5\frac{1}{2}$

Note: If an equation is written as 26 = 3x + 2, rewrite it as 3x + 2 = 26 before you begin to solve it.

Exercise 6   Use a method of your choice to solve these.

1. $2x + 4 = 10$ 2. $4y - 6 = 22$ 3. $3m + 2 = 14$ 4. $7x + 5 = 33$
5. $4d + 6 = 24$ 6. $2n - 11 = 6$ 7. $2x + 3 = 22$ 8. $5p + 2 = 10$
9. $9m - 5 = 67$ 10. $15 = 6x + 3$ 11. $11 = 3n - 4$ 12. $18 = 4x - 5$
13. $17 = 8x + 3$ 14. $24 = 5x - 2$ 15. $2x - 3 = -1$ 16. $4x - 10 = -2$

Equations with brackets

To solve an **equation with brackets**, first write the equation without brackets. Then use a method of your choice to solve the equation.

Example

$$5(x - 3) = 9$$
$$5 \times x - 5 \times 3 = 9 \qquad \text{Remove the brackets.}$$
$$5x - 15 = 9$$
$$5x - 15 + 15 = 9 + 15 \qquad \text{Add 15 to both sides.}$$
$$5x = 24$$
$$\frac{5x}{5} = \frac{24}{5} \qquad \text{Divide both sides by 5.}$$
$$x = 4.8 \quad \text{or} \quad 4\tfrac{4}{5}$$

Exercise 7   Solve these equations.

1. $3(x + 1) = 12$ 2. $6(y - 3) = 18$ 3. $4(p - 2) = 24$
4. $8(w - 6) = 32$ 5. $10(d + 4) = 40$ 6. $5(x + 2) = 20$
7. $2(a - 7) = 18$ 8. $7(y + 3) = 42$ 9. $20 = 5(f + 3)$
10. $36 = 9(y - 4)$ 11. $2(2x + 1) = 6$ 12. $3(2y - 7) = 9$
13. $3(3b + 2) = 33$ 14. $3(4t - 1) = 27$ 15. $5(4x + 1) = 60$
16. $7(5b - 3) = 42$ 17. $3(6x + 1) = 21$ 18. $3(4y - 2) = 24$

Equations with letters on both sides

Sometimes **equations** have **letters on both sides** of the equals sign.

To solve these equations we must get all of the letters on to the same side. We do this by subtracting or adding letters using the balance method.

Example

Use the balance method to remove letters from the side with the **smaller** number of them. $2x < 5x$ so subtract $2x$.

$$5x - 3 = 2x + 6$$
$$5x - 3 - 2x = 2x + 6 - 2x \qquad \text{Subtract } 2x \text{ from each side.}$$
$$5x - 2x - 3 = 6$$
$$3x - 3 = 6$$
$$3x - 3 + 3 = 6 + 3 \qquad \text{Add 3 to both sides.}$$
$$3x = 9$$
$$\frac{3x}{3} = \frac{9}{3} \qquad \text{Divide both sides by 3.}$$
$$x = 3$$

Example

$$3(3 - x) = 10 - 5x$$ First remove the brackets.
$$9 - 3x = 10 - 5x$$

$$9 - 3x + 5x = 10 - 5x + 5x$$ Add 5x to both sides
$$9 + 2x = 10$$

$$9 + 2x - 9 = 10 - 9$$ Subtract 9 from both sides
$$2x = 1$$

$$\frac{2x}{2} = \frac{1}{2}$$ Divide both sides by 2.

$$x = \tfrac{1}{2} \quad \text{or} \quad 0.5$$

−5x is less than −3x so remove the letters on the −5x side.

Exercise 8

A   Solve these equations.

1. $3x - 4 = 2x + 6$
2. $4y + 2 = 3y + 4$
3. $7w - 10 = 6w + 4$
4. $5a + 2 = 3a + 6$
5. $8n - 3 = 6n + 5$
6. $2b - 5 = 10 - b$
7. $2p + 5 = 10 + p$
8. $5m - 9 = 2m + 3$
9. $4 + 3x = 12 - x$
10. $5n - 4 = n + 8$
11. $6x - 8 = 4x + 2$
12. $2x + 5 = 15 - 2x$
13. $6x + 3 = 4x - 1$
14. $7y + 8 = 5y - 4$
15. $12 - x = 3x - 4$
16. $6x + 8 = 8x + 2$
17. $x - 3 = 2x + 5$
18. $2x + 5 = 4x + 7$

B   Solve these equations.

1. $3x = 2(x + 4)$
2. $4x = 3(x + 7)$
3. $5x = 3(x + 4)$
4. $3x + 1 = 2(x + 5)$
5. $5x - 6 = 4(x - 1)$
6. $3(x + 2) = 2x + 10$
7. $3(x - 2) = 12 - x$
8. $6b - 7 = 4(b + 1)$
9. $5y + 17 = 3(y + 6)$
10. $4(3 - b) = 15 - 9b$
11. $3(5 - x) = 20 - 8x$
12. $2(4 - y) = 19 - 10y$

Worked Exam Question

Solve the equations

(a) $3y + 2 = 11$ **MEG**   *(2)*
(b) $4p - 7 = p + 11$.   *(3)*

Answer   (a) $3y + 2 = 11$

$$3y + 2 - 2 = 11 - 2$$ Subtract 2 from both sides.
$$3y = 9$$

$$\frac{3y}{3} = \frac{9}{3}$$ Divide both sides by 3.

$$y = 3$$

Remember to remove the letters from the side which has the smaller number of them.

(b) $4p - 7 = p + 11$

$$4p - 7 - p = p + 11 - p$$ Subtract p from both sides.
$$3p - 7 = 11$$

$$3p - 7 + 7 = 11 + 7$$ Add 7 to both sides.
$$3p = 18$$

$$\frac{3p}{3} = \frac{18}{3}$$ Divide both sides by 3.

$$p = 6$$

Exercise 9

A Solve the following equations.

1. $2x = 12$ 2. $3x + 2 = 8$ 3. $3x + 2 = 17$
4. $x + 7 = 18$ 5. $5y = 45$ 6. $4(p - 3) = 20$
7. $4x - 1 = 11$ 8. $3(4x - 1) = 27$ 9. $3(2x - 1) = 9$
10. $2x + 5 = 11 - x$ 11. $31 - x = 13$ 12. $4y + 3 = 17$
13. $2n + 1 = 3n - 2$ 14. $3(x + 1) = 2x - 4$ 15. $3(2x - 4) = 8x - 1$

B
LONDON
Solve the following equations.
(a) $4x - 7 = 20$ *(3)*   (b) $3(y + 5) = 42$ *(4)*   (c) $3x = 24$ *(1)*   (d) $18 + 3y = 6 - y$ *(3)*

C
WJEC
Solve the equation $6x - 7 = 4(x + 1)$ *(3)*

D
NEAB
Solve the equations
(a) $2x + 10 = 29$ *(2)*   (b) $5x - 4 = 8 - x$ *(2)*

E If $4p - 3 = 15$, find the value of $2p - 3$.

Solving problems using equations

Worked Exam Question

NEAB

(a) Kevin has 8 windows cleaned.
How much does Wendy charge? *(1)*

(b) Betty has W windows cleaned.
Which of the following expressions represents Wendy's charge, in pence, for cleaning Betty's windows? *(1)*
        $60 + 50W$ $110W$ $60W + 50$

(c) Wendy charges Ali C pence to clean his windows.
Use your expression in (b) to form an equation for this charge. *(1)*

(d) Bert pays Wendy £5.10 to clean his windows.
How many windows does Wendy clean? *(2)*

Wendy
THE WINDOW WASHER
Only 60p
plus 50p for every window cleaned

Answer (a) $60p + 8 \times 50p = 60p + 400p$ (b) $60 + 50W$
                $= £4.60$

(c) $C = 60 + 50W$

(d) £5.10 must be changed into pence. $£5.10 = 510p$
        $510 = 60 + 50W$
        $510 - 60 = 60 + 50W - 60$ Subtract 60 from both sides.
        $450 = 50W$
        $\dfrac{450}{50} = \dfrac{50W}{50}$ Divide both sides by 50.
        $9 = W$

So Wendy cleans **9** windows.

Exercise 10

A

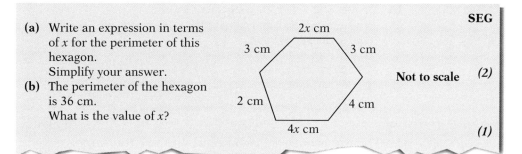

(a) Write an expression in terms of x for the perimeter of this hexagon. Simplify your answer.
(2)

(b) The perimeter of the hexagon is 36 cm. What is the value of x?
(1)

Labels on hexagon: 2x cm, 3 cm, 3 cm, 2 cm, 4 cm, 4x cm. **Not to scale**

B The cost, S pounds, of a cabinet with d drawers can be calculated using the formula $S = 50 + 20d$.
A cabinet costs £150. Calculate the number of drawers this cabinet has.

C Use the formula $v = 2u + 32$ to work out the following.
1. Find v when $u = -7$.　　**2.** Find u when $v = 40$.

D An approximate rule for changing degrees Celsius (C) into degrees Fahrenheit (F) is $F = 2 \times C + 30$.　　Find C when $F = 54$.

E

Mrs Brown is making a collection of china jugs. Each jug costs £15.
(a) Write down an expression for the cost, in £, of n jugs. *(2)*
(b) Mrs Brown displays the jugs in a cabinet which costs £68.
　(i) Write down an expression, in terms of n, for the total cost of the cabinet and n jugs. *(2)*
　(ii) The total cost of the cabinet and n jugs is £188. Use your answer to part **(b)(i)** to form an equation. *(2)*
　(iii) Solve your equation to find the number of jugs in Mrs Brown's collection. *(3)*

F The three angles of a triangle are given as x, $2x$ and $3x$.
Calculate the value of x.
(**Remember:** The interior angles of a triangle add to 180°.)

G A pencil costs n pence. A pen costs $n + 1$ pence.
Mrs Brown buys 6 pens and 6 pencils. She pays £3.06.
1. Form an equation in n.
2. Solve your equation to find the cost of a pencil.

H This picture shows some packets of sugar in the pans of a weighing machine.
The pans are balanced.
Each packet of sugar weighs x kg.
In Pan A there are 8 packets of sugar and a 5 kg weight.
In Pan B there are 6 packets of sugar and a 15 kg weight.

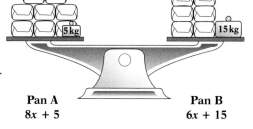

Pan A
8x + 5

Pan B
6x + 15

1. Write down an equation in terms of x to represent this information.
2. Use your equation to calculate the weight, x kg, of one packet of sugar.

I

SEG

Two rectangles, P and Q, have the same perimeter.
The perimeter of P is $4x + 8$.
The perimeter of Q is $12x + 2$.
(i) Solve the equation $4x + 8 = 12x + 2$. *(2)*
(ii) What is the perimeter of P in centimetres? *(1)*

J The areas of these two rectangles are the same.

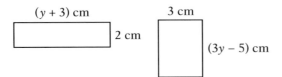

$(y + 3)$ cm

2 cm

3 cm

$(3y - 5)$ cm

By solving the equation $2(y + 3) = 3(3y - 5)$ find the area of one of these rectangles.

K

SEG

The perimeters of these triangles are equal.

x cm $(x + 2)$ cm

A   B   **Not to scale**

$(x + 2)$ cm $(3x - 1)$ cm

(a) Triangle A is equilateral. Its perimeter is $3(x + 2)$ cm.
     Multiply out $3(x + 2)$. *(1)*
(b) Solve the equation $3(x + 2) = x + (x + 2) + (3x - 1)$. *(3)*
(c) Calculate the perimeter of triangle B. *(1)*

L Elizabeth is 6 years older than her brother Tom.
In three years time Elizabeth will be twice as old as Tom.
Let Tom's age now be x years.
1. Write an expression for Elizabeth's age now.
2. Write down an equation using the children's ages in three year's time.
3. Solve your equation to find x.

Homework/Review

A

MEG

Consider this simple function machine.   IN → ×4 → −3 → OUT
(a) Put in the number 5 and find the number that comes out. *(2)*
(b) Find the number that has been put into the machine if the number 9 comes out. *(2)*

B

SEG

A function machine is shown.

Input $\longrightarrow$ [+ 3] $\longrightarrow$ [   ] $\longrightarrow$ Output

box A

(a) What goes in **box A** so that the output is always the same as the input? *(1)*

(b) A second function machine subtracts 3 and then adds 7.

Input $\longrightarrow$ [– 3] $\longrightarrow$ [+ 7] $\longrightarrow$ Output

David draws a function machine that will have the same effect as this machine but he only uses one box.
What goes on David's function machine?

Input $\longrightarrow$ [   ] $\longrightarrow$ Output *(1)*

C

WJEC

(a) When a number is multiplied by 3 and then 8 is added to the result, the answer is 35.
What is the number? *(2)*

(b) When 5 is taken away from a number and the result is divided by 9, the answer is 7.
What is the number? *(2)*

D

LONDON

Solve (a) $3x = 15$ *(1)*   (b) $4y + 6 = 26$ *(2)*

E

MEG

Solve the equations
(a) $3w = -18$ *(1)*   (b) $3(x - 4) = 12$ *(2)*   (c) $3y + 7 = 13 - y$ *(2)*

F Solve these equations.

1. $5b - 6 = 21$ 2. $4(y + 6) = 64$ 3. $15 + 3n = 5 - n$ 4. $8x - 3 = 4(x + 2)$

5. $3(x + 2) = -6$ 6. $x - 4 = 3x + 12$ 7. $\dfrac{a}{1.6} = 4.2$ 8. $5t + 11 = 2t + 2$

G

LONDON

A shop sells two types of lollipops.
The shop sells Big lollipops at 80p each and
Small lollipops at 60p each.
Henry buys x Big lollipops.

Big 80p   Small 60p

(a) Write down an expression, in terms of x, for the cost of Henry's lollipops. *(1)*

Lucy buys r Big lollipops and t Small lollipops.

(b) Write down an expression, in terms of r and t, for the total cost of Lucy's lollipops. *(1)*

The cost of g Big lollipops and 2 Small lollipops is £10.80.

(c) Write this as an equation in terms of g. *(2)*

(d) Use your equation to find the value of g. *(2)*

☑ KEY POINTS

☑ **Subtracting undoes adding** and **adding undoes subtracting**.
Multiplying undoes dividing and **dividing undoes multiplying**.

☑ To find the **output from a function machine**, follow the rules of the machine.
To find the **input** when you are given the output, use an undoing machine.

Example   Input $\longrightarrow$ ☐ × 2 ☐ → ☐ – 3 ☐ → ☐ × 4 ☐ → Output

'undoing machine'

Input ← ☐ ÷ 2 ☐ ← ☐ + 3 ☐ ← ☐ ÷ 4 ☐ ← Output

☑ We can use **function machines** to solve **'think of a number'** problems.

☑ We can solve **equations** using **'look and see'**, **function machines** or **the balance method**.

Example $x + 7 = 10$ We can see by looking that $x = 3$.

Example $4a + 3 = 16$ We can solve this using a function machine as follows.

$a \longrightarrow$ ☐ × 4 ☐ → $4a \longrightarrow$ ☐ + 3 ☐ → $4a + 3$

$3.25 \longleftarrow$ ☐ ÷ 4 ☐ ← $13 \longleftarrow$ ☐ – 3 ☐ ← 16

$a = 3.25$

When we use the **balance method** we do the same to both sides of the equation.

Example

$$3y + 2 = -1$$

$$3y + 2 - 2 = -1 - 2 \qquad \text{Subtract 2 from both sides.}$$

$$3y = -3$$

$$\frac{3y}{3} = \frac{-3}{3} \qquad \text{Divide both sides by 3.}$$

$$y = -1$$

☑ When an equation has **brackets**, multiply out the brackets first and then solve the equation using a method of your choice.

☑ When there are **letters on both sides of the equation** we must use the balance method to remove letters from the side which has the smaller number of them.

Example

$$5y + 7 = 8 + 3y \qquad \text{3y is less than 5y so remove the 3y}$$

$$5y + 7 - 3y = 8 + 3y - 3y \qquad \text{Take 3y from both sides.}$$

$$2y + 7 = 8$$

$$2y + 7 - 7 = 8 - 7 \qquad \text{Take 7 from both sides.}$$

$$2y = 1$$

$$\frac{2y}{2} = \frac{1}{2} \qquad \text{Divide both sides by 2.}$$

$$y = \tfrac{1}{2} \text{ or } 0.5$$

◄◄ CHAPTER REVIEW ◄◄

◄◄
Exercise 1
on page 111

A

| INPUT | → | add 5 | → | multiply by 2 | → | OUTPUT |

WJEC

Copy the following table.
Use the above instructions to
complete the table.

INPUT	OUTPUT
3	
−2	

(2)

◄◄
Exercise 2
on page 113

B

Ian thought of a number.
He doubled his number and added 5.
His answer was 19.
What number did Ian think of?

LONDON

(2)

◄◄
Exercise 2
on page 113

C

Think of a number.
Multiply it by three.
Now add seven.

The number I
think of is 14

My answer is 94

NEAB

Teacher   Tina   Abel

(a) What answer does Tina get? *(1)*
(b) What is the number Abel thinks of? *(3)*

◄◄
Exercises 6, 8
and 9 on
pages 116, 117
and 118

D

1. Solve the equations (a) $5x - 3 = 7$ *(2)* (b) $5x + 5 = 7 + x$ *(3)* **NEAB**
2. Solve the equations (a) $3x - 4 = 11$ *(2)* (b) $5x + 17 = 3(x + 6)$ *(3)* **WJEC**

◄◄
Exercises 2 and 10
on pages 113
and 119

E

(a) When a number is divided by 4 and then 2 is subtracted from the
result, the answer is 7.
What is the number? **WJEC** *(2)*

(b) The square lids of three gift boxes have perimeters $4x$ cm, $8x$ cm and
$12x$ cm.

Perimeter = $4x$ cm   Perimeter = $8x$ cm   Perimeter = $12x$ cm

The total length of the perimeters of the three lids is 96 cm.

(i) Write down an equation in x.
(ii) Solve your equation to find the value of x.
(iii) Write down the lengths of the sides of the three lids. *(4)*

9 Angles

By the end of this chapter you will be able to:

- name acute, obtuse, reflex and right angles
- draw and measure angles using a protractor
- use the properties of the angles made with intersecting lines (lines that cross each other)
- use the properties of angles made with parallel lines.

Getting started ....

You will need · a group to work with

1. Take turns to draw an angle.

   Example

2. Everyone else in the group estimates its size.
3. Measure the angle.
4. The person with the closest estimate gets 5 points.
5. The winner is the person with the most points after everyone has had 2 turns at drawing an angle.

Angles

Types of angle

There are 360° in a full turn.	There are 180° in a straight angle.	There are 90° in a right angle.	An acute angle is less than 90°.	An obtuse angle is greater than 90° but less than 180°.	A reflex angle is greater than 180° but less than 360°.

Naming angles

We **name** angles using letters.

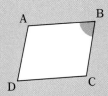
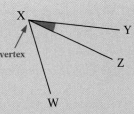

The shaded angle
is ∠ ABC
or ∠ CBA.

The shaded angle
is ∠ ZXY
or ∠ YXZ.

Sometimes angles are named like this: AB̂C ZX̂Y
The ^ is put over the middle letter.

Measuring and drawing angles using a protractor

We use a **protractor** to measure and draw angles.

To **measure an angle** we

• put the middle of the protractor on
  the vertex
• read the scale that starts at 0°.

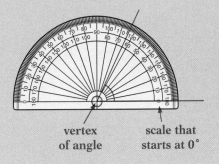

vertex
of angle

scale that
starts at 0°

To draw an angle of 72° follow these steps.

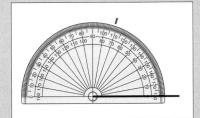

Draw a straight line.

Put the middle of the protractor
on the end of the line.
Put a mark at 72°.

Remove the protractor.
Draw a line through the mark.

Worked Exam Questions

1. On the diagram mark and label

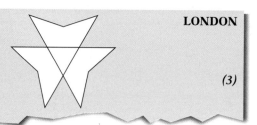
LONDON

(i) an acute angle with a letter A,
(ii) a reflex angle with a letter B,
(iii) an obtuse angle with a letter C.

(3)

Answer (i) An acute angle is less than 90°.
You have to label **just one** acute angle with the letter **A**.
You could put it in any **one** of the places shown.

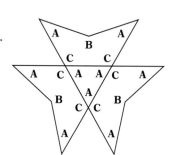

(ii) A reflex angle is greater than 180° but less than 360°.
You could put the letter **B** in any **one** of the places shown.

(iii) An obtuse angle is greater than 90° but less than 180°.
You could put the letter **C** in any **one** of the places shown.

2.

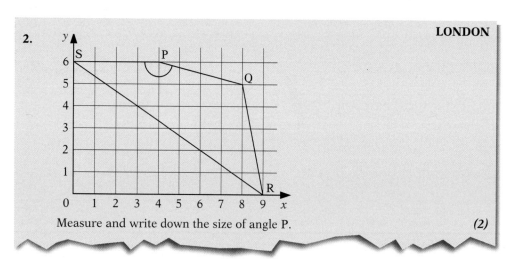
LONDON

Measure and write down the size of angle P.

(2)

Answer We use a protractor to measure angles.
To measure angle P you will have to place your protractor as shown.
The line PQ needs to be made longer so you can read the protractor.
Read the scale that starts at zero.
The angle is **165°**.

read this scale

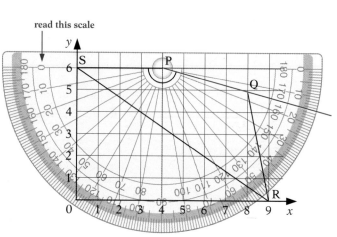

Exercise 1   **A**   Name these angles. Choose from the box.

1.   **2.**   **3.**

> acute
> obtuse
> reflex
> right

4.   **5.**   **6.**

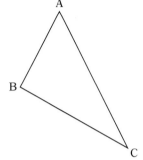

B   **1.**   Measure angle ABC and write it down.
     2.   Measure angle ACB and write it down.
     3.   Write down the special names of angles ABC
        and ACB.

C   Use a copy of the diagram.

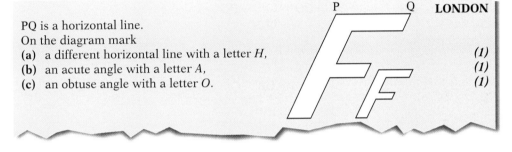

PQ is a horizontal line.
On the diagram mark
(a)   a different horizontal line with a letter *H*,   *(1)*
(b)   an acute angle with a letter *A*,   *(1)*
(c)   an obtuse angle with a letter *O*.   *(1)*

D   Draw these angles.
   1.   65°   **2.**   121°   **3.**   204°   **4.**   274°

Angles made with intersecting lines (lines that cross)

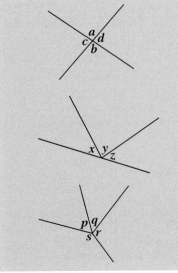

Angles *a* and *b* are called vertically opposite angles.
Angles *c* and *d* are also vertically opposite angles.
a = b   and   **c = d**
Vertically opposite angles are equal.

Angles *x*, *y* and *z* are adjacent angles on a straight line.
x + y + z = 180°
Adjacent angles on a straight line add to 180°.

Angles *p*, *q*, *r* and *s* are angles at a point.
p + q + r + s = 360°
Angles at a point add to 360°.

Worked Exam Question

The diagram shown has not been drawn accurately. When drawn accurately, **SEG** POQ is a straight line, angle ROS is a right angle and $a + b + c = 218°$.

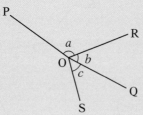

Work out the sizes of angle a and angle c. *(2)*

Answer We usually find the letters in alphabetical order.
$$a + b + c = 218°$$
$$a + 90° = 218°$$
$$a + 90° - 90° = 218° - 90°$$
$$a = 128°$$

There is often more than one way to find an angle.

POQ is a straight line so $a + b = 180°$.
$$128° + b = 180°$$
$$b = 52°$$

$$a + b + c = 218°$$
$$128° + 52° + c = 218°$$
$$c = 38°$$

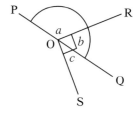

Example Find the value of x.

Answer $x + 2x + x = 180°$
$$4x = 180°$$
$$\frac{4x}{4} = \frac{180}{4} \quad \text{Divide both sides by 4.}$$
$$x = 45°$$

Exercise 2 **A** Find the size of angle a.
Give a reason.

1.

2.

3.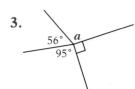

4.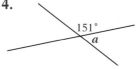

5.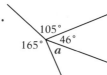

B   Find the size of the angles marked with letters in these diagrams.

1.

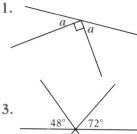

2.

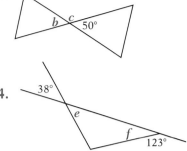

3.

4.

5.

6.

Angles made with parallel lines

Parallel lines never meet.
We use arrows to show parallel lines.
AB is parallel to CD.
EF is parallel to GH.

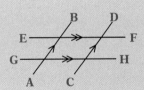

Task

You will need   a protractor

Measure the angles *a* and *b* in each of these diagrams.

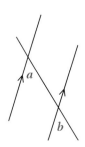

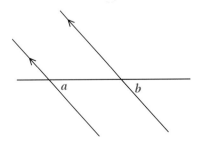

What do you notice?
Take a close look at the positions of *a* and *b* in each diagram.

Angles **x** and **y** are called **corresponding angles**.

Corresponding angles are equal.

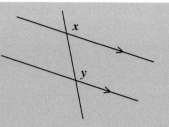

If we are asked to say why **x** and **y** are equal we write:
Corresponding angles, parallel lines, are equal.

Example   **a** and the 38° angle are corresponding angles.
$a = 38°$
Reason: Corresponding angles, parallel lines, are equal.

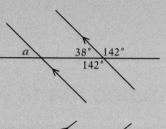

Example   Find the size of angles x and y.

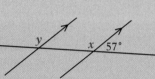

Answer $x + 57° = 180°$ **Adjacent angles on a straight line add to 180°.**
$x = 180° - 57°$
$x = 123°$

$y = x$ **Corresponding angles, parallel lines, are equal.**
So $y = 123°$

Exercise 3   **A**   Find the size of angle b.

1.

2.
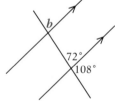

3.
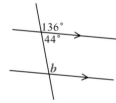

4.
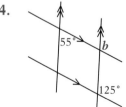

5.
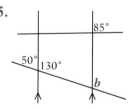

6.
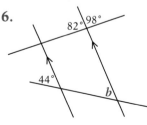

B Find the size of angles *c* and *d*.

1.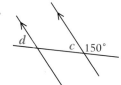

2.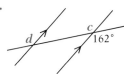

3.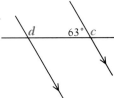

4.

5.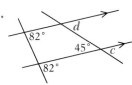

C The diagram shows part of a map.

Palm Road and Short Road are parallel.

What is the size of the shaded angle between Meadow Lane and Short Road?

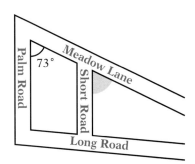

Task

You will need   a protractor

Measure the angles *f* and *g* in each of these diagrams.

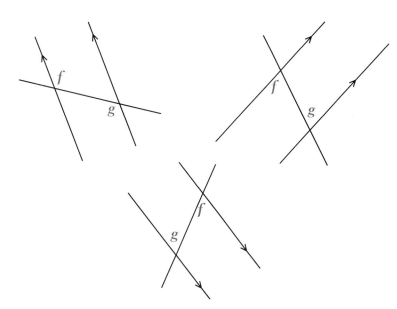

What do you notice?
Take a close look at the positions of *f* and *g* in each diagram.

Angles *p* and *q* are called **alternate angles**.

Alternate angles are equal.

If we are asked to say why *p* and *q* are equal we write:
   Alternate angles, parallel lines, are equal.

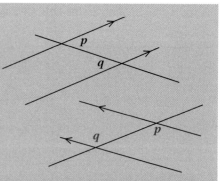

Example   *d* and the 154° angle are alternate angles.
d = 154°
Reason: Alternate angles, parallel lines, are equal.

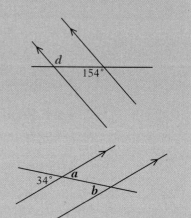

Example   Find the sizes of angles *a* and *b*.
Give reasons.
a = 34°
Reason: Vertically opposite angles are equal.

b = 34°
Reason: Alternate angles, parallel lines, are equal.
   or   Corresponding angles, parallel lines, are equal.

Exercise 4   **A**   Find the size of angle *w*.

1.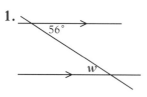

2.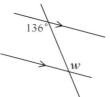

3.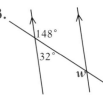

4.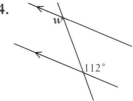

5.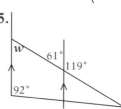

6.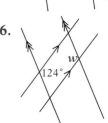

B   Find the size of all of the marked angles.

1.

2.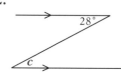

3.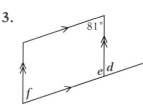

4.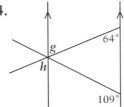

5.

C Are lines AB and CD parallel? Give a reason.

1.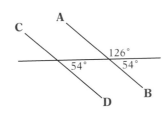

2.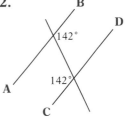

Task

You will need a protractor

Measure the angles *j* and *k* in each of these diagrams.
Add *j* and *k* together.

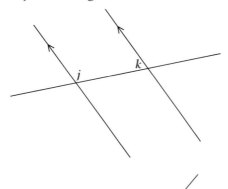

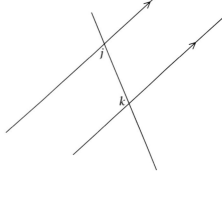

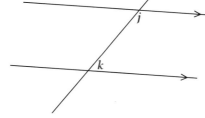

What do you notice?
Take a close look at the positions of *j* and *k* in each diagram.

Angles *e* and *f* are called **interior angles**.

Interior angles add to 180°.

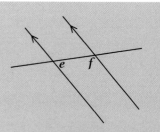

If we are asked to say why $e + f = 180°$, we write:
  interior angles, parallel lines, add to 180°.

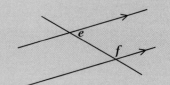

Example   *x* and the 72° angle are interior angles.
$$x + 72° = 180°$$
$$x + 72° - 72° = 180° - 72°$$
$$x = 108°$$
Reason: Interior angles, parallel lines, add to 180°.

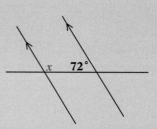

Example   Find the size of *w* and *y*.

Answer $w = 82°$
Reason: Corresponding angles, parallel lines, are equal.

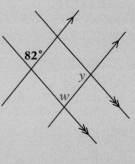

$$w + y = 180°$$
$$82° + y = 180°$$
$$82° + y - 82° = 180° - 82°$$
$$y = 98°$$
Reason: Interior angles, parallel lines, add to 180°.

Exercise 5   **A**   Find the size of angle *r*.

1.

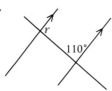

110°

2.

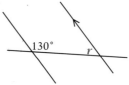

130°

3.

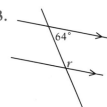

64°

4.

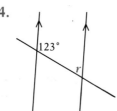

123°

5.

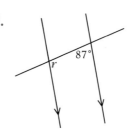

87°

6.

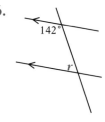

142°

B   Find the size of angles x and y.

1.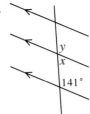

2.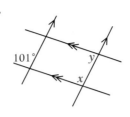

3.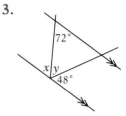

4.

5.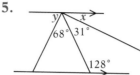

Worked Exam Question

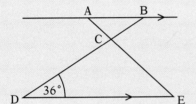

MEG

Not to scale

In the diagram DE is parallel to AB, DB meets AE at C and angle BDE = 36°.
(i)   Find angle ABD.   *(1)*
(ii) What property of parallel lines did you use in order to answer part (i)?   *(1)*
(iii) If angle DEC = 42°, calculate angle DCE and angle BCE.   *(1)*

Answer   **(i)**   Angles ABD and the 36° angle are alternate angles and so they are equal.
Angle ABD = 36°

(ii)   Alternate angles, parallel lines, are equal.

(iii)   DCE is a triangle.
The interior angles of a triangle add to 180°.
$$\angle DCE + 36° + 42° = 180°$$
$$\angle DCE + 78° = 180°$$
$$\angle DCE + 78° - 78° = 180° - 78°$$
$$\angle DCE = 102°$$

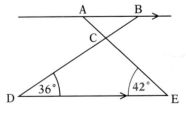

There is sometimes more than one way of finding the answer.

$\angle DCE$ and $\angle BCE$ are adjacent angles on a straight line.
$$\angle BCE + \angle DCE = 180°$$
$$\angle BCE + 102° = 180°$$
$$\angle BCE + 102° - 102° = 180° - 102°$$
$$\angle BCE = 78°$$

Exercise 6 **A** Find the size of angles marked with letters in these diagrams.

1.

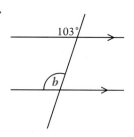

2.

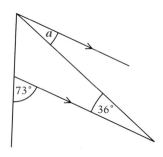

B

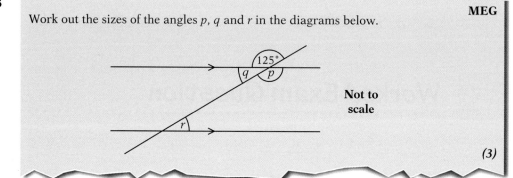

Work out the sizes of the angles *p*, *q* and *r* in the diagrams below.

MEG

Not to scale

(3)

C On the diagram the lines PQ and RS are parallel.

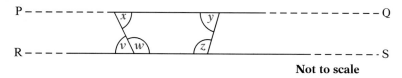

Not to scale

Angle *x* = 67° and angle *z* = 115°.
1. What is the size of angle *v*?
2. Work out the size of angle *y*.

D This diagram shows the side view of some scaffolding.
It is symmetrical about BF.
The bars GE, HD and AC are parallel.
Angle HGF = 74° and angle GHF = 56°.
1. What is the size of angle *e*?
2. Work out the size of angle *f*.

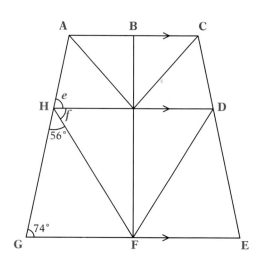

Not to scale

Homework/Review

A Use a copy of the diagram.
  1. Mark and label an acute angle with a cross, X.
  2. Mark and label an obtuse angle with a triangle, △.
  3. Mark and label a reflex angle with a circle, ○.
  4. Mark and label a right angle with a square, □.

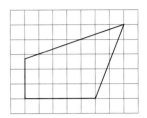

B Measure the acute angle in the diagram in **A**.

C

(a) (i) Measure and write down the size of angle P.
  (ii) Write down the mathematical name for angle P.

(2)

(b) (i) Measure and write down the size of angle Q.
  (ii) Write down the mathematical name for angle Q.

(2)

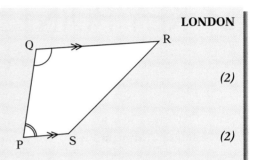

LONDON

D What do two oceans say when they meet?

	i																		
100°	125°	50°	36°	55°	100°	117°		50°	36°	27°	54°		130°	30°	25°	50°		38°	80°	142°	27°

Use a copy of this box.
Find the size of the angles marked with letters in these diagrams.

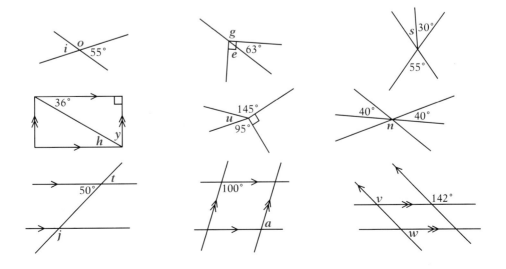

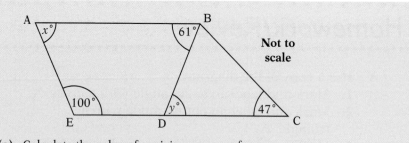

(a) Calculate the value of x, giving a reason for your answer. (2)
(b) Calculate the value of y, giving a reason for your answer. (2)

☑ KEY POINTS

| full turn 360° | straight angle 180° | right angle 90° | acute angle less than 90° | obtuse angle greater than 90° but less than 180° | reflex angle greater than 180° but less than 360° |

☑ We **name angles** using letters.
We can name the shaded angle ∠ CDE or ∠ EDC or CD̂E or ED̂C.

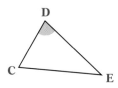

☑ We **measure** and **draw angles** using a **protractor**.

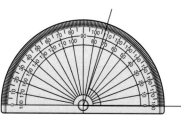

a = b
a and b are vertically opposite angles and are equal.

x + y + z = 180°
x, y and z are adjacent angles on a straight line and add to 180°.

c + d + e = 360°
c, d and e are angles at a point and add to 360°.

a = b
a and b are corresponding angles, parallel lines, and are equal.

c = d and e = f
c and d are alternate angles. e and f are also alternate angles. Alternate angles, parallel lines, are equal.

x + y = 180°
x and y are interior angles, parallel lines, and add to 180°.

◀◀ CHAPTER REVIEW ◀◀

◀◀
Exercise 1
on page 127

A

MEG

For each of the following statements, pick one of the words listed below as your answer. The first one has been done for you.
OBTUSE,   PERPENDICULAR,   HORIZONTAL,   REFLEX,
VERTICAL,   ACUTE,   PARALLEL.

(a) A flagpole is <u>VERTICAL</u>.
(b) An angle between 0° and 90° is _____ .   *(1)*
(c) Two lines which are always the same distance apart must be _____ .   *(1)*
(d) Two lines that cross each other at 90° are _____ .   *(1)*
(e) An angle which is greater than 180° but less than 360° is _____ .   *(1)*

◀◀
Exercise 1
on page 127

B

WJEC

Measure and record the size of the angles marked x and y in the diagram.   *(2)*

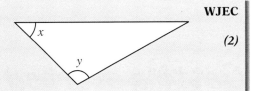

◀◀
Exercise 1
on page 127

C

WJEC

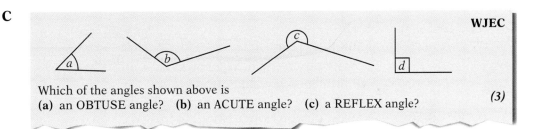

Which of the angles shown above is
(a) an OBTUSE angle?   (b) an ACUTE angle?   (c) a REFLEX angle?   *(3)*

◀◀
Exercises 2 and
6 on pages 128
and 136

D   Find the size of the angles with the marked letters.

1.
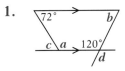

2.
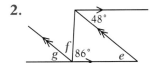

3.
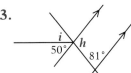

4.

◀◀
Exercise 6
on page 136

E

NEAB

A sketch of a six-sided symmetrical shape is shown. It has three pairs of parallel lines.
An angle of 60° is shown.
Work out the sizes of the angles marked a, b and c.

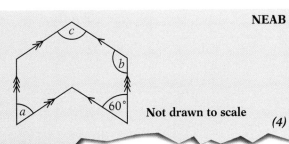

Not drawn to scale   *(4)*

10 Special Numbers

By the end of this chapter you will be able to:

- understand odd, even, prime, factor, multiple, prime factor, square, cube, power, square root, cube root
- find factors, multiples and prime factors of a number
- find the square or cube of a number
- find the square root or cube root of a number using a calculator where necessary
- understand the meaning of $a \times 10^n$.

Getting started ....

This shows the first 6 rows of **Pascal's Triangle**.

1. Find the pattern.
   Write down the next 4 rows.
2. Find the sum of the numbers in each row.
   What do you notice about them?
3. Which rows of the triangle will contain only odd numbers?

Row										
1					1					
2				1		1				
3			1		2		1			
4		1		3		3		1		
5	1		4		6		4		1	
6	1	5		10		10		5		1

Special numbers

The **odd numbers** are 1, 3, 5, 7, 9, 11, 13, ...
The **even numbers** are 2, 4, 6, 8, 10, 12, 14, ...
The **factors** of a number are all the numbers that will divide exactly into that number.

Example 30 can be divided by 1, 2, 3, 5, 6, 10, 15 and 30.
The factors of 30 are 1, 2, 3, 5, 6, 10, 15 and 30.

The **multiples** of a number are found by multiplying the number by 1, 2, 3, 4, 5, ...

Example The first 6 multiples of 8 are 8, 16, 24, 32, 40, 48.

A **prime number** has only two factors, itself and 1.

Example   17 is a prime number. It has only two factors, 17 and 1.
Note: 1 is not a prime number.

A **prime factor** is a factor that is a prime number.

Example   20 has factors 1, 2, 4, 5, 10 and 20.
The prime factors of 20 are 2 and 5.

We can find **prime factors** using a **tree diagram**.
We keep dividing the number by the smallest possible prime number.

Example   Divide by 3
Divide by 5

3 and 5 are the prime factors of 75.

When we multiply a number by itself we get a **square number**.

Examples $6 \times 6 = 36$ $9 \times 9 = 81$ $14 \times 14 = 196$
36, 81 and 196 are square numbers.
Note: We write 6×6 as 6^2. 6^2 is read as six squared or six to the power of 2.

When we multiply a number by itself and then by itself again, we get a **cube number**.

Examples $3 \times 3 \times 3 = 27$ $5 \times 5 \times 5 = 125$ $10 \times 10 \times 10 = 1000$
27, 125 and 1000 are cube numbers.
Note: We write $5 \times 5 \times 5$ as 5^3. 5^3 is read as five cubed or five to the power of 3.

Worked Exam Questions

1. Here are the first five multiples of 3:   NEAB
    3   6   9   12   15
    (a) Write down the first five multiples of 5.   (1)
    (b) The number 15 is a multiple of both 3 and 5.
         Write down two more numbers that are multiples of both 3 and 5.   (2)
    (c) Find a number that is a multiple of both 3 and 5 and is also bigger than
         100.   (1)

Answer   (a)   5, 10, 15, 20, 25
          (b)   Multiples of both 3 and 5 are the multiples of 15.
                 So 30, 45, 60, ... are multiples of 3 and 5.
          (c)   The multiples of 3 and 5 are the multiples of 15.
                 These are 15, 30, 45, 60, 75, 90, 105, 120, 135 ...
                 105, 120, 135, ... are bigger than 100.

2. The first four prime numbers are given.

SEG

2, 3, 5, 7, ...

(a) What is the next prime number? *(1)*
(b) Explain why 2 is the only even prime number. *(1)*

Answer **(a)** 11 is the next prime number. It has two factors, 11 and 1.

(b) 2 is the only even prime number because **every other even number has at least 3 factors:** 1, 2 and itself.

Exercise 1 **A**

WJEC

1	2	3	4	5	6	7	8	9	10
11	12	13	14	15	16	17	18	19	20
21	22	23	24	25	26	27	28	29	30
31	32	33	34	35	36	37	38	39	40
41	42	43	44	45	46	47	48	49	50

From the numbers shown above, write down
(a) the square numbers which lie between 1 and 50, *(2)*
(b) the multiples of 9 which lie between 1 and 50. *(1)*

B Is 47 a multiple of 7?
Explain your answer.

C Debbie uses each of the digits 6, 5, 7 and 8 to make a four figure number, for example 7568.
1. What is the smallest four figure odd number she can make?
2. Debbie now makes a three figure number using each of the digits 7, 6 and 5. The number she makes is a multiple of 8. What is her number?

D

Below is a list of all the prime numbers that are less than 50.

MEG

	2	3	5	7	
11		13		17	19
		23			29
31				37	
41		43		47	

(a) Find four different pairs of prime numbers that each add up to 50. *(4)*
(b) Find a set of three prime numbers which add up to 50. *(2)*

E

Here are the first five numbers of a sequence.

MEG

1, 4, 13, 40, 121, ...
Three of these numbers are square numbers.
Write down the three square numbers. *(2)*

F Which of the numbers greater than one but less than six are prime numbers?

G   A number is less than 20.
It is a multiple of 2.
It can be divided exactly by 5.
What is the number?

H   Write these down:
1. the square of 7   2. all the multiples of 6 which are less than 40
3. the prime factors of 36   4. the prime factors of 70
5. the value of 3^3 6. the value of 8^2.

I   Here is a number pattern.
  8, 16, 24, 32, 40, 48, 56, 64
What goes in the gap?
Choose from the box.

> prime factors square
> multiples cube

1. These numbers are _____ of 8.
2. The numbers 16 and 64 are _____ numbers.
3. 8 and 16 are _____ of 32.
4. 64 is a _____ number but 16 is not.

J

1	2	3	4	5	6	7	8	9	10
11	12	13	14	15	16	17	18	19	20
21	22	23	24	25	26	27	28	29	30
31	32	33	34	35	36	37	38	39	40
41	42	43	44	45	46	47	48	49	50

From the numbers in the table write down
1. a square number   2. a factor of 60, other than 1
3. a factor of 100, other than 1   4. a multiple of 8
5. a multiple of 5   6. a multiple of 7
7. a cube number   8. three prime numbers
9. the numbers that 5 will divide into exactly
10. a square number bigger than 45
11. an even prime number
12. a number which is a multiple of 3 and also a multiple of 8
13. a number which is a multiple of 6 and also a multiple of 7
14. a prime factor of 30.

K   Write down the answers to these.
1. 2^3 2. 3^2 3. 9^2 4. 5^3 5. 3^3

L

1	2	3	5	8	24	27	36	49	64	100

Which numbers from the box are:
1. multiples of 6   2. factors of 9
3. prime numbers   4. prime factors of 100
5. square numbers   6. cube numbers?

M

MEG

The factors of 21 are 1, 3, 7 and 21.
Write down all the factors of 28.

(2)

N   Draw a tree diagram to find the prime factors of
1. 28 **2.** 50 **3.** 30 **4.** 42

Squares and cubes

Find out how to use your **calculator** to find squares and cubes of numbers.

We sometimes have to work out squares and cubes in a calculation.

Example   Work out the value of $5^2 \times 2^3$.

$$5^2 = 5 \times 5 \qquad\qquad 2^3 = 2 \times 2 \times 2$$

Note: You could use your calculator

$$= 25 \qquad\qquad\qquad = 8$$

to work out the answer.

$$5^2 \times 2^3 = 25 \times 8$$
$$= 200$$

Exercise 2

A   Use your calculator to find these.
1. 14^2 **2.** 19^2 **3.** 11^3 **4.** 8^3 **5.** 24^2
6. 12^3 **7.** 32^2 **8.** 16^2 **9.** 20^2 **10.** 51^2
11. 2.3^2 **12.** 3.3^2 **13.** 1.8^3 **14.** 1.4^3 **15.** 4.9^2

B   Work out the value of these.
1. $2^2 \times 3$ **2.** 4×2^2 **3.** 3×2^3 **4.** $4^2 \times 2^3$ **5.** $4^2 \times 3^3$
6. $3^3 \times 2^3$ **7.** $3^2 \times 2.1$ **8.** 10×3^2 **9.** 2.2×2^2

Investigation

To square a number ending in 5 follow these steps.

Example
65×65

1. Write down the part before the 5.
2. Add 1 to the number you wrote down in part **1**.
3. Multiply the number from part **1**. by the number from part **2**.
4. Write 25 on the end of this answer.

1. 6
2. 7

3. $6 \times 7 = 42$
4. **4225**

Can you square all these numbers ending in 5 using this method?

75^2 95^2 115^2 135^2 105^2

Make up some numbers ending in 5.
Can you square them using the steps given above?

Square roots and cube roots

Examples The **square root** of 25 is 5 because $5 \times 5 = 25$.
The **square root** of 49 is 7 because $7 \times 7 = 49$.
The square root of 25 is written as $\sqrt{25}$.

$$\sqrt{25} = 5 \qquad \sqrt{100} = 10 \qquad \sqrt{36} = 6 \qquad \sqrt{144} = 12$$

Find out how to use your calculator to find the square root of a number.

The **cube root** of 8 is 2 because $2 \times 2 \times 2 = 8$.
The **cube root** of 64 is 4 because $4 \times 4 \times 4 = 64$.
The cube root of 8 is written as $\sqrt[3]{8}$.

$$\sqrt[3]{8} = 2 \qquad \sqrt[3]{125} = 5 \qquad \sqrt[3]{1} = 1 \qquad \sqrt[3]{64} = 4$$

Find out how to use your calculator to find the cube root of a number.

Exercise 3

A Without using your calculator, find these:

1. $\sqrt{9}$ 2. $\sqrt{4}$ 3. $\sqrt[3]{1000}$ 4. $\sqrt[3]{27}$ 5. $\sqrt{100}$
6. $\sqrt{1}$ 7. $\sqrt[3]{1}$ 8. $\sqrt{64}$ 9. $\sqrt{49}$ 10. $\sqrt[3]{8}$

B Use your calculator to find these.

1. $\sqrt{256}$ 2. $\sqrt{961}$ 3. $\sqrt{1.21}$ 4. $\sqrt{2.56}$ 5. $\sqrt{1.69}$
6. $\sqrt[3]{64}$ 7. $\sqrt[3]{10.648}$ 8. $\sqrt[3]{0.08}$ 9. $\sqrt[3]{2.197}$

C Use your calculator to find these. Round the answers to the nearest whole number.

1. $\sqrt{78}$ 2. $\sqrt{2000}$ 3. $\sqrt{4 \times 6}$ 4. $\sqrt{8 \times 5}$ 5. $\sqrt{3 \times 9}$
6. $\sqrt[3]{80}$ 7. $\sqrt[3]{100}$ 8. $\sqrt[3]{6.85}$ 9. $\sqrt[3]{500}$ 10. $\sqrt[3]{158}$

Other powers

$$5 \times 5 = 5^2 \qquad 8 \times 8 \times 8 = 8^3$$

$8 \times 8 \times 8$ is called **expanded** form. 8^3 is called **exponent** form.

Examples

Expanded Form	Exponent Form
$6 \times 6 \times 6 \times 6$	6^4
$7 \times 7 \times 7 \times 7 \times 7$	7^5
$9 \times 9 \times 9 \times 9 \times 9 \times 9$	9^6
4	4^1

Exercise 4

A Write these in their expanded form.
The first one is done for you.

1. $3^5 = 3 \times 3 \times 3 \times 3 \times 3$ 2. 8^4 3. 12^5 4. 15^5
5. 9^1 6. 7^6 7. 6^1 8. 20^4

B Write in exponent form.
The first one is done for you.

1. $2 \times 2 \times 2 \times 2 \times 2 \times 2 = 2^6$ 2. $5 \times 5 \times 5 \times 5$
3. $8 \times 8 \times 8 \times 8 \times 8$ 4. $7 \times 7 \times 7 \times 7 \times 7 \times 7 \times 7$
5. $4 \times 4 \times 4 \times 4 \times 4 \times 4$ 6. $6 \times 6 \times 6 \times 6$
7. $9 \times 9 \times 9 \times 9 \times 9$ 8. $3 \times 3 \times 3 \times 3 \times 3 \times 3 \times 3 \times 3$
9. $2 \times 2 \times 2 \times 2 \times 2 \times 2 \times 2 \times 2 \times 2$ 10. $10 \times 10 \times 10 \times 10 \times 10 \times 10 \times 10$

Investigation

You will need   a calculator

1. Use a copy of this table.
   Finish filling it in.

	2^1	2^2	2^3	2^4	2^5	2^6	2^7	2^8	2^9	2^{10}	2^{11}	2^{12}	2^{13}	2^{14}
Value	2	4	8	16	32	64								
End digit	2	4	8	6	2	4								

The end digits form a repeating pattern.
Write down the repeating pattern.

2. Do the end digits of the powers of 3 form a repeating pattern?
   Use a copy of this table and fill it in.

	3^1	3^2	3^3	3^4	3^5	3^6	3^7	3^8	3^9	3^{10}	3^{11}	3^{12}	3^{13}	3^{14}	3^{15}
Value	3	9	27												
End digit	3	9	7												

3. Do the end digits of the powers of 4, 5 and 6 form a repeating pattern?

Index notation

$$10^1 = 10 \qquad 10^2 = 10 \times 10 \qquad 10^3 = 10 \times 10 \times 10 \qquad 10^4 = 10 \times 10 \times 10 \times 10$$

$$\begin{aligned} 3 \times 10^4 &= 3 \times 10 \times 10 \times 10 \times 10 \\ &= 3 \times 10\,000 \\ &= 30\,000 \end{aligned} \qquad \begin{aligned} 2.5 \times 10^3 &= 2.5 \times 10 \times 10 \times 10 \\ &= 2.5 \times 1000 \\ &= 2500 \end{aligned}$$

Exercise 5   **A** Write down the value of these.

1. 10^2 2. 10^1 3. 10^4 4. 10^3

B Write down the value of these.
1. 2×10^2 2. 3×10^1 3. 5×10^4 4. 8×10^3
5. 7×10^1 6. 4.2×10^2 7. 3.1×10^3 8. 6.8×10^4
9. 5.2×10^3 10. 0.8×10^2 11. 0.2×10^4 12. 3.25×10^3
13. 13×10^4 14. 2.1×10^5 15. 8.3×10^4 16. 0.01×10^3

C Write down the value of these.
1. $2 \times 10^2 \times 3 \times 10^1$ 2. $4 \times 10^1 \times 3 \times 10^2$ 3. $4 \times 10^3 \times 2 \times 10^2$
4. $5 \times 10^1 \times 3 \times 10^2$ 5. $2 \times 10^3 \times 2.2 \times 10^2$ 6. $3.1 \times 10^2 \times 4 \times 10^1$

The calculator gives big numbers in **index notation**.
Sometimes we get an answer on the calculator that
looks like this.
This is read as 4×10^2 or 4×100 or 400.

$$4.^{02}$$

Examples

$\boxed{8.^{03}}$ is read as 8×10^3 or 8×1000 or 8000.

$\boxed{7.5^{05}}$ is read as 7.5×10^5 or $7.5 \times 100\,000$ or 750 000.

$\boxed{9.63^{10}}$ is read as 9.63×10^{10} or $9.63 \times 10\,000\,000\,000$ or 96 300 000 000.

Exercise 6   **A**   1. $\boxed{3.^{04}}$ is the number

                      A 3.04   **B** 1.2   **C** 30 000

        2. $\boxed{7.^{10}}$ is the number

                      A 7.10   **B** 70   **C** 70 000 000 000

        3. $\boxed{5.2^{05}}$ is the number

                      A 5.200 000   **B** 520 000   **C** 5 200 000

        4. $\boxed{8.2^{07}}$ is the number

                      A 82 000 000   **B** 8.207   **C** 820 000 000

        5. $\boxed{7.62^{05}}$ is the number

                      A 7.620 00   **B** 762 000   **C** 7 620 000

B   Jay worked out the distance from the sun to Neptune

and got this answer. $\boxed{4.5^{09}}$

He thought this was the number 4.5^9.
1. Explain why he is wrong.
2. Maurice thought it was the number 45 000 000 000.
    Daniel thought it was the number 4 500 000 000.
    Who is correct?

C   Do these calculations on your calculator.
Write down the answer.
1. 40 000 × 6000
2. 500 000 × 30 000
3. 420 000 × 50 000
4. 6 800 000 × 300

Homework/Review

A 1. Write down the first 6 multiples of 4.
2. Write down the first 6 multiples of 6.
3. Write down 2 numbers that are a multiple of 4 *and* a multiple of 6.

B From the numbers in the cloud write down
1. the prime numbers which lie between 10 and 20
2. the square numbers which lie between 20 and 80
3. the factors of 100
4. the multiples of 8 which lie between 1 and 60
5. the prime factors of 64.

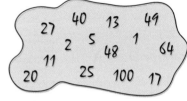

27   40   13   49
      2   5   1
11   48   64
20   25   100   17

C

| 48 | 27 | 8 | 64 | 1 | 100 |

Which of the numbers in the box are cube numbers?

D

Work out the value of   **LONDON**
(i) 5^3 (ii) $\sqrt{36}$ (iii) $2^3 \times 3^2$.   *(4)*

E

                                                                WJEC

(a) Write down, in figures, the number nine thousand and seventy-three.   *(1)*
(b) Write down the value of four squared.   *(1)*
(c) Write down the value of 3^3.   *(1)*

F Use your calculator to work these out.
1. 16^2 2. 8^3 3. 13^2 4. 5.2^2 5. 6.1^3
6. 2.01^2 7. 3.4^3 8. $\sqrt{225}$ 9. $\sqrt{625}$ 10. $\sqrt{2.25}$
11. $\sqrt{11.56}$ 12. $\sqrt{5.76}$ 13. $\sqrt[3]{0.512}$ 14. $\sqrt[3]{4.096}$

G $4^7 = 4 \times 4 \times 4 \times 4 \times 4 \times 4 \times 4$
Write 5^8 in expanded form.

H Write these in exponent form.
1. $4 \times 4 \times 4$ 2. $6 \times 6 \times 6 \times 6 \times 6 \times 6 \times 6$
3. $10 \times 10 \times 10 \times 10 \times 10 \times 10$ 4. $12 \times 12 \times 12 \times 12 \times 12$

I Find the value of these.
1. 5×10^3 2. 7×10^4 3. $2 \times 10^2 \times 3 \times 10^3$

J 3.2^{08} is the number

      A 3.208   **B** 320 000 000   **C** 25.6   **D** 3 200 000 000

KEY POINTS

☑ The **odd numbers** are 1, 3, 5, 7, 9, 11, 13, 15, 17, ...
The **even numbers** are 2, 4, 6, 8, 10, 12, 14, 16, ...

☑ The **factors** of a number are all of the numbers that will divide into that number leaving no remainder.
Example The factors of 24 are 1, 2, 3, 4, 6, 8, 12 and 24.

☑ The **multiples** of a number are found by multiplying the number by 1, 2, 3, 4, 5, ...
Example The **multiples** of 8 are 8, 16, 24, 32, 40, 48, 56, 64, ...

☑ A **prime number** has only two factors, itself and 1. 1 is not a prime number.
Example 23 can only be divided by 23 and 1 so it is a prime number.
The first six prime numbers are 2, 3, 5, 7, 11, 13.

☑ A **prime factor** is a factor that is a prime number.
We can find prime factors using a tree diagram.
The prime factors of 12 are 2 and 3.
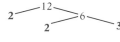

☑ The **square numbers** are found by multiplying a number by itself.
$1 \times 1 = 1$ $2 \times 2 = 4$ $3 \times 3 = 9$ $4^2 = 16$ $5^2 = 25$ $6^2 = 36$
1, 4, 9, 16, 25 and 36 are the first 6 square numbers.

☑ The **cube numbers** are found by multiplying a number by itself and then by itself again.
$1 \times 1 \times 1 = 1$ $2 \times 2 \times 2 = 8$ $3^3 = 27$ $4^3 = 64$
1, 8, 27, 64 are the first 4 cube numbers.

☑ $9 \times 9 = 81$. 9 is the **square root** of 81. $\sqrt{81} = 9$

☑ $3 \times 3 \times 3 = 27$. 3 is the **cube root** of 27. $\sqrt[3]{27} = 3$

☑ $8 \times 8 \times 8 \times 8 \times 8$ is in **expanded form**. It can be written as 8^5 which is **exponent form**.

☑ 2.2×10^4 is written in **index notation**. $2.2 \times 10^4 = 2.2 \times 10\ 000$
$$= 22\ 000$$

☑ On a **calculator** is read as 4.2×10^3. $4.2 \times 10^3 = 4.2 \times 1000$
$$= 4200$$

 # Investigation

If we add the digits of a number together we get a one digit **reduced number**.

Example   16 $1 + 6 = 7$ 7 is the reduced number from 16.
Sometimes we have to do this more than once to get a single digit.

Example   128 $1 + 2 + 8 = 11$ and $1 + 1 = 2$ 2 is the reduced number from 128.

1.   Copy this table and finish filling it in.

Number	1	2	3	4	5	6	7	8	9	10	11	12	13	14	15	16	17	18	19	20
Square Number	1	4	9	16	25	36	49	64	81	100	121	144	169	196	225	256	289	324	361	400
Reduced Number																				

These reduced numbers form a repeating pattern.
Does this repeating pattern continue if you find more reduced numbers?

2.   Do the reduced numbers made from the cube numbers form a repeating pattern?
Make a table like the one in *part* **1** to help you answer this.

◀◀ CHAPTER REVIEW ◀◀

◀◀
Exercise 1
on page 142

A

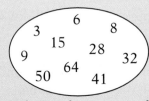

LONDON

From the numbers in the ring write down all the
(a) square numbers, (2)
(b) cube numbers, (2)
(c) prime numbers, (2)
(d) factors of 56. (2)

◀◀
Exercise 1 on
page 142

B From the box write down
1. the multiples of 9
2. the factors of 60
3. the prime factors of 24.

1	60	2	18
20	9	5	30
81	4	3	54

◀◀
Exercises 2, 3
and 5 on pages
144, 145
and 146

C

SEG

1. (i) What is the value of 3^2? (1)
   (ii) What is the value of 2^3? (1)

MEG

2. Work out
   (a) 7 squared (b) 3 cubed (c) 2^4 (d) 5×10^3 (e) 3.2×10^2 (5)

NEAB

3. Work out
   (a) the cube of 5 (b) 2^6 (2)

◀◀
Exercises 2
and 3 on pages
144 and 145

D

LONDON

Write down the value of
(a) $\sqrt{25}$ (1)
(b) the cube of 4. (1)

◀◀
Exercise 6 on
page 147

E Gordon used his calculator and the display gave the answer 5.6^{10}.
Beth said that this was the number 5.6.
Mohini said that this was the number 56 000 000 000.
Rachel said that this was the number 5.6000000000.
Who was correct?
Explain how you got your answer.

11 Probability

By the end of this chapter you will be able to:

- understand and use the words even chance, certain, likely, unlikely, impossible, fair and unfair
- list the outcomes of one or two events
- calculate the probability of equally likely outcomes
- understand mutually exclusive events
- understand that the probabilities of mutually exclusive events add up to 1
- find the probability of an event not happening
- use relative frequency to estimate probability
- estimate probabilities by studying past data or by making a sensible guess
- use a probability scale
- find the expected number of times an event will occur.

Getting started...

You will need   a copy of these
2 paper fasteners

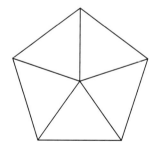  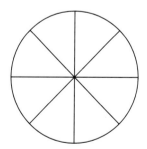

Paste each of these onto thin card.
Attach the pointers to the spinners with a split pin.
Make one of the spinners a **fair** spinner and the other an **unfair** spinner.
Explain why each of your spinners is fair or unfair.
Test each of your spinners to see if it is fair or unfair.

Likelihood

We use the following words to describe the probability of an event happening.

even chance   unlikely   likely   certain   impossible

Examples   There is an **even chance** a coin will land on heads.
It is **unlikely** that the spinner shown will stop on grey.
It is **likely** that the spinner shown will stop on red.
It is **certain** that the sun will rise tomorrow.
It is **impossible** that you will be born tomorrow.

Exercise 1

A   Pick one of these words to describe the probability of each of these events.

certain   likely   evens   impossible   unlikely

1. The sun will set today.
2. You will grow another arm.
3. A die will land on an even number.
4. The next person you speak to will have brown or black hair.

B   Put these events in order of likelihood with the most likely first.
1. The next child born in London will be a boy.
2. It will snow at the North Pole next winter.
3. Someone in your class will cough tomorrow.
4. Someone in your class will be Prime Minister one day.

C   Which colour is this spinner least likely to stop on?

D   This table shows the colours of hats sold at a fête.
I walk around the fête. Which colour hat am I most likely to see?

Colour	Number
Red	14
Green	2
Yellow	7
Blue	10

E

Sita	Sally	Johnny	Joyce	Jafar	Tom	Paul
50	49	50	48	50	47	50

This table shows the marks seven students got in a test.
One of these students is chosen at random.
Use one of the words in the box below to describe the probability that the student chosen will have a mark of

1. 50   2. 48   3. 40.

| likely   impossible   unlikely   certain   even chance |

Calculating probability

When we toss a die there are 6 possible **outcomes**.
These are: 1, 2, 3, 4, 5 or 6.
If the die is **fair** these outcomes are all **equally likely**.

We can calculate the probability of an event happening if the outcomes are equally likely.

> **Probability of an event** = $\dfrac{\text{number of ways the event can happen}}{\text{total number of possible outcomes}}$

Example The probability of getting a 2 when a die is tossed is $\frac{1}{6}$.

Probabilities can be written as fractions, decimals or percentages.
A fraction is usually written in its simplest form.

Sometimes the probability of an event happening is written as P (event).

Example The probability of getting a 4 when a die is tossed is $\frac{1}{6}$.
This may be written $P(4) = \frac{1}{6}$.

Worked Exam Question

Two fair spinners each have their edges numbered one to four. When the two spinners are spun, there are 16 possible ways in which they can land. Five of the ways are shown in the table.   **MEG**
(a) Complete the table.   (2)
(b) From your table, find the probability of getting two numbers that are the same.   (2)
(c) Find the probability of getting two numbers that are different.   (2)

1, 1	2, 1		
1, 2			
1, 3			
1, 4			

Answer

(a) We complete the table to show all the possible outcomes.

1, 1	2, 1	3, 1	4, 1
1, 2	2, 2	3, 2	4, 2
1, 3	2, 3	3, 3	4, 3
1, 4	2, 4	3, 4	4, 4

(b) There are 16 possible outcomes altogether.
4 of these have two numbers the same.

Probability of two numbers the same = $\dfrac{\text{number of ways event can happen}}{\text{total number of possible outcomes}}$

$= \dfrac{4}{16}$

$= \dfrac{1}{4}$ (or 25% or 0.25)

(c) There are 12 ways of getting two numbers that are different.
Probability of two different numbers = $\dfrac{12}{16}$

$= \dfrac{3}{4}$ (or 75% or 0.75)

Exercise 2 **A** In a cage there are four white kittens and one black kitten.
One kitten is to be taken out at random.
Write down the probability that the kitten taken from the cage will be: **1.** black **2.** white.

B A game is played with two fair spinners. They are spun at the same time.

The result shown in the diagram is **Red, 1**.
1. List all the possible results when the spinners are spun.
2. Use your list to work out the probability of getting the following when both spinners are spun.
    (a) Red, 2   **(b)** Yellow, 1   **(c)** Blue and an odd number

C
NEAB

  (a) Veena has three necklaces: a cream, a green and a yellow one.
     She also has three blouses: a black, a purple and a white one.
     She wears one necklace with one blouse.
     One pair of colours Veena could wear is cream, black.
     List all the other pairs of colours Veena could wear. *(3)*
  (b) Veena takes one of her blouses at random.
     What is the probability that she takes the white one? *(1)*
  (c) Veena takes a blouse and a necklace at random.
     What is the probability that she takes the green necklace and the white
     blouse? *(1)*

D Two fair triangular spinners each have their edges numbered 1, 2 and 3.
The two spinners are spun together. Three ways in which they can land are shown in the table.
1. Copy and complete the table.
2. Work out the probability that
    (a) both spinners land on the number 2
    (b) both spinners land on an odd number.

1, 1	1, 2	1, 3

E
WJEC

In a game two fair 6 sided dice are thrown.
The score is determined by finding the **difference** between the two numbers uppermost on the dice.
(a) Copy and complete this table to show the possible scores. *(2)*
(b) What is the probability of obtaining a score of 1? *(2)*

	1	2	3	4	5	6
...	...	...	...	...	...	...
...	...	...	...	...	...	...
4	...	...	...	...	...	...
3	2	1	0	1	2	3
2	1	0	1	2	3	4
1	0	1	2	3	4	5

F

SEG

David throws a dice and spins a four sided spinner.
He multiplies the numbers together to get his score.

(a) (i) Copy and complete the table to show all the possible scores. *(1)*

Number on spinner (columns); **Number on dice** (rows)

×	1	2	3	4
1	1	2		
2		4		
3				12
4			12	16
5		10	15	20
6	6	12	18	24

(ii) What is the probability of getting a score of seven when this game is played? *(1)*

(b) What is the probability of David scoring more than 11? *(2)*

G I have two bags containing numbered balls.
In the first bag there are four balls numbered 1, 2, 3 and 4.
In the second bag there are three balls numbered 2, 4 and 6.
I take one ball at random from each bag.

1st bag	2nd bag
1	2
1	4
1	6
2	2

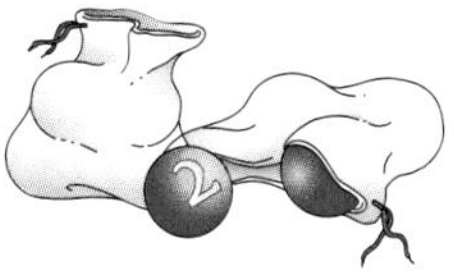

1. Copy and complete the table to show all the possible combinations of numbers that I might get.
2. What is the probability that
   (a) the numbers are the same (b) the numbers add up to 8 or more
   (c) the numbers add to 3 or more (d) the numbers add to 12?

H

SEG

The table shows the results of a survey in a class.

Eye colour	Boys	Girls
Blue eyes	5	8
Green eyes	1	2
Brown eyes	19	12

(a) What is the probability that one of the girls has blue eyes? *(2)*
(b) What is the probability that one of the students has brown eyes? *(2)*

I Rachel has bought 5 tickets in the 'Instant National Lottery'. She won a prize with one of them. She says, 'This shows that the chance of winning a prize in the Instant National Lottery is $\frac{1}{5}$.'
Is she correct? Give a reason for your answer.

J The 300 children in a school each bought one ticket for the school's prize draw.
The 300 tickets numbered 1 to 300 are put in a barrel and one winning ticket is drawn.

1. Natalie has ticket number 150.
   What is the probability that she will win the prize?
2. What is the probability that the winning ticket number will be greater than 150?
3. Iman says, 'Either a boy or a girl must win, so the probability that a girl will win is $\frac{1}{2}$.' Explain why she may be wrong.

K   NEAB

Connor and Georgia are brother and sister.
Say whether you agree or do not agree with each of the following things they say.
Give a reason for your answer each time.

(a) Georgia has bought a box of chocolates for her mother.
    There are 3 white chocolates and 5 milk chocolates in the box.
    Georgia: 'If Mother chooses a chocolate at random, the probability that it will be white is $\frac{3}{5}$.'   *(1)*

(b) Every evening Connor and Georgia spin a coin to see who does the washing up.
    Georgia has won on the last four evenings.
    Georgia: 'The probability that I will win tonight is $\frac{1}{32}$.'   *(1)*

(c) There is a biscuit tin on the table.
    It contains only chocolate biscuits, shortbread biscuits and ginger biscuits.
    Connor: 'If one biscuit is taken out at random the probability that it will be a chocolate biscuit is $\frac{1}{3}$.'   *(1)*

L The diagram shows two sets of cards, A and B.

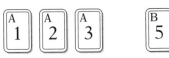

1. One card is chosen at random from each set.
   List all the possible outcomes.
2. The two numbers are added together.
   What is the probability of getting a total of 6?
3. A new card is added to set B. It is

   One card is chosen at random from set A and one card is chosen at random from the new set B.
   (a) How many possible outcomes are there now?
   (b) Explain why adding the new card **does not** change the number of outcomes that have a total of 6.
   (c) Adding the new card does change the probability of getting a total of 6.
       What is the probability of getting a total of 6 now?

Mutually exclusive events

Events which cannot happen at the same time are called **mutually exclusive**.

Examples When you toss a die you cannot get a 1 *and* a 4 on the same toss.
If you take one card at random from this set you cannot get a red *and* a black card.

If all of the outcomes of an event are mutually exclusive, the probabilities of these events add to 1.

Examples Getting a 1 or 2 or 3 or 4 or 5 or 6 when you toss a die are mutually exclusive events. They cannot happen at the same time.
The probabilities of getting these add to 1.

One of these cards is chosen at random.
The probability of getting a grey card is $\frac{1}{4}$.
The probability of getting a white card is $\frac{3}{4}$.
The events 'getting a grey card' and 'getting a white card' are mutually exclusive.
The probabilities of getting a grey or a white card add to 1. $\frac{1}{4} + \frac{3}{4} = 1$

Exercise 3

A Are events A and B mutually exclusive? Write Yes or No.
1. A die is tossed.
   Event A: getting an even number
   Event B: getting an odd number
2. A die is tossed.
   Event A: getting a number less than 3
   Event B: getting a 1
3. A card is picked at random from this set.

   | 3 | 5 | 8 | 10 | 16 | 19 |

   Event A: getting an odd number
   Event B: getting a number less than 10
4. The spinner shown is spun.
   Event A: landing on red
   Event B: landing on grey

B

Alison, Brenda, Claire and Donna are the only runners in a race.   **LONDON**
The probabilities of Alison, Brenda and Claire winning the race are shown below.

Alison	Brenda	Claire	Donna
0.31	0.28	0.24	

Work out the probability that Donna will win the race.   *(2)*

Probability of an event not happening

> Probability of an event *not* happening = 1 – probability of the event happening

Worked Exam Question

• •

A bag contains 6 red counters, 3 blue counters and 2 yellow counters.   **WJEC**
Howell takes a counter from the bag without looking.
(a) What is the probability that he takes a blue counter?   *(2)*
(b) Some green and some orange counters are put into the bag so that
   the probability of taking an orange counter is $\frac{3}{16}$. What is the
   probability of not taking an orange counter?   *(2)*

Answer   (a)   There are $6 + 3 + 2 = 11$ possible outcomes altogether.
             There are 3 blue counters.
             Probability of getting a blue counter $= \frac{3}{11}$

             (b) $P(\text{not orange counter}) = 1 - P(\text{orange counter})$
                   $= 1 - \frac{3}{16}$
                   $= \frac{13}{16}$

Exercise 4   **A**   A spinner is spun twice.
                       The probability that the spinner lands on red both times is 0.36.
                       What is the probability that both spins do *not* land on red?

                 B   A packet contains 8 yellow counters and 5 green counters.
                       A counter is taken at random from the packet.
                       What is the probability that it is *not* yellow?

                 C   Tim buys some tickets in a raffle.
                       1. The probability that he wins a prize is 15%.
                           What is the probability that he will *not* win a
                           prize?
                       2. 100 tickets were sold.
                           How many tickets did Tim buy?

                 D   Two cubes with numbers on them are tossed.
                       The probability of the two numbers adding to 6 is $\frac{7}{36}$.
                       What is the probability of getting two numbers that do *not* add up to 6?

Estimating probability

> We can **estimate the probability** of an event happening from the **relative
> frequency** of the event.
>
> | Relative frequency = | $\dfrac{\text{no of successful trials}}{\text{total number of trials}}$ |
> |---|---|

Example A company tested 1000 light bulbs.
130 of them lasted more than 5000 hours.
Relative frequency of a light bulb lasting more than 5000 hours $= \frac{130}{1000}$.
From this we can estimate the probability that the next light
bulb tested will last more than 5000 hours as $\frac{130}{1000}$ or $\frac{13}{100}$.
We could also write this as 13% or 0.13.

Note: The greater the number of trials, the more accurate the
estimate of the probability will be. If only 10 light bulbs
had been tested, the relative frequency would not give a
very accurate estimate of the probability.

Example Reena made a six-sided spinner. She spun it 50 times.
The table shows the results.

Score	1	2	3	4	5	6
Frequency	3	10	9	15	6	7

Is Reena's spinner fair? Give a reason for your answer.

Answer We can use the relative frequency to get an estimate of the probability.
If the spinner is fair then it would be equally likely to land on 1, 2, 3, 4,
5 or 6.
The probabilities would then be about the same.
The probabilities are not **about** the same.
$P(1) = \frac{3}{50}$, $P(2) = \frac{10}{50}$, $P(3) = \frac{9}{50}$, $P(4) = \frac{15}{50}$, $P(5) = \frac{6}{50}$, $P(6) = \frac{7}{50}$
So the spinner is not fair.
Note: The relative frequencies do not have to be *exactly* the same for the
spinner to be fair.

Exercise 5

A This table shows the colours of 200 skateboards at a skateboard
competition.

A skateboard is chosen at random.
Estimate the probability it will be

Colour	Black	Grey	Gold	Other
Frequency	49	32	17	102

1. black   **2.** grey   **3.** gold   **4.** other.

B This table shows the results of a survey of the
number of phone calls made each week by 100
16-year-old girls.
One of these girls is chosen at random.
What is the probability she made
1. 11–20 calls   **2.** 21–30 calls
3. greater than 20 calls?

Number of calls	Frequency
1 – 10	18
11 – 20	33
21 – 30	36
31 – 40	13

C Paul tossed a die 200 times.
His results are shown.
Was Paul's die a fair die?
Explain your answer.

Score	1	2	3	4	5	6
Frequency	32	31	34	35	33	35

D

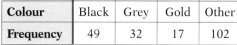

MEG

You are given 2 dice. You are told one is unfair, but not which one.
How could you find out which of the 2 dice is unfair?   *(4)*

We can also estimate probability from **past data** or by making a **sensible guess**.

Example Estimate the probability that it will snow in London in July.

Answer We can look at past data or make a sensible guess. July is a summer month so the probability of it snowing in London will be very close to 0.

Exercise 6 Estimate the probability of these events.
Give a reason for your answer.
1. It will snow tomorrow.
2. There will be an earthquake somewhere in the world next week.
3. It will rain in London tomorrow.
4. A girl chosen at random from 16-year-olds will have her hair tied up.
5. Your teacher will be away one day next week.

Probability scales

All probabilities **are greater than or equal to 0 and less than or equal to 1**.
We can show probabilities on a **probability scale**.

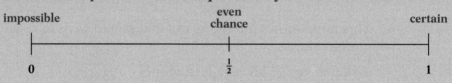

impossible		even chance		certain
0		$\frac{1}{2}$		1

Worked Exam Question

The table shows the bus fares paid by some pupils to travel to school. **LONDON**

Name	Neil	Daksha	Tarik	Sarah	Marc	Tom	Rob	Sita
Bus fare to school in pence	45	60	35	35	60	35	35	40

One of these pupils is to be chosen at random.
(a) What is the most likely bus fare of the chosen pupil? *(1)*
(b) Mark with an X on the number line below the probability that the chosen pupil pays a 40 pence bus fare. *(1)*

0		$\frac{1}{2}$		1

Answer (a)   The fare that happens most often is 35p. So the most likely fare is **35p**.

(b)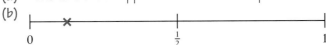

1 out of 8 pupils had a bus fare of 40p.
So the probability of a pupil chosen at random having a bus fare of 40p = $\frac{1}{8}$.
The cross must be $\frac{1}{8}$ of the way along the line.

Exercise 7

A

NEAB

A pupil uses a regular hexagon to make a spinner for a game.
(a) On a probability scale like the one below draw an arrow
to show how likely it is to score '0' with one spin.

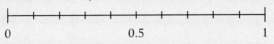

(1)

(b) A player thinks the spinner might be biased.
He does 100 spins and records the results.

Score	−3	−2	−1	0	2	3
Frequency	15	19	13	16	19	18

Do you think the spinner is biased? Give a reason for your answer.   (2)

B

SEG

(a) Show on this line, an estimate of the probability that a person chosen at
random is left-handed.

(1)

(b) Show on this line, an estimate of the probability that a person chosen at
random is **not** left-handed.

(1)

C

MEG

A bag contains some red balls, some green balls and some blue balls.
A ball is taken from the bag at random.
The diagram shows the probability that the ball is red and the probability that
the ball is green.

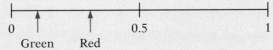

Green   Red

(a) Estimate the probability that the ball taken is
   (i)   green,
   (ii) red.   (3)
(b) What is the probability that the ball taken is not red?   (2)
(c) What is the probability that the ball taken is yellow? Explain your answer.   (2)

D

Probability Scale

LONDON

0 ───┼───┼───┼───┼───┼───┼───┼─── 1

      ↑   ↑ ↑

   Yellow   Red Blue

In a game you spin an arrow. The arrow stops on one of sixteen equal sectors of a circle. Each sector of the circle is coloured. The probability scale shows how likely it should be for the arrow to stop on any one colour.
Copy the circles below.
Shade them to show how many sectors should be
(i) coloured red   (ii) coloured blue

(2)

Expected number

If we know the probability of an event occurring we can work out the **expected number** of times this event will occur in a given number of trials.

Example The probability of Ron scoring under 72 in a round of golf is 0.35.
Ron plays 100 rounds of golf.
We would expect he would score under 72 in 0.35×100 or 35 rounds of golf.

> **Expected Number = probability × number of trials**

Exercise 8

A The probability of a pupil at Stratford School being left-handed is 0.18.
There are 550 pupils at the school.
How many would you expect to be left-handed?

B The probability of winning a prize in a raffle is 0.1.
If 350 people have a ticket, how many will win a prize?

C The spinner shown is spun 500 times.
How many times would you expect it to stop on red?

D There are six possible equally likely outcomes when a cube is rolled.
One of these is ★.
The cube is rolled 300 times.
How many times would you expect it to land on the star?

Homework/Review

A

Polly has kept records of the weather for five years.
She works out that the probability that it will rain on
any day in September is 0.2.
- **(a)** What is the probability that it will **not** rain on
  September 15th?
- **(b)** On how many September days could it be expected
  to rain?

MEG

September 1998
6 13 20 27
7 14 21 28
1 8 15 22 29
2 9 16 23 30
3 10 17 24
4 11 18 25
5 12 19 26

(1)

(2)

B

Two pupils are doing a survey on the makes of cars
passing their school.
The results so far are shown in this table.
Using this data, answer true or false to the following
statements, giving a reason for your answer.
- **(a)** The probability that the next car will be a Ford is
  roughly $\frac{1}{2}$.
- **(b)** The probability that the next car will be a
  Rolls-Royce is zero.
- **(c)** The probability that the next car will be a Renault is $\frac{1}{6}$.

MEG

Ford	136
Vauxhall	35
Renault	18
Nissan	41
Rover	17
Other makes	22

(1)

(1)

(1)

C

Two fair spinners are used for a game.
The scores from each spinner are added
together.
For example: The total score from the two
spinners shown is $4 + 5 = 9$
- **(a)** Copy and complete this table to show all the
  possible totals for the two spinners.
- **(b)** What is the probability of scoring
  (i)   a total of 3
  (ii) a total of more than 8?

NEAB

	1	2	3	4	5
2	3	4			
3	4	5			
4					
5					
6					

(2)

(1)

(2)

D

- **(a)** Graham estimated that the probability of a girl having blue eyes is 0.2 and
  that the probability of a boy having blue eyes is 0.24.
  (i)   What is Graham's estimate of the probability of a girl not having blue eyes?
  (ii) In a school of 800 children, 350 children are girls. About how many of
        these children would Graham expect to have blue eyes? *(5)*
- **(b)** A bag contains 4 toffees, 6 mints and 5 chocolates. Jill takes a sweet at
  random from the bag.
  What is the probability that the sweet she takes out is **not** a mint? *(2)*
- **(c)** The events A and B are described below.
  - A   One red sweet is picked at random from a bag containing 3 red
        and 7 white sweets.
  - B   Water will overflow when 2 litres of water are poured into a 1 litre
        container.
  Write A and B at approximate positions of their probabilities on a scale like
  this one. *(1)*

WJEC

```
|─────────────────────┼─────────────────────|
0                    0.5                    1
```

✔ KEY POINTS

✔ We can use the following words to describe the probability of an event happening.

   even chance   **unlikely**   **likely**   **certain**   **impossible**

✔ **Equally likely outcomes** all have an equal chance of happening.

   Examples   The outcomes red, green and blue for this spinner are equally likely.
   The outcomes red, green and blue for this spinner are *not* equally
   likely.

✔ We can calculate the probability of an event if the outcomes are equally likely.

$$\textbf{Probability of an event} = \frac{\textbf{number of ways an event can happen}}{\textbf{total number of possible outcomes}}$$

✔ **Mutually exclusive** events are events that cannot happen at the same time.

   Example You cannot roll a 4 *and* a 6 in the same roll of a die.

   If all the outcomes of an event are mutually exclusive, the probabilities of these events
   will add up to 1.

✔ P (event *not* happening) = 1 − P (event happening)

✔ We can **estimate probabilities** from the relative frequency of an event.

$$\textbf{Relative frequency} = \frac{\textbf{number of successful trials}}{\textbf{total number of trials}}$$

   The greater the number of trials, the more accurate the estimate.

✔ Sometimes we have to **estimate the probability** of an event by looking at **past data** or by
   making a **sensible guess**.

   Example We can estimate the probability that we will see stars tonight by looking at the
   sky and the weather forecast and making a sensible guess.

✔ **All probabilities** are **greater than or equal to 0 and less than or equal to 1**.
   A probability of 0 means the event is impossible.
   A probability of 1 means the event is certain.

✔ We can show probabilities on a **probability scale**.

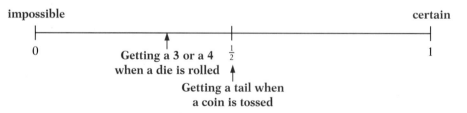

✔ **Expected number** of times an event will occur in a given number of trials
   = probability event will occur × number of trials.

◄◄ CHAPTER REVIEW ◄◄

◄◄

A

Exercises 1, 2, 3 and 7 on pages 152, 154, 157 and 161

SEG

(a) Below are five words that describe probability.
Write each word in the right place next to the probability scale.
The first one is done for you.

Evens   Unlikely   Certain   Likely   Impossible

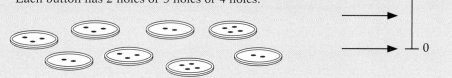

Evens   **(2)**

(b) Yvonne has eight buttons as shown.
Each button has 2 holes or 3 holes or 4 holes.

Yvonne takes a button at random.
(i) What is the probability that she takes a button with 2 holes?   **(2)**
(ii) What is the probability that she takes a button with 2 holes or with 4 holes?   **(2)**

A bag contains red, blue, white and yellow buttons only.
A button is taken at random from the bag.
The probability of getting each colour is shown in the table.

Colour	Red	Blue	White	Yellow
Probability	0.2	0.1	0.4	

(c)   What is the probability of getting a yellow button?   **(2)**

◄◄

Exercise 7 on page 161

B Rachel said, 'The probability that it will rain tomorrow is $\frac{7}{6}$.'
What is wrong with Rachel's statement?

◄◄

Exercises 1, 2, and 7 on pages 152, 154 and 161

C

LONDON

The spinner is spun.
(a) (i) Which colour is least likely?
(ii) Give a reason for your answer.   **(2)**
(b) On the probability line, mark with an X the probability that the colour will be Red.   **(1)**

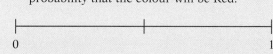

0   1

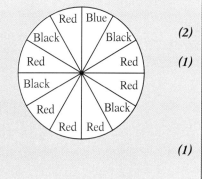

(c) Write down the probability that the colour will be Blue.   **(1)**

◀◀ **D**
Exercises 2 and 8
on pages 154 and
162

WJEC

(a) Three coins are tossed in the air. When they land Andrew records the heads (H) and the tails (T) obtained in the following way.
  HHH   HHT   HTH   ...   ...
List all the other possible results.
Hence write down the probability of obtaining two tails and a head, in any order. *(2)*

(b) In one turn of a game at a fête, a contestant spins two spinners. Each spinner is numbered 1 to 5 and these numbers are equally likely to occur. A contestant's score is the sum of the two numbers shown on the spinners.

(i) Copy and complete the table to show the possible outcomes of a contestant's score on one turn.

Second spinner					
5	...	...	...	...	...
4	...	...	...	...	...
3	4	...	...	...	...
2	3	4	5	6	7
1	2	3	4	5	6
	1	2	3	4	5

First spinner

(ii) What is the probability of scoring 2 on one turn?

(iii) Contestants win a prize if they score 8 or more. Jennifer has one turn at the game. What is the probability that she wins a prize?

(iv) At the fête, 200 people each have one turn at the game. Approximately how many of them will win a prize? *(7)*

◀◀ **E**
Exercises 2 and 4
on pages 154 and
158

SEG

The table shows information about a group of children.

(a) A boy in the group is chosen at random. What is the probability that he wears glasses?

		Boys	Girls
Wears glasses	Yes	5	3
	No	14	10

(2)

(b) A child in the group is chosen at random. The probability that the child wears glasses is 0.25. What is the probability that the child does **not** wear glasses? *(1)*

◀◀ **F**
Exercise 3
on page 157

LONDON

Martin bought a packet of mixed flower seeds.
The seeds produce flowers that are Red or Blue or White or Yellow.
The probability of a flower seed producing a flower of a particular colour is:

Colour	Red	Blue	White	Yellow
Probability	0.6	0.15		0.15

(a) Write down the most common colour of a flower. *(1)*

Martin chooses a flower seed at random from the packet.
(b) (i) Work out the probability that the flower produced will be White.
(ii) Write down the probability that the flower produced will be Orange. *(3)*

12 Using Decimals, Fractions and Percentages

By the end of this chapter you will be able to:

- add and subtract decimals
- multiply and divide decimals
- use fractions and percentages
- find fractions and percentages of a quantity
- carry out percentage calculations involving VAT, interest, profit, loss, discount, percentage increase and percentage decrease.

Getting started ....

Rate %	£5000		£25 000		£50 000		£100 000	
5.00	20.83	29.56	104.17	147.81	208.33	295.63	416.67	591.27
5.50	22.92	31.06	114.58	155.31	229.17	310.62	458.33	621.24
6.00	25.00	32.59	125.00	162.97	250.00	325.94	500.00	651.88
6.50	27.08	34.15	135.42	170.79	270.83	341.58	541.67	683.17
7.00	29.17	35.75	145.83	178.77	291.67	357.54	583.33	715.08
7.50	31.25	37.37	156.25	186.89	312.50	373.79	625.00	747.58
8.00	33.33	39.03	166.67	195.16	333.33	390.32	666.67	780.65
8.50	35.42	40.71	177.08	203.56	354.17	407.13	708.33	814.26
9.00	37.50	42.41	187.50	212.09	375.00	424.19	750.00	848.38
9.50	39.58	44.14	197.92	220.74	395.83	441.49	791.67	882.99
10.00	41.67	45.90	208.33	229.51	416.67	459.03	833.33	918.06

Amount borrowed

Interest only mortgage figures are in black.

Repayment mortgage over 25 years figures are in red.

This table shows how much a mortgage costs *per month* at different interest rates.

1. Mr Sinclair borrowed £50 000 at 7.5%.
   He chose to repay the mortgage over 25 years.
   How much are his mortgage payments each year?
   How much would he pay in total over 25 years?

2. Mrs Young borrowed £50 000 at 7.5%.
   She chose an interest only mortgage.
   How much are her mortgage payments each year?
   How much would she pay over 25 years? Include the £50 000 she has to pay back at the end.

Using decimals

Adding and subtracting

When we **add and subtract decimals** we line up the decimal points.

Examples $86.3 + 5.78$

$$
\begin{array}{r}
86.30 \\
+\,{}_{1}5.78 \\
\hline
92.08 \\
\end{array}
$$

$£85.70 - £38.59$

$$
\begin{array}{r}
{}^{7}\!\!{}_{1}8\overset{6}{5}.\overset{1}{7}0 \\
-\,38.59 \\
\hline
47.11 \\
\end{array}
$$

The answer is £47.11.

Worked Exam Question
• •

WJEC

John buys a 10 m roll of heavy duty tape to repair cracks in his garage roof.
He uses 4.75 m on one crack, and 2.6 m on another crack.
Find the length of tape that is left.   *(2)*

Answer   In total, John used 4.75 m + 2.6 m.
4.75 m + 2.6 m = 7.35 m
He had 10 m to start with.
10 m − 7.35 m = 2.65 m
There is **2.65 m** of tape left.

$$
\begin{array}{r}
4.75 \\
+\,2.60 \\
\hline
7.35 \\
\end{array}
\qquad
\begin{array}{r}
{}^{0}\!\!\overset{9}{1}\overset{9}{0}.\overset{9}{0}\overset{1}{0} \\
-\,7.35 \\
\hline
2.65 \\
\end{array}
$$

Exercise 1   **A**   Find the answers to these.

1. $16.7 + 4.25$
2. $104.68 + 0.96$
3. $42 + 8.34$
4. $51.58 + 62.79$
5. $42.5 - 3.6$
6. $5.8 - 4.37$
7. $12 - 8.72$
8. $15 - 9.64$

B   A length of ribbon was cut into sections of length 3.4 cm, 4.6 cm and 5.9 cm. What was the original length of the ribbon?

C   A length of rope was cut into sections of length 4.2 m, 3.6 m and 7.9 m. What was the original length of the rope?

D   Melissa had £8. She spent £4.65 on a pair of earrings and £1.89 on food. How much did she have left?

E

   £2.99

   £2.49

   £1.29

1. Emma bought a Sara Lee dessert and a cheesecake. How much did this cost altogether?
2. How much change should she get from a £5 note?
3. Dipesh bought two pavlovas. How much change did he get from £10?

Multiplying and dividing

Example   A maths teacher buys 92 text books, costing £4.85 each.
Work out the exact total cost.

Answer   We must find the answer to 4.85 × 92.

```
  4.85
×   92
──────
  970
43650
──────
44620
```

1. Multiply the numbers as if
the decimal point wasn't there.

2. Estimate the answer.   4.85 × 92 is about 5 × 100.
5 × 100 = 500.

3. Put the decimal point in so that the answer is close to
the estimate.

Note: 446.20 is the closest number to 500.

```
  4.85
×   92
──────
446.20
```

Example   Sirah bought 24.6 kg of apples.
She divided these equally into 8 bags.
How many kilograms were in each bag?

Answer   We must find 24.6 ÷ 8.

There were 3.075 kg in each bag.

line up the decimal points

```
      3.075
     ───────
8 │ 24.600
         4
```

add zeros
when you run
out of numbers

If we are asked to divide using money, it is best to change the pounds
into pence.

Example   How many 55p donuts can you buy for £10?

Answer   Change £10 to 1000p.

1000 ÷ 18 = 18r10
You can buy 18 donuts with £10.

```
        18r10
      ───────
55 │ 1000
       55
      ───
      450
      440
      ───
       10
```

Exercise 2

A   Find the answers to these.

1. 47 × 3.8   2. 6.9 × 57   3. 804 × 5.8   4. 1.05 × 6.2
5. 18.4 ÷ 4   6. 125.8 ÷ 5   7. 84.6 ÷ 6   8. 118.75 ÷ 19

B   Jean buys 86 sandwiches at £1.55 each. What is the total cost?

C

1.   Which of these is the cheapest per kilogram?
2.   How much dearer per kilogram are 'Peanuts' than 'Mixed Nuts'? Give
your answer in pounds.

D Look at this calculation. $86 \times 134 = 11\,524$

Use it to find the exact value of

1. 86×0.134　　2. $0.086 \times 13\,400$　　3. $11\,524 \div 860$

E

WJEC

Anthony has £10. He uses this money to buy as
many roses as he can for his mother.
Each rose costs 65p.

(a)　How many roses does he buy?
(b)　How much money does he have left?

(3)

F Two cans of cola and one small cake cost £1.70.

One can of cola and one small cake cost £1.10.

(a)　What is the cost of one can of cola?
(b)　What is the total cost of 5 cans of cola and 5 small cakes?

G

WJEC

A carpenter stores sheets of plywood on top of each other.
(a)　The height of 56 sheets of plywood is 25.2 cm.
　　　Find the thickness of **one** sheet of plywood.　　*(2)*
(b)　Calculate the height of 75 sheets of plywood.　　*(2)*

H Naim bought 25 pumpkins to sell at a stall.
He paid £22.50 in total for them.
How much did he pay for each pumpkin?

I 1.　Anne bought a ribbon 71.25 cm long. She cut it into 15 equal pieces.
　　How long was each piece?
2.　Selma travelled 298.2 miles on 42 litres of petrol.
　　How many miles did she travel on each litre?

Using fractions and percentages

We often have to find **fractions and percentages of a quantity.**

Example　Find $\frac{3}{5}$ of £35.

Answer　'of' means multiply.
$\frac{3}{5}$ **of** £35 $= \frac{3}{5} \times$ £35
Without the calculator, we find $\frac{3}{5}$ by dividing by 5 and multiplying by 3.
$35 \div 5 = 7$ and $7 \times 3 = 21$
$\frac{3}{5}$ of £35 = £21.

Using the calculator, key ⟨3⟩ ⟨÷⟩ ⟨5⟩ ⟨×⟩ ⟨3⟩ ⟨5⟩ ⟨=⟩ to get ⟨21.⟩

Example Find $17\frac{1}{2}\%$ of £680.

Answer $17\frac{1}{2}\% = 0.175$

So $17\frac{1}{2}\%$ of £680 $= 0.175 \times £680$
$= £119$

Worked Exam Question

MEG

Pupils on a school trip were given the choice between cola and lemonade.
(i)   There were 260 girls on the trip. 65% of them chose cola.
      How many girls chose cola?   *(2)*
(ii) There were 210 boys on the trip. Two fifths of them chose cola.
      How many boys chose cola?   *(2)*
(iii) There were 470 pupils altogether on the trip.
      What percentage of them chose cola?   *(3)*

In part (iii) we must express one quantity as a percentage of another.

Answer (i)   We must find 65% of 260.
             65% of 260 $= 0.65 \times 260$
             $= 169$
             169 girls chose cola.

Change 65% to $\frac{65}{100}$ or 0.65

(ii) We must find $\frac{2}{5}$ of 210.
      $\frac{2}{5}$ of 210 $= \frac{2}{5} \times 210$
      $= 84$
      84 boys chose cola.

$210 \div 5 = 42$
$42 \times 2 = 84$

To find one quantity as a percentage of another
1. Write the quantities as a fraction.
2. Multiply by 100%.

(iii) $169 + 84 = 253$
      253 altogether chose cola.
      So $\frac{253}{470}$ chose cola.
      We must multiply this fraction by 100%.
      $\frac{253}{470} \times 100\% = 53.8$ to 1 d.p. or **54% to the nearest %**.

Key [2][5][3][÷][4][7][0][×][1][0][0][=] to get **53.829787**

Exercise 3   **A**   Find
1. $\frac{1}{3}$ of 240   2. $\frac{5}{6}$ of 138   3. 10% of 58.4   4. 20% of £68.50
5. 38% of 452   6. $\frac{3}{8}$ of 12   7. $12\frac{1}{2}\%$ of 600   8. $17\frac{1}{2}\%$ of £199.

B

MEG

Work out $\frac{1}{8}$ of 40.   *(1)*

C

SEG

On one day 186 pupils use the school tuck shop.
(i)   Half of these pupils buy a biscuit.
      What percentage of pupils buy a biscuit?   *(1)*
(ii) One sixth of the pupils buy crisps.
      How many pupils buy crisps?   *(1)*

D

WJEC

(a) In a box of 200 apples 40 are rotten.
What fraction of the apples are rotten? *(1)*

(b) Find $\frac{3}{10}$ of 50 litres. *(1)*

> Note:
> If you are asked to give the answer as a fraction, reduce it to its lowest terms.

E

WJEC

Find $\frac{4}{7}$ of £56. *(1)*

F

MEG

Find **(a)** 20% of £70 *(2)*   **(b)** $17\frac{1}{2}$ of £440. *(2)*

G

LONDON

There are 560 pupils going on a trip.
45% of the pupils are boys.
Work out the number of boys going on the trip. *(2)*

H

WJEC

Calculate 46% of 350 kg. *(2)*

I

A group of 80 students applied to go on a ski course.
Only 80% of the students who applied went on the course.
How many students went on the course?

J

WJEC

An aeroplane can seat 300 passengers. What percentage of the seats are occupied when the aeroplane has 150 passengers who are all seated? *(1)*

K

LONDON

Peter gets 56 marks out of 80 marks for his test.
Work out his percentage mark for the test. *(2)*

L

WJEC

Anil earns £800 each month.
Each month, one quarter of his monthly income is used to pay the rent on his flat. One fifth of the income that he has left after paying the rent is put into a savings account in a building society.
What **fraction** of his monthly income is left after the above amounts have been taken away? *(4)*

M   MEG

The number of new cars registered in August 1994 was 460 000.
(i)   One quarter of the cars were red. Find the number of red cars.   *(2)*
(ii)   36% of the cars were blue. Find the number of blue cars.   *(2)*
(iii)   There were 2400 black cars. What fraction of the cars were black?   *(2)*

N   SEG

Only 18 pieces, each 32 m long, can be cut from 592 m of cable.
(i)   How much cable is left over?   *(2)*
(ii)   What percentage of the original cable is left over?   *(2)*

O   SEG

Peter and Simon take part in a long jump
competition.
Peter makes two jumps.
His first jump is 350 cm long.
The length of his second jump is $\frac{9}{10}$ of his first.
What is the length of Peter's second jump?   *(1)*

P   Calculate 1.5% of 4 kg, giving your answer in grams.

Q   MEG

The number of seriously overweight Americans increased from a quarter
of the population in 1985 to a third of the population in 1995.
(i)   Write a quarter and a third as numerical fractions.   *(1)*
(ii)   Find a quarter of 264.   *(1)*
(iii)   264 million people lived in America in 1985, and the same number
lived there in 1995.
How many more were seriously overweight in 1995 than in 1985?   *(4)*

R   There are 100 grams of tea in a partly used packet.
There are 125 grams of tea in a full packet.
Express the weight of tea in the partly used packet as a percentage of the
weight of tea in the full packet.

S   SEG

The price per kilogram for two different sorts of cheese is:
           Brie   £4.80
           Edam   £4.00
Alistair buys some Brie.
He pays £1.60.
What fraction of a kilogram did he buy?
Give your answer in its simplest form.   *(2)*

VAT, interest, profit, loss, discount, % increase and % decrease

Percentages are used to calculate **VAT**, **interest**, **profit**, **loss**, **discount**, **% increase** and **% decrease**.

Worked Exam Questions

1. Kitty invests £1500 in an account for 3 years at 8% per annum simple interest.
Calculate the total amount in the account at the end of the 3 years.

WJEC

(3)

Answer   Simple interest means that Kitty earns the same amount of interest each year.
We must find 8% of £1500.
8% of £1500 = 0.08 × 1500
              = 120
Kitty earns £120 each year for 3 years.
£120 × 3 = £360
At the end of 3 years there will be £1500 + £360.
£1500 + £360 = **£1860**.

2. (a) How much is saved by paying the cash price instead of the credit price?
(b) Another television set costs £550.
In a sale the price is reduced by 12%.
Calculate the new price of the television set.

SEG

(5)

(3)

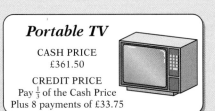

Portable TV

CASH PRICE
£361.50

CREDIT PRICE
Pay $\frac{1}{3}$ of the Cash Price
Plus 8 payments of £33.75

Answer (a) $\frac{1}{3}$ of the cash price is $\frac{1}{3}$ of £361.50
$\frac{1}{3}$ of £361.50 = $\frac{1}{3}$ × 361.50
               = £120.50
8 payments of £33.75 is 8 × 33.75
8 × £33.75 = £270
Total credit price = £120.50 + £270
                 = £390.50
Saving = credit price − cash price
        = £390.50 − £361.50
        = **£29**

Key $\boxed{1}$ $\boxed{÷}$ $\boxed{3}$ $\boxed{×}$ $\boxed{361.5}$ $\boxed{=}$

Find the credit price. Subtract cash price from the credit price.

(b)   12% of £550 = 0.12 × 550
                = £66
The television set is reduced by £66.
New price = old price − reduction
          = £550 − £66
          = **£484**

New price = old price − reduction

3. In 1993 a 'CHOCO EASTER EGG' cost £1.60.   **SEG**
   (a) In 1994 a 'CHOCO EASTER EGG' cost 10% more.
       How much more did one of these eggs cost in 1994?   *(1)*
   (b) In 1995 a 'CHOCO EASTER EGG' cost £1.90.
       Calculate the percentage increase in the price of one of these   *(2)*
       eggs from 1993 to 1995.

Answer   **(a)**   We must calculate 10% of £1.60.

$$10\% \text{ of } £1.60 = 0.1 \times 1.6$$
$$= 0.16$$

In 1994 the egg cost **£0.16 or 16p more**.

  (b)   Actual increase $= £1.90 - £1.60$

$$= £0.30 \text{ or } 30p$$

To find % increase
1. Calculate actual increase
2. Find $\dfrac{\text{increase}}{\text{original}} \times 100\%$.

$$\% \text{ increase} = \frac{\text{increase}}{\text{old price}} \times 100\%$$

$$= \frac{0 \cdot 3}{1 \cdot 6} \times 100\% \left(\text{or } \frac{30}{160} \times 100\% \right)$$

$$= \textbf{18.75\%}$$

Exercise 4   **A**

Mary buys a television set in this sale.   **WJEC**
The usual price of the television is £480.
Calculate the sale price of the television.   *(2)*

SALE sale SALE sale

Prices down by 15%

B   **SEG**

A theatre has 2100 seats.
The number of seats is increased by 5%.
Calculate the total number of seats after the increase.   *(2)*

C   Rod receives £5 pocket money. How much pocket money does he get
     when it is increased by 5%?

D

                                Tigers   Cheetahs   **LONDON**

Jugdev pays to see the Tigers.
It normally costs £2.40 but there is
20% off the price.
(a) Work out how much he pays.   *(2)*
Jugdev then pays to see the
Cheetahs.
It normally costs £2.70 but there is $\frac{1}{3}$
off the price.
(b) Work out how much he pays.   *(1)*

Admission. £2.40   Admission. £2.70

SPECIAL OFFER   SPECIAL OFFER

20% off $\frac{1}{3}$ off

E The average cost to run a fridge for a year is £75. If the fridge has been fitted with Plugsaver, how much would be saved over the year?

Cut electricity costs by 15% with **Plugsaver**

F The marked price of a shirt is £15.99. What is its sale price, to the nearest penny?

Sale
25% off all marked prices

G Jill earns £20.40 a week. She is given a pay rise of 15%. How much will Jill earn each week now?

H The recommended price of a book is £9.60. Two shops have special offers. At which shop is the book cheaper? By how much?

TREES   TREES

SHOP A $\frac{1}{3}$ off   SHOP B   35% off

I 1. Rachel's kitchen is 4 m long. She wants it to be 60% bigger. Calculate the length that Rachel wants it to be.
   2. The cost to make it bigger is estimated at £9000. She says, 'We must reduce the cost by $\frac{1}{5}$.' Calculate what Rachel thinks the cost should be.

J Mr Patel has a faulty cooker. He calls out an electrician who replaces some parts which cost £17.80. Copy and complete the bill.

SAM'S ELECTRICAL	£
Fixed call charge	25.50
$1\frac{1}{4}$ hours at £22 per hour	
Parts	
Total before VAT	
VAT at $17\frac{1}{2}\%$	
Total due	

K This shows the meter readings for three months on an electricity bill.

Previous meter reading	**58 324**
Present meter reading	**59 864**

The cost per unit is 9 pence.
The fixed charge per quarter is £14.00
1. Find the total cost of the electricity.
2. VAT of 8% is charged on electricity bills. How much is the total bill, including VAT?

L 1. Bradley was given a pay rise of 8%. He earned £176 per week before the rise. What was his pay after the rise?
   2. Natasha was also given a pay rise. Her pay rose from £180 to £216 per week. Express this as a percentage increase.

M 1. Tom stays for 6 nights at the Kings Hotel.
   How much more would it cost to stay for a week?

2. Jasmine stays at the hotel for one week and three more nights.
   If you pay in advance, there is a 15% discount.
   How much will Jasmine save by paying in advance?

KINGS HOTEL
£82 per night
Special weekly rate £495

N Skirts were priced at £13.80.
In a sale they cost £12.30.
What percentage discount is this?
Give your answer to an appropriate degree of accuracy.

O 1. Interest is 8% per annum.
   How much would be in an account at the end of the year if £470 was put in at the beginning of the year?

2. How much interest is earned on £500 at a simple interest rate of 8% per annum for 3 years?

P 1. Apples cost 45p per kilogram.
   Pears cost 20% more per kilogram.
   How much does 5 kg of pears cost?

2. Oranges were 18p each yesterday. Today each costs 19p.
   Calculate the percentage increase in price.

Q 1. Brett bought a car for £2400.
   He sold it and made a profit of 8%.
   How much did he sell the car for?

2. Rose bought a car for £3670.
   She sold it for £3490.
   What percentage loss did she make?

Puzzles

1. Andrew is allowed a 10% discount on goods because he works at a store.
   In a sale at the store everything is reduced by 10%.
   Does Andrew now get a 20% discount on things he buys?
   How much would he pay for an item that was £100 before the sale?

2. Louise bought two bikes.
   She sold them each for £300.
   On one bike she made a 10% profit.
   On the other she made a 10% loss.
   Did she make or lose money overall?

Homework/Review

A Chocolate bars cost 35p each.
   (a) Jason buys 5 bars.
       How much change does Jason get from £5?
   (b) How many bars of chocolate can Jason buy with £5?

SEG

(2)
(2)

B

MEG

In Year 11 of a school, $\frac{1}{4}$ of the students support City and $\frac{3}{8}$ of them support Rovers. There are 160 students in Year 11.
(i) How many of them support City? *(1)*
(ii) How many of them support Rovers? *(2)*

C Find, without using a calculator.
1. $3.86 + 0.92$ 2. 4.23×24 3. $896 - 4.97$ 4. $170.1 \div 7$

D Find
1. 25% of 400 2. 35% of 80 g 3. $17\frac{1}{2}\%$ of £620
4. $\frac{2}{3}$ of £480 5. $\frac{3}{5}$ of 48 kg 6. 33% of 570 miles

E A bus can seat 50 passengers. 32 seats are occupied.
What percentage of seats are occupied?

F Mrs Smith charged £28 for a ticket for a tour.
196 people bought a ticket.
The total cost of the tour to Mrs Smith was £5000.
1. How much profit did Mrs Smith make?
2. Express the profit as a percentage of the total cost of the trip.

G

WJEC

(a) The Government stated that the cost of living rose by 4% during the past year. Leah earned £15 400 last year. By how much should her salary increase in order to keep up with this rise in the cost of living? *(2)*
(b) A 2 kg piece of beef contains 320 g of fat. What percentage of the beef is fat? *(2)*

H

WJEC

(a) In an examination Robert scored 56 marks out of a total of 70. What percentage of the total mark did Robert achieve? *(2)*
(b) The normal price of a bicycle is £240. In a sale, its price is reduced to £204. Express the reduction as a percentage of the normal price. *(3)*

I

LONDON

The Standard monthly payment for an insurance scheme for Tom is £7.20.
This is reduced for the Discount monthly payment to £6.12.
Work out the percentage reduction. *(3)*

J Mrs Tan bought a stereo.
She borrowed £800 from the bank at 8% interest per year.
1. How much interest does she have to pay each year?
2. The stereo cost £680 plus $17\frac{1}{2}\%$ VAT.
What was the total cost of the stereo?

K

MEG

(a) Before the last World Athletics championship, one woman's personal best
for the triple jump was 14.80 metres.
During the championship she increased this by 3%.
Calculate her new personal best.
Give your answer to an appropriate degree of accuracy.   *(3)*

(b) At the same championship the record for the men's triple jump increased
from 17.98 metres to 18.29 metres.
Calculate the percentage increase.   *(3)*

✔ KEY POINTS

✔ To **add and subtract decimals** line up the decimal points.

✔ **Multiply decimals** as follows.
Multiply as if the decimal point wasn't there.
Estimate the answer to find where the decimal point goes.

✔ To **divide into a decimal** put the decimal points underneath each other.

$$6\overline{)18.72} = 3.12$$

✔ To find the **fraction of an amount** multiply the amount by the fraction.
Example $\frac{2}{3}$ of 15 $= \frac{2}{3} \times 15$ **15 × 2 = 30 and 30 ÷ 3 = 10**
$= 10$

✔ Find the **percentage of an amount** as follows.
Step 1   Write the percentage as a fraction or decimal. e.g. 15% is written as $\frac{15}{100}$ or 0.15.
Step 2   Multiply the amount by this fraction or decimal.
Example $17\frac{1}{2}\%$ of £65 = 0.175 × £65
Key `0.175` × `65` = to get `11.375`
So $17\frac{1}{2}\%$ of £65 = £11.38 to the nearest penny.

✔ Write **one quantity as a fraction or percentage of another** as follows.
Step 1   Write the two quantities as a fraction.
Make sure they have the same units.
Step 2   Multiply the fraction by 100% to get a percentage as the answer.

✔ When money invested receives the same amount of interest each year this is called **simple interest**. It is calculated by multiplying the amount invested by the interest per year.

✔ **Increase or decrease by a fraction or percentage** as follows.
Step 1   Find the actual increase or decrease.
Step 2   Add it on if it is an increase. Subtract it if it is a decrease.
Example A tie costs £21.60 before the sale. We find the sale price as follows.
35% of £21.60 = 0.35 × £21.60
= £7.56
£21.60 − £7.56 = £14.04
The tie costs £14.04 in the sale.

TODAY ONLY SALE **35%** discount

✔ Find a **fractional or percentage increase or decrease** as follows.
Step 1   Calculate the actual increase or decrease.
Step 2   Write this increase or decrease over the *original* amount.
Step 3   To get the percentage increase or decrease, multiply the fraction from **Step 2** by 100%.

◀◀ CHAPTER REVIEW ◀◀

◀◀
Exercise 3
on page 171

A

WJEC

Find 25% of 200.

(1)

◀◀
Exercise 3
on page 171

B

SEG

In York, Usuf visits the
Jorvik Centre.
The admission prices are
shown.
Usuf is 15 years old.
Work out how much Usuf
paid to get in.

JORVIK CENTRE
Prices
ADULTS £8.00
UNDER 16 years old ...... $\frac{3}{4}$ of the Adult Price

(2)

◀◀
Exercises 1, 2, 3
and 4
on pages 168,
169, 171 and 175

C

LONDON

Mark has a market stall.
He sells apples at 56p for each
kilogram.
Bianca buys 4 kilograms of apples.
She pays for her apples with a £5
note.
(a) How much change should she
get?

(3)

Mark bought 25 melons for his stall.
He paid £16 for 25 melons.
(b) Work out the price Mark paid for
each melon.

(3)

Two of the melons were bad.
Mark sold the other 23 melons for 149p each.
(c) Work out the total amount for which Mark sold the melons.

(3)

Mark usually sells oranges for 40p each.
He reduces the price to $\frac{7}{8}$ of this.
(d) Work out the new price of an orange.

(2)

Mark bought his potatoes for 30p for each kilogram.
He sold the potatoes and made a profit of 40%.
(e) At what price did Mark sell the potatoes?

(3)

◀◀
Exercise 3
on page 171

D

SEG

A geography test is marked out of 80.
(a) Georgina gets 60% of the marks.
How many marks does she get?

(2)

(b) Alfie gets 36 marks.
What percentage does he get?

(2)

◀◀
Exercises 1, 2 and
3 on pages 168,
169 and 171

E

NEAB

(a) Korky cat food costs 44p a tin.
Alec buys 18 tins of Korky cat food.
He pays with a £10 note.
How much change should he receive? *(3)*
(b) Alec's cat eats $\frac{2}{3}$ of a tin of Korky each day. What is
the least number of tins Alec needs to buy to feed
his cat for 7 days? *(3)*

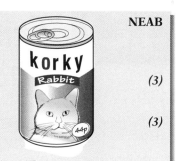

◀◀
Exercises 1, 2 and
4 on pages 168,
169 and 175

F

WJEC

Christopher has received his gas bill for the period June to August.
The details of the bill are as follows.
   Number of units of gas used is 7939.
   The cost of one unit of gas is 1.52 pence.
   Number of days in this period is 92.
   The standing charge is 10.39 pence per day.
(a) Find, in pounds, the cost of the gas, including the standing charge, for the
   June to August period. Show your working. *(4)*
(b) VAT at 5% is charged on gas bills.
   How much is Christopher's gas bill including VAT? Give your answer in
   pounds, correct to the nearest penny. *(2)*

◀◀
Exercise 4
on page 175

G

LONDON

Two shops sell the same
make of calculator.
At **Calculators are Us**, the
price of a calculator is
£7.50 plus VAT.
At **Top Calculators**, the
price is £8.75. This includes
VAT.
VAT is charged at a rate of
17.5%.
Work out the difference in cost between the two prices. *(3)*

Calculators are Us	**Top Calculators**
Model HX 130 £7.50 VAT not included	Model HX 130 £8.75 VAT included

◀◀
Exercises 1 and 3
on pages 168
and 171

H

NEAB

In a competition there is a total of £1500 in prize money.
(a) Sue wins $\frac{1}{2}$ of the total prize money.
   How much does she win? *(1)*
(b) Ben wins 25% of the total prize money.
   How much does he win? *(2)*
(c) How much money is left for the other prizes? *(2)*

13 Triangles, Quadrilaterals and Polygons

By the end of this chapter you will be able to:

- understand that angles in a triangle add up to 180°
- recognise special triangles
- solve problems involving special triangles
- name and know the properties of the special quadrilaterals
- name polygons
- recognise a regular polygon
- find a missing interior angle of a polygon
- find a missing exterior angle of a polygon
- find the size of each interior or exterior angle of a regular polygon.

Getting started ....

You will need some matchsticks

1. Make these 4 squares using 12 matchsticks. Move 3 matchsticks to make 3 squares all the same size.
2. Make the 4 squares again using 12 matchsticks. Move 4 matchsticks to make 3 squares all the same size.

Triangles

Remember The **interior angles of any triangle add up to 180°.**

> The shaded angles are interior angles.

If we tear the angles of a triangle off, they fit along a straight line.

Example

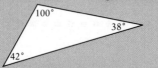

100° + 42° + 38° = 180°

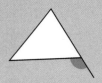

The shaded angle is called an **exterior angle** of a triangle.

Special triangles

Remember   An **isosceles** triangle has **two equal sides** and **two equal angles**.
The dashes show the two equal sides.
The equal angles are at the base of the two equal sides.

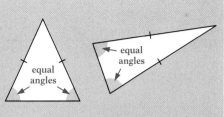

An **equilateral** triangle has **three equal sides** and **three equal angles**, each 60°.

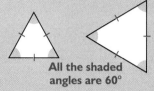

All the shaded angles are 60°

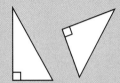

A **right-angled triangle** has one right angle.

A **right-angled isosceles** triangle has one right angle and two equal angles, each of 45°.

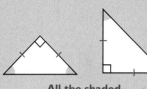

All the shaded angles are 45°

Example   Find the size of $A\hat{C}B$.
  Note: $A\hat{C}B$ means angle ACB.

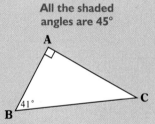

Answer   This is a right-angled triangle.

$$90° + 41° + A\hat{C}B = 180°$$
$$131 + A\hat{C}B = 180°$$
$$A\hat{C}B = 49°$$

Example   Find the size of y.

Answer   This is an isosceles triangle.
The other angle at the base also equals y.

$$50° + y + y = 180°$$
$$50° + 2y = 180°$$
$$2y = 130° \qquad \text{subtracting 50 from both sides}$$
$$y = 65° \qquad \text{dividing both sides by 2}$$

Example   The angles of a triangle are $(2x - 2)$, $(x + 6)$ and $(x - 8)$.
Find the value of the smallest angle.

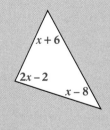

Answer   The angles add to 180°.

$$\text{So} \quad (2x - 2) + (x + 6) + (x - 8) = 180°$$
$$2x - 2 + x + 6 + x - 8 = 180° \qquad 2x + x + x = 4x$$
$$4x - 4 = 180° \qquad -2 + 6 - 8 = -4$$
$$4x = 184°$$
$$x = 46°$$

The smallest angle is $x - 8$.
$$x - 8 = 46° - 8$$
$$= 38°$$

Exercise 1   **A**   Find the size of x.

1.

2.

3.

4.

5.

6.

7.

8.

9.

10.

11.

12.

B   Write an expression in terms of x for the sum of the angles.
Write down an equation in x.
Solve your equation to find the size of the **smallest** angle in the triangle.

1.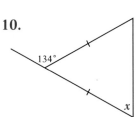

2.

3.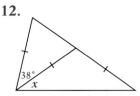

4.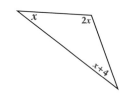

5.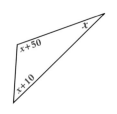

6.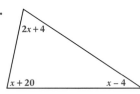

C   ABC is an isosceles triangle.
  1. State the size of angle ABC.
      Give a reason for your answer.
  2. Calculate the size of angle ACB.
  3. State the size of angle DCE.
      Give a reason for your answer.

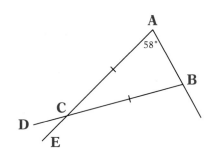

Worked Exam Question

SEG

AB is parallel to CD.
CP = DP. Angle CPD = 110°.

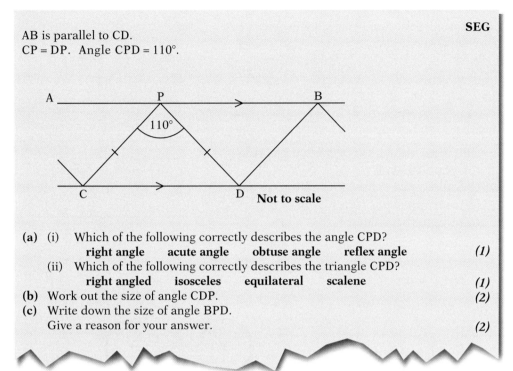

Not to scale

(a) (i)   Which of the following correctly describes the angle CPD?
           right angle   **acute angle**   **obtuse angle**   **reflex angle**   *(1)*
    (ii) Which of the following correctly describes the triangle CPD?
           right angled   **isosceles**   **equilateral**   **scalene**   *(1)*
(b) Work out the size of angle CDP.   *(2)*
(c) Write down the size of angle BPD.
    Give a reason for your answer.   *(2)*

Answer   (a)   (i)   *obtuse angle*
               (ii) *isosceles*

        (b) $110° + C\hat{D}P + P\hat{C}D = 180°$

                    $C\hat{D}P + P\hat{C}D = 70°$

                           $C\hat{D}P = P\hat{C}D$ (isosceles triangle)

                  So $C\hat{D}P = \dfrac{70°}{2}$

                           $= \mathbf{35°}$

        (c) $B\hat{P}D = \mathbf{35°}$ (alternate angles, parallel lines, are equal)

Exercise 2   **A** In the diagram AB = AC and AD = DB.

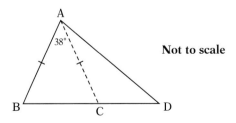

Not to scale

Angle BAC = 38°
1. Find angle ABC.
2. Find angle DAC.

B

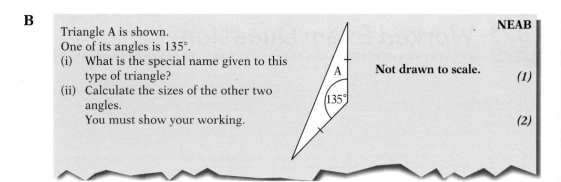

Triangle A is shown.
One of its angles is 135°.
(i)   What is the special name given to this
      type of triangle? *(1)*
(ii) Calculate the sizes of the other two
      angles.
      You must show your working. *(2)*

NEAB

Not drawn to scale.

C 1. Calculate the value of x, giving a reason
           for your answer.
       2. Calculate the value of y, giving a reason
           for your answer.
       3. Calculate the value of z.

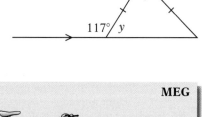

D

Not to scale

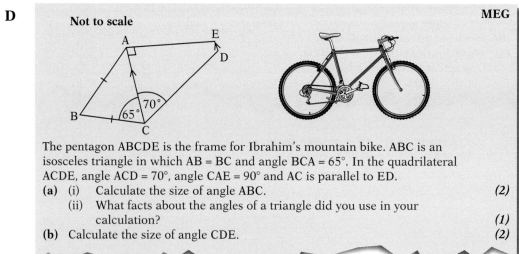

MEG

The pentagon ABCDE is the frame for Ibrahim's mountain bike. ABC is an
isosceles triangle in which AB = BC and angle BCA = 65°. In the quadrilateral
ACDE, angle ACD = 70°, angle CAE = 90° and AC is parallel to ED.
(a) (i)   Calculate the size of angle ABC. *(2)*
    (ii) What facts about the angles of a triangle did you use in your
          calculation? *(1)*
(b) Calculate the size of angle CDE. *(2)*

Quadrilaterals

Quadrilaterals have 4 straight sides.
Some quadrilaterals have special names.

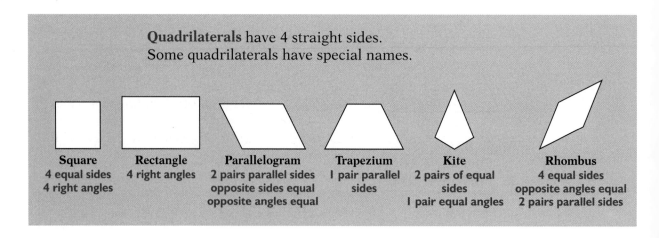

Square	Rectangle	Parallelogram	Trapezium	Kite	Rhombus
4 equal sides 4 right angles	4 right angles	2 pairs parallel sides opposite sides equal opposite angles equal	1 pair parallel sides	2 pairs of equal sides 1 pair equal angles	4 equal sides opposite angles equal 2 pairs parallel sides

Investigation

You will need   3 large copies of each of these special quadrilaterals
a copy of the tables

| Square | Rectangle | Parallelogram | Rhombus | Trapezium | Kite |

1. A square has 4 lines of symmetry.
    Check this by folding your square.
    It should fold in half along each line
    shown.

    By folding, check how many lines of
    symmetry these have.
    Rectangle   Parallelogram   Trapezium   Kite   Rhombus

2. A parallelogram has rotational symmetry of order 2.
    As you turn it around, it looks the same in 2 different
    positions.

    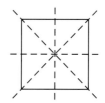

    Turn each of your other shapes.
    What is the order of rotational symmetry of each?

    Use a copy of this table. Fill it in.

Quadrilateral	Number of lines of symmetry	Order of rotational symmetry
Parallelogram		
Rectangle		
Square		
Rhombus		
Kite		
Trapezium		

3. On a copy of each of the special quadrilaterals, draw the diagonals.
    (a)   Measure the diagonals on each to see if they are equal.
    (b)   Measure the angle between the diagonals.
        Is it a right angle?
    (c)   Measure to see if the diagonals cut each other in half (**bisect** each
        other).
    (d)   Measure to see if the diagonals cut the angles at the corners in
        half.

Bisect means
cut in half.

Use a copy of this table. Fill it in.

Quadrilateral	Diagonals equal	Diagonals cross at right angles	Diagonals cut each other in half	Diagonals cut the angles in half
Parallelogram				
Rectangle				
Square				
Rhombus				
Kite				
Trapezium				

Exercise 3

A What goes in the gap?

1. A parallelogram has opposite .... and opposite .... equal.
2. The diagonals of a .... and a .... bisect each other at right-angles.
3. A .... and a .... have equal diagonals.
4. A .... has equal diagonals that bisect each other at right angles.

B Name all the special quadrilaterals which have

1. 2 lines of symmetry
2. no rotational symmetry
3. all sides equal
4. 4 lines of symmetry
5. all angles equal
6. diagonals that cut each other in half.

Angles in quadrilaterals

Example Find the value of *a*.

1.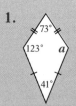
2.

Answer 1. $a = 123°$ one pair of **opposite angles in a kite is equal.**
2. $a = 90°$ **diagonals of a rhombus cut each other at right angles.**

Exercise 4   Find the value of the angles marked with letters.

1.

2.

3.

4.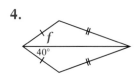

Homework/Review 1

A **What would you get if you crossed a dwarf and a computer?**

$$\frac{\text{a}}{60°} \qquad \frac{\quad}{108°}\frac{\quad}{78°}\frac{\quad}{73°}\frac{\quad}{72°}\frac{\quad}{116°} \qquad \frac{\quad}{52°}\frac{\quad}{112°}\frac{\quad}{72°}\frac{\quad}{52°}\frac{\quad}{68°}\frac{\quad}{112°}\frac{\quad}{116°}$$

Use a copy of this box.
Find the sizes of the angles marked with letters.

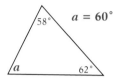 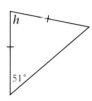

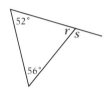 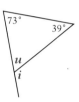

B

LONDON

(a)   Draw in all the lines of symmetry for this rectangle. *(2)*

(b)   Write down the name of a four sided shape that has rotational symmetry of order 4. *(1)*

C Find the value of x.

D

WJEC

(a)   Jahal has three cardboard shapes: a parallelogram, a kite and a rhombus. He labels them **A**, **B** and **C** but **not in that order**.
Shape **A** has one line of symmetry and no rotational symmetry.
Shape **B** has two lines of symmetry and rotational symmetry order two.
Shape **C** has rotational symmetry order two but no lines of symmetry.
Which letter refers to which shape? *(2)*

(b)   Complete the following sentence.
A **square** has .... lines of symmetry and rotational symmetry order .... *(2)*

E   Write down the names of the three special quadrilaterals shown below.

1.   **2.**   **3.**

Polygons

A **polygon** is a closed shape with three or more straight sides.

A **3-sided** polygon is a **triangle**.   A **4-sided** polygon is a **quadrilateral**.
A **5-sided** polygon is a **pentagon**.   A **6-sided** polygon is a **hexagon**.
A **7-sided** polygon is a **heptagon**.   An **8-sided** polygon is an **octagon**.
A **9-sided** polygon is a **nonagon**.   A **10-sided** polygon is a **decagon**.

A **regular** polygon has all sides and all angles equal.

regular pentagon   regular hexagon   regular octagon

Interior angles of a polygon

The sum of the interior angles of a polygon is found as follows.
Step 1   From *one* corner draw all the diagonals.
Step 2   Count the number of triangles.
Step 3   Multiply the number of triangles by 180°.
This gives the sum of the interior angles.

The sum of the interior angles of the polygon shown is 4 × 180° or 720°.

Note: The number of triangles is always two less than the number of sides.

Worked Exam Question

ABCD is a kite.
Angle ABC = 90° and angle ADC = 54°.
Calculate the size of angle BAD.

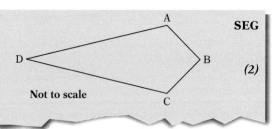

SEG

(2)

Not to scale

Answer

> Write the angles you are given on the diagram.

Angles DAB and BCD are equal because ABCD is a kite.
Call them both *x*.
ABCD is a 4-sided polygon.
We can divide it into 2 triangles.
So the sum of the interior angles is 2 × 180° or 360°.

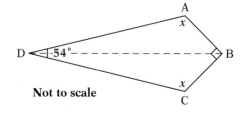

Not to scale

$$54° + 90° + x + x = 360°$$
$$144 + 2x = 360°$$
$$2x = 216°$$
$$x = 108°$$

So angle BAD = **108°**

Exercise 5

A Find the sum of the interior angles of these.
   1. a pentagon   **2.** an octagon   **3.** a 9-sided polygon
   4. a quadrilateral   **5.** a 12-sided polygon

B Find the size of *x*.

1.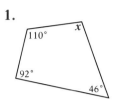

2.

3.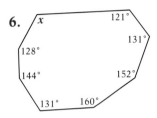

4.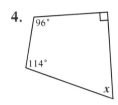

5.

6.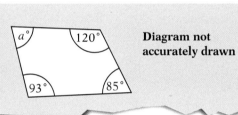

C

LONDON

The diagram shows a
quadrilateral.
Work out the size of the angle
marked *a*°.

a°   120°   **Diagram not
accurately drawn**

93°   85°

(2)

D

MEG

Work out the sizes of the
angles *s* and *t* in the
diagrams.

s   120°   110°

64°   80°   *t*

(2)

Not to scale

E This is a regular pentagon.

   1. What goes in the gap?
        The angles of a regular pentagon are
        all ....
   2. Find the size of *y*.

F This is a regular octagon.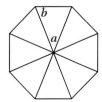
   It is divided into 8 equal sectors.
   1. Work out the value of angle *a*.
   2. Work out the value of angle *b*.

G

These tiling patterns have been made using regular polygons.

SEG

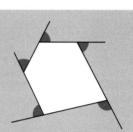

Work out the size of the angles marked *a* and *b*.

(2)

Exterior angles of polygon

This diagram shows the exterior angles of a polygon.
The **exterior angles of any polygon add to 360°.**

Example Find the value of *y*.

Answer $62° + 58° + 76° + 84° + y = 360°$

$$280° + y = 360°$$
$$y = 80°$$

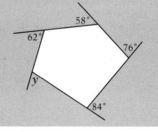

Exercise 6

A What is the sum of the exterior angles of
1. an octagon
2. a 10-sided polygon
3. a pentagon?

B Find the size of angle *x*.

1.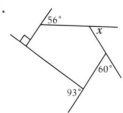
2.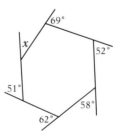
3.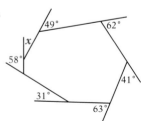

C 1. This is a regular hexagon.
What is the size of each exterior angle?

2. What is the size of angle *y*?

Homework/Review 2

A **If you drop a white hat into the red sea, what will it become?**
Use a copy of this box.
Find the value of *x*.

T.

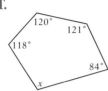

W.

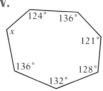

E.

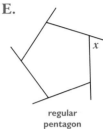

B

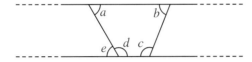

Not to scale

What is the sum of the angles marked *a, b, c* and *d*?

C O is the centre of rotational symmetry of the regular pentagon ABCDE.
 1. Calculate angle AOB.
 2. Write down the number of lines of symmetry of a regular pentagon.

D This is a tiling pattern made from pentagons and rhombuses.
Calculate the size of the angle marked *x*.

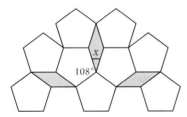

E Find the value of *x*.

1.

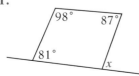

2.

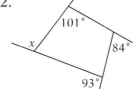

✔ KEY POINTS

✔ The **interior angles of any triangle add up to 180°**.

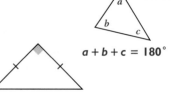

$a + b + c = 180°$

isosceles triangle   **equilateral triangle all angles = 60°**   **right-angled triangle**   **right-angled isosceles triangle**

✔ This table gives the **properties of quadrilaterals**.

Property	Square	Rhombus	Rectangle	Parallelogram	Trapezium	Kite
opposite sides parallel	✓	✓	✓	✓	1 pair	
opposite sides equal	✓	✓	✓	✓		
opposite angles equal	✓	✓	✓	✓		1 pair
all sides equal	✓	✓				
all angles equal	✓		✓			
diagonals equal	✓		✓			
diagonals bisect each other	✓	✓	✓	✓		
diagonals meet at right angles	✓	✓				✓
diagonals bisect the angles at the vertices	✓	✓				just 1 diagonal
number of lines of symmetry	4	2	2	0	0 or 1	1
order of rotational symmetry	4	2	2	2	1	1

✔ A **polygon** is a closed shape with three or more straight sides.
A polygon   with **3** sides is a **triangle**   with **4** sides is a **quadrilateral**
           with **5** sides is a **pentagon**   with **6** sides is a **hexagon**
           with **7** sides is a **heptagon**   with **8** sides is an **octagon**
           with **9** sides is a **nonagon**   with **10** sides is a **decagon**.

✔ A **regular polygon** has equal sides and equal angles.

✔ To find the **sum of the interior angles of a polygon**
divide the polygon into triangles as shown
multiply the number of triangles by 180°.

✔ The **sum of the exterior angles of a polygon is 360°**.

 ## Investigation

· ·

1. Draw polygons with 3, 4, 5, ... 10 sides.
2. For each polygon draw in **all** the diagonals.
3. Copy and complete this table.

Number of sides	3	4	5	6	7	8	9	10
Number of diagonals			5					

4. Write a rule, in words, for finding the next term in the pattern from the previous term.

◄◄ CHAPTER REVIEW ◄◄

◄◄
Exercises 1 and
2 on pages 184
and 185

A

(a) Write down the special name
given to this sort of triangle. *(1)*
(b) Work out the size of the angles
marked (i) *x* (ii) *y*. *(3)*

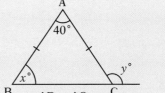

LONDON

◄◄
Exercises 1 and
2 on pages 184
and 185

B

This diagram is not drawn to scale.
It shows an isosceles triangle PQR and a line RS.
PQ is equal to PR.
Angle QPR is 70°
PQ is parallel to RS.
(a) Calculate the size of angle PQR. You must show
your working. *(2)*
(b) State the size of angle QRS.
Give a reason for your answer. *(1)*

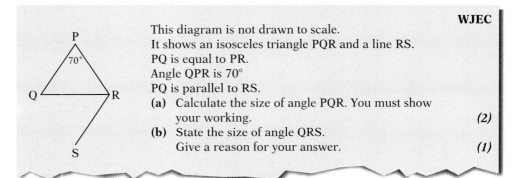

WJEC

◄◄
Exercise 1
on page 184

C

The angles of a triangle are $(2x - 3)°$, $(x + 4)°$ and $(x + 19)°$.   **SEG**

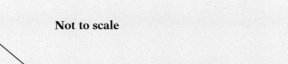

Not to scale

(a) Write an expression, in terms of *x*, for the sum of the angles.
Write your answer in its simplest form. *(2)*
The sum of the angles is 180°.
(b) (i) Write down an equation in *x*. *(1)*
(ii) Solve your equation to find the size of the **smallest** angle in the triangle. *(3)*

◄◄
Exercise 3
on page 188

D WXYZ is a quadrilateral.
WY is a line of symmetry.
Which of the following correctly describes the
quadrilateral WXYZ?
**square   rhombus   trapezium   rectangle
parallelogram   kite**

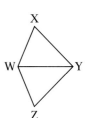

◄◄

Exercise 6
on page 192

E   Find the size of **b**.

1.

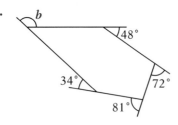

2.

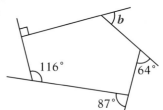

◄◄

Exercises 1 and 5
on pages 184 and
191

F

(a) Calculate the size of x in each.   **WJEC**

(i)   (ii)

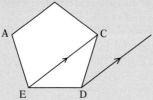

(2)

(b)

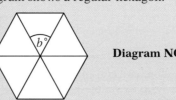

The above diagram shows a regular pentagon ABCDE, a diagonal EC and
a line DF which is parallel to EC. Each interior angle of the regular
pentagon is 108°.

(i)   Calculate the size of EĈD.   (ii)   Calculate the size of CD̂F.   *(3)*

◄◄

Exercise 5
on page 191

G

(a) The diagram shows a regular hexagon.   **LONDON**

Diagram NOT accurately drawn

Work out the size of the angle marked $b°$.   *(2)*

(b) The diagram shows a regular octagon.

Diagram NOT accurately drawn

Work out the size of the angle marked $c°$.   *(2)*

14 Patterns

By the end of this chapter you will be able to:

- find the next number in a sequence
- write in words or symbols, the rule for a sequence
- write, in symbols, the *n*th term of a sequence
- describe and write rules for patterns made with pictures.

Getting started ....

You will need   squared paper

A 3 by 10 rectangle is made using 30 square tiles, as shown.
Where the corners of four tiles meet, there is a dot.
This rectangle has 18 dots.

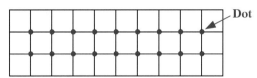
Dot

Investigate the number of dots seen when 36 tiles are arranged in different rectangles.

Sequences

A **sequence** is a number pattern. The numbers in the sequence are connected by a rule.

Examples

Sequence	Rule
7, 12, 17, 22, ...	Add 5
5, 10, 20, 40, 80, ...	Multiply by 2
100, 97, 94, 91, 88, ...	Subtract 3
5000, 1000, 200, 40, 8, ...	Divide by 5

Sometimes sequences are made by adding a different number each time. The numbers added form a pattern.

Examples

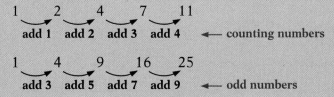

1   2   4   7   11
  add 1 add 2 add 3 add 4   ◄—— counting numbers

1   4   9   16   25
  add 3 add 5 add 7 add 9   ◄—— odd numbers

The numbers in a sequence are called **terms**.

5,   8,   11,   14 . . . . . t_n

↑   ↑   ↑
First Second   nth
term   term   term

Sometimes sequences are made by adding the two previous terms together.

Example   1, 1, 2, 3, 5, 8, 13
This sequence has a special name.
It is called the **Fibonacci sequence**.

Worked Exam Question

• •

(a) (i) Write down the next two terms of the following sequence.   **MEG**
           3, 6, 12, 24, 48,   *(1)*
    (ii) What is the rule for finding the next term?   *(1)*
(b) (i) Write down the next term of the following sequence.
           1, 4, 13, 40, 121,   *(1)*
    (ii) Explain how you found this term.   *(2)*

> Find the rule for the sequence.
> 1. Is the rule
>   add ...
>   subtract ...
>   multiply by ...
>   divide by ...?
> 2. Is a different number added each time to form a pattern?
> 3. Are the terms added together?

Answer (a)(i)   3,   6,   12,   24,   48,   96,   192
                  ×2   ×2   ×2   ×2   ×2   ×2
             The next two terms are **96, 192**.
       (ii) The rule for finding the next term is '**multiply the previous term by 2**'.
    (b)(i)   1,   4,   13,   40,   121
  and (ii)   +3 +9 +27 +81
             The numbers added form the pattern   3,   9,   27,   81
                                                        ×3   ×3   ×3

             To find the next term, add 81 × 3, which is 243.
             121 + 243 = 364

Exercise 1   **A**   This is a sequence of odd numbers.
        What are the missing numbers?
                     ___, ___, 13, 15, 17, ___, ___

        B   **(a)** Write down the next two terms in the sequence
                     6, 12, 18, 24, ___, ___.
             (b) Describe the sequence in words.

C

LONDON

(a) Write down the next two numbers in this number sequence. *(2)*

1, 7 13, 19, 25, ... , ...

(b) Write down a number in the sequence that divides exactly by 5. *(1)*

D

LONDON

Here is a number pattern.
Two numbers are missing.

6, 12, 18, ... , ... , 36.

(a) Write in the missing numbers. *(2)*

(b) Describe, in words, the rule that you used to find the missing
numbers in the pattern. *(2)*

E

MEG

The rule to form a sequence of numbers is

'Multiply the previous number by 2 and then add 3'.

(a) (i) Write down the next two numbers in the sequence

2, 7, 17, 37 .... , ... , *(2)*

(ii) What is the first number in this sequence that is NOT prime? *(1)*

(b) Use the same rule to write down the next two numbers in the sequence
which starts

(i) 0, -- *(2)*

(ii) −6, −9, -- *(2)*

F

MEG

Here are the first five numbers of a sequence.

1, 4, 13, 40, 121,

(a) Three of these numbers are square numbers.
Write down the three square numbers. *(2)*

(b) To continue the sequence, multiply the previous number by 3, then add 1.
Write down the next two numbers of the sequence. *(3)*

G

LONDON

Here are the first five numbers in a simple number sequence.

1, 3, 7, 13, 21, ... , ... ,

(a) Write down the next two numbers in the sequence. *(2)*

(b) Describe, in words, the rule to continue this sequence. *(2)*

H

WJEC

2, 5, 7, 12, 19, 31, ----------------

The first six numbers of a sequence are shown above. Each term in the sequence, except the first and second, is found by adding together the two previous terms.

For example 19 = 12 + 7

(a) Find the next three numbers in the sequence. *(3)*

(b) (i) The difference between the first two terms is 3, the difference between the second and third terms is 2, and so on. This is shown in the diagram below.

Work out the next two differences in the diagram below. *(1)*

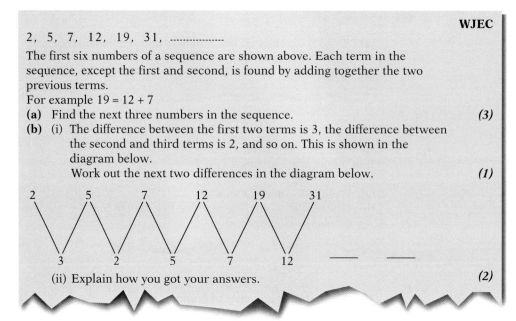

(ii) Explain how you got your answers. *(2)*

I

SEG

The first two terms of a sequence are:

4, 8

(a) Using the rule:

ADD THE TWO PREVIOUS NUMBERS AND DIVIDE BY TWO

write down the third and fourth terms in the sequence. *(1)*

(b) If the sequence had begun 8, 4 instead of 4, 8 would the third and fourth terms be the same as those in part (a)?

Give a reason for your answer. *(1)*

J

SEG

A sequence of numbers is

, a, 9, 3, 1, $\frac{1}{3}$, b,

In the sequence two numbers are shown as a and b.

(a) Describe how to find the number a. *(1)*

(b) Describe how to find the number b. *(1)*

K

WJEC

(a) In the following pattern, write down the next number

$$\frac{1}{2}, \quad \frac{3}{4}, \quad \frac{5}{6}, \quad \frac{7}{8}, \quad \frac{9}{10}, \quad \text{-----------------}$$

(1)

(b) In the following pattern, write down the next number and explain in words what you think is the rule for finding the next number.

$$2, \quad 7, \quad 13, \quad 20, \quad 28, \quad \text{-----------------}$$

(2)

Investigations

A

Show all your working.

MEG

Look at the pattern

$$1 \times 8 + 1 = 9$$
$$12 \times 8 + 2 = 98$$
$$123 \times 8 + 3 = 987$$

(a) Work out $1234 \times 8 + 4 =$ _____

(1)

(b) Investigate how much further the pattern goes on. Write down each line of your working.

(5)

(c) Explain why the pattern stops.

(2)

B The Fibonacci sequence is made by adding together the two previous terms in the sequence. It begins with 1, 1.

The sequence is:

1, 1, 2, 3, 5, 8, 13, 21, 34, 55, 89, 144, 233, 377, 610, ...

1. What type of number is every 3rd number?
2. What number will divide evenly into every 4th number?
3. Find these sums.

$$T_2 + T_6 =$$
$$T_2 + T_6 + T_{10} =$$
$$T_2 + T_6 + T_{10} + T_{14} =$$

What special name is given to these answers?
Does this pattern continue?

4. Choose any three consecutive Fibonacci terms.
   (a) Square the middle number.
   (b) Multiply the other two numbers together.
   (c) Subtract the answer to (b) from the answer to (a).

Do you get the same answer whichever three consecutive terms you choose?

Finding the rule for the *n*th term

Example 3, 7, 11, 15, 19, ...
Write down the rule for finding the *n*th term.

Answer To find the rule for the *n*th term follow these steps.

Step 1 **Find the difference between each term.**
In this example, the difference is **4**.

Step 2 **Multiply *n* by the difference found in Step 1.**
This gives **4*n*.**

Step 3 **To finish the rule look to see what must be added or subtracted to the expression you found in Step 2.**
For the first term, $n = 1$ so $4n = 4 \times 1$
$$= 4.$$
But since term 1 is 3, the rule must be $4n - 1$.

Step 4 **Check the rule for some other terms.**
term 2 $n = 2$ $4n - 1 = 4 \times 2 - 1$
$$= 7$$
term 3 $n = 3$ $4n - 1 = 4 \times 3 - 1$
$$= 11$$
These are correct, so $t_n = 4n - 1$ is the rule for this sequence.

Exercise 2

A Write down the *n*th term of these sequences.
1. 1, 4, 7, 10, ...
2. 5, 7, 9, 11, 13, ...
3. 4, 6, 8, 10, ...
4. 2, 6, 10, 14, ...
5. 2, 5, 8, 11, ...
6. 3, 8, 13, 18, ...
7. 7, 13, 19, 25, ...
8. 6, 9, 12, 15, ...
9. −1, 1, 3, 5, 7, ...
10. −2, 2, 6, 10, 14, ...

B Look at this sequence of numbers.
5, 9, 13, 17, 21, ...
1. Write down, in words, the rule for getting each number from the one before it.
2. Write down a formula, in terms of *n*, for the *n*th number in the sequence.

C A sequence begins 4, 10, 16, 22, ...
1. Write an expression for the *n*th term in this sequence.
2. What is the 20th term of the sequence?

D A sequence begins 7, 12, 17, 22, ...
1. Write an expression for the *n*th term in this sequence.
2. Find these
   (a) the 10th term (b) the 25th term (c) the 100th term

E Write down the 30th term of these sequences.
1. −3, 0, 3, 6, 9, ... 2. −2, 4, 10, 16, ... 3. −50, −40, −30, −20, ...

Patterns with pictures

Worked Exam Question

SEG

Sticks are used to make a sequence of patterns.
The first four patterns are shown.

Pattern 1   Pattern 2   Pattern 3   Pattern 4

(a) (i)   How many sticks are needed for Pattern 5? *(1)*
    (ii)   How many extra sticks are needed to make Pattern 6 from Pattern 5? *(1)*
(b) The patterns are used to make a sequence of shapes as shown.

     Shape 1   Shape 2   Shape 3

    (i)   How many sticks will Shape 4 have? *(1)*

The rule for finding the number of sticks, s, needed for Shape n, is $s = 3n + 4$.
    (ii)   Use this rule to find the number of sticks needed for Shape 50. *(1)*
    (iii) Solve the equation $20 = 3n + 4$. *(2)*
    (iv)   Use your answer to part (iii) to explain why one of these shapes cannot have 20 sticks. *(1)*

Answer (a)(i) The sequence formed by the number of sticks is:
        3, 5, 7, 9,...
      Pattern 5 will need **11 sticks**.

You could draw
Pattern 5

      (ii) **2**
    (b)(i) The sequence formed by the number of sticks is:
        7, 10, 13 ...
      Shape 4 will have **16 sticks**.

You could draw
Shape 4

      (ii) $s = 3n + 4$
          $= 3 \times \mathbf{50} + 4$
          $= \mathbf{154}$

$n = 50$ so put
50 instead
of n in the
expression.

      (iii) $20 = 3n + 4$
        $20 - \mathbf{4} = 3n + 4 - \mathbf{4}$
          $16 = 3n$

This has been
solved using the
balance
method.

          $\dfrac{16}{3} = \dfrac{3n}{3}$

         $5.3 = n$
          $n = \mathbf{5.3}$ **to 1 dp**.

    (iv)   *n is not a whole number so it cannot be a shape number.*

Exercise 3 **A**

Here are some patterns made out of matchsticks.

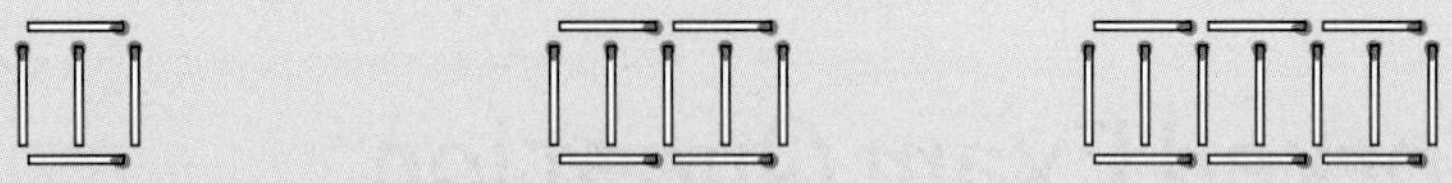

pattern number 1   pattern number 2   pattern number 3

(a) Draw a diagram of pattern number 4. *(1)*

(b) Copy and complete the table to show the number of matchsticks needed for pattern number 4 and pattern number 5. *(2)*

Pattern number	Number of matchsticks
1	5
2	9
3	13
4	
5	

(c) Work out the pattern number that needs exactly 41 matchsticks. *(2)*

(d) (i) How many matchsticks are needed for pattern number 100?
(ii) Describe how you found this answer. *(2)*

B

Rose bushes are planted in a park so that every white rose (✪) is surrounded by four red roses (✳). Two of the possible ways of planting are shown below. Pattern A is shown below for 1, 2 and 3 white roses.

(a) How many red roses are needed when 6 white roses are planted? *(3)*

Pattern B is shown below for 1, 2 and 3 white roses.

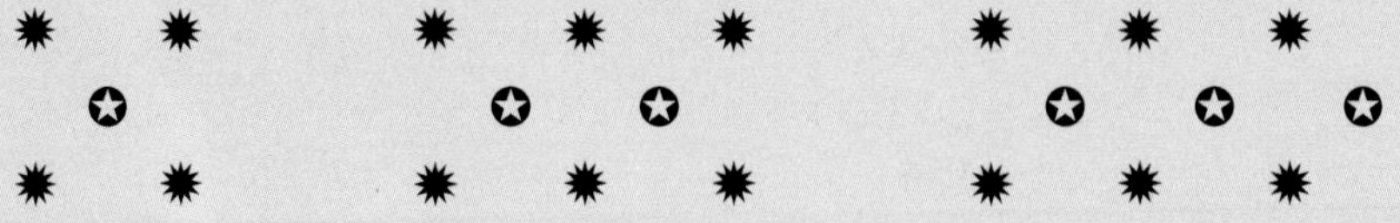

(b) Twenty red roses are planted in Pattern B. How many white roses are planted? *(3)*

(c) Which pattern uses fewer red roses in general? Explain your answer. *(3)*

C

WJEC

These patterns are made using black and white square tiles.

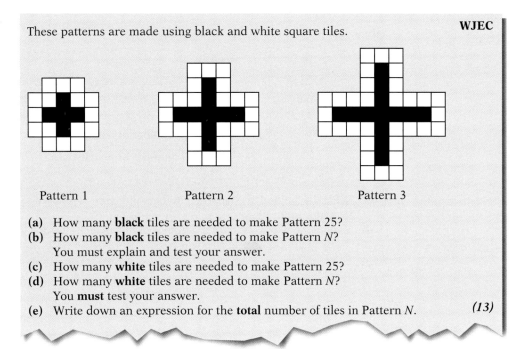

Pattern 1   Pattern 2   Pattern 3

(a) How many **black** tiles are needed to make Pattern 25?
(b) How many **black** tiles are needed to make Pattern *N*?
    You must explain and test your answer.
(c) How many **white** tiles are needed to make Pattern 25?
(d) How many **white** tiles are needed to make Pattern *N*?
    You **must** test your answer.
(e) Write down an expression for the **total** number of tiles in Pattern *N*.   *(13)*

D

LONDON

Mr McDonald is making sheep pens. He uses fences to make pens as shown in the diagram below. The pens are arranged in pairs in a row.

Number of pens	2 pens	4 pens	6 pens

Number of fences   7   12   17

(a) Draw diagrams to show the number of fences needed for
    (i) 8 pens,   (ii) 10 pens.   *(2)*
(b) Explain how you could work out the number of fences needed for twelve pens, without drawing a diagram.   *(2)*

The table below shows the number of fences needed for different numbers of pens.

Number of pens	2	4	6	8	10	12	14	16
Number of fences	7	12	17					

(c) Copy and complete the table.   *(2)*
(d) Work out the number of fences needed for 30 pens.   *(2)*

E

WJEC

June makes rows of triangles using matchsticks.

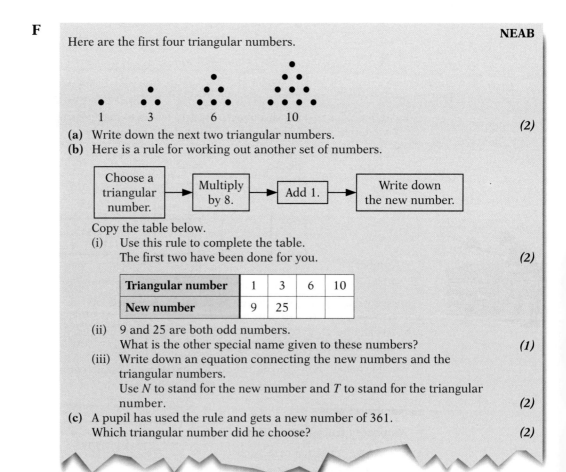

1 triangle   2 triangles   3 triangles   4 triangles

(i)   Copy and complete the table.

Number of triangles	1	2	3	4	5	6
Number of matchsticks		5		9		

(ii) What do you notice about the numbers of matchsticks used to make the triangles in this way?

(iii) Explain how to work out the number of matchsticks needed to make a row of 20 triangles in this way.

(9)

F

NEAB

Here are the first four triangular numbers.

1   3   6   10

(2)

(a) Write down the next two triangular numbers.

(b) Here is a rule for working out another set of numbers.

Choose a triangular number.	→	Multiply by 8.	→	Add 1.	→	Write down the new number.

Copy the table below.

(i)   Use this rule to complete the table.
The first two have been done for you.

(2)

Triangular number	1	3	6	10
New number	9	25		

(ii) 9 and 25 are both odd numbers.
What is the other special name given to these numbers?

(1)

(iii) Write down an equation connecting the new numbers and the triangular numbers.
Use N to stand for the new number and T to stand for the triangular number.

(2)

(c) A pupil has used the rule and gets a new number of 361.
Which triangular number did he choose?

(2)

More patterns

Sometimes we can work out the answers to problems by using **patterns**.

Worked Exam Question

The table shows the number of bacteria growing on a piece of cheese over a period of time on a particular morning.
SEG

(a) Complete the table. *(1)*

Time	Number of bacteria
0900	80
0920	160
0940	320
1000	640
1020	
1040	

(b) Explain how you got your answers. *(1)*

Answer (a) The missing part of the table is:

Time	Number of bacteria
1020	1280
1040	2560

(b) The number of bacteria forms the pattern, 80, 160, 320, 640, ...
The rule is 'multiply the previous number by 2.'

Exercise 4

A

Row 1	1	Sum = $1 = 1^3$
Row 2	3 5	Sum = $8 = 2^3$
Row 3	7 9 11	Sum = $27 = 3^3$

1. Write down the numbers and the sum for the next 2 rows.
2. Which row will have sum = 1000?
3. What is the sum of row 8?
4. The first number in a row is n.
   Write an expression, in terms of n, for the second number in the row.

B

MEG

The diagram shows part of a computer spreadsheet.
The number 10, in column B row 4, is labelled B4.
The rule for finding the numbers in column B is

     B1 = 1
     B2 = B1 + A2
     B3 = B2 + A3
     B4 = B3 + A4, and so on.

(a) Find the numbers B6 and B7. *(2)*

(b) The numbers C2, C3, C4, ... can be found from the numbers in column B. Write down the rule for finding these numbers using column B. *(2)*

(c) The pattern in column C is continued.
    (i) What number will be C20? *(1)*
    (ii) Describe in words the pattern of numbers in column C. *(1)*

		Column		
		A	B	C
Row	1	1	1	1
	2	2	3	4
	3	3	6	9
	4	4	10	16
	5	5	15	
	6	6		
	7	7		

C

MEG

Show all your working.

Set A	Set B
12	32
14	40
16	48
18	56
20	64
22	72
24	80
26	88
⋮	⋮

(a) Write down the next three terms in each set. *(4)*

(b) Set B is part of the eight times table.
    Copy and complete the statement below.
       Set A is part of the _____ times table. *(1)*

(c) **(i)** The units digits in Set A, reading down the column, are
        2, 4, 6, 8, 0, 2, 4, 6, ...
      Write down the units digits of Set B, reading down the column. *(1)*

    (ii) Look at the two lists of digits in part (c)(i).
      Write down three things that you notice about them. *(4)*

D

NEAB

Look at this number pattern.

$$7^2 = 49$$
$$67^2 = 4489$$
$$667^2 = 444889$$
$$6667^2 = 44448889$$

This pattern continues.
(a) Write down the next line of the pattern. *(2)*
(b) Use the pattern to work out 6666667^2. *(1)*

Homework/Review

A Look at the sequence 1, 6, 11, 16
  1. Write down the next number in the sequence.
  2. Explain how you found your answer.

B Rob started this number pattern.   1, 1, 2, 3, 5, 8, ...
  1. What is the next number in this pattern?
  2. Explain how you would find the ninth number in this pattern.

C

SEG

(a) (i) What is the next number in the pattern? *(1)*
  28, 23, 18, 13, ...
  (ii) Explain how you found your answer to part (i). *(1)*
(b) (i) What is the missing number in the pattern?
  3, 6, 12, ..., 48, 96. *(1)*
  (ii) Explain how you found your answer to part (b)(i). *(1)*

D

LONDON

The diagrams show patterns made out of sticks.

Pattern number   1   2   3

(a) Draw a diagram to show pattern number 4. *(1)*

The table below can be used to show the number of sticks needed for a pattern.

Pattern number	1	2	3	4	5	6	7
Number of sticks	3	5					

(b) Copy and complete the table. *(2)*

(c) (i) Work out the number of sticks needed for pattern number 15.
  (ii) Explain how you obtained your answer. *(4)*

(d) Write down a formula which can be used to calculate the number of sticks, S, in terms of the pattern number, n. *(2)*

E

NEAB

Look at the number pattern below.
  $1 \times 2 - 1 = 1$ line 1
  $2 \times 3 - 2 = 4$ line 2
  $3 \times 4 - 3 = 9$ line 3
  $4 \times 5 - 4 = 16$ line 4
  $5 \times 6 - 5 = p$ line 5
  $\_\_ \times \_\_ - \_\_ = q$ line 6

(a) (i) Calculate the value of p in line 5. *(1)*
  (ii) Write down line 6 and calculate the value of q. *(1)*
(b) Write down line 20 of this number pattern. *(2)*
(c) What special name is given to the numbers 1, 4, 9, 16, ...? *(1)*

☑ KEY POINTS

☑ A **sequence** is another name for a number pattern.

☑ The numbers in a sequence are called **terms**.

$$1, \quad 4, \quad 7, \quad 10, \quad \ldots \quad t_n$$

first term, second term, nth term

☑ To **continue a sequence**: work out the rule
use the rule to find the next numbers.

☑ To find the **nth term** of a sequence follow these steps.

Step 1 Find the difference between each term.
Step 2 Multiply n by the difference found in Step 1.
Step 3 Work out what to add or subtract to this expression to make the rule true for all terms.

Example 7, 10, 13, 16, 19, ...

Step 1 3 is added each time.
Step 2 Rule begins as **$3 \times n$** or **$3n$**.
Step 3 For term 1 the rule must be $3n + 4$ because $3 \times 1 + 4 = 7$.
This rule also works for terms 2, 3, 4 and 5.
So the rule is $3n + 4$.

☑ Rules can be found for **picture patterns**.

☑ Answers to some problems can be found by using patterns.

◄◄ CHAPTER REVIEW ◄◄

A

Exercise 1
on page 198

A sequence begins 1, 3, 7, 15, ...   **SEG**
The rule for continuing the sequence is shown.

> MULTIPLY THE LAST NUMBER BY 2 AND ADD 1

(a) What is the next number in the sequence?   *(1)*
(b) This sequence uses the same rule.
$-2, -3, -5, -9, \ldots$
What is the next number in this sequence?   *(2)*

B

Exercises 1 and 2
on pages 198
and 202

Here are the first five numbers of a simple number sequence.   **LONDON**
1, 5, 9, 13, 17, ..., ...,
(a) Write down the next two numbers in the sequence.   *(2)*
(b) Describe, in words, the rule to continue this sequence.   *(1)*
(c) Write down, in terms of n, the nth term of this sequence.   *(2)*

◄◄
Exercise 4
on page 207

C

Here is a rectangle made from 36 square tiles.

NEAB

Its length is 18 tiles and its width is 2 tiles.
(a) Copy the table below. In the table, write the length and width of two
different rectangles which could be made using 36 square tiles. *(2)*

Length	Width
18	2

(b) I have a single row of 72 square tiles.
Give the length and width of two more rectangles which could be made
using all these 72 tiles. *(2)*

◄◄
Exercise 1
on page 198

D **1.** Fill in the missing numbers in this pattern.

$$12^2 - 11^2 = \boxed{23}$$
$$11^2 - 10^2 = \text{..........}$$
$$10^2 - \boxed{\text{..........}} = \boxed{\text{..........}}$$

2. Write down the next line of this pattern.

◄◄
Exercise 3
on page 204

E

Black tiles and white tiles are used to make tiling patterns.

SEG

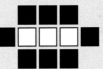

Pattern 1   Pattern 2   Pattern 3

(a) How many black tiles will Pattern 4 have? *(1)*
(b) **(i)** Explain the rule for finding the number of black tiles in a Pattern
when you know the Pattern number. *(2)*
(ii) How many black tiles will Pattern 50 have? *(2)*

15 Displaying and Analysing Data

By the end of this chapter you will be able to:

- display data on a bar chart, pictogram or bar-line graph
- display data on a frequency diagram
- display data on a frequency polygon
- find the mean, median, mode and range of a set of data
- find the mean, median, mode and range from a frequency table
- use the mean, median, mode and range to compare two sets of data.

Getting started ....

A What is misleading about these statements?
   1. Brite Colour washes your clothes 50% better.
   2. Tests prove Kittydins is best.
   3. Come to the Sunshine Resort. Annual mean rainfall only 200 mm.

B 1.

2.

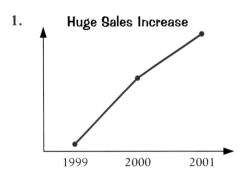

3.

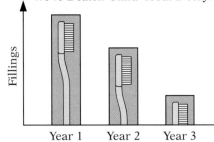

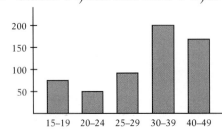

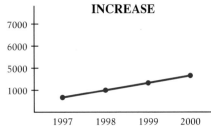

Write some sentences about why these graphs are misleading.

Bar charts, pictograms, bar-line graphs

Bar charts, pictograms and bar-line graphs are used to display discrete data.

Worked Exam Questions

1. The diagram is part of a pictogram. The pictogram shows the number of lorries which crossed the North Sea by ferry during a week in 1996.

   LONDON

Monday	🚌 🚌 🚌 🚌 🚌
Tuesday	🚌 🚌 🚌 🚌 🖢
Wednesday	🚌 🚌
Thursday	🚌 🚌 🚌 🚌
Friday	

   🚌 = 100 lorries

   (a) How many lorries crossed the North Sea on the Tuesday? *(1)*

   On the Friday 300 lorries crossed the North Sea by ferry.

   (b) Complete the pictogram to show this information. *(2)*

   Look at the key carefully.

   Answer (a) Each 🚌 represents 100 lorries.
   There are $4\frac{1}{2}$ symbols on Tuesday.
   4 symbols represent 400 lorries. Half a symbol represents 50 lorries (half of 100).
   So on Tuesday **450** lorries crossed.

Monday	🚌 🚌 🚌 🚌 🚌
Tuesday	🚌 🚌 🚌 🚌 🖢
Wednesday	🚌 🚌
Thursday	🚌 🚌 🚌 🚌
Friday	🚌 🚌 🚌

   🚌 100 lorries

   Draw the symbols quickly – don't spend too much time on them.

   (b) 300 lorries is represented by 3 symbols. We draw them underneath the other ones.

2. Zeeshan counts the number of vowels in a sentence. The results are shown in the table.   **LONDON**

Vowel	a	e	i	o	u
Number	14	17	8	9	6

   (2)

   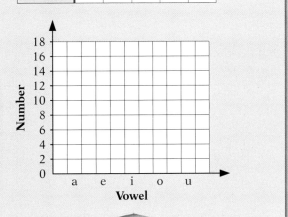

   Draw a bar chart to show this information.

Answer The vertical scale goes up in twos.

Draw the height of the bars carefully.

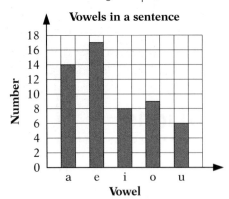

Vowels in a sentence

Whenever you draw a bar chart, make sure
- the axes are labelled
- the chart has a title
- the vertical scale goes up in equal steps.

Bar-line graphs are similar to bar charts.

Example This bar-line graph shows the number of people, in thousands, attending a health resort each month.

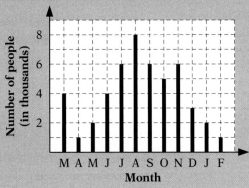

1. How many people attended the resort in August?
2. How many more people used the resort in November than in December?
3. Which four months were the most popular?

Answer
1. The scale is in thousands.
   So 8000 people attended in August.
2. 6000 used it in November. 3000 used it in December.
   So 3000 more used it in November.
3. July, August, September and November.

Exercise 1 **A**

In Cwmgwely Comprehensive School, mathematics pupils in each year are arranged in sets.
The bar chart shows the number of pupils in each set in year 9.
(i) Which set has the smallest number of pupils?
(ii) How many pupils are there in the largest set?
(iii) How many more pupils are there in set E than in set F?

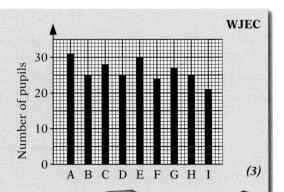

WJEC

(3)

B This graph shows the number of pupils who liked Maths in eleven Year 10 and Year 11 classes.

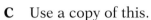

Pupils who like Maths

1. Which class had the greatest number of pupils who liked Maths?
2. Which class had the least number who liked Maths?
3. Which classes had fewer than 20 pupils who liked Maths?
4. Which three classes had the same number of pupils who liked Maths?

C Use a copy of this.

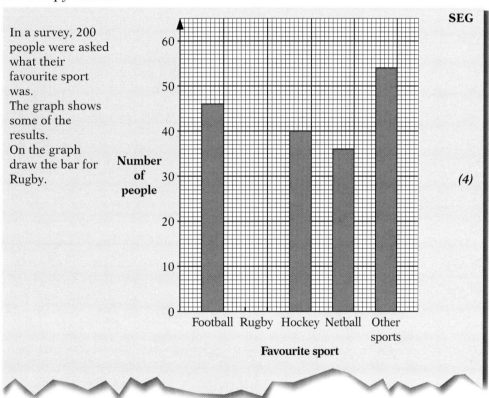

In a survey, 200 people were asked what their favourite sport was.
The graph shows some of the results.
On the graph draw the bar for Rugby.

SEG

(4)

D Use a copy of this.

LONDON

The pictogram shows the number of golfers who played at the local golf club last week.

(a) How many golfers played on Sunday? *(1)*

(b) How many golfers played on Monday? *(1)*

On Tuesday 35 golfers played.

(c) Complete the pictogram to show this. *(1)*

Saturday
Sunday
Monday
Tuesday

Represents 20 golfers

E

WJEC

Class 3P carry out a survey to find the number of lorries passing the school gates. The results are shown below.

Time	Number of Lorries
10 a.m.–noon	35
noon–2 p.m.	20
2 p.m.–4 p.m.	30

Copy the diagram.
Draw a pictogram to represent the above data.

(3)

F You will need some 0.1 cm graph paper for this question.

WJEC

(a) This bar chart below shows the marks obtained by seven boys in an examination.
  (i) Write down the name of the boy who had the highest mark.
  (ii) What was the lowest mark obtained by a boy?
  (iii) Sam had more marks than Jim. How many more?

(3)

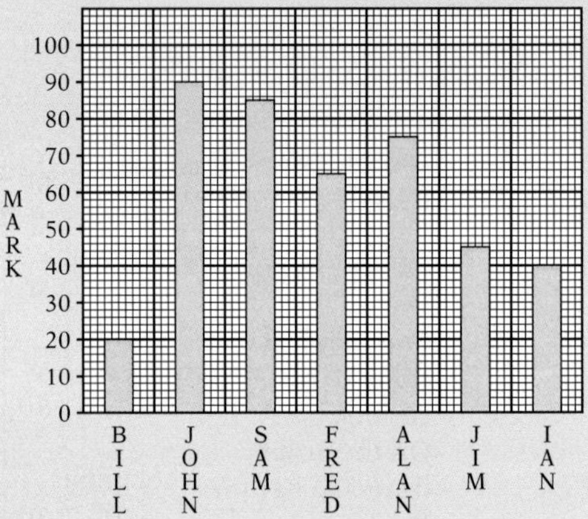

(b) The marks obtained by ten girls taking the same examination are given below.

Jane	Ann	Kate	Sue	Enid	Sian	Emma	Lynn	Mary	Rose
70	85	55	95	60	40	70	75	65	55

On 0.1 cm graph paper draw a bar chart to show these marks.

(4)

G

WJEC

George has carried out a survey about favourite colours. He asked 50 teenagers to state their favourite colour. Here are the results of George's survey.

Colour	Tally	Frequency
Red	ⅢⅢⅢ Ⅲ	
Blue	Ⅲ Ⅲ	
Yellow	Ⅲ I	
Pink	III	
Black	Ⅲ Ⅲ IIII	
Brown	IIII	
Green	II	

(a) Display the results of George's survey using a diagram of your own choice.
(b) Write **two** sentences about the results of George's survey.

(5)

H

NEAB

A survey was conducted to find out which activities 11-year-old pupils do after school.
The results are displayed below.

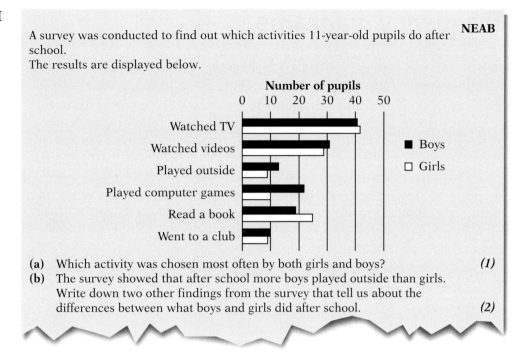

(a) Which activity was chosen most often by both girls and boys? *(1)*
(b) The survey showed that after school more boys played outside than girls.
Write down two other findings from the survey that tell us about the differences between what boys and girls did after school. *(2)*

I

NEAB

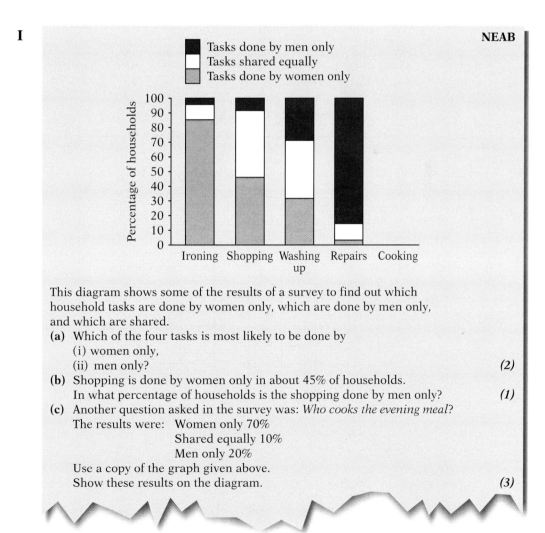

This diagram shows some of the results of a survey to find out which household tasks are done by women only, which are done by men only, and which are shared.
(a) Which of the four tasks is most likely to be done by
 (i) women only,
 (ii) men only? *(2)*
(b) Shopping is done by women only in about 45% of households.
In what percentage of households is the shopping done by men only? *(1)*
(c) Another question asked in the survey was: *Who cooks the evening meal?*
The results were: Women only 70%
 Shared equally 10%
 Men only 20%
Use a copy of the graph given above.
Show these results on the diagram. *(3)*

Frequency diagrams

When grouped data is displayed in a table it is often called a **frequency distribution**.
A **frequency diagram** is used to display **grouped data**.
It is like a bar chart with the bars touching each other.
Sometimes a frequency diagram is called a **histogram**.

Example This table shows the grouped frequency distribution of the heights, measured to the nearest centimetre, of all the pupils in Moha's dance class.

Height (to nearest cm)	140 –	150 –	160 –	170 –	180 –	190 – 200
Number of pupils	4	10	16	12	6	2

(a) How many people are there in Moha's dance class?
(b) On the grid given below, draw a grouped frequency diagram to show the distribution of the heights.
(c) The grouped frequency diagram shows the distribution of the heights, measured to the nearest centimetre, of the girls in Moha's dance class.

Find the number of boys in Moha's dance class whose heights measured to the nearest centimetre, are 170 cm or more.

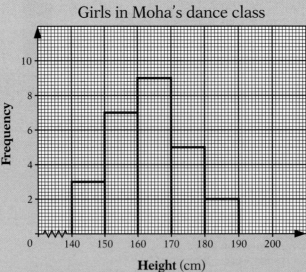

Girls in Moha's dance class

A frequency diagram has the bars touching.

Answer (a) To find the total number of pupils in Moha's dance class we must add up the 'number of pupils' row in the table.
4 + 10 + 16 + 12 + 6 + 2 = 50
There are 50 pupils in Moha's dance class.

(b)

All pupils in Moha's dance class

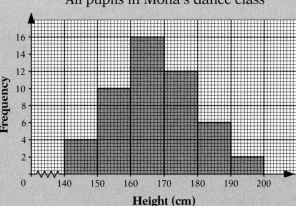

Make sure the bars are clear. It is best to shade them.

(c) From the table or the graph you drew for (b), we can find the total number of pupils whose heights are 170 cm or more.

Pupils 170 cm or more = 12 + 6 + 2

= 20

From the graph in (c) we can work out the number of **girls** that are 170 cm or more.

Girls 170 cm or more = 5 + 2

= 7

So there must be 20 – 7 = 13 boys whose height is 170 cm or more.

Exercise 2   A

SEG

The 'Early Bird' bus company conducts a survey of bus arrival times.

If a bus arrives late in the bus station, the number of minutes late is recorded.

The frequency diagram shows the results of the survey.

Part of the table of results is shown.

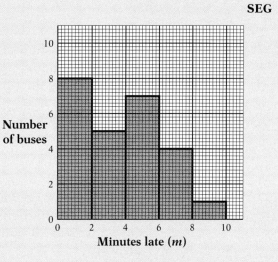

Use a copy of the table.

(a) Use the frequency diagram to complete the table of results.

(b) The next bus to arrive in the bus station is 5 minutes late. How many buses are between 2 and 6 minutes late altogether?

Minutes late (m)	Number of buses
$0 \leq m < 2$	
$2 \leq m < 4$	
$4 \leq m < 6$	
$6 \leq m < 8$	
$8 \leq m < 10$	

(2)

(1)

B Use a copy of this.

This table shows the times that contestants took to complete a general knowledge test.

Age (years)	56	60	20	23	43	42	26	24	55	70	30	35	19	54
Time (minutes)	11	8	12	9	16	23	19	14	15	9	21	7	6	19

(a) Complete the table below to show the grouped frequency distribution of the times taken by the contestants.

Time (minutes)	5 –	10 –	15 –	20 – 25
Tally				
Frequency				

(b) On the axes, draw a grouped frequency diagram to show the distribution of the time taken by the contestants.

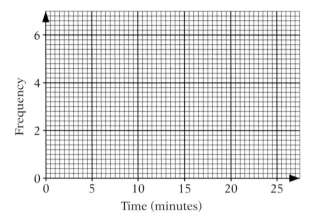

(c) This diagram shows the grouped frequency distribution of the times taken by the same contestants to do a second general knowledge test.

Which general knowledge test do you think was the harder? Give a reason for your answer.

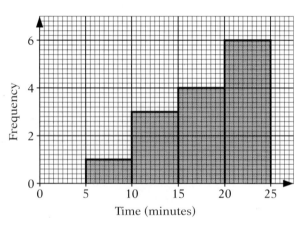

C   Use a copy of this.

On one day twenty people booked a package holiday with a travel agent.   **SEG**
The frequency distribution of the cost of the holidays booked is shown below.

Cost	£300–	£310–	£320–	£330–	£340–	£350–	£360–	£370–	£380–	£390–£400
Frequency	0	1	2	1	4	2	3	4	1	2

(a) Draw a frequency diagram for these data.   *(2)*

(b) How many people booked a holiday costing less than £330?   *(1)*

Frequency polygons

A **frequency polygon** is another way of displaying data.
We draw a frequency polygon as follows.

1.   Draw a frequency diagram.
2.   At each end, add class intervals which have zero frequency.
3.   Complete the polygon by joining the midpoints of all class intervals, including those added at each end.

Example This frequency table gives the ages, to the nearest year, of members of a circus troupe.

Age	Frequency
10 –	12
20 –	15
30 –	10

This diagram shows a frequency polygon for the data given above.

Note: A polygon is formed with one side being the *x*-axis.

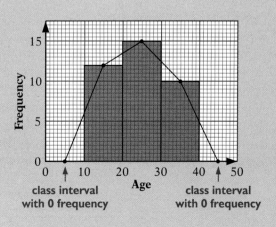

Exercise 3   **A**   Use a copy of this.
The lengths, in centimetres, of some duck eggs are given below.

4.1	4.5	4.3	4.3	4.5	4.2	3.9	4.3	4.1
4.7	4.3	4.0	4.2	4.5	4.2	4.0	4.4	4.4

1. Fill in this frequency table.

Length (cm)	Frequency
3.85 –	
4.05 –	
4.25 –	
4.45 –	
4.65 – 4.85	

2. Draw a frequency polygon for the data.

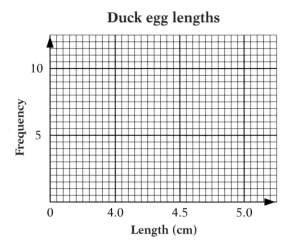

Duck egg lengths

B   The following times (in seconds) are recorded for a speed test.

28	63	88	79	42	46	57	33	50	40	68	76	46	81
92	77	84	76	66	49	75	81	58	57	82	67	78	70
61	65	94	79	52	82	77	51	65	70	74	63		

1. Use a copy of this frequency table. Fill it in.

Time (in seconds)	20 –	30 –	40 –	50 –	60 –	70 –	80 –	90 – 100
Frequency								

2. Draw a frequency diagram for this data.
   Use 0.1 cm graph paper.
3. On the same grid as question **2** draw a frequency polygon for the data.
4. What was the most common time interval?
5. How many people took more than 50 seconds?

C   The following data are the test marks for two different tests sat by the same class.
1. Draw a frequency polygon for each set of data.
2. Comment on the different shapes.

Score	10 –	15 –	20 –	25 –	30 –	35 –	40 –	45 – 50
Frequency Test 1	1	3	5	10	4	5		
Frequency Test 2		1	2	4	6	8	4	3

Homework/Review 1

A The pictogram shows the time it takes a train to travel from London to three other cities.

NEAB

(a) How long does it take to travel from London to Glasgow? *(1)*

(b) How much longer does it take to go from London to Liverpool than to go from London to Birmingham? *(1)*

(c) The train from London to Manchester takes 2 hours 30 minutes. Use a copy of the pictogram. Draw this information on the pictogram. *(1)*

	Key represents 30 minutes
London to Glasgow	
London to Liverpool	
London to Birmingham	
London to Manchester	

B Use a copy of this.

WJEC

Freda has carried out a survey about pupils' favourite types of film. She asked one hundred Junior school pupils and fifty High school pupils about their favourite type of film.

Here are the results of Freda's survey.

Type of film	Results for the Junior school pupils		Results for the High school pupils	
	Tally	Frequency	Tally	Frequency
Cartoon	ԼԱ ԼԱ ԼԱ ԼԱ ԼԱ ԼԱ ԼԱ ԼԱ		I	
Comedy	ԼԱ ԼԱ ԼԱ ԼԱ ԼԱ		ԼԱ II	
Horror	I		ԼԱ ԼԱ ԼԱ I	
Science fiction	ԼԱ ԼԱ ԼԱ I		ԼԱ ԼԱ	
Historical	II		II	
Fantasy	ԼԱ ԼԱ IIII		I	
Thriller	II		ԼԱ ԼԱ III	
		100		50

(a) Complete the frequency column for each table.

(b) Display Freda's survey results for the Junior school pupils using a chart or diagram of your own choice.

(c) Display Freda's survey results for the High school pupils using a chart or diagram of your own choice.

(d) Why do you think Freda has collected the data for Junior and High school pupils separately?

(e) Is it fair to say that the historical films are as popular with Junior school pupils as they are with High school pupils?
You **must** give a reason for your answer.

(f) Write **three** more conclusions which would be fair to make about Freda's results. *(12)*

C Use a copy of this.

WJEC

In this question all times are given in minutes rounded down to the nearest whole number of minutes.

Twenty boys undertook two tasks. The times taken to complete Task 1 are given.
  19 26 45 25 37 31 34 18 35 43
  29 33 34 41 39 15 36 47 28 20

(a) One of the 20 boys is selected at random. What is the probability that he took 18 minutes to complete Task 1? *(1)*

(b) Complete this grouped frequency table to show the distribution of these
times.   *(2)*

Time	At least 10 Less than 20	At least 20 Less than 30	At least 30 Less than 40	At least 40 Less than 50
Tally				
Frequency				

(c) Draw a grouped frequency diagram to show the distribution of the times.   *(2)*

D   Draw a frequency polygon for the data given in **C**.

Mean, median, mode and range

The **mode** of a set of data is the **value that occurs most often**.

Examples   3   4   4   7   7   7   8   9   mode = 7

12°C   14°C   12°C   13°C   10°C   14°C   mode 12°C and 14°C

4 kg   3 kg   2.5 kg   7.6 kg   5 kg   8 kg   9 kg   no mode

Example   This table shows the time taken by 25
pupils in a pizza-eating competition.

The **modal class** or **modal group** is 20–.

Time (seconds)	Tally	Frequency
0–	III	3
20–	IIII IIII IIII III	18
40–60	IIII	4

The **median** is the **middle value** of a set of data which have been put in
order.

Example   16   17   17   ⑱   20   24   28   median = 18

When there are an even number of data values, there are two middle
values. The median is halfway between these.

Example   Emma measured the height in metres, of eight shrubs. They were:

1.4   1.6   1.8   (1.9   2.3)   2.6   2.6   2.8

The median $= \dfrac{1.9 + 2.3}{2}$

$= 2.1$ m

The **mean** of a set of data is often called the average.

$$\text{Mean} = \frac{\text{sum of all data values}}{\text{number of values}}$$

Example   Nadine weighed six school bags.

5.1 kg   3.1 kg   4.5 kg   2.6 kg   1.9 kg   3.2 kg

$$\text{Mean} = \frac{\text{sum of all data values}}{\text{number of values}}$$

$$= \frac{5.1 + 3.1 + 4.5 + 2.6 + 1.9 + 3.2}{6}$$

$$= 3.4 \text{ kg}$$

The **range** measures the spread of the data.
Range = highest data value – lowest data value

Example   The range for the six school bags Nadine weighed in the previous example is:
Range = 5.1 – 1.9
= 3.2 kg

Exercise 4

A   Here is the number of goals scored by Rovers hockey team in its matches this season.

3	3	1	0	3	2
1	3	3	0	3	

Work out these for the number of goals scored.
1. mode   **2.** median   **3.** mean   **4.** range

B   The number of pupils in each set in year 8 is given below.   **WJEC**

SET	A	B	C	D	E	F	G	H	I
SET SIZE	24	26	28	25	28	30	24	24	25

(i)   What is the range of the set sizes for mathematics for year 8?
(ii)   What is the mode of the set sizes?
(iii) Calculate the mean of the set sizes.
(iv)   Use 0.1 cm graph paper. Draw a bar chart to show these set sizes.   *(8)*

C   **MEG**

The weights, in kilograms, of members of a rowing crew are
80,   83,   83,   86,   89,   91,   93,   99.

(a) Calculate the mean of these weights.   *(2)*
(b) Calculate the range of these weights.   *(2)*

D   **LONDON**

Ten teams took part in a quiz.
Their scores are shown below.
15,   13,   17,   11,   14,   15,   16,   15,   16,   8.
Work out the mean score.   *(3)*

E

MEG

The first 20 letters of the alphabet are numbered as follows.

A	B	C	D	E	F	G	H	I	J	K	L	M	N	O	P	Q	R	S	T
1	2	3	4	5	6	7	8	9	10	11	12	13	14	15	16	17	18	19	20

(a) Under each of the letters of the word BANANAS, write its number. *(1)*

    B   A   N   A   N   A   S

(b) (i)   Arrange the seven letters of the word BANANAS in the order of their
numbers, smallest first. *(2)*

    (ii)   Which letter is the mode? *(1)*

    (iii)   Which number is the median? *(1)*

F   Olivia plays in her school netball team.
She will be selected to play for the county team
next season if her mean score of goals after the
first 7 games is at least 12.
After 6 games her mean score is 11.5.

1. What is the total number of goals Olivia has
scored in these 6 games.
2. What is the least number of goals she must
score in the next game in order to be chosen?
3. In the seventh game she scores 13 goals.
Has her mean score of goals increased or decreased?

G

SEG

Birdpool Park held its annual fishing competition in September.
The number of fish caught by each of fifteen competitors in the time allowed
was as follows:

    1,   2,   2,   4,   4,   7,   7,   8,   9,   9,   9,   10,   10,   11,   11.

(a) What was the modal number of fish caught? *(1)*

(b) What was the median number of fish caught? *(1)*

The numbers of fish caught by five more competitors were:

    2,   10,   7,   11,   7.

(c) For the twenty results now available calculate:

    (i)   the mode, *(1)*

    (ii)   the median. *(2)*

H

SEG

There are 24 people in an old people's home.
There are 15 women.
Their ages are shown below.

98	85	87	75	71	69	76	82
93	94	78	77	91	90	79	

(a) (i)   What is the range of the ages of the women? *(1)*

    (ii)   Calculate the mean age of the women. *(2)*

All the people in the home are 65 years old or more.
The men have a mean age of 71 years.
The range of the ages of the men is 34 years.

(b) What is the sex of the oldest person in the home?
Give a reason for your answer. *(1)*

Finding the mean, median, mode and range from a frequency table

Worked Exam Question

Number of tickets	Number of teachers	
0	2	
1	7	
2	5	*(1)*
3	2	*(3)*
4	0	*(2)*
5	3	
6	1	

LONDON

Some teachers were asked how many National Lottery tickets they bought last week.
The results are shown in the table.

(a) Which number of tickets is the mode?
(b) Work out the mean number of tickets.
(c) Find the median number of tickets.

Answer (a) **1** is the mode number of tickets because this is the most common number of tickets bought.

(b) Mean $= \dfrac{\text{sum of all the data values}}{\text{number of values}}$

The sum of all the data values is found by multiplying each data value by its frequency and then adding them up.

The number of values is found by adding up the number of teachers.

$= \dfrac{0 \times 2 + 1 \times 7 + 2 \times 5 + 3 \times 2 + 4 \times 0 + 5 \times 3 + 6 \times 1}{20}$

$= \dfrac{0 + 7 + 10 + 6 + 0 + 15 + 6}{20}$

$= \dfrac{44}{20}$

$= \mathbf{2.2}$

(c) 20 teachers were asked.
The median is halfway between the 10th and 11th values.
9 teachers bought 0 or 1 ticket. The 10th and 11th teachers bought 2 tickets.
So the median number of tickets bought is **2**.

We find the **range** from a **frequency table** using:
Range = highest data value – lowest data value.
The range in the worked exam question above is 6 – 0 or 6.

Exercise 5   **A**   Find the mean, median, mode and range of:

1. the number of pets   **2.** the number of goals   **3.** the marks in a test.

Number of pets	Number of families
0	12
1	11
2	4
3	2
4	0
5	1

Number of goals	Number of pupils
0	5
1	8
2	4
3	1
4	0
5	1
6	2

Mark in test	Number of pupils
10	5
20	3
30	10
40	8
50	4

B Some pupils were asked how many items they bought at the school canteen at lunchtime. The results are shown in the table.

1. Which number of items is the mode?
2. Work out the mean number of items.
3. Find the median number of items.

Number of items	Number of pupils
1	11
2	26
3	24
4	16
5	9
6	4

C Some families were asked how many times the phone rang in their house one evening. The results are shown in the table.

1. What is the mode of this data?
2. Work out the mean number of times the phone rang. Give your answer to 1 decimal place.
3. Find the median of the number of times the phone rang.

Number of times phone rang	Number of families
0	1
1	3
2	6
3	8
4	12
5	16
6	10
7	8
8	3

Comparing data

The mean, median, mode and range are often helpful when we want to compare two sets of data.

Worked Exam Question

SEG

A survey was carried out on the shoe sizes of 25 men.
The results of the survey were

10	6	9	8	9	8	6	7	9
9	7	7	9	10	9	8	9	8
5	8	8	9	10	8	7.

(a) **(i)** What is the mode of the shoe sizes? *(1)*
　　 (ii) What is the median of the shoe sizes? *(1)*

This frequency diagram shows the results of a survey of the shoe sizes of 25 women.

(b) Using your answers from part **(a)** make two different comparisons between the shoe sizes of men and women.

SEG

(2)

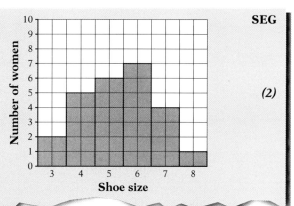

Number of women

Shoe size

Answer (a) (i) The most common shoe size is 9, so the mode shoe size is **9**.

(ii) We must put the shoe sizes in order.

5, 6, 6, 7, 7, 7, 7, 8, 8, 8 ,8, 8, ⑧ , 8, 9, 9, 9, 9, 9, 9, 9, 10, 10, 10

The median is the 13th value.

The median shoe size is **8**.

(b) The mode shoe size for women is 6.

The median shoe size for women is also the 13th value.

On the diagram, we count along adding the frequencies until we find the 13th value.

The 13th value is 5.

So the median shoe size for women is **5**.

We can use the mode and median to compare the shoe sizes for men and women.

Possible answers are:

Comparison 1 The modal shoe size for men is 3 sizes larger than the modal shoe size for women.

Comparison 2 The median shoe size for men is 3 sizes larger than the median shoe size for women.

Exercise 6

A

Two groups take the same Maths test.

The test is marked out of 50.

Graham writes down the marks for his group.

NEAB

 25,   47,   49,   31,   38,   24,   19,   22,   38,   25.

(a) Calculate the mean mark for this group. *(2)*

(b) What is the range of marks for this group? *(1)*

Arpita writes down the marks for her group. The lowest mark is 12. The range is 30.

(c) What is the highest mark for her group? *(1)*

The mean for her group is 25.

(d) Compare the results of the two groups. *(1)*

B

At the end of a typing course all the students are tested on their typing speeds. The number of words typed per minute by each student is shown.

SEG

 43   49   56   56   57   57   61   61   61   62   79

(a) What is the range of their typing speeds? *(1)*

(b) Calculate the mean typing speed for these students. *(3)*

At the start of the course the mean typing speed of these students is 42 words per minute and the range is 67.

(c) What do these statistics suggest about the changes in the students' typing speeds?

You must comment on both the mean and the range. *(1)*

C

NEAB

Pauline's class and Rekha's class both go swimming regularly.

Pauline's class uses a 'Rapids' bus.
Rekha's class uses a 'Streamline' bus.

The two classes decide to do a survey to find out which bus service is best.
The two girls record the journey times (in minutes) of 20 journeys from school to the swimming pool.
Here are the results.

Rapids buses					
	18	26	28	29	31
	25	25	19	21	22
	26	33	25	28	27
	24	24	24	23	22

Streamline buses					
	31	29	27	31	31
	23	31	24	33	25
	31	29	30	33	31
	31	32	33	32	33

Pauline calculated the mean and the range of the times for each bus:

Rapids   Mean time = 25 minutes
                        Range = 15 minutes

Streamline   Mean time = 30 minutes
                        Range = 10 minutes

(a) Describe in words how she calculated the mean times.   *(2)*
(b) Describe in words how she calculated the range of the times.   *(2)*
(c) Which bus is best for getting them to the swimming pool?
    Explain your choice, using both the mean and the range in your answer. *(2)*

D

SEG

(a) The fifteen members of a hockey squad were asked what size of boot they wore.

    The replies were:

    6, 3, 7, 8, 7, 6, 3, 5, 4, 6, 3, 7, 5, 4, 7.

    For these sizes, find
    (i)   the mode,   *(1)*
    (ii) the median,   *(2)*
    (iii) the range.   *(1)*

(b) The fifteen members of a rugby team were asked what size of boot they wore.
    For their replies, the mode was 8, the median was 7 and the range was 3.
    Comment on how the boot sizes for the rugby team differ from those of the hockey squad in part (a).   *(2)*

Homework/Review 2

A
LONDON

Edwina had 5 boxes of matches. She counted the number of matches in each box.
Here are the numbers   28,   30,   31,   28,   27
(a) Work out the mean number of matches per box.   *(3)*
(b) Work out the range of Edwina's numbers.   *(2)*

B
LONDON

Twenty five people took part in a competition.
The points scored are grouped in the frequency table.
Write down the modal class of points scored.

Points scored	Number of people
1 to 5	1
6 to 10	2
11 to 15	5
16 to 20	7
21 to 25	8
26 to 30	2

(1)

C
SEG

The handspans of some children were measured.
The measurements, in centimetres, are shown.

    15   13   16   15   14   14   15   12
    12   14   13   15   13   15   13

(a) **(i)**   What is the range of the children's handspans?   *(2)*
    (ii) Calculate the mean handspan.   *(3)*

A second group of children have handspans with the same mean as the first group.
The range of their handspans is 7 cm.
(b) Describe **one** difference between the handspans of the two groups.   *(1)*

D   What is the median handspan of the first group of children in **C**?

E
NEAB

A teacher asks all his class.
Here are their replies.
(a) How many children are in the class?   *(1)*
(b) What is the most common number of children in the family for this class?   *(1)*
(c) Calculate the mean number of children per family in this class?
    Give your answer to 1 decimal place.   *(3)*

How many children are there in your family?

Number of children in the family	Number of replies
1	7
2	12
3	5
4	2
5	0

F   Find the median number of children in the families in **E**.

☑ KEY POINTS

☑ **Pictograms, bar charts** and **bar-line graphs** are used to display ungrouped discrete data.

☑ We use **frequency diagrams** to show grouped data.

☑ A **frequency polygon** is a line graph joining midpoints of class intervals, including the class intervals with zero frequency which are added at each end.

☑ The **mode** of a set of data is the value that occurs most often.

☑ When data is grouped we find the **modal class** rather than the mode.

☑ The **median** is the middle value of a set of data once the data has been put in order. If there is an even number of data values, there are two middle values. We find the number halfway between them.

Example   The median of   2   8   12   16   24   28   is $\dfrac{12 + 16}{2} = 14$

☑ **Mean** $= \dfrac{\textbf{sum of data values}}{\textbf{number of values}}$

☑ **Range = highest data value – lowest data value**

☑ To find the **mean** from a frequency table:
    multiply each frequency by its data value and add up the answers
    divide by the sum of the frequencies (the number of data values).

☑ To find the **median** from a frequency table:
    work out which value is the median
    count along the table to find this value.

• •

◄◄ CHAPTER REVIEW ◄◄

• •

◄◄
Exercise 6
on page 229

A

LONDON

Mrs Chowdery gives her class a Maths test.
Here are the test marks for the girls.

   7, 5, 8, 5, 2, 8, 7, 4, 7, 10, 3, 7, 4, 3, 6

(a) Work out the mode.   *(1)*
(b) Work out the median.   *(2)*

The median mark for the boys was 7 and the range of the marks of the boys was 4.
The range of the girls' marks was 8.
(c) By comparing the results explain whether the boys or the girls did
     better in the test.   *(2)*

B   Use a copy of this.

◀◀
Exercise 1
on page 214

The pictogram shows the number of parcels posted at the High Street Post Office on Monday, Tuesday and Wednesday.

| Monday | ⊞ ⊞ ⊞ | **LONDON** |

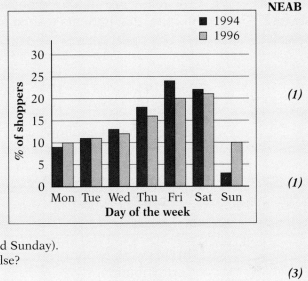

(a) How many parcels were posted on
  (i) Monday,   (ii) Wednesday?   *(2)*
25 parcels were posted on Thursday.
(b) Show this on the pictogram.   *(2)*

◀◀
Exercise 6
on page 229

C   The bar chart shows which day of the week shoppers went to a supermarket in 1994 and 1996.

NEAB

(a) Which day of the week was the most popular day for shopping in 1994?   *(1)*
(b) Did the shoppers choose different days to shop in 1996 compared with 1994?
  Give a reason for your answer.   *(1)*
(c) In 1996 about half the shoppers did their shopping at the end of the week (Friday, Saturday and Sunday).
  Is this statement true or false?
  Show all your working.   *(3)*

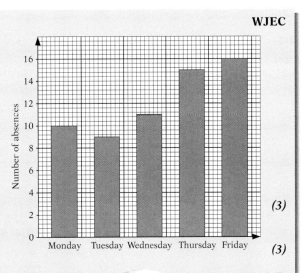

◀◀
Exercises 1, 5
and 6 on pages
214, 227 and 229

D
(a) The following diagram shows the number of pupils who were absent from Aberglas Primary School each day for one week in April.
  (i)   On which day was the least number of pupils absent?
  (ii) How many pupils were absent on Thursday?
  (iii) How many more pupils were absent on Friday than on Monday?   *(3)*
(b) Calculate the mean of the numbers of daily absences for the week in April.   *(3)*

WJEC

(c) The daily absences during a week in June are shown in the following table.

Monday	Tuesday	Wednesday	Thursday	Friday
12	14	8	18	23

(i) Using 1 mm graph paper, draw a bar chart for this data.
(ii) Write down the range of daily absences for this week in June.
(iii) The mean of the numbers of daily absences for the week in June is 15. Which of the two weeks given above had the better attendance rate? Give a reason for your answer. *(6)*

◀◀ Exercise 2 on page 219

E The following numbers show the times in minutes, correct to the nearest minute, that patients waited at a dentist's before seeing the dentist.

14	12	15	25	32	17	45	23	27	13
28	18	21	13	45	26	16	17	28	24
26	45	13	17	42	24	25	14	31	20
15	30	17	19	11	24	22	27	13	32

(a) Complete the following table to show a grouped frequency distribution of the waiting times of the patients.

Time (minutes)	0–	10–	20–	30–	40–50
Tally					
Frequency					

(b) On graph paper draw a grouped frequency diagram to show this distribution.
(c) What is the modal class interval for the waiting time of the patients?

◀◀ Exercise 3 on page 222

F Draw a frequency polygon for the data in **E**.

◀◀ Exercise 5 on page 227

G The results of a History test for 25 pupils are shown.
(a) Which mark is the mode?
(b) Find the median mark.
(c) Calculate the mean mark.

Mark	Number of pupils
4	1
5	3
6	2
7	2
8	7
9	8
10	2

2-D and 3-D Shapes

By the end of this chapter you will be able to:

- draw squares, rectangles, circles, triangles and quadrilaterals
- name the parts of a circle
- draw parallel and perpendicular lines using a ruler and set square
- recognise congruent shapes
- name these 3-D shapes
  cube, cuboid, cylinder, sphere, pyramid, cone, prism, triangular prism
- write down the number of faces, edges and vertices of any 3-D shape
- draw a net for a cube, cuboid, pyramid or prism
- draw a 3-D shape on isometric dot paper.

Getting started ....

A photograph is 15 cm by 9 cm.
Aaron's photo album has pages which are
36 cm by 27 cm.
How can he arrange four photos on a page
so that they are evenly spaced?
Each photo must be the same distance from
each other as from the edges.

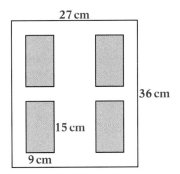

Drawing 2-D shapes

Squares and rectangles

We use a ruler and set square to draw **squares** and **rectangles**.
Check the accuracy of your drawing by measuring the diagonals.
They should be equal.

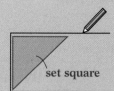

set square

Circles

Use a compass to draw a **circle**.
The parts of a circle are:

radius   diameter   circumference   arc   sector

You should also be able to recognise a **chord** and **tangent**.
A **chord** is a straight line which joins any two points on the circumference.
A **tangent** is a straight line which touches a circle at just one point.

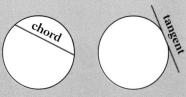

chord   tangent

Triangles and quadrilaterals

We use a ruler and compass or ruler and protractor to draw a **triangle** or **quadrilateral**.

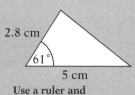

2.8 cm   61°   5 cm

Use a ruler and protractor to draw this.

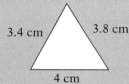

3.4 cm   3.8 cm   4 cm

Use a ruler and compass to draw this.

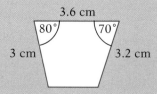

3.6 cm   80°   70°   3 cm   3.2 cm

Use a ruler and protractor to draw this.

Worked Exam Question

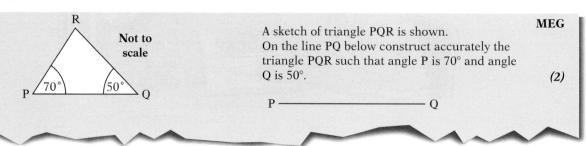

R   Not to scale   P 70°   50° Q

A sketch of triangle PQR is shown.
On the line PQ below construct accurately the triangle PQR such that angle P is 70° and angle Q is 50°.

MEG

(2)

P ——————————— Q

Answer

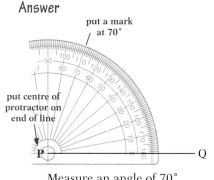

put a mark at 70°

put centre of protractor on end of line

Measure an angle of 70° at P.

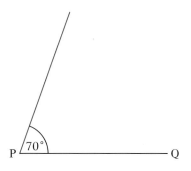

Draw a line through the mark.

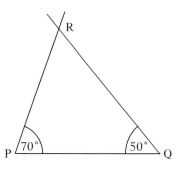

Measure and mark an angle of 50° at Q. Draw a line through the mark.

Exercise 1

A Draw these accurately.
Check by measuring the diagonals.

1. A rectangle 4 cm long and 2.8 cm wide
2. A square with sides of 3 cm
3. A rectangle 5.5 cm long and 3.2 cm wide
4. A square with sides of 28 mm
5. A rectangle with sides 3.6 cm long and 2.5 cm wide

B Name the parts of the circle which are drawn in red.

1.   2.   3.   4.

5.   6.   7.   8.

C Draw these accurately.
1. A circle of diameter 4.5 cm
2. A circle of radius 6 cm
3. A circle with diameter AB (trace AB into your book)

A ——————————————— B

4. A circle of diameter 28 mm
5. A circle of radius PQ (trace PQ into your book)

P ————————— Q

D

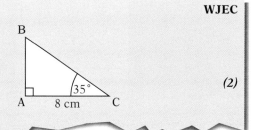

This diagram is not drawn to scale. It shows a triangle ABC. AC is 8 cm long. Angle ACB is 35°.
Draw triangle ABC accurately, full sized.

WJEC

(2)

E   Use your ruler, compass and protractor to make an accurate construction of the following.
     On your diagram, measure the length of the red line.

1.
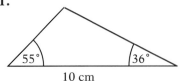

2.
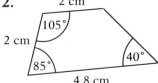

F

WJEC

Draw a semicircle of radius 5 cm.

(1)

G   Measure the diameters of the following circles.
     Give your answer to the nearest millimetre.

1.
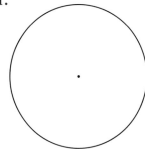

2.
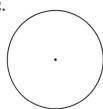

3.

4.

H

MEG

(a) Draw accurately the triangle ABC which has the following measurements:
           AC = 6 centimetres; angle A = 31°; AB = 8.2 centimetres.   *(2)*
(b) Measure the size of the angle at C, and the length of the line BC.   *(2)*

Drawing parallel and perpendicular lines

We can use a ruler and set square to draw **parallel** and **perpendicular** lines.

Parallel lines

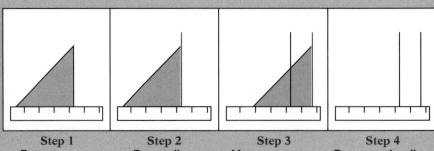

Step 1	Step 2	Step 3	Step 4
Put set square on a ruler.	Draw a line.	Move set square along the ruler.	Draw another line.

Perpendicular lines

Example   Draw a line through the point R which is perpendicular to PQ.

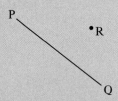

Answer

Put your set square along PQ so that the side goes through R.

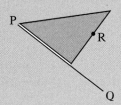

Draw a line along the side of the set square.

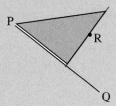

Exercise 2   **A**   Use a copy of this.

On the diagram given below,

(i)   draw a line through the point Q which is perpendicular to MN,
(ii) draw a line through the point R which is parallel to MN.

WJEC

(2)

B   Use a copy of this.

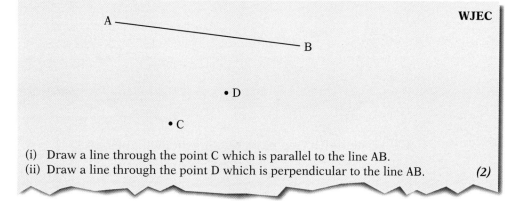

(i)   Draw a line through the point C which is parallel to the line AB.
(ii) Draw a line through the point D which is perpendicular to the line AB.

WJEC

(2)

Congruence

Shapes which have exactly the same size and shape are called **congruent**.

Example

A and C are congruent.

Exercise 3   **A**   Which triangle is congruent to triangle X?

B

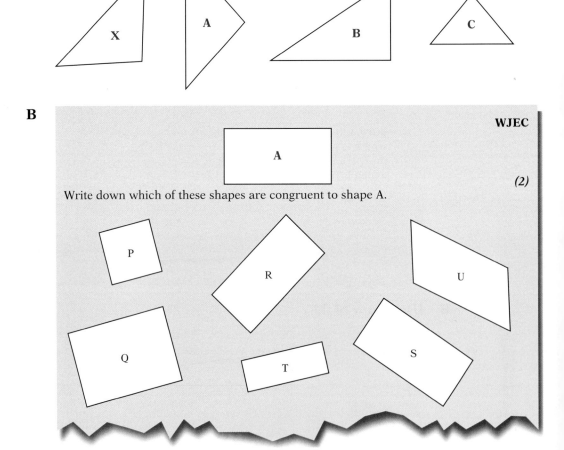

WJEC

Write down which of these shapes are congruent to shape A.

(2)

C   Write down two pairs of congruent shapes.

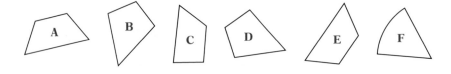

3-D shapes

Naming 3-D shapes

Remember   You should know the names of these solids.

Cube   **Cuboid**   **Cylinder**   **Sphere**   **Triangular-based pyramid**   **Square-based pyramid**   **Cone**

You should also recognise a **prism**.
A **prism** has two congruent parallel faces.
All **cross sections** which are cut parallel to the congruent faces are identical.
A prism with a triangular end is called a **triangular prism**.

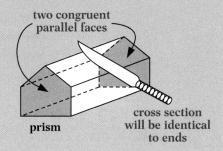

two congruent parallel faces

prism

cross section will be identical to ends

Faces, edges, vertices

Remember

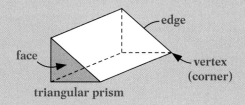

edge

face

vertex (corner)

triangular prism

This prism has 5 faces, 9 edges and 6 vertices.

Example   1.   Name the **two** 3-D shapes which make up this shape.
2.   Write down the number of
(a)   faces   (b)   edges
(c)   vertices.

Answer   1.   A square based pyramid and a cube.
2.   (a)   9   (b)   16   (c)   9

> You could mark the faces, edges and vertices on the diagram as you count them.

Note: You can check your answers using:
faces + vertices = edges + 2

Exercise 4   **A**   Write down the names of these shapes.

1.   2.   3.   4.

5.   6.   7.   8.

B For each of the following shapes, write down the number of:

(a) faces   (b) edges   (c) vertices.

1.   2.   3.   4.

C The names of some shapes are given.

cube, prism, square-based pyramid, square, cylinder

Choose one of these names for each description below.
1. It has six faces and eight vertices and twelve edges.
2. It has two flat faces and one curved face.
3. It has two pairs of sides of equal length and four right-angles.
4. It has five faces and five vertices and eight edges.

Task

You will need thin card
a copy of the diagram below

1. Paste the diagram onto thin card.
2. Cut along the solid lines.
3. Fold along the dashed lines and fit the shape together.
4. Use sticky tape to help keep the tabs in place.

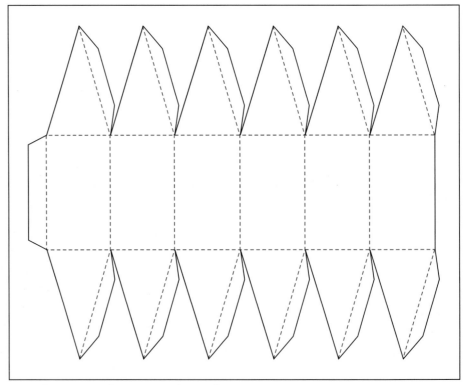

How many faces, edges and vertices does your shape have?

Nets

A **net** folds to make a 3-D shape.
You are often asked to draw a net.

Worked Exam Question

The cross section of a prism is a right angled triangle.   **SEG**

5 cm   8 cm   **Not to scale**

3 cm

4 cm

The triangle is part of the net of the prism.
(i) Measure accurately the smallest angle of the triangle.
(ii) Complete an accurate net of the prism.

3 cm

4 cm

(1)
(3)

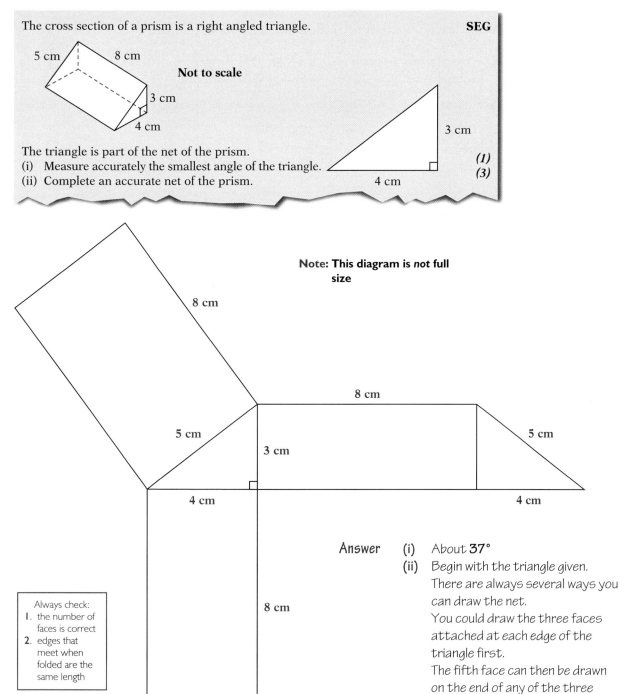

Note: **This diagram is *not* full size**

8 cm

8 cm

5 cm

5 cm

3 cm

4 cm

4 cm

8 cm

4 cm

Always check:
1. the number of faces is correct
2. edges that meet when folded are the same length

Answer
(i) About **37°**
(ii) Begin with the triangle given. There are always several ways you can draw the net.
You could draw the three faces attached at each edge of the triangle first.
The fifth face can then be drawn on the end of any of the three faces already drawn.

Exercise 5 **A**

NEAB

Here is a net that is used to make a fair dice for a game.
When the dice is made, which number will be on the face opposite the face with the number 8?

	5		
4	6	9	8
	7		

(1)

B Write down which of the following are nets of a cube.

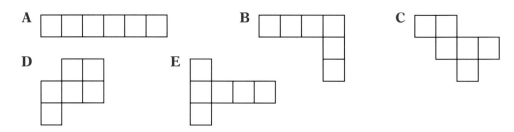

C **A**, **B**, **C** and **D** are drawn accurately.

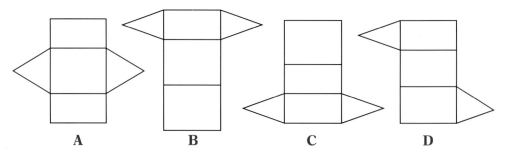

A   B   C   D

1. Which diagram shows the net of a triangular prism?
2. Which diagram has rotational symmetry?

D **You will need 1 cm squared paper**
The dimensions of a box are shown.
Draw an accurate net of the box.
Use a scale of 1 cm to 10 cm.
Use 1 cm squared paper.

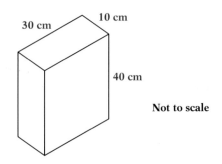

30 cm   10 cm   40 cm

Not to scale

E **You will need 1 cm squared paper**
Here is a sketch of an open box.
Draw a net for the open box.
Use 1 cm squared paper.

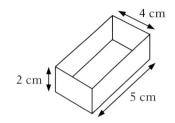

F 1. What name is given to this solid?
2. Draw the net for this solid.

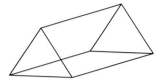

G

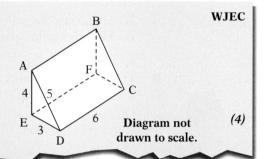

The diagram shows a small gift box in the form of a triangular prism.
The length of the prism is 6 cm.
The sides of the triangular cross-section are 3 cm, 4 cm, and 5 cm respectively.

Draw the net of the prism accurately.

WJEC

Diagram not drawn to scale.

(4)

H This diagram shows part of the net for a pyramid with a rectangular base.
1. Copy and complete the net accurately.
2. Sketch the pyramid the net would make.

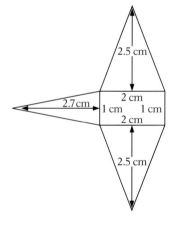

Isometric drawing

We can draw 3-D shapes on **isometric** dot paper.

Worked Exam Question

WJEC

This diagram is drawn to scale. All measurements are in centimetres. It shows one end of a prism. The prism is 2 cm long.

On the isometric grid given below, draw the prism. The line AB has been drawn for you.

(3)

Remember a prism has two congruent parallel faces.

Answer   First, draw the end given in the
question.
Then make the prism 2 cm long.

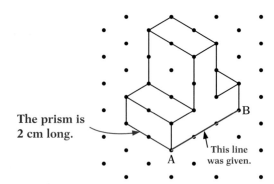

The prism is
2 cm long.

A

This line
was given.

B

Exercise 6   **You will need 1 cm isometric dot paper and triangular paper for this
exercise.**

A   **1.**   On isometric dot paper, draw a diagram of a cuboid.
   2.   On triangular paper, draw a diagram of a cuboid.

B   This diagram shows a piece of wood.
   All of the angles are right angles.
   On isometric dot paper, draw a full size
   isometric drawing of the wood.

4 cm

4 cm

2 cm

6 cm

4 cm

2 cm

C

NEAB

A cuboid has sides of lengths 4 cm, 6 cm and 8 cm.
Make an accurate 3-D drawing of the cuboid.
Use 1 cm isometric dot paper.

(3)

D

NEAB

The diagram shows a block of Starlight
Soap. Its volume is 24 cm^3.

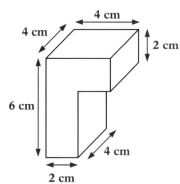

Starlight
Soap

2 cm

3 cm

4 cm

(a) (i)   On isometric dot paper, sketch
         another block of soap with
         different dimensions which also
         has a volume of 24 cm^3.   *(1)*
      (ii)   Give the dimensions of your block
         of soap.   *(1)*
(b) (i)   On isometric dot paper, draw a diagram of a box whose dimensions
         are **twice** those of the block of Starlight Soap.   *(2)*
      (ii)   What is the largest number of blocks of Starlight Soap which will fit
         into this box?   *(1)*

Homework/Review

A Draw these accurately.

1.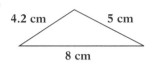

2.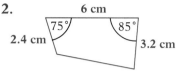

3. A circle with diameter 5 cm.
4. A rectangle 4.5 cm long and 3 cm wide.

B (a) Name each of the solids given below.
   (b) Write down the number of faces, edges and vertices each has.

1.   2.   3.   4.

C

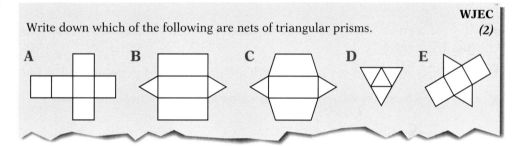

Write down which of the following are nets of triangular prisms.   **WJEC** *(2)*

A   B   C   D   E

D You will need squared paper.

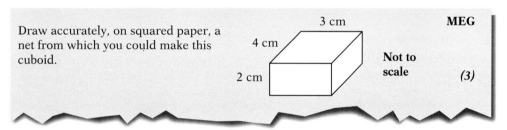

Draw accurately, on squared paper, a net from which you could make this cuboid.   **MEG**

3 cm   4 cm   2 cm   Not to scale   *(3)*

E You will need isometric dot paper.

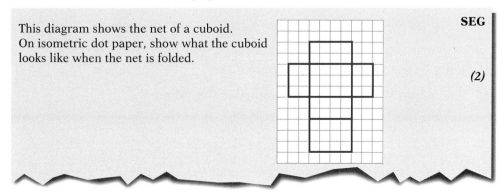

This diagram shows the net of a cuboid. On isometric dot paper, show what the cuboid looks like when the net is folded.   **SEG** *(2)*

F You will need isometric dot paper.

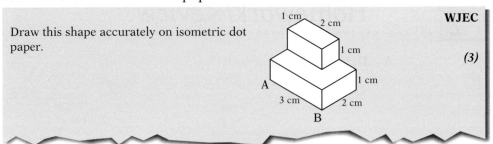

Draw this shape accurately on isometric dot paper.

WJEC

(3)

✔ KEY POINTS

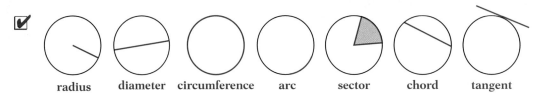

radius   diameter   circumference   arc   sector   chord   tangent

✔ We use a set square and ruler to draw **squares and rectangles**.

✔ We use a **compass** to draw a **circle**.

✔ We use a **ruler** and **protractor** or **ruler** and **compass** to draw **triangles** and **quadrilaterals**.

✔ We use a ruler and set square to draw **parallel** and **perpendicular** lines.

✔ Shapes which are exactly the same size and shape are **congruent**.

✔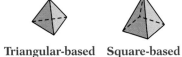

    Cube   **Cuboid**   **Cylinder**   **Sphere**   **Triangular-based**   **Square-based**   **Cone**
                                              pyramid   **pyramid**

✔ A **prism** has two end faces which are parallel and congruent (exactly the same).

                                                  prism   triangular prism

✔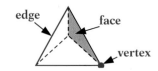

✔ A slice through a shape gives a **cross-section**.

✔ A **net** folds to make a 3-D shape.

✔ We can draw 3-D shapes on **isometric dot paper**.

◄◄ CHAPTER REVIEW ◄◄

◄◄
Exercises 1 and 2
on pages 237 and
239

A

(a) Draw a square with sides equal to the length of AB.   **WJEC**

A ——————————————————————— B   *(1)*

(b) Draw a circle with **diameter** RS.

R ——————————————— S   *(1)*

(c) Use a copy of this.
   On the diagram given,
   (i) draw a line through P which is
        parallel to ST,
   (ii) draw a line through S which is perpendicular to ST.   *(2)*

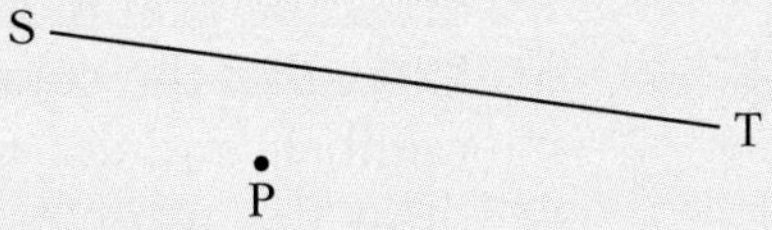

◄◄
Exercise 3
on page 240

B Which two shapes are congruent?

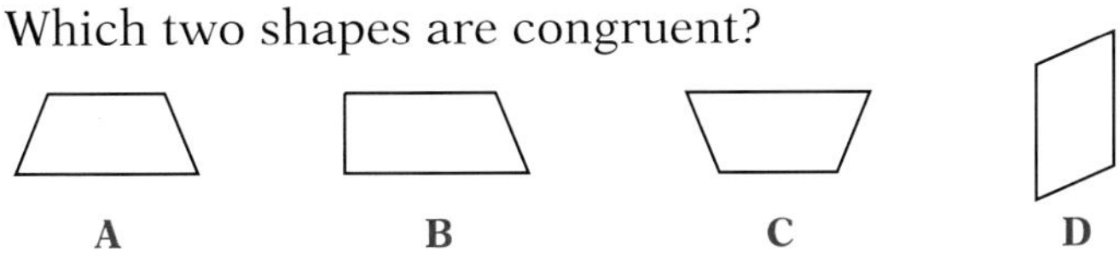

   A   B   C   D

◄◄
Exercise 4
on page 241

C   **MEG**

Below are four diagrams showing some three dimensional objects.

   A   B   C   D

(a) Give the mathematical name for (i) object A   (ii) object B   *(2)*
(b) How many edges has object C?   *(1)*
(c) How many faces has object D?   *(1)*
(d) Sketch a triangular prism.   *(2)*
(e) How many vertices has a triangular prism?   *(1)*

◄◄
Exercise 5
on page 244

D The diagram shows a triangular prism.
Draw an accurate net of the prism.
Use 1 cm squared paper.

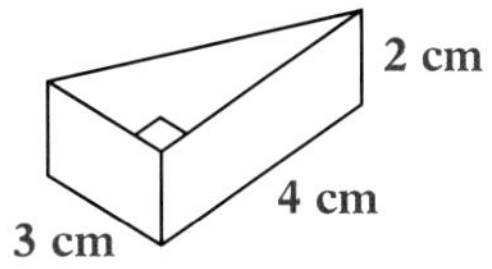

2 cm
4 cm
3 cm

◄◄
Exercise 5
on page 244

E   **WJEC**

What name is given to the object shown.
Draw a sketch of the net of this object.   *(2)*

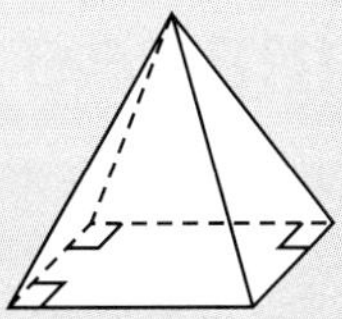

◄◄
Exercise 6 on
page 246

F Use 1 cm isometric dot paper.
Draw a full size drawing of this.

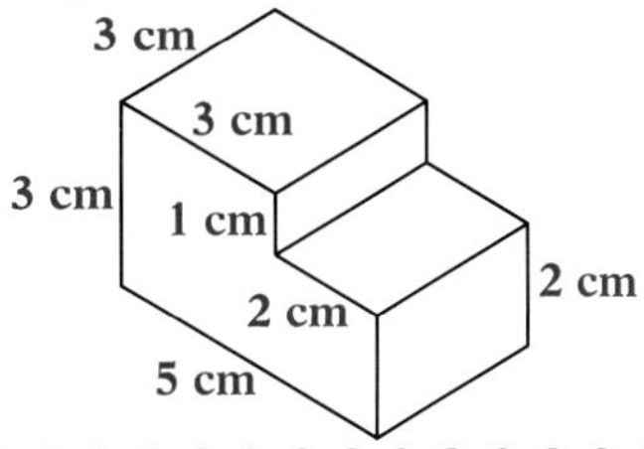

3 cm
3 cm
3 cm   1 cm
2 cm
2 cm
5 cm

17 Graphs

By the end of this chapter you will be able to:

- plot and read coordinates
- draw the graph of a straight line by plotting points
- know that the equation of a horizontal line is $y = a$, where a is any number, and the equation of a vertical line is $x = b$, where b is any number
- draw the graph of a curve with equation $y = x^2 + a$ where a is any number
- read and draw conversion graphs
- read and draw graphs of real-life situations
- read and draw distance–time graphs.

Getting started ....

Use a copy of this.
Use the grid to fill in the letters above the coordinates in the box below.
What does the message say?

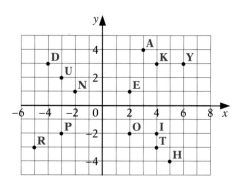

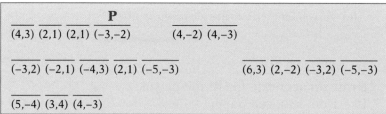

$$\underset{(4,3)}{\rule{1cm}{0.4pt}} \underset{(2,1)}{\rule{1cm}{0.4pt}} \underset{(2,1)}{\overset{P}{\rule{1cm}{0.4pt}}} \underset{(-3,-2)}{\rule{1cm}{0.4pt}} \qquad \underset{(4,-2)}{\rule{1cm}{0.4pt}} \underset{(4,-3)}{\rule{1cm}{0.4pt}}$$

$$\underset{(-3,2)}{\rule{1cm}{0.4pt}} \underset{(-2,1)}{\rule{1cm}{0.4pt}} \underset{(-4,3)}{\rule{1cm}{0.4pt}} \underset{(2,1)}{\rule{1cm}{0.4pt}} \underset{(-5,-3)}{\rule{1cm}{0.4pt}} \qquad \underset{(6,3)}{\rule{1cm}{0.4pt}} \underset{(2,-2)}{\rule{1cm}{0.4pt}} \underset{(-3,2)}{\rule{1cm}{0.4pt}} \underset{(-5,-3)}{\rule{1cm}{0.4pt}}$$

$$\underset{(5,-4)}{\rule{1cm}{0.4pt}} \underset{(3,4)}{\rule{1cm}{0.4pt}} \underset{(4,-3)}{\rule{1cm}{0.4pt}}$$

Using coordinates

The **coordinates** of the vertices of the triangle are; $(-3, 2)$, $(4, 1)$ and $(-2, -3)$.
The x-**coordinate** is always written **first** in the bracket.

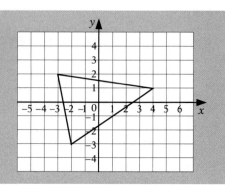

Worked Exam Question

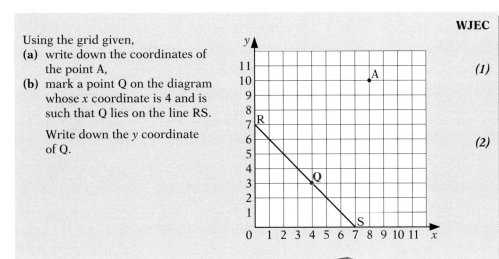

WJEC

Using the grid given,
(a) write down the coordinates of the point A, *(1)*
(b) mark a point Q on the diagram whose *x* coordinate is 4 and is such that Q lies on the line RS.

Write down the *y* coordinate of Q. *(2)*

Answer (a) **(8, 10)**
(b) *Q is shown in red.*
The y coordinate of Q is **3**.

Exercise 1 A

NEAB

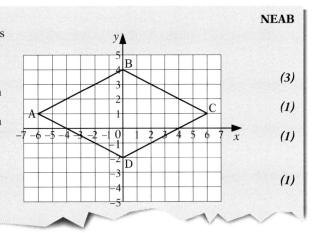

(a) Write down the coordinates of
(i) point C (ii) point A
(iii) point D. *(3)*
(b) What special name is given to triangle ABC? *(1)*
(c) What special name is given to quadrilateral ABCD? *(1)*
(d) What is the order of rotational symmetry for shape ABCD? *(1)*

B Use a copy of this.

MEG

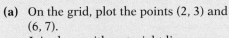
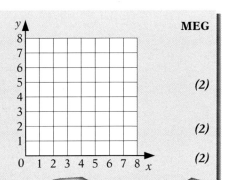

(a) On the grid, plot the points (2, 3) and (6, 7).
Join them with a straight line. *(2)*
(b) On the same grid, plot the points (3, 0) and (3, 5).
Join them with a straight line. *(2)*
(c) Write down the coordinates of the point where the two lines cross. *(2)*

C Use a copy of this.

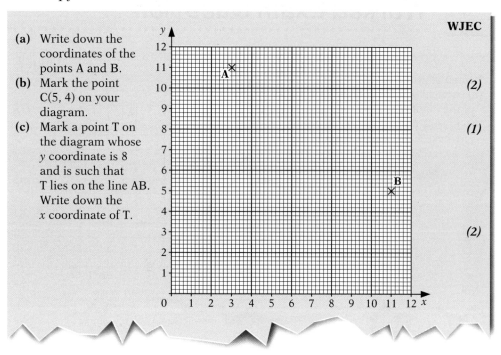

(a) Write down the coordinates of the points A and B.

(b) Mark the point C(5, 4) on your diagram.

(c) Mark a point T on the diagram whose y coordinate is 8 and is such that T lies on the line AB. Write down the x coordinate of T.

(2)

(1)

(2)

WJEC

D Draw a grid with x-values and y-values from −6 to 6.
   (a) On the grid, plot the three points A(−2, −5), B(4, 1) and C(2, 3).
   (b) Join the points A and B with a straight line.
       Write down the coordinates of the mid-point of line AB.
   (c) A, B and C are three corners of a rectangle. Mark and label the fourth corner D. Write down the coordinates of D.

E Use a copy of this.
   (a) Draw a line OP such that OP is 3.9 cm long and OP makes an angle of 53° with the x axis.
       M is the mid-point of the line joining P and Q.
       Mark the position of M on the diagram.

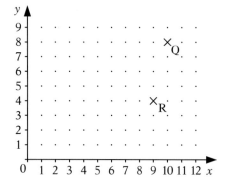

   (b) Specify the position of the point R by finding the distance of R from O and the angle that OR makes with the x-axis.

Straight line graphs

$$y = x + 4 \qquad y = 2x - 3 \qquad y = -3x + 4 \qquad y = 6 - x$$

These are all **equations of straight lines**.
We can use the equation to find some points that lie on the line.

Example Complete this table of values for $y = 4 - x$.

x	-4	-3	-2	-1	0	1	2	3	4
y									

Answer We must find the y-value for each x-value given in the table.

when $x = -4$	**when $x = -3$**	**when $x = -2$**
$y = 4 - (-4)$	$y = 4 - (-3)$	$y = 4 - (-2)$
$\quad = 4 + 4$	$\quad = 4 + 3$	$\quad = 4 + 2$
$\quad = 8$	$\quad = 7$	$\quad = 6$

> Sometimes, once a few values have been found, a pattern may become clear.

Then fill in the table.

x	-4	-3	-2	-1	0	1	2	3	4
y	8	7	6	5	4	3	2	1	0

These points could then be plotted and joined with a straight line to give the graph of $y = 4 - x$.

Note: Sometimes you have to make and fill in the table yourself to find the points to plot.

Worked Exam Question

SEG

(a) On the diagram draw and label the following lines.
   $y = 2x$ and $x + y = 5$ *(4)*
(b) Solve the equation $2x = 5 - x$.   *(2)*

Answer **(a)** Draw up a table of points to plot.
The grid given has x-values from -5 to 6.
Choose some values of x between -5 and 6 for the tables.

x	-5	-3	0	2	4	6
y	-10	-6	0	4	8	12

$y = 2x$

Now plot the points for each table.
Join the points with a straight line.

> Always put equations into the form $y = ...$ using the balance method.

$$x + y = 5$$
$$x + y - x = 5 - x \qquad \text{Subtract } x \text{ from both sides.}$$
$$y = 5 - x$$

x	-5	-3	0	2	4	6
y	10	8	5	3	1	-1

$y = 5 - x$

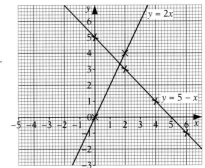

Note: Draw the lines carefully using a sharp pencil.
Note: We only need to plot 2 or 3 points to draw a straight line.

> Just write down the x coordinate when asked to solve an equation using graphs.

(b)   The **x coordinate** of the point where the graphs $y = 2x$ and $y = 5 - x$.
meet is the solution to the equation $2x = 5 - x$.
The solution is **$x = 1.7$** to 1 d.p.

Remember   The graphs of **horizontal** lines have equations $y = a$, for example $y = 5$ or $y = -2$.
The graphs of **vertical** lines have equations $x = b$, for example $x = 7$ or $x = -1$.

Exercise 2   **A**

The graph of the straight line $y = 20 - 4x$ is drawn by plotting the points given in this table and joining them with a straight line.

x	0	2	5
y	20	12	0

WJEC

Draw a grid with x-values from 0 to 6 and y-values from 0 to 20.
(a) (i)   Draw the graph of the straight line $y = 20 - 4x$,
    (ii)   Mark the points A(1, 5) and B(6, 15) and join these points with a straight line.   *(4)*
(b) The line AB meets the line $y = 20 - 4x$ at C.
    (i)   Mark the point C on the diagram.
    (ii)   Write down the coordinates of C.   *(2)*

B   Copy and complete these tables for the equations given.

1. $y = x + 2$

x	-3	-2	0	2	3	4
y						

2. $y = 10 - x$

x	-2	-1	0	1	2
y					

3. $y = 2x + 4$

x	-2	-1	0	1	3
y					

C   Draw a grid with x-values from −4 to 4 and y-values from −2 to 12.
(a)   On your grid, draw the lines $y = x + 2$, $y = 10 - x$ and $y = 2x + 4$ using the tables in question **B**, and label them.
(b)   Write down the coordinates of the point where $y = x + 2$ and $y = 10 - x$ meet.
(c)   Use your graph to solve the equation $10 - x = 2x + 4$.

D   Use a copy of this.
(a) (i)   Plot the points (3, 1) and (7, 5).
        Join the points with a straight line.
    (ii)   The point P(a, 4) lies on the line.
        What is the value of a?
    (iii) The line is extended.
        Complete the following mapping
        for points on the line.
        $3 \rightarrow 1$ $4 \rightarrow 2$
        $10 \rightarrow \ldots$ $x \rightarrow \ldots$

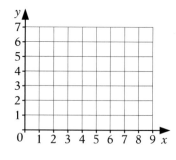

(b)   On the same axes, draw the graph of $y = 6 - x$.
(c)   Solve the equation $x + 2 = 6 - x$.

E   Draw 6 grids with x-values from −5 to 6 and y-values from −10 to 10.
Draw a pair of lines on each grid.
1. $y = x + 1$ and $x = 2$ 2. $x = 3$ and $y = x - 4$
3. $y = 2x + 2$ and $y = 10 - x$ 4. $y = -2$ and $y = 2x - 2$
5. $y = 2x$ and $y = 5 - x$ 6. $y = x + 3$ and $y = 8 - 2x$

F   Use the graph you drew in **E4** to solve the equation $2x - 2 = -2$.

Graphs of $y = x^2 + a$

Graphs of equations which have an
x^2 **term** are **curves**.
We draw them in a similar way to straight line
graphs.

1.   Draw up a table of values for x and y.
2.   Plot these points on a grid.
3.   Join with a **curve**.

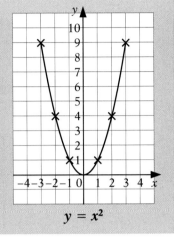

$y = x^2$

Worked Exam Question

NEAB

(a) Complete these tables of values:
  (i)   for the equation $y = 2x$ *(1)*

x	−1	1	3
y			

  (ii) for $y = x^2$.   *(1)*

x	−1	0	1	2	3
y					

(b) On the grid draw graphs of $y = 2x$ and $y = x^2$.   *(3)*

Answer   **(a)** **(i)** When $x = -1$ When $x = 1$ When $x = 3$ **(b)**
                   $y = 2 \times (-1)$ $y = 2 \times 1$ $y = 2 \times 3$
                   $= -2$ $= 2$ $= 6$

So the table is filled in as:

x	−1	1	3
y	−2	2	6

  (ii) When $x = -1$ When $x = 0$ When $x = 1$
            $y = (-1)^2$ $y = 0^2$ $y = 1^2$
            $= -1 \times -1$ $= 0$ $= 1$
            $= 1$

When $x = 2$ When $x = 3$
$= 2^2$ $y = 3^2$
$= 4$ $= 9$

So the table is filled in as:

x	−1	0	1	2	3
y	1	0	1	4	9

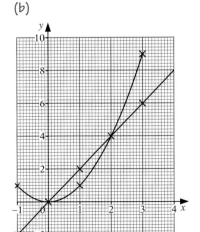

Exercise 3

A   Copy and complete these tables of values for the equation given.

1. $y = x^2 + 1$

x	-2	-1	0	1	2
y					

2. $y = x^2 - 4$

x	-2	-1	0	1	2	3
y						

3. $y = x^2 + 3$

x	-2	-1	0	1	2	3
y						

B   Draw a grid with x-values from -3 to 3 and y-values from -4 to 10.
On your grid draw the graphs of
$$y = x^2 + 1, \qquad y = x^2 - 4 \qquad \text{and} \qquad y = x^2 + 3$$

C   Write down the coordinates of the points where $y = x^2 - 4$ crosses the x-axis.

D   Use a copy of this.

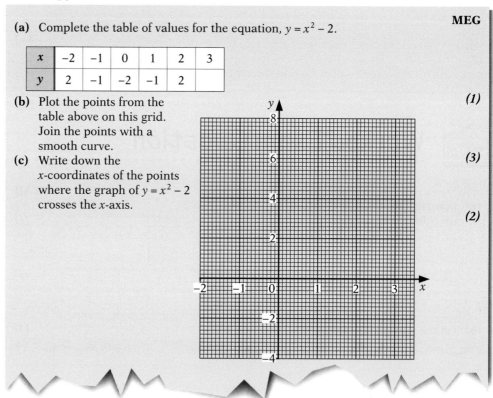

MEG

(a) Complete the table of values for the equation, $y = x^2 - 2$.

x	-2	-1	0	1	2	3
y	2	-1	-2	-1	2	

(b) Plot the points from the table above on this grid. Join the points with a smooth curve.   *(1)*

(c) Write down the x-coordinates of the points where the graph of $y = x^2 - 2$ crosses the x-axis.   *(3)*

(2)

E   The graph of $y = x^2 - 1$ is drawn by plotting the points given in the following table and joining these points with a smooth curve.

x	1	2	3	4	5	6
y	1	3	8	15	24	35

(a) Draw a grid with x-values from 0 to 6 and y-values from 0 to 40.
Use 1 mm grid paper.
On your grid draw the graph of $y = x^2 - 1$.

(b) Plot the points R(1, 25) and S(5, 5).
Join these points with a straight line.
This line meets the curve $y = x^2 - 1$ at P.
Mark the position of P on the diagram.
Write down the coordinates of P.

Homework/Review 1

A This diagram shows a square.
Write down the coordinates of A, B, C and D.

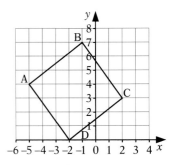

B Write down the equations of these vertical and horizontal lines.

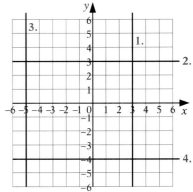

C (a) Given that $y = x - 1$, copy and complete the table of values.

x	−3	−2	−1	0	1	2	3
y							

(b) Draw a grid with x-values from −3 to 3 and y-values from −4 to 3.
Draw the graph of $y = x - 1$.

D Draw a grid with x-values from −6 to 6 and y-values from −10 to 10.
(a) Draw these lines on your grid. Label them.
$$y = 2x - 3 \qquad y = 3 - x$$
(b) Use your graph to solve the equation $2x - 3 = 3 - x$.

E Use a copy of this.

(a) Complete the table of values for the function $y = x^2 - 1$.   *(2)*

x	−2	−1	0	1	2
$y = x^2 - 1$	3			0	

(b) Draw the graph of $y = x^2 - 1$.   *(2)*

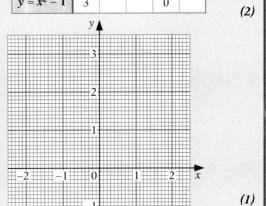

(c) Find the value of y when $x = 1.5$.   *(1)*

Real-life graphs

Conversion graphs

We often use a graph to **convert** between one unit and another.

Examples   Kilojoules and Calories   Pounds Sterling and Deutschmarks

Worked Exam Question

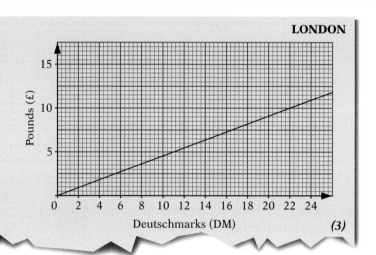

The diagram shows a conversion graph between Pounds (£) and German Deutschmarks (DM). Use the graph to write down how many

(i) Deutschmarks can be exchanged for £10,
(ii) Pounds can be exchanged for 14 Deutschmarks.

(3)

Answer   (i)   Go to £10 on the vertical axis. Draw a horizontal line across to the line given. Draw a vertical line down to the DM scale.
22 Deutschmarks can be exchanged for £10.

(ii)   Go to 14 DM on the horizontal axis. Draw a vertical line up to the line given. Draw a horizontal line across to the £ scale.
Each square is 50p, so **£6.50** can be exchanged for 14 DM.

Exercise 4   **A**   Use the graph given in the **Worked Exam Question** above to answer these.
1. How many pounds can be exchanged for
    (a)   12 DM   (b)   24 DM   (c)   100 DM?
2. How many Deutschmarks can be exchanged for
    (a)   £5   (b)   £9.50   (c)   £100?

B

SEG

Jenny weighs three objects in both kilograms and pounds.
The table shows her results.

Object	A	B	C
Weight in kilograms	2	5	10
Weight in pounds	4.4	11	22

(a) Use Jenny's results to draw a conversion graph between kilograms and pounds.
(2)
(b) A fourth object weighs 15 pounds.
Use your graph to find its weight in kilograms.
(1)

C Penny wrote down how many litres and gallons she used on three journeys.

Litres	13.5	22.5	4.5
Gallons	3	5	1

1. Use this data to draw a conversion graph for changing gallons into litres.
2. Use the conversion graph to convert
   (a) 4 gallons into litres   (b) 27 litres into gallons
   (c) 2 gallons into litres   (d) 17.5 litres into gallons.

Graphs of practical situations

Worked Exam Question

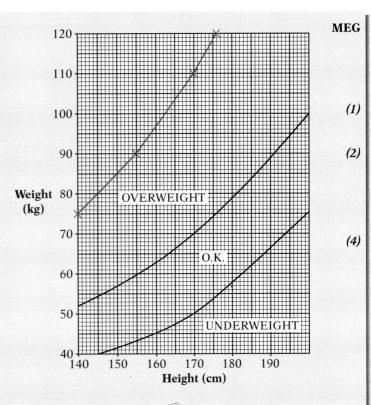

This diagram can be used to divide people into three groups – underweight, O.K. and overweight – according to their heights.

(i) Alphonse is 170 cm tall and weighs 80 kg.
Which group is he in? *(1)*

(ii) Betty is 155 cm tall. If she is in the 'O.K.' group, between what limits does her weight lie? *(2)*

(iii) The line between 'Overweight' and 'Seriously Overweight' passes through the points (140, 75), (155, 90), (170, 110) and (176, 120). Plot these points on the diagram and join them up with a smooth curve. *(4)*

Answer (i) **Overweight**
(ii) Each square on the vertical axis is 1 kg.
The limits are about **43 kg** and **60 kg**.
(iii) This line is shown in red on the diagram.

Exercise 5　A

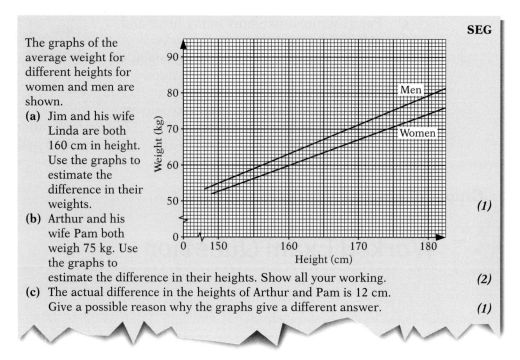

SEG

The graphs of the average weight for different heights for women and men are shown.

(a) Jim and his wife Linda are both 160 cm in height. Use the graphs to estimate the difference in their weights. *(1)*

(b) Arthur and his wife Pam both weigh 75 kg. Use the graphs to estimate the difference in their heights. Show all your working. *(2)*

(c) The actual difference in the heights of Arthur and Pam is 12 cm. Give a possible reason why the graphs give a different answer. *(1)*

B The table shows the charge for using different units of electricity.

Units	0	100	250	350	450	500
Charge (£)	5	17	35	47	59	65

1. Plot these points on a grid.
   Have 'Units' along the horizontal axis.
2. Use your graph to find the charge for using
   (a) 300 units　(b) 400 units　(c) 480 units.
3. How many units of electricity have you used if you are charged
   (a) £25　(b) £40　(c) £60?

C

WJEC

In some rectangles the length is twice the width. If the width of such a rectangle is denoted by x cm, and its area by y cm^2, then x and y are connected by the equation:　$y = 2x^2$

(a) Complete the table which shows the values of y for some values of x.

x	0	0.5	1	1.5	2	2.5	3	3.5
y	0	0.5	2		8	12.5		24.5

(2)

(b) Use a copy of the grid on the next page.
Plot the points represented in the table and draw the graph of y against x. *(3)*

You must show on your graph how you obtain your answer to (c).
(c) Use your graph to find the width of such a rectangle which has an area of 11 cm^2. *(1)*

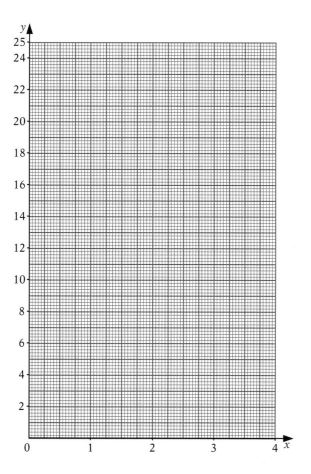

Travel graphs

Travel graphs or distance–time graphs tell us about journeys.

Example This distance–time graph shows the car journey Mrs Brown took to pick up her daughter.

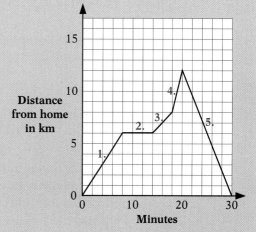

1. The car travels 6 km in the first 8 minutes.
2. Then it stops for 6 minutes.

Note: **A horizontal part of the graph means no distance is being covered. The vehicle must be stopped.**

3. The car travels 2 km in 4 minutes.
4. The car speeds up and travels 4 km in 2 minutes.

Note: **A steeper slope means the speed is faster.**

5. The car travels back home. It travels 12 km in 10 minutes.

Note: **When the slope of the line is to the right (\\) travel is in the opposite direction.**

Worked Exam Question

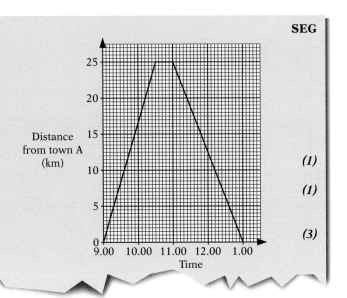

SEG

A cyclist leaves town A at 9.00 a.m., cycles to town B, then returns to town A. The distance–time graph of the cyclist's journey is shown.

(a) What is the distance between town A and town B?   *(1)*

(b) How long did the cyclist stay in town?   *(1)*

(c) How far was the cyclist from town B at 12.30 p.m.?   *(3)*

Distance from town A (km)

Time

Answer   (a)   The furthest distance the cyclist is from town A is 25 km.
So town B must be **25 km** from town A.

(b)   The graph is horizontal from 10.30 a.m. to 11 a.m.
The cyclist stopped in town for **30 minutes** or $\frac{1}{2}$ **an hour.**

(c)   At 12.30 p.m. the cyclist was 6 kilometres from town A.
Town B is 25 km from town A, so the cyclist was $25 - 6 = $ **19 km** from town B.

Exercise 6   **A**   Rachel walks to the park, plays a game of soccer and walks home.

1. How far from home is the park?
2. How many minutes did it take Rachel to walk to the park?
3. How long did she stay at the park?
4. Did she walk to the park faster than she walked home?

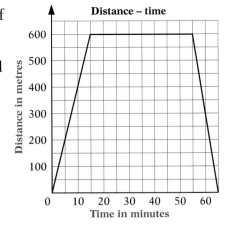

B   This graph shows Arshard's car journey from home to his aunt's, and back home again.

1. How far away does his aunt live?
2. For how long did he stop during the journey to his aunt's?
3. How long did he stay at his aunt's?
4. How far did he travel in the first hour?
5. What was his average speed on the way home?

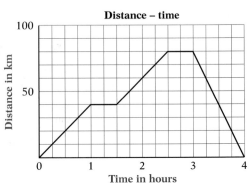

C   Use a copy of this.

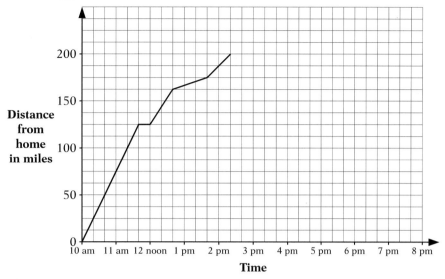

The graph represents Guy's journey from home to London.

1. Guy stopped for lunch on the way.
   (a) Write down the time at which he stopped.
   (b) For how long did he stop?
2. At 12.40 Guy had to slow down because of slow traffic.
   For how many miles did he travel at this slower speed?
3. Guy spent an hour visiting friends in London. He then returned home, travelling at a steady speed of 50 miles an hour.

Use this information to complete the graph of his journey.

D   Use a copy of this.

The graph represents the journey of a train from town A to town B and then to town C.

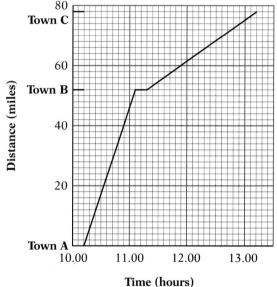

1. What was the average speed of the train from town A to town B?
2. How long did the train wait at town B?
3. The average speed of the train between town A and town B is greater than its average speed between town B and town C. Without calculating any average speed, explain how the graph shows this.
4. Another train starts at town B at 10.30 and travels nonstop to town A at an average speed of 60 m.p.h. Draw the graph of its journey on the grid.
5. Use your graph to write down the time this train arrives at town A.
6. Write down how far from town B the trains were when they passed each other.

Homework/Review 2

A

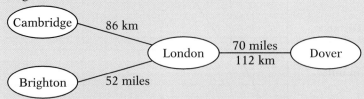

The road distances between London and three other towns are shown on the diagram.   **SEG**

Cambridge — 86 km

London — 70 miles / 112 km — Dover

Brighton — 52 miles

(a) Using the data from the London–Dover route draw a graph for converting miles into kilometres.   *(2)*
(b) How many kilometres is it from London to Brighton?   *(1)*
(c) How many miles is it from London to Cambridge?   *(1)*

B Use a copy of this.
This is a graph for working out an approximate cost of a certain type of lino.

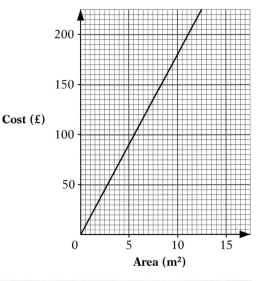

1. Use the graph to find the cost of lino for an area of 11 m². **Cost (£)**
2. Find the cost per square metre of this lino.
3. Another type of lino costs £8 per square metre.
   Draw a line on the grid which can be used to find the cost of different sizes of this lino.

Area (m²)

C

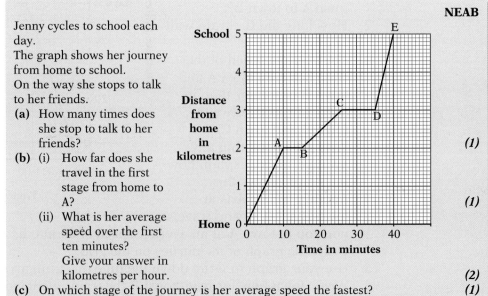

NEAB

Jenny cycles to school each day.
The graph shows her journey from home to school.
On the way she stops to talk to her friends.

(a) How many times does she stop to talk to her friends?   *(1)*

(b) (i) How far does she travel in the first stage from home to A?   *(1)*

   (ii) What is her average speed over the first ten minutes?
   Give your answer in kilometres per hour.   *(2)*

(c) On which stage of the journey is her average speed the fastest?   *(1)*

✔ KEY POINTS

- ✔ The **coordinates** of a point are given as (x, y). The first number is the x coordinate. The second number is the y coordinate.

  Example   For the point $(3, -2)$ the x coordinate is 3 and the y coordinate is -2.

- ✔ A **straight line** graph can be described by an equation.
  We use the equation to draw the graph by following these steps.

    1. Choose x-values and put them in a table.
       Sometimes this is done for you.
    2. Using the equation, work out the y-values.
    3. Plot the points in the table onto a grid.
    4. Join the points with a straight line.

- ✔ **Vertical lines** have the equation $x = b$ where b is a number.

  Example $x = 2$ $x = -3$

- ✔ **Horizontal lines** have the equation $y = a$ where a is a number.

  Example $y = -1$ $y = 5$

- ✔ $y = x^2 + a$ is the equation of a curve.
  We draw the graph in the same way as for a straight line except we join the points with a smooth curve.

- ✔ We can draw the graph of a **real-life situation** by plotting the points given on a table and joining them with a straight line.

- ✔ **Conversion graphs** can be used to convert between one unit and another.

  Example   Pounds Sterling and Deutschmarks
            Degrees Fahrenheit and degrees Celsius

- ✔ **Distance–time graphs** give us information about a journey.
  The steeper the slope the faster the speed.
  When the line is horizontal the movement has stopped.
  If a line slopes to the right (╲) the person or vehicle is travelling in the opposite direction.

◄◄ CHAPTER REVIEW ◄◄

Ask your teacher for the grids that go with questions D and E.

◄◄

Exercise 1
on page 251

A   Use a copy of this.

MEG

(i)   On the grid on the next page, plot the points A(20, 10) and B(20, 50).   *(1)*
(ii) Join AB with a straight line.
      Draw the circle with AB as the diameter.   *(1)*
(iii) Two points on the circle have y coordinate 18.
      Write down the x coordinates of these points.   *(2)*

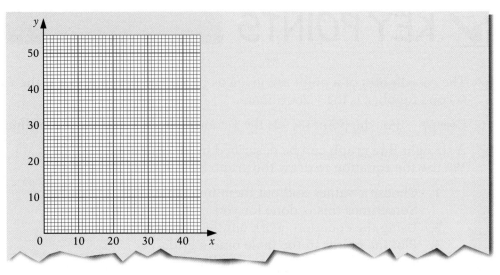

◄◄

Exercise 2
on page 254

B Use a copy of this.

(a) On the graph draw the line $y = 4 - x$ for values of x from −4 to 4.

(b) What are the coordinates of the points where the graph $y = 4 - x$ meets the curve?

SEG

(3)

(2)

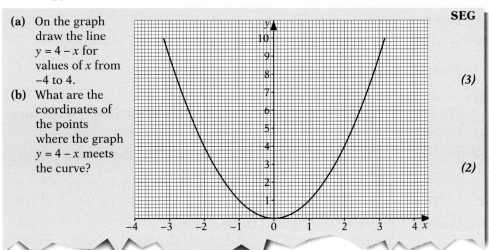

◄◄

Exercise 3
on page 256

C Use a copy of this.

(a) Complete this table, which gives values of $x^2 + 2$ for values of x from −2 to 4.

(b) On the graph paper draw the graph of $y = x^2 + 2$ for values of x from −2 to 4.

WJEC

x	−2	−1	0	1	2	3	4
$x^2 + 2$	6		2	3	6		18

(1)

(3)

◀◀
Exercise 4
on page 258

D

WJEC

At the bottom of a CEEFAX page is the following table which shows how ° Celsius can be changed into ° Fahrenheit.

°C	−5	0	5	10	15	20	25	30	35
°F	23	32	41	50	59	68	77	86	95

(i)   Use the above information to draw a conversion graph for changing °C into °F.

Use your graph to
(ii)   change 80°F to °C,
(iii) change −10°C to °F. **(5)**

◀◀
Exercise 5
on page 260

E

WJEC

When you look into a glass of water, the depth of the water appears to be less than the real depth. The depth that the water appears to have is called the apparent depth. The real depth of water in the glass is denoted by r cm and the apparent depth is denoted by a cm. The table below gives five values of r

r	2	4	7	9	12
a	1.5	3	5.25	6.75	9

and the corresponding values of a.
(a)   Plot the points represented in the table and draw the graph of a against r. **(3)**

You must show on your graph how you obtain your answers to (b) and (c).
(b)   Use your graph to find the apparent depth of water when the real depth is 5 cm. **(1)**
(c)   Use your graph to find the real depth of water when the apparent depth is 8.5 cm. **(1)**

◀◀
Exercise 6
on page 262

F

MEG

The graph shows Philip's cycle journey between his home and the sports centre.

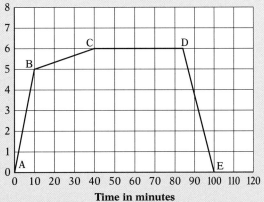

(a)   Explain what happened between C and D. **(1)**
(b)   Explain what changed at B. **(1)**
(c)   Explain what happened at E. **(1)**
(d)   Work out the total distance that Philip travelled. **(1)**

18 Ratio and Proportion

By the end of this chapter you will be able to:

- write a ratio in its simplest form
- solve ratio and proportion problems
- read scales on drawings and maps
- share in a given ratio.

Getting started ....

This small hand print was left behind
at the scene of a crime.
How could you use the hand print to
estimate the height of the person?
How tall do you estimate the person
to be?

Ratio

A **ratio** compares quantities of the same kind.

Example There are 28 boys and 23 girls in a club.
The ratio of boys to girls is 28 : 23.

A ratio must be written in its **simplest form**.
To **simplify a ratio**, divide both parts by the same number.

Example The ratio of red to white squares is 6 : 3.

$$\overset{\div 3}{\underset{\div 3}{6 : 3 = 2 : 1}}$$
          Divide both numbers by 3.

2 : 1 is a ratio in its simplest or lowest terms.

The quantities in a ratio must have the **same units**.

Example Sonal had £4.20. Jennifer had 70p.
To find the ratio of what Sonal had to what Jennifer had we must
change £4.20 into pence.
£4.20 = 420p
The ratio is
420 : 70 = 6 : 1   Divide both numbers by 70.

Exercise 1

A For each of these diagrams, write the ratio of red parts to white parts. Simplify the ratio if possible.

1.   2.   3.   4.   5.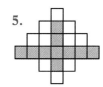

B

Write these as ratios in their lowest terms
1. amount Lennie has to the amount Mia has
2. amount Mia has to the amount Jake has
3. amount Jake has to the amount Lennie has

C In a tennis club there are 63 junior players.
27 of these are boys.
Write, in its simplest form, the ratio of junior girls
to junior boys.

D Write these ratios in their lowest terms.
1. 60 cm to 1 metre   2. 60p to £2   3. £8 to 25p
4. 400 g to 2 kg   5. 150 ml to 3 ℓ   6. 8p to £3

E Jan used 150 g of sugar and 240 g of flour.
Write the grams of sugar to the grams of flour as a ratio in its lowest terms.

F The ratio of boys to girls at a party was 2 : 3.
Write down the number of boys and girls that could have been at the party.

G If $\frac{1}{4}$ of a class of 36 is boys, what is the ratio of boys to girls?

Proportion

2 : 3	4 : 6	20 : 30	24 : 36

All of the ratios in the box are **equivalent**.
They all equal 2 : 3 when put in their simplest form.

We use equivalent ratios to solve **proportion** problems.

Example   Find x if $5 : 8 = 30 : x$.

Answer   5 : 8 and 30 : x are equivalent.

         ×6

$5 : 8 = 30 : x$ **5 was multiplied by 6 to get 30.**

         ×6

$5 : 8 = 30 : 48$ **8 must also be multiplied by 6 to find the value of x.**
$x = 48$

Worked Exam Question

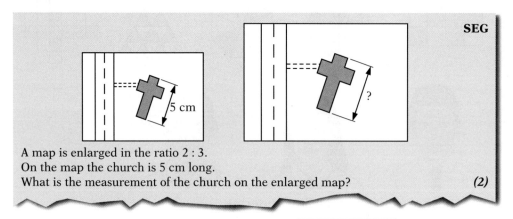

SEG

5 cm

?

A map is enlarged in the ratio 2 : 3.
On the map the church is 5 cm long.
What is the measurement of the church on the enlarged map? *(2)*

Answer

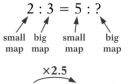

2 : 3 = 5 : ?

small big small big
map   map map   map

> We must be careful to write a proportion with the equivalent ratios in the correct order.

×2.5

2 : 3 = 5 : 7.5   2 × 2.5 = 5

×2.5

So the church is **7.5 cm** *on the enlarged* map.

Exercise 2

A Work out the value of x.

1. $1 : 2 = 5 : x$ 2. $4 : 3 = 12 : x$ 3. $4 : 7 = x : 28$
4. $5 : 3 = 25 : x$ 5. $1 : 2 = x : 320$ 6. $7 : 3 = x : 51$

B The ratio of nurses to doctors in a ward is 7 : 2.
There are 14 nurses in the ward.
How many doctors are there?

C The ratio of the number of butterflies to the
number of bugs in a Bugs and Butterflies
Exhibition is 1 : 3.
There are 120 butterflies in the exhibition.
How many bugs are there?

D The ratio of men to women at a concert was 4 : 5.
There were 240 men at the concert.
How many women were there?

E A photo is enlarged in the ratio 5 : 9.
On the original photo a bridge is 2.5 cm long.
How long is the bridge in the enlarged photo?

F The ratio of the number of cats in a show this year to the number of cats
last year is 3 : 2.
Last year there were 38 cats in the show.
How many cats were there this year?

Worked Exam Question

. . . .

SEG

A sponge cake for five people needs 75 g of sugar.
John makes a sponge cake for eight people.
(a) Calculate the weight of sugar he needs. *(2)*
The small cake serves five people.
The larger cake serves eight people.
(b) Calculate the percentage increase in the number of people served by
making the larger cake. *(2)*

Answer **(a)** The ratio of the number of people the cakes will serve is 5 : 8.
So the ratio of sugar needed is 75 : ?
These are equivalent ratios, so 5 : 8 = 75 : ?

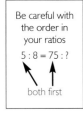

Be careful with
the order in
your ratios

5 : 8 = 75 : ?

both first

$$\overset{\times 15}{5 : 8 = 75 : 120}\underset{\times 15}{}$$

$5 \times 15 = 75$
$8 \times 15 = 120$

So **120 g** of sugar are needed for 8 people.

(b) Actual increase = 3 people.

$$\% \text{ increase} = \frac{\text{actual increase}}{\text{original amount}} \times 100\%$$

$$= \frac{3}{5} \times 100\%$$

$$= 60\%$$

The percentage increase is **60%**.

Exercise 3 **A**

MEG

The recipe below is for a cheesecake for 8 people.

Wheatmeal biscuit crumbs	160 g
Butter	50 g
Cream cheese	640 g
Caster sugar	70 g

(i) Calculate the amount of butter required to make a cheesecake for 4
people. *(1)*
(ii) Calculate the amount of caster sugar required to make a cheesecake for
12 people. *(2)*

B This is a recipe for 12 scones.

> 300 g flour
> 125 g butter
> 50 g dried fruit
> water to mix

(a) How much dried fruit is needed for 24 scones?
(b) How much flour would you need for 50 scones?

C   The recipe shows the ingredients needed to make some small cakes.

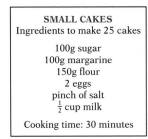

> **SMALL CAKES**
> Ingredients to make 25 cakes
>
> 100g sugar
> 100g margarine
> 150g flour
> 2 eggs
> pinch of salt
> $\frac{1}{2}$ cup milk
>
> Cooking time: 30 minutes

1. How much sugar is needed to make 60 cakes?
2. How much flour is needed to make 108 cakes?
3. How many eggs are needed to make 60 cakes?

D   **MEG**

Here is a recipe for chocolate pudding for 4 people.

Nadia is making the pudding for 6 people.
(i)   How many eggs will she need?   **(1)**
(ii)   Find the amount of milk she needs.   **(1)**
(iii) Find the amount of vanilla essence she needs.   **(1)**

> *Rich chocolate pudding*
>
> 100 g   Flour
> 75 g   Plain chocolate
> 50 g   Butter
> 300 ml   Milk
> 65 g   Sugar
> $\frac{1}{2}$ tsp   Vanilla essence
> 2   eggs

Scale drawing

> **Scales** on maps or plans are often written as ratios.
>
> **Example**   1 : 500
> This means every centimetre on the map represents 500 cm in real life.

Worked Exam Question

· ·

A map has a scale of 1 : 5000.   **WJEC**
(a) The distance between two places on the map is 6 cm. What is the real life distance, in metres, between these two places?   **(2)**
(b) The real life distance between two landmarks is 1.2 kilometres. What is the distance, in cm between these landmarks on the map?   **(2)**

Answer   (a)   1 : 5000 = 6 : ?
                     1 : 5000 = 6 : 30 000
                        ×6   ×6

                       So 6 cm represents 30 000 cm or **300 m**.

             30 000 cm = 30 000 ÷ 100 m
                         = 300 m

         (b)   1.2 km   = 1200 m
                       = 120 000 cm
             1 : 5000 =   ? : 120 000
             1 : 5000 = 24 : 120 000   *So 1.2 km is represented by* **24 cm**.
                   ×24   ×24

Exercise 4

A A map has a scale of 1 : 100.
   1. What is the real life distance if the distance on the map is
       (a) 4 cm   **(b)** 10 cm   **(c)** 15.2 cm   **(d)** 24.6 cm   **(e)** 0.8 cm?
   2. What is the distance, in centimetres, on the map if the real life distance
       is   **(a)** 800 cm   **(b)** 6 m   **(c)** 4.7 m   **(d)** 12.3 m   **(e)** 60 cm?

B The plan of a house is drawn to a scale of 1 : 200.
   1. On the plan the length, in metres, of the house is 12 cm.
       What is the actual length of the house?
   2. The actual length of one of the bedrooms is 4 m.
       How long will this be on the plan?
       Give your answer in centimetres.

C This diagram shows the plan for
      a new classroom.
   1. What is the actual length, in
       metres, of the classroom?
   2. What is the actual width, in
       metres, of the classroom?
   3. What is the actual width, in
       metres, of the doorway?
   4. What is the actual length, in
       metres, of the whiteboard?

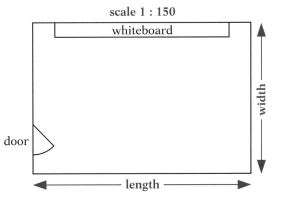

D

SEG

The plan of a house is drawn to a scale of 1 : 50.
On the plan the length of the hall is 15 cm.
What is the actual length of the hall in metres?

(2)

E This shows Mrs Todd's plans for a new kitchen.
      The scale is 1 : 50.

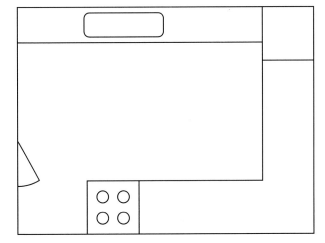

   1. What is the actual length, in metres, of the kitchen?
   2. What is the actual width of the door?
   3. How wide would the door be if it was made 20% bigger?

Finding the value of 1 unit

We can solve proportion problems by finding **the value of 1 unit**.

Example   Eight chocolate bars cost £2.48.
Find the cost of 5 chocolate bars.

Answer   **Step 1**   Find the cost of *one* chocolate bar.
One chocolate bar costs 31p. $248 \div 8 = 31$

Step 2   Multiply the cost of one chocolate bar by 5. $31 \times 5 = 155$
Five chocolate bars cost £1.55.

Exercise 5

A   Nine cakes cost £4.95.
1. How much does one cake cost?
2. How much do these cost?
(a) 4 cakes   (b) 7 cakes   (c) 15 cakes

B   Kishan bought 15 raffle tickets for £22.50.
1. How much does one raffle ticket cost?
2. How much do these cost?
(a) 8 raffle tickets   (b) 12 raffle tickets   (c) 19 raffle tickets

C   The accommodation for 30 students on a sports trip is £1050.
How much would the same accommodation cost for these numbers of students?
1. 10   **2.** 35   **3.** 64   **4.** 23

D   This recipe is for steamed pudding.
It serves 8 people.
1. How much butter would be needed to make a steamed pudding for 10 people?
2. How many eggs would be needed to make a steamed pudding for 28 people?

STEAMED PUDDING (8 people)
100 g butter
$\frac{1}{2}$ cup sugar
2 eggs
1 tsp vanilla
230 g flour
$\frac{1}{2}$ tsp baking powder

E   A car travels at 80 km per hour.
1. How long, in minutes, does it take to travel 1 km?
2. The car keeps travelling at the same speed.
How long does it take to travel
(a) 50 km   (b) 120 km   (c) 325 km?

F   Rose had a recipe that used 470 g flour and made 60 cakes.
She had only 1 kg of flour but plenty of the other ingredients needed.
What is the maximum number of cakes she can make?

Puzzles

1.   Ron can clean his car in 3 hours.
His little brother takes 6 hours to clean the same car.
How long will they take if they both work together?

2.   Chris needs 2 hours to do a job. His brother can do the same job in 1 hour.
How long would it take both of them working together to do the job?

Sharing in a given ratio

Often things are **shared in a given ratio**.

Example   Menna shared her sweets with her sister in the ratio 3 : 1.
This means Menna got 3 times as many sweets as her sister.

Example   Three brothers shared some money in the ratio 3 : 2 : 1.
This means one brother got 3 shares, another got 2 and the third got 1 share.
Out of every £6, £3 went to one brother, £2 to another and £1 to the third brother.

To share in a given ratio, follow these steps.

Step 1   Add the shares or parts in the ratio.
Step 2   Find the size of one share or part.
Step 3   Multiply the answer to **Step 2** by each number of shares or parts given in the ratio.

Worked Exam Questions

1.   A test is taken by a class of 28 pupils.
The ratio of the number of boys to the number of girls in the class is 3 : 4.
How many boys take the test?

SEG

(2)

Answer   Step 1   The class is divided into $3 + 4 = 7$ parts.
Step 2   One part is $28 \div 7 = 4$.
Step 3   The boys make up 3 parts.
$3 \times 4 = 12$

There are **12** boys taking the test.

2.   In a TV game show, the winners share the prize money, £2400, in proportion to their scores.
Lee, Siân and Heulwen are the winners with scores of 24, 28 and 12 respectively.
Calculate how much money **each** person wins.

WJEC

(3)

Answer   The prize money is shared in the ratio 24 : 28 : 12.

Step 1   There are $24 + 28 + 12 = 64$ shares in total.
Step 2   One share is $£2400 \div 64 = £37.50$.
Step 3   **Lee** gets 24 shares.
She gets $24 \times £37.50 = £\mathbf{900}$.
Siân gets 28 shares.
She gets $28 \times £37.50 = £\mathbf{1050}$.
Heulwen gets 12 shares.
She gets $12 \times £37.50 = £\mathbf{450}$.

Check that £900 + £1050 + £450 add up to £2400.

Exercise 6

A
1. Share £100 in the ratio 2 : 3.
2. Share £6800 in the ratio 5 : 3.
3. Share £621.50 in the ratio 4 : 7.
4. Share £348 in the ratio 3 : 2 : 1.
5. Share £806 in the ratio 6 : 3 : 1.
6. Share £6234 in the ratio 5 : 2 : 3.
7. Share £784 in the ratio 4 : 3 : 1.
8. Share £321.30 in the ratio 4 : 5.

B   Olivia and Lucy buy a house for £48 000.
They pay for it in the ratio 3 : 5.
How much did each pay?

C   Bill and Joan save £1200 for a holiday. They
divide the money in the ratio 3 : 2. How much
money did each get?

D   Trish and Jason share £800 in the ratio 5 : 3.
1. How much does each of them receive?
2. Jason gives £90 of his share to his mother.
What percentage is this of his share?

E

> Malika's father won £128.   **LONDON**
>
> He shared the £128 between his three children in the ratio 6 : 3 : 1.
> Malika was given the biggest share.
>
> Work out how much money Malika received.   *(3)*

F

> A family packet of Crunchy Crispies weighs 500 g.   **SEG**
> Crunchy Crispies contain nuts and cornflakes.
> The nuts and cornflakes are mixed by weight in the ratio 1 : 3.
> What is the weight of the nuts in each family packet?   *(2)*

G   There are 32 people on a bus.
The ratio of adults to children is 3 : 5.
How many children are on the bus?

H   Marcus and Betty bought a £2 raffle ticket.
Marcus paid 80p and Betty paid £1.20.
The raffle ticket won a prize of £225.
How should Marcus and Betty share this prize?

I   The ratio of length of advertisements to length of
programmes on TV one evening from 6 p.m. to
11 p.m. was 3 : 7.
1. How long in total were the advertisements?
2. How much of the time from 6 p.m. to 11 p.m. was programmes?

Homework/Review

A 1. Write the number of shaded squares to the number of white squares as a ratio in its lowest terms.
  2. The ratio is to be changed so that the ratio of shaded squares to white squares is 4 : 1. How many more squares must be shaded?

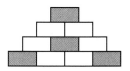

B Tina had 2 m of fabric. She used 40 cm of it.
Write as a ratio in its lowest terms the amount she used to the amount she has left.

C

A cake is made from fat, flour and sugar.
The cake weighs 110 g.
The weight of the sugar is 42 g.

  (a) The ratio of the weight of flour to the weight of sugar is 3 : 2. What is the weight of the flour?

SEG

(2)

D 1. The ratio of paperback to hardback books in a sale is 5 : 2.
There are 2750 paperback books in the sale.
How many hardback books are there?
  2. A map is enlarged in the ratio 2 : 9.
On the original map, town A and town B are 3.5 cm apart.
How far apart are these towns on the enlarged map?

E

The seating plan of a theatre is drawn to a scale of 1 : 80.
On the plan the width of a seat is 0.5 cm.
What is the actual width of a seat?

SEG

(2)

F

NEAB

Money from the lottery was given to good causes.
Two of the good causes were swimming and athletics.
80 million pounds was shared between these two sports in the ratio

　　　swimming : athletics
　　　　　3 : 1

Calculate the amount that was given to swimming.

(2)

G

WJEC
(2)

Share £140 in the ratio 5 : 2.

---

278 Ratio and Proportion

H | George has £80.50 to share between his two nieces. | **NEAB**

He decides to divide the money in the ratio of their ages.
Ann is 8 years old and Joan is 15 years old.

How much will Ann receive? *(3)*

I Share £2800 in the ratio 2 : 3 : 2.

✔ KEY POINTS

✔ A **ratio** compares quantities of the same kind.
 Example In a cage there are 5 black kittens and 3 ginger ones.
 The ratio of black kittens to ginger kittens is 5 : 3.

✔ We always write ratios in their **lowest terms**.
 We can simplify a ratio if we can divide both parts by the same number.
 Example

 $21 : 14 = 3 : 2$ **Divide both parts by 7.** ($\div 7$)

21 : 14 and 3 : 2 are **equivalent** ratios.

✔ The quantities in a ratio must have the same units.
 The units are not put in the ratio.
 Example To find the ratio of 25p to £2.50, £2.50 must be changed to 250p.

 $25 : 250 = 1 : 10$ ($\div 25$)

✔ We can use **equivalent ratios** to solve **proportion** problems.
 Example $3 : 2 = ? : 8$

 $3 : 2 = 12 : 8$ ($\times 4$)

✔ We can solve **proportion** problems by finding the value of **one** unit.
 Example To find the cost of 15 pies if 9 pies cost £10.80 follow these steps.
 Step 1 **Find the cost of one pie**.
 One pie costs £1.20. $10.80 \div 9 = 1.2$
 Step 2 **Find the cost of 15 pies**.
 Multiply the cost of one pie by 15. $1.20 \times 15 = 18$
 15 pies cost £18.

✔ To **share in a given ratio** follow these steps.
 Step 1 Find the total number of shares.
 Step 2 Find the value of one share.
 Step 3 Find the value of the shares given by the ratio.

 Example Mr Begum left £16 650 to his 3 daughters to be shared in the ratio 4 : 3 : 2.
 How much did each get?
 Step 1 There are 4 + 3 + 2 = 9 shares.
 Step 2 One share is £16 650 ÷ 9 = £1850.
 Step 3 One daughter gets 4 × £1850 = £7400.
 Another daughter gets 3 × £1850 = £5550.
 The third daughter gets 2 × £1850 = £3700.

◄◄ CHAPTER REVIEW ◄◄

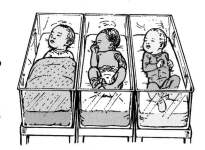

◄◄ Exercise 1 on page 269

A In a hospital, 400 babies were born during August.
220 of them were girls.
What is the ratio   Boy babies : Girl babies?
Give your answer in its lowest terms.

◄◄ Exercise 2 on page 270

B At a rally, the ratio of classic cars to modern cars was 2 : 7.
There were 120 classic cars.
How many modern cars were at the rally?

◄◄ Exercise 4 on page 273

C

> Terry is making a doll's house as a model of his own house to a scale of 1 : 30.   **WJEC**
> **(a)** He measures the height of the front door in his own house and finds it is 210 cm.
>   Calculate the height of the front door in the doll's house.   **(2)**
> **(b)** The height of the doll's house is 29 cm. Calculate the height, in metres, of Terry's house.   **(2)**

◄◄ Exercise 5 on page 274

D 1. Find the cost of 17 jam rolls if 8 jam rolls cost £14.80.
2. How long will it take a lorry travelling at 100 km/h to travel 120 km?

◄◄ Exercise 6 on page 276

E

> Ann, Tony and Peter serve in a restaurant. They agree to share tips in the   **WJEC**
> ratio of the money spent on meals at the tables at which they serve.
> The amounts of money spent on meals served by Ann, Tony and Peter are
> £180, £130 and £90 respectively. The total amount received in tips was
> £36. What share should each get?   **(3)**

◄◄ Exercise 3 on page 271

F

> Fred has a recipe for 30 biscuits.   **LONDON**
>
> Here is a list of ingredients for 30 biscuits
>
> Self-raising flour   :   230 g
> Butter   :   150 g
> Caster sugar   :   100 g
> Eggs   :   2
>
> Fred wants to make 45 biscuits.
> **(a)** Copy and complete his new list of ingredients for 45 biscuits,
>
> Self-raising flour   :
> Butter   :
> Caster sugar   :
> Eggs   :   **(3)**
>
> Gill has only 1 kilogram of self-raising flour. She has plenty of the other ingredients.
> **(b)** Work out the maximum number of biscuits that Gill could bake.   **(3)**

19 Transformations

By the end of this chapter you will be able to:

- reflect a shape in a mirror line
- write down the equation of the mirror line for a given reflection
- rotate a shape about a given centre of rotation by a $\frac{1}{4}$, $\frac{1}{2}$ or $\frac{3}{4}$ turn
- describe and carry out a translation
- enlarge a shape by a positive scale factor
- enlarge a shape with a given centre of enlargement
- describe transformations
- tessellate a shape.

Getting started ....

Tangrams

You will need   thin card, scissors

Paste a copy of this square onto thin card.
Cut out the seven pieces.
Use all of your seven pieces to make the shapes below.

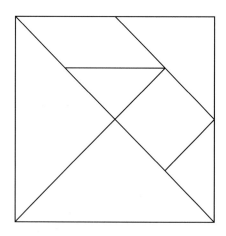

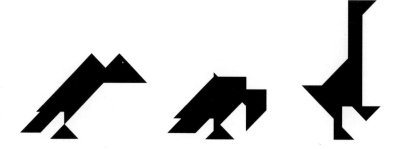

Reflection

We are often asked to **reflect** a shape in a **mirror line**.

Example   The red E has been reflected in the mirror line to get the black E.

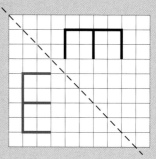

Sometimes we are given the **equation of the mirror line**.

Example   The square ABCD is reflected in the line $x = -1$.
What are the new coordinates of D?

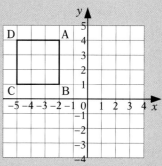

Answer   First draw the line $x = -1$.
Reflect ABCD in this line.
The new coordinates of D are (3, 4).

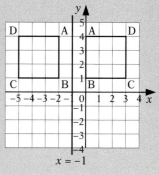

> **Note:** Sometimes the **image** of **ABCD** is called **A′ B′ C′ D′**.
> The dash on the letter means it is an image point.

Exercise 1   **A**   Use a copy of this.
Reflect each shape in the mirror line.

1.

mirror line

2.

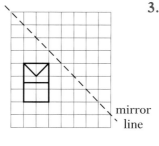

mirror line

3.

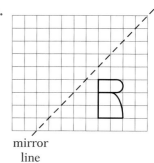

mirror line

B Use a copy of this.

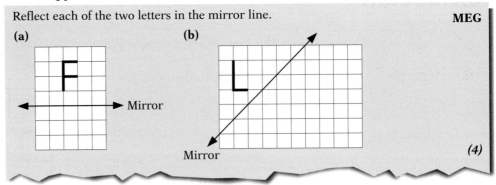

Reflect each of the two letters in the mirror line. **MEG**

(a)   (b)

Mirror

Mirror

(4)

C Use a copy of this.
Reflect the shape P in the mirror line.
Label the reflected shape Q.

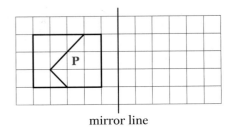

mirror line

D Copy this diagram.
The rectangle ABCD is reflected
in the line $y = -1$.
Write down the coordinates of
A′, B′, C′ and D′.

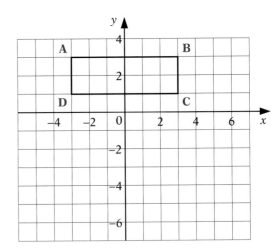

E Triangle PQR is reflected in the y-axis to
give triangle STU.

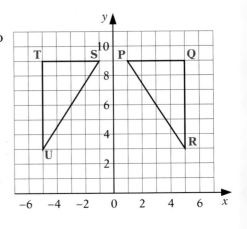

Points	Coordinates	Points	Coordinates
P	(1,9)	S	
Q	(5,9)	T	
R		U	

1. Copy and complete this table for the
   coordinates.
2. If the point A(23, 12) was reflected
   in the y-axis what would be the
   coordinates of the reflected point?
3. If the point (−7, −21) was reflected in the y-axis, what would be the
   coordinates of the reflected point?

Sometimes we are asked to write down the **equation of the mirror line**.

Example

Mirror lines usually have equations such as:
$y = a$ (a horizontal line)
$x = b$ (a vertical line)
where a and b are numbers.
$y = x$
$y = -x$

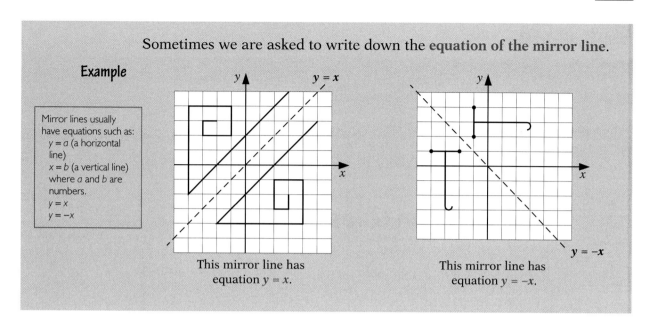

This mirror line has equation $y = x$.

This mirror line has equation $y = -x$.

Exercise 2

Shape A is reflected to give shape B.
Write down the equation of the mirror line.

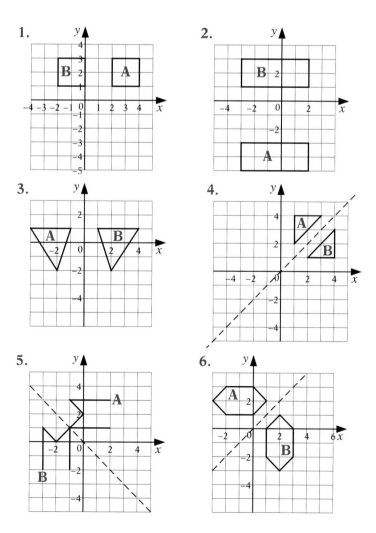

1.

2.

3.

4.

5.

6.

Rotation

When we **rotate** a shape we turn it around a fixed point.
It is best to use tracing paper.

Remember Clockwise is the direction hands move on a clock.

$\frac{1}{4}$ turn = 90° $\frac{1}{2}$ turn = 180° $\frac{3}{4}$ turn = 270°

 # Worked Exam Question

(a) (i) Rotate triangle *PQR* through 180° about the point *O*. Label as *S* the image of *Q*.

MEG
(2)

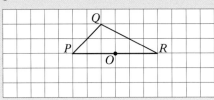

(ii) Name the special quadrilateral *PQRS*. *(1)*
(b) Draw, and name, **two** other special types of quadrilateral. *(4)*

Answer   (a) (i)   180° is a half turn.

Use tracing paper to help.

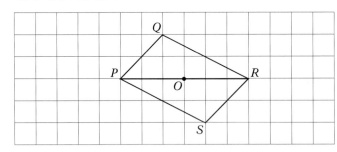

(ii) Parallelogram

(b) You could draw and name two of these.

square   rectangle   kite   trapezium   rhombus

**Note: The centre of rotation is the point about which a shape is rotated.
The centre of rotation in the worked exam question above is O.**

Exercise 3   **A**   Use a copy of this.

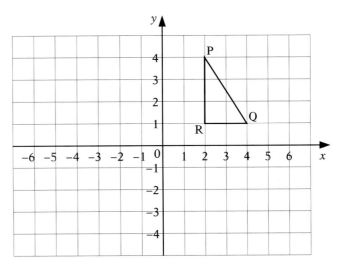

1. Rotate triangle PQR 90° clockwise about (0, 0).
    Label the new triangle ABC.
2. Reflect triangle PQR in the *x*-axis.
    Label the new triangle LMN.
3. Rotate triangle PQR 270° clockwise about (0, 0)
    Label the new triangle DEF.

B   Use a copy of this.

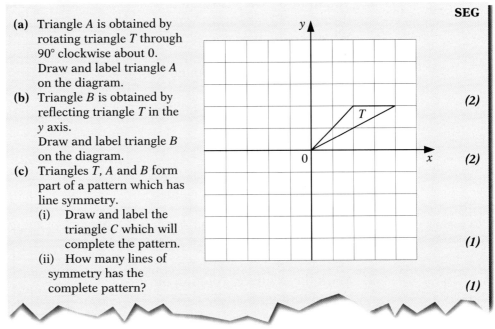

SEG

(a) Triangle *A* is obtained by rotating triangle *T* through 90° clockwise about 0. Draw and label triangle *A* on the diagram.

(b) Triangle *B* is obtained by reflecting triangle *T* in the *y* axis. Draw and label triangle *B* on the diagram.

(c) Triangles *T*, *A* and *B* form part of a pattern which has line symmetry.

(i)   Draw and label the triangle *C* which will complete the pattern.

(ii) How many lines of symmetry has the complete pattern?

(2)

(2)

(1)

(1)

C   Complete the following figures so that they will look the same when rotated through a half-turn about the point O.

1.

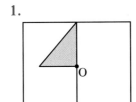

2.

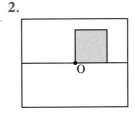

D Use a copy of this.
The diagram shows an equilateral triangle PQR.

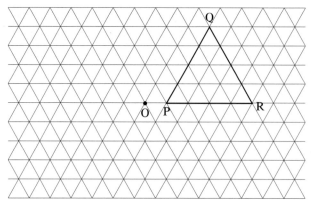

The triangle PQR is rotated 180° about O.
Draw the new triangle on the diagram.

E 1. The square PQRS is reflected in the line x = 2.
What are the new coordinates of Q?
2. The square PQRS is rotated through 180° about S.
What are the new coordinates of Q?
3. The square PQRS is rotated 270° clockwise about S.
What are the new coordinates of Q?

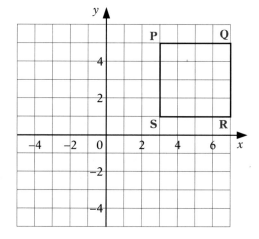

F Use a copy of this.
1. Triangle ABC has been rotated to triangle A'B'C'.
Draw two more triangles so that the complete pattern has rotational symmetry of order 4.
2. Mark the centre of rotation on the pattern with an X.

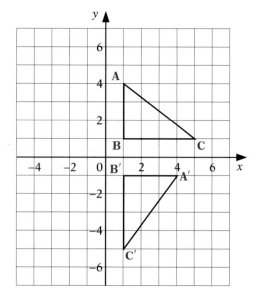

Translation

When we **translate** a shape we slide it without turning it or reflecting it.

Example   The red shape has been translated 5 units to the right and 2 units down.

Exercise 4   **A**   The red shape has been translated to the grey shape.
Describe the translation.

1.

2.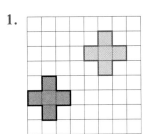

3.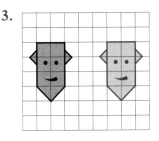

B   Copy each shape onto squared paper.

1. Translate the shape
3 units to the left
and 2 units down.

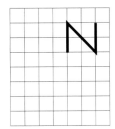

2. Translate the shape
3 units to the right and
2 units up.

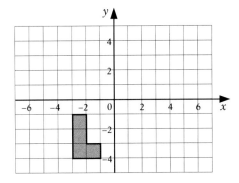

C   The shape PQRS is translated
4 units to the left and 3 units
down.
What are the new coordinates of
P, Q, R and S?

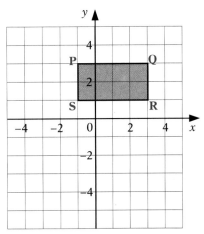

Enlargement

Remember Each side on the red shape is **two times** longer than that side on the grey shape.
We say the grey shape has been enlarged by a **scale factor** of 2 to give the red shape.

Worked Exam Question

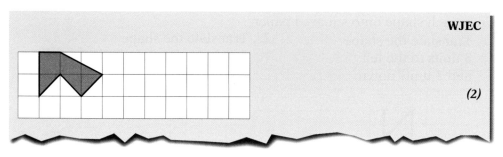

WJEC

(2)

Answer

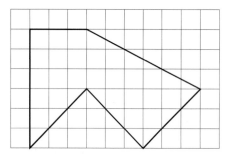

Exercise 5 **A** Copy these shapes onto grid paper.
Enlarge each by the scale factor written beside it.

1.

scale
factor
2

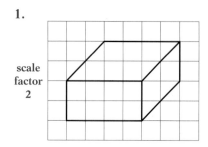

2.

scale
factor
3

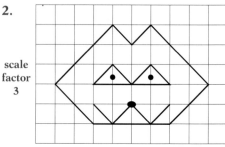

B Use a copy of this.

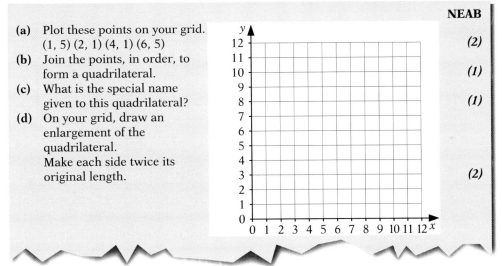

NEAB

(a) Plot these points on your grid.
    (1, 5) (2, 1) (4, 1) (6, 5)   *(2)*
(b) Join the points, in order, to
    form a quadrilateral.   *(1)*
(c) What is the special name
    given to this quadrilateral?   *(1)*
(d) On your grid, draw an
    enlargement of the
    quadrilateral.
    Make each side twice its
    original length.   *(2)*

Investigation

You will need   some squared paper.

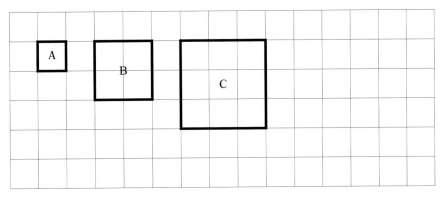

Square A is enlarged by a scale factor of 2 to square B.
Count squares to find the area of A.
Count squares to find the area of B.

Square A is enlarged by a scale factor of 3 to square C.
Count squares to find the area of C.
Make a table like this one.

Area of shape	Scale factor	Area of image	$\dfrac{\text{area image}}{\text{area of shape}}$
	2		
	3		

Draw some squares and rectangles on
squared paper.
Enlarge them by scale factors of 2, 3
and 4.
Fill in your table for your shapes.
Copy and complete this sentence.

When a shape is enlarged by a scale factor of n, the area of the image is
_____ *times bigger than the shape.*

Centre of enlargement

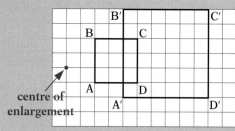 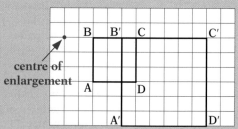

In each of the diagrams above, the square ABCD has been enlarged by a scale factor of 2.

Each enlargement has a different **centre of enlargement**.

If the scale factor is 2, then each point on the image is two times further from the centre of enlargement than the corresponding point on the shape.

Note: **We label the image of ABCD as A,B,C,D,.**

Example Using the point P as the centre of enlargement, enlarge the triangle ABC by a scale factor of 3.

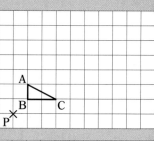

Answer Make the distance from P to the image of A 3 times as long as the distance PA.

Do the same for the distances from P to the images of B and C.

The sides of the image will be 3× as long as the sides on the shape.

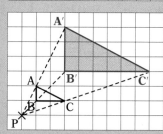

Note: **You could find the correct distance by counting squares or by measuring.**

On the given triangle, A is 1 square to the right and 2 squares up from P.

So on the image triangle, A must be 3 squares to the right and 6 squares up from P.

Once you have placed one or two points you can then draw the rest of the shape.

Exercise 6 **A** Make a copy of this.

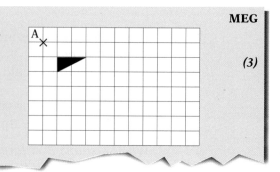

Using point A as centre of enlargement, enlarge the shaded triangle with scale factor 3.

MEG

(3)

B Copy this diagram onto grid paper.
Place point E carefully.
Enlarge the shaded figure, using scale factor 3 and
centre of enlargement E.

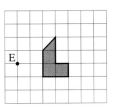

C Copy each diagram onto grid paper.
Enlarge each shape, using scale factor 2 and centre of enlargement X.

1. 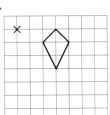 2. 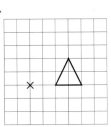 3.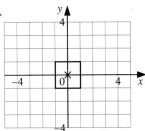

Describing transformations

To describe transformations fully, give these details.
 reflection   mirror line
 rotation   centre of rotation, clockwise or anticlockwise, angle
 translation   units right or left, units up or down
 enlargement   centre of enlargement, scale factor

Note: Sometimes it is not possible to give all of these
details.

Example The transformation that mapped A onto B
is a rotation of 180° about (0, 0).

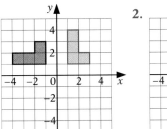

Exercise 7 **A** The red shape is transformed to the grey shape.
Describe these transformations fully.

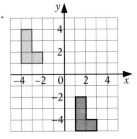

B The red shape is transformed to the black shape.
Describe these transformations.

1. 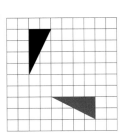 2. 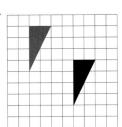 3.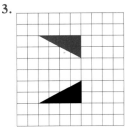

Tessellations

Worked Exam Question

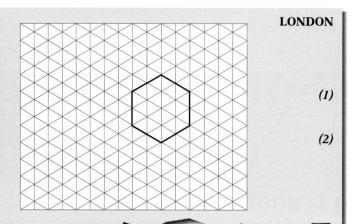

(a) On the grid show how regular hexagons tessellate. One hexagon has been drawn.

(b) Explain why regular pentagons will not tessellate.

LONDON

(1)

(2)

Answer (a)

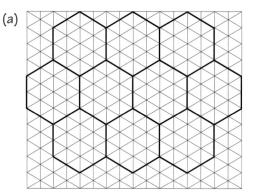

(b) The interior angle of a regular pentagon is 108°.
To tessellate, the sum of the angles at the point where the pentagons meet must equal 360°.
A regular pentagon will not tessellate because 360° is not a multiple of 108°.

Exercise 8   **A**

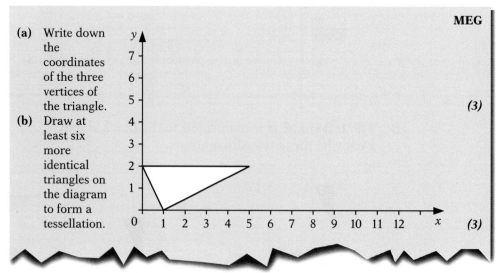

(a) Write down the coordinates of the three vertices of the triangle.

(b) Draw at least six more identical triangles on the diagram to form a tessellation.

MEG

(3)

(3)

B

SEG
(2)

Explain why a tiling pattern *cannot* be made with regular pentagons.

C You will need squared paper.
Show how each of these shapes tessellates.

1. 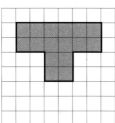   2. 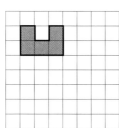   3.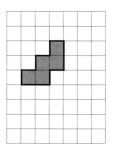

Homework/Review

A Copy these diagrams onto grid paper.

(a) Draw a reflection of this letter in the mirror line.

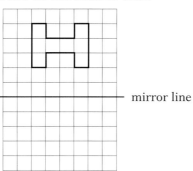

mirror line

(b) Rotate this shape ½ a turn about the centre X.

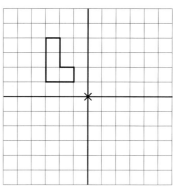

B Copy this diagram.

(i) Reflect triangle ABC in the x-axis.
Label the new triangle PQR.

(ii) Rotate triangle ABC anticlockwise 90° about the origin (0, 0).
Label the new triangle STU.

WJEC

(3)

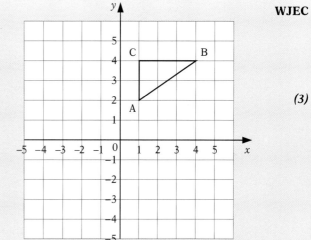

C

Using only one of the words, 'rotation, reflection or translation', describe the single transformation which maps:
(i)   the shape A onto shape B;   *(1)*
(ii) the shape A onto shape C.   *(1)*

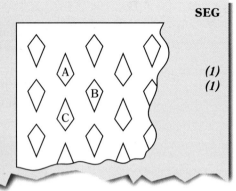

SEG

D   Use a copy of this diagram.
The position of a point Q is shown.
1.   What are the coordinates of Q?
2.   Q is reflected in the *x*-axis.
On the diagram, mark the new position of Q with a cross.

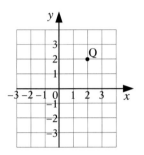

E   In each of these, shape A has been mapped onto shape B.

(a) Describe this
translation.

(b) Write down the equation
of the mirror line.

(c) Describe this
transformation.

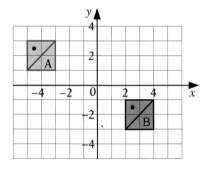

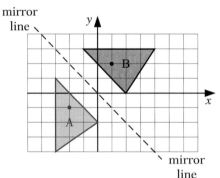

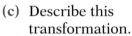

F   Use squared paper to show how this kite tessellates.

G

Enlarge the triangle *ABC* from the point marked *P*.
Use a scale factor of 3.
The new position of corner *A* is shown as *A'*.

NEAB

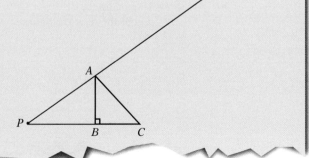

☑ KEY POINTS

☑ The triangle ABC has been **reflected** in the **mirror line** to give the image of ABC. We sometimes call the **image A'B'C'**. Each point on the triangle ABC is the same distance from the mirror line as the corresponding point on the triangle A′B′C′.

The **equation of the mirror line** is $y = x$.

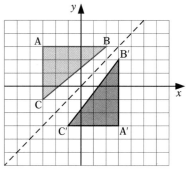

☑ When we turn a shape about a point it is called a **rotation**.

Example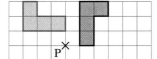

The red shape has been turned 90° clockwise (a quarter turn clockwise) about P, to the grey shape. The grey shape is the image.
P is called the **centre of rotation**.

☑ Sliding movements are called **translations**.

Example

The red shape has been translated 5 squares to the right and 1 square down to give the grey shape.

☑ When we **enlarge** a shape, each length is enlarged by the same amount. This is called the **scale factor** of the enlargement.

Example PQR has been enlarged by scale factor 2 and centre of enlargement X.
Each point on the image, P′Q′R′, is 2 times as far from X as the same point on PQR.

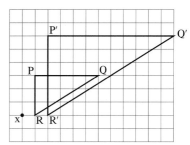

☑ A **tessellation** pattern is formed when shapes fit together without any gaps.

◀◀ CHAPTER REVIEW ◀◀

◀◀
Exercise 1
on page 281

A (i) Reflect triangle *ABC* in the line *AC*. Label as *D* the image of *B*. **MEG**

(ii) Name the special quadrilateral *ABCD*.

(2)
(1)

◄◄

Exercises 3 and 4
on pages 285 and
287

B Use a copy of this.

1. Rotate ABCD 90°
   anticlockwise about (0, 0).

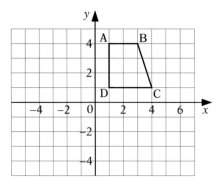

2. Translate ABC 4 units to the
   right and 2 units down.

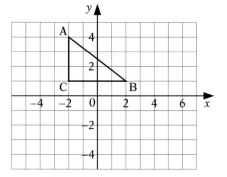

◄◄

Exercises 1 and 2
on pages 281 and
283

C Use a copy of this.

The grid shows a quadrilateral PQRS
and a line AB.
   (a) What type of quadrilateral is
       PQRS? *(1)*
   (b) The quadrilateral PQRS is
       reflected in line AB.
       Draw the reflected quadrilateral
       on the grid. *(3)*
   (c) Write down the equation of
       line AB. *(1)*

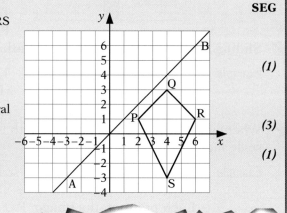

SEG

◄◄

Exercises 5 and 6
on pages 288 and
290

D Copy this shape onto squared paper.
   Enlarge the shape by a scale factor of 2, centre X.

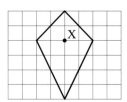

◄◄

Exercise 8
on page 292

E Draw a tiling pattern using regular hexagons only.
   Draw at least six hexagons.

◄◄

Exercises 2 and 7
on pages 283 and
291

F Use a copy of this.

   (a) Triangle A is a reflection of the
       shaded triangle.
       Draw the mirror line for this
       reflection on your diagram. *(1)*
   (b) Describe fully the transformation
       that maps the shaded triangle onto
       triangle B. *(3)*

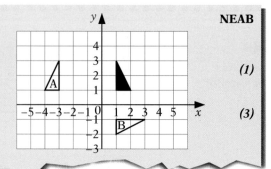

NEAB

Pie Charts and Scatter Graphs

By the end of this chapter you will be able to:

- read a pie chart
- draw a pie chart
- recognise positive, negative, perfect and no correlation
- read and draw a scatter graph
- read and draw a two-way table.

Getting started..

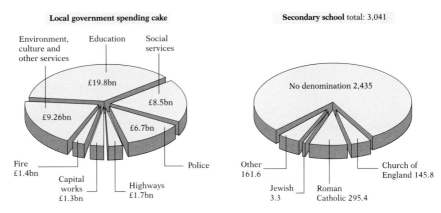

Local government spending cake

Environment, culture and other services

Education

Social services

£19.8bn

£8.5bn

£9.26bn

£6.7bn

Fire £1.4bn

Capital works £1.3bn

Highways £1.7bn

Police

Secondary school total: 3,041

No denomination 2,435

Other 161.6

Jewish 3.3

Roman Catholic 295.4

Church of England 145.8

These pie charts come from the newspaper.
Write a sentence about what each tells us.

Find some more pie charts in newspapers.
What does each tell you?

Reading pie charts

A **pie chart** shows us how something is **shared** or **divided**.
Each sector is a **fraction or percentage of the whole**.
The **angle** at the centre of each sector represents the fraction or percentage of the whole.

Example　The whole circle is 360°.
90° out of 360° or $\frac{90}{360}$ said YES.

126° out of 360° or $\frac{126}{360}$ said NO.

144° out of 360° or $\frac{144}{360}$ said MAYBE.
We can reduce the fractions to their lowest terms or make them into a percentage.
$\frac{90}{360} = \frac{1}{4}$ or 25%　　$\frac{126}{360} = \frac{7}{20}$ or 35%　　$\frac{144}{360} = \frac{2}{5}$ or 40%

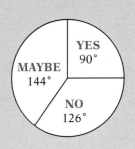

YES 90°

MAYBE 144°

NO 126°

If you are given the fraction or percentage for a sector you can work out the angle.

Example The angle for red is 45% of 360°.
$$45\% \text{ of } 360° = \frac{45}{100} \times 360°$$
$$= 162°$$

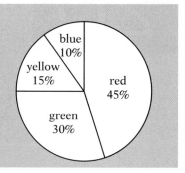

Worked Exam Questions

. . . .

MEG

1. The pie chart shows how the cereal Brekki Flakes is made up.
   (i) What fraction of the cereal is protein? *(1)*
   (ii) Mattie helps herself to 45 grams of the cereal. How many grams of fibre are in this helping? *(2)*

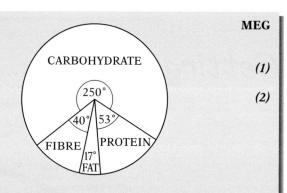

Answer (i) The angle at the centre of the sector gives us the fraction.
$\frac{53}{360}$ of the cereal is protein.

(ii) The fraction that is fibre is $\frac{40}{360}$.
We must find $\frac{40}{360}$ of 45.
$$\frac{40}{360} \text{ of } 45 = \frac{40}{360} \times 45$$
$$= 5 \text{ grams}$$

NEAB

2. The selling price of a CD is £12.99. The diagram below shows how the £12.99 is divided between the people who are involved in the sale of a CD.
   (a) What fraction of the selling price goes to the Record Company? *(1)*
   (b) How much money does the shopkeeper get from the sale of this CD? *(2)*
   (c) The artist receives 88p for each CD sold. What percentage of the £12.99 is this? *(2)*

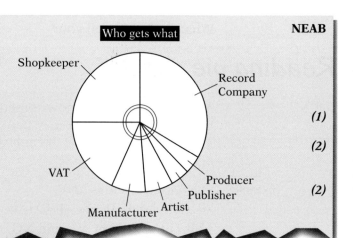

Answer (a) The angles are not given. You must measure them.
The angle for the Record Company sector is 120°.
The fraction for the Record Company is $\frac{120}{360}$ or $\frac{1}{3}$.

(b) The angle for the shopkeeper sector is 90°.
The fraction for the shopkeeper is $\frac{90}{360}$ or $\frac{1}{4}$.
So we must find $\frac{1}{4}$ of £12.99.
$\frac{1}{4}$ of £12.99 = $\frac{1}{4}$ × £12.99
        = **£3.25 to the nearest penny**.

(c) To find a percentage we multiply the fraction by 100%.
Remember to change £12.99 to pennies.
$\frac{88}{1299}$ × 100% = **6.8% to 1 d.p.**

Exercise 1   **A**   A survey was
carried out in two
different classes
to show the
popularity of
different soap
operas.
These pie charts
show the results.

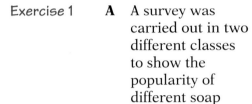
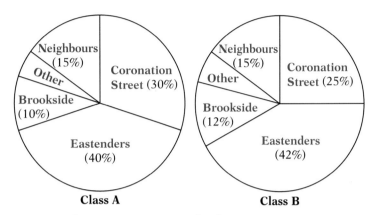

Class A   **Class B**

1. Which was the most popular programme with class A?
2. Which programme was **less** popular with class B than with class A?
3. Which programme had the same popularity with both classes?

B   200 members of a sports club were asked what
their favourite sport was.
This pie chart shows the results.
1. How many of the 200 members chose
    tennis?
2. Calculate the size of the angles for
    swimming and football.
    Show all your working.

C   This pie chart shows how Joel spent a
whole day.
1. What fraction of the day did Joel spend
    sleeping?
2. How many hours of the day did Joel
    spend on
    (a) sport and free time
    (b) school?

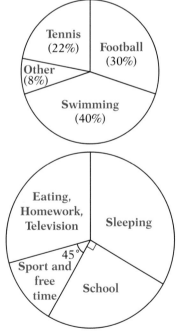

D   The pie chart shows the reasons given by 48 pupils
for being late to school.
Use the pie chart to work out how many pupils said
1. they slept in
2. they missed the bus
3. they had a flat tyre.

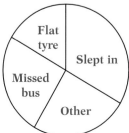

E

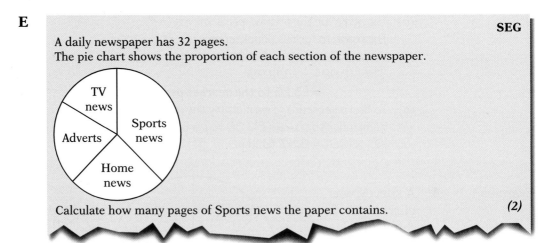

SEG

A daily newspaper has 32 pages.
The pie chart shows the proportion of each section of the newspaper.

Calculate how many pages of Sports news the paper contains. *(2)*

Drawing pie charts

To draw a **pie chart** we must calculate the angle at the centre of each sector.

Worked Exam Question

WJEC

Jill records the nationalities of 18 rugby fans. Her results are given in this table.

Nationality	Welsh	Scottish	English	Irish
Frequency	7	4	1	6

In a blank circle, draw a pie chart to show these results.
You must show how you calculate the angles of your pie chart. *(3)*

Answer   We must find the angles at the centre of each sector.
There were 18 rugby fans in total.
To find the angle for Welsh.

7 out of 18 or $\frac{7}{18}$ are Welsh.

$$\frac{7}{18} \text{ of } 360° = \frac{7}{18} \times 360°$$
$$= 140°$$

So the angle at the centre of the sector for Welsh is 140°.

> Fraction × 360°
> gives angle at
> centre of
> sector.

We work out the other angles in a similar way.

Scottish	$\frac{4}{18} \times 360°$	$= 80°$
English	$\frac{1}{18} \times 360°$	$= 20°$
Irish	$\frac{6}{18} \times 360°$	$= 120°$

Note: All the angles should add to 360°.

Draw a pie chart with these angles at the centre.

Exercise 2

A Lufta spent £180.
This table shows what she spent it on.
Lufta wanted to construct a pie chart to show her
spending.

Items	Amount spent
Train fares	£24
Going out	£50
Clothes	£60
CDs	£30
Other	£16
Total	£180

1. Use a copy of this table.
   Work out the angle of each sector of the
   pie chart.
2. Draw a circle of radius 4 cm.
   Construct the pie chart in the circle.

Items	Angle of sector
Train fares	
Going out	
Clothes	
CDs	
Other	

B   **LONDON**

In a town 1800 cars were stolen in
a year. The table shows
information about the times of day
when they were stolen.

Time	Number of cars
Midnight to 6 am	700
6 am to midday	80
Midday to 6pm	280
6 pm to midnight	470
Time unknown	270

This information can be shown in
a pie chart.
Use a copy of this table
(a) Work out the angle of each
    sector of the pie chart.

Time	Angle of sector
Midnight to 6 am	
6 am to midday	
Midday to 6pm	
6 pm to midnight	
Time unknown	
Total of angles	360°

(3)

(b) Draw a circle of radius 4 cm.
    Construct the pie chart in the circle. *(3)*
(c) What fraction of the number of cars was stolen between Midday and
    6 pm? Write your fraction in its simplest terms. *(2)*

C The table shows the number of different types of plants in a garden.

Type of plant	Rose	Annual	Shrub	Vegetable
Number of plants	35	52	33	60

Draw a clearly labelled pie chart to show this information.

D

WJEC

A survey of the types of fuel used to heat the homes of people living in a town was carried out. The results are shown in this table.

Fuel	Gas	Electricity	Coal	Wood
Number of homes	20	10	5	1

Draw a circle of radius 4 cm.
In the blank circle, draw a pie chart to show this information.
You must show how you calculate the angles of your pie chart. *(3)*

E   A group of students took a test. Their results were given as comments.
$\frac{1}{6}$ had Excellent $\frac{1}{4}$ had Very good $\frac{3}{8}$ had Good
The rest had no comment.
1. Draw a circle of radius 4 cm.
   Draw accurately, on the circle, a clearly labelled pie chart to represent this information.
2. Twenty four students took the test.
   How many students had the comment
   (a) Excellent   **(b)** Very good   **(c)** Good?

F   Use a copy of this.

SEG

In a school canteen the price of a banana depends on its weight.
The weights of 24 bananas for sale are recorded to the nearest gram as follows.

128	120	184	113	170	206	179	99
92	156	234	192	106	163	180	100
119	150	173	232	115	200	166	196

(a)   The bananas are sold as small, medium or large.
Complete the grouped frequency table for these bananas. *(2)*

Size	Weight (g)	Tally	Frequency
Small	$80 \leqslant g < 120$		
Medium	$120 \leqslant g < 180$		
Large	$180 \leqslant g < 250$		

(b)   Draw a pie chart to show the proportion of each size of banana. *(3)*

G

MEG

This question is about the way water is used in two Mozambique villages.
(a)   In village A, 324 litres of water are used each day. The pie chart shows how the water is used.
   (i)   How much water is used each day for cooking?
   (ii)   What fraction of the water used is given to animals?
   Give the fraction in its lowest terms. *(2)*

(2)

Use of water in village A

(b)   In village B, the water is used as follows:

Cooking	20%
Drinking and washing themselves	50%
Washing clothes	20%
Washing pots	10%

Draw a circle of radius 4 cm.
Using this circle, represent the information on a pie chart. *(3)*

Homework/Review 1

A

WJEC

A school has 720 pupils in Years 7 to 11.
The pie chart shows the proportion of these
pupils in each Year.
(a) Calculate the number of pupils in Year 7.
(b) (i) Measure and record the size of the
angle for Year 10.
(ii) What fraction of the total number of
pupils is in Year 10?

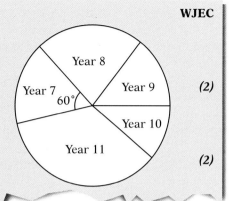

(2)

(2)

B

LONDON

30 people used a Sports Centre one evening.
Here is a list of the activities in which they took part.

Gym	Swimming	Squash	Swimming	Aerobics
Swimming	Aerobics	Aerobics	Aerobics	Gym
Aerobics	Gym	Gym	Gym	Squash
Squash	Gym	Squash	Gym	Gym
Gym	Aerobics	Aerobics	Squash	Gym
Gym	Aerobics	Squash	Gym	Aerobics

(a) Copy and complete the
table to show this
information.

Activity	Tally	Frequency
Gym		
Swimming		
Squash		
Aerobics		
	Total	30

(3)

(b) Draw a pie chart to show this information. *(5)*

C

MEG

180 students in Year 11 were asked what
they intended to do during the following
year.
The results are shown in the table.
Draw a circle of radius 4 cm.
In the circle, draw and label a pie chart to
show these choices.

School 6th Form	81
F.E. College	40
Training	28
Employment	12
Other	19

(4)

D

SEG

One Saturday a newsagent sells the following:

National daily newspapers   510
Echo   360
Magazines and comics   210

Draw a clearly labelled pie chart to represent these sales. *(4)*

Scatter graphs

Sometimes there is a relationship between **two** sets of data.
We can draw a **scatter graph** or **scatter diagram** to show this.
A relationship between two sets of data is called a **correlation**.

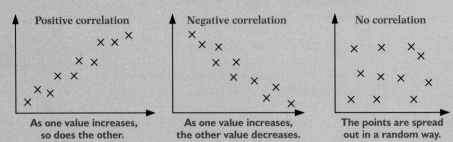

Positive correlation	Negative correlation	No correlation
As one value increases, so does the other.	As one value increases, the other value decreases.	The points are spread out in a random way.

Note: **If there is perfect correlation then a straight line can be drawn through the plotted points.**

Example The number of students at school against the number of students absent from school shows a perfect correlation.

Worked Exam Question

A bird watcher counts the number of pigeons and the number of hawks he sees each day. **WJEC**
This table shows his results.

Pigeons	5	32	18	29	33	12	21	15	35	8	22	22
Hawks	20	5	11	8	4	16	9	14	3	17	10	11

(a) Draw a scatter diagram to show this information. (2)
(b) Does your scatter diagram show positive correlation, negative correlation or no correlation? (1)
(c) About how many pigeons would the bird watcher expect to see if he sees 15 hawks? (1)

Answer (a)

Plot the points on the grid.

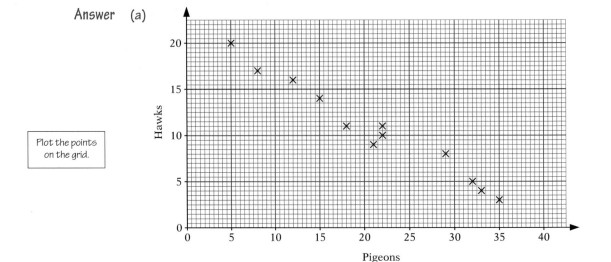

(b) **negative correlation**

(c) We can estimate this by drawing a line across from 15 hawks.
Somewhere **between 12 and 16** pigeons would be seen by the bird watcher.

Exercise 3 **A** Fifteen girls of different ages were given a reading test.
The results in the table have been plotted on the scatter graph below.

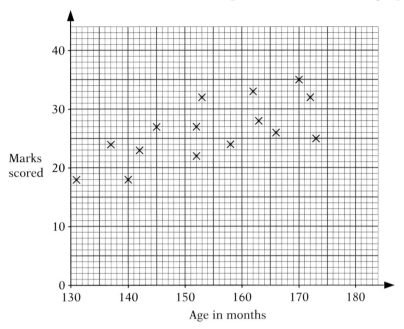

Does the scatter graph show the sort of result you would expect? Explain your answer.

B Use a copy of this.

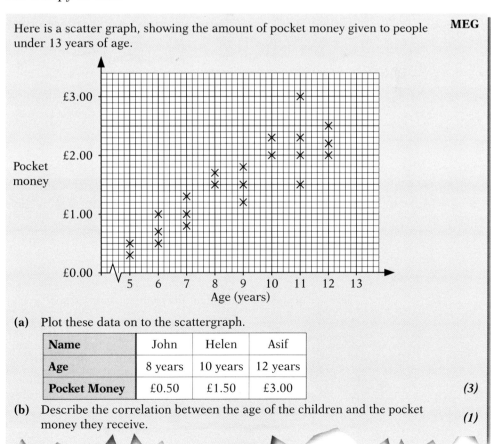

Here is a scatter graph, showing the amount of pocket money given to people under 13 years of age. **MEG**

(a) Plot these data on to the scattergraph.

Name	John	Helen	Asif
Age	8 years	10 years	12 years
Pocket Money	£0.50	£1.50	£3.00

(3)

(b) Describe the correlation between the age of the children and the pocket money they receive.

(1)

Ask your teacher for the grids for Questions C–I

C   **LONDON**

Information about oil was recorded each year for 12 years.
The table shows the amount of oil produced (in billions of barrels) and the average price of oil (in £ per barrel).

Amount of oil produced (billions of barrels)	7.0	11.4	10.8	11.3	9.6	8.2	7.7	10.9	8.0	9.9	9.2	9.4
Average price of oil (£ per barrel)	34	13	19	12	23	33	30	12.5	28.5	13.5	26.5	15.5

(a) Draw a scatter graph to show the information in the table.   *(3)*
(b) Describe the correlation between the average price of oil and the
     amount of oil produced.   *(1)*

D   **LONDON**

The table lists the weights of twelve books and the number of pages in each one.

Number of pages	80	155	100	125	145	90	140	160	135	100	115	165
Weight (g)	160	330	200	260	320	180	290	330	260	180	230	350

(a) Draw a scatter graph to show the information in the table.   *(3)*
(b) Describe the correlation between the number of pages in these books
     and their weights.   *(1)*

E   **SEG**

The table shows the ages and weights of ten babies.

Age (weeks)	2	7	9	4	10	16	6	14	13	12
Weight (kg)	4	4.6	4.3	3	4.7	5.7	4.1	5.5	5	5.6

(a) Use this information to draw a scatter graph.   *(2)*
(b) Comment on the relationship between the ages of these babies and their
     weights.   *(1)*

F   **NEAB**

These are the prices charged for different journeys by taxi.

Length of journey (km)	1	2	3	5	8	13	14	18
Cost (£)	1.80	2.30	2.50	2.80	5.40	7.50	8.40	10.30

(a) On a grid, draw a scatter diagram to show this information.   *(2)*
(b) What does this diagram tell you about the relationship between the length
     of a journey and its cost?   *(1)*

G   **NEAB**

Annie asked a group of teenagers to say how much time they spent doing
homework one evening and how much time they spent watching TV.
Here is a scatter diagram to show the results:

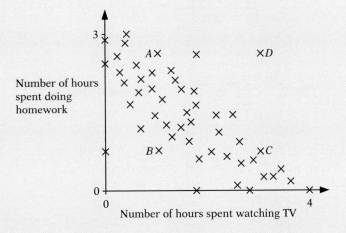

(a) Which of the four points *A*, *B*, *C* or *D* represents each of the statements
shown below? Write one letter next to each statement.

1. I watched a lot of TV last night and I also did a lot of homework.

2. I spent most of my evening doing homework. I only watched one programme on TV.

3. I went out last night. I didn't do much homework or watch much TV.

(b) Make up a statement which matches the fourth point.   *(3)*
(c) What does the graph tell you about the relationship between time spent
    watching TV and time spent doing homework?   *(2)*
(d) Annie also drew scatter diagrams which showed that: *(2)*

> Older students tend to spend more time doing homework than
> younger students.
>
> There is no relationship between the time students spend watching
> TV and the time students spend sleeping.

Copy the axes below.
Show what Annie's scatter diagrams may have looked like.

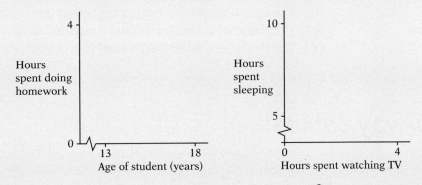

H

The table shows the time taken by each of seven motorists to complete a journey.

Length of journey (km)	25	40	48	65	90	90	100
Time taken (hours)	0.5	0.8	1.2	1	1.3	1.8	1.2

(a) Draw a scatter graph for these data. *(2)*
(b) Give one reason why the length of journey and time taken are not perfectly correlated. *(1)*

I Melissa did a survey to find the prices of second hand cars in her town. Here are her results for Honda Civics.

Age (years)	2	1	5	3	$5\frac{1}{2}$	5	6	$3\frac{1}{2}$	2	$4\frac{1}{2}$	3	4
Cost (£)	7000	8500	4000	6250	3700	3800	3200	5600	6800	4500	6000	4500

1. Draw a scatter diagram to show her results.
2. About how much would you expect to pay for a $2\frac{1}{2}$ year old Honda Civic in Melissa's town?
3. About how old would you expect a Honda Civic that cost £8000 to be?
4. About how much would you expect to pay for a Honda Civic that is
   (a) $4\frac{1}{2}$ years old (b) $1\frac{1}{2}$ years old (c) $6\frac{1}{2}$ years old.

J This table gives information about the age and value of nine similar radio controlled boats.

Age of boat (to the nearest year)	1	7	6	2	6	4	3	2	4
Value of boat (to the nearest £10)	270	40	60	230	100	110	190	200	160

1. Use this information to draw a scatter graph.
2. What does the scatter graph tell you about the connection between the age of radio controlled boats and their value?
3. Use the graph to estimate:
   (a) the value of a similar radio controlled boat which is 5 years old
   (b) the age of a similar radio controlled boat with a value of £250
   (c) the value of a similar radio controlled boat which is $2\frac{1}{2}$ years old
   (d) the age of a similar radio controlled boat with a value of £130.

Two-way tables

A **two-way table** displays two data sets.

Worked Exam Question

A gym club has 69 members.
38 of these members are boys.
There are 19 members who are girls under 15 years old.
There are 23 members who are boys 15 years old or over.

LONDON

	Under 15 years old	15 years old or over	Totals
Boys		23	38
Girls	19		
Totals			69

(a) Complete the two-way table.   *(1)*
(b) Work out how many members of the gym club are girls 15 years old or over.   *(1)*

Answer   (a)   Fill in the table in the order shown by the numbers.

	Under 15 years old	15 years old or over	Totals
Boys	15	23	38
Girls	19	12	31
Totals	34	35	69

1. These must add to 38. 15 + 23 = 38
3. These must add to 31. 19 + 12 = 31
4. Add these. 15 + 19 = 34
5. Add these. 23 + 12 = 35
2. These must add to 69. 38 + 31 = 69

(b)   **12**

Exercise 4   **A**   The two-way table shows the number of students achieving grades A to E in examinations in Maths and Science.

Maths Grade

		A	B	C	D	E
	A	5	3	2	0	0
	B	3	4	4	1	0
Science Grade	**C**	1	5	7	0	1
	D	0	1	0	6	5
	E	0	0	0	4	6

1. How many students achieved the same grade in both subjects?
2. How many of the students who achieved grade B in Maths achieved a different grade in Science?
3. What does the table suggest about the grades achieved by these students in Maths and Science?

B   Use a copy of this. This two-way table shows the results of males and females who sat driving tests.

	Passed 1st time	Passed 2nd time	Passed 3rd time	Totals
Male	14	12		34
Female	26		0	
Totals				68

1. Complete the two-way table.
2. How many females passed on their 2nd attempt?

C   Use a copy of this. This two-way table shows the numbers of pizzas delivered, taken away and the number eaten in on a Friday and Saturday night.

	Delivered	Take away	Eaten in	Totals
Friday	41		22	119
Saturday		25		114
Totals			58	

1. Complete the two-way table.
2. How many pizzas were taken away on Friday night?

Homework/Review 2

A

WJEC

The table below shows the scores of six pupils in Paper 1 and Paper 2 of a mathematics examination.

Score in Paper 1	20	32	15	6	25	16
Score in Paper 2	14	21	11	4	15	13

  (a) Draw a scatter diagram to show these scores.   *(2)*
  (b) What kind of correlation does your scatter graph show?   *(1)*

B

MEG

A shop manager keeps a record of the number of days each of her employees was absent.

Employee	Anne	Bill	Cath	Del	Emma	Fred	Gaz	Hugh	Ian	Jim
Number of years worked	2	4	10	9	1	5	4	8	3	1
Number of days off last year	12	9	2	5	16	8	13	4	14	12

  (i) Draw a scatter diagram.   *(2)*
  (ii) What does your diagram show?   *(2)*

C   This table gives you the marks scored by 15 contestants in Part A and Part B of a quiz.

Part A	15	35	34	23	35	27	36	34	23	24	30	40	25	35	20
Part B	20	37	35	25	33	30	39	36	27	20	33	35	27	32	28

  1. Draw a scatter graph of the marks scored in Part A and Part B.
  2. Describe the relationship between the marks scored in the two tests.
  3. Jenni scored 32 in Part A.
      Use the scatter graph to estimate the mark she scored in Part B.

D   Use a copy of this.
  This is a two-way table.
  It shows the number of days it rained and the number it did not rain in December and January.

	Rained	Did not rain	Totals
December		16	31
January	19		31
Totals			

  1. Complete the two-way table.
  2. How many days did it rain in December?
  3. How many days did it rain in total?
  4. How many days did it not rain in January?

Task

  1. Collect data from 20 people on one of the following.
     • age and head circumference
     • height and length of ears
     • length of thumb and length of big toe
     • handspan and shoe size
  2. Use your data to draw a scatter graph or two-way table.
  3. Comment on the relationship shown by your display.

KEY POINTS

✔ A **pie chart** is used to show how something is shared or divided.

✔ The **angle at the centre** of each sector can be used to find the fraction or percentage that sector represents.

✔ We find the **angle at the centre** of each sector of a pie chart as follows:
  find what fraction (or percentage) of the whole the sector represents
  multiply this fraction (or percentage) by 360°.

✔ To **draw a pie chart**, calculate the angle at the centre of each sector.
  Then construct these angles in the centre of a circle.

✔ A **scattergraph** shows the relationship between two sets of data.
  The relationship between the two sets of data is called **correlation**.

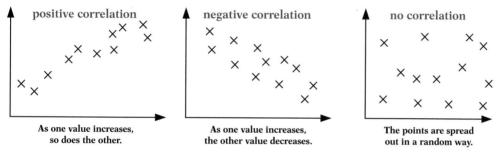

✔ **Perfect correlation** exists if a straight line can be drawn through all of the points.

✔ A **two-way table** displays two data sets in a table.

Example   This two-way table shows the number of males and females who play various sports in a club.

	Soccer	Netball	Squash	Tennis	Total
M	104	98	52	83	337
F	7	12	47	51	117
Total	111	110	99	134	454

• •

◄◄ CHAPTER REVIEW ◄◄

• •

◄◄
Exercise 1
on page 299

A

NEAB

The pie chart shows how the cost of a pint of milk is shared amongst the milkman, the dairy and the farmer.
The farmer receives half of the cost of a pint of milk.
What fraction does the milkman receive?

(1)

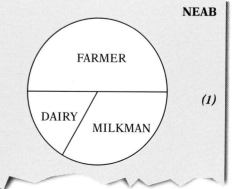

◄◄ **B**

Exercise 4
on page 309

SEG

The number of medals won
by the top six countries in
the 1984 Winter Olympics
is shown.

	GOLD	SILVER	BRONZE
Germany	9	9	6
Soviet Union	6	10	9
United States	4	4	0
Finland	4	3	6
Sweden	4	2	2
Norway	3	2	4

(a) How many Silver
medals did Finland
win?

(b) How many medals did
Germany win alto-
gether?

(1)

(1)

(c) Which country won a total of 12 more medals than Finland? *(2)*

◄◄ **C**

Exercise 2
on page 301

NEAB

In one week Ronnie rents out 90 items from his shop as shown in the table
below.
Draw a circle of radius 4 cm.
In the circle, draw a pie chart
for all the week's rentals.

Item	Frequency	
Televisions	35	
Videos	30	
Computers	17	
Other equipment	8	

(4)

Ask your teacher for the grids for D and E.

◄◄ **D**

Exercise 3
on page 305

SEG

The Mathematics scores and Science scores of 8 students are shown in the
table.

Student	A	B	C	D	E	F	G	H
Mathematics score	44	18	51	60	25	10	35	40
Science score	34	21	46	50	18	15	29	39

(a) Use the data to plot a scatter diagram. *(2)*

(b) What does the scatter diagram suggest about the connection between the
scores in Mathematics and Science? *(1)*

◄◄ **E**

Exercise 3
on page 305

LONDON

9 different models of car were tested to see how long it took each car to
travel 500 metres from a standing start.
The times, together with the size of each engine, are shown in the table.

Model	A	B	C	D	E	F	G	H	I
Engine size cc	1000	1200	1250	1400	1450	1600	1800	1950	2000
Time (seconds)	26	23	23	21	21	19	18	16	14

(a) Plot these on a scatter diagram. *(2)*

(b) Describe the relationship between the time a car takes to travel
500 metres and the size of its engine. *(1)*

(c) Use your scatter diagram to estimate the time taken to travel
500 metres by a car with an engine size of 1700 cc. *(1)*

21 Directions, Maps and Bearings

By the end of this chapter you will be able to:

* give and read directions using N, E, S, W, NE, NW, SE, SW
* give and follow directions using angles, distances, clockwise and anticlockwise
* use a scale on a map
* make a scale drawing
* read and use bearings
* find the position of a point using its bearing from two other points.

Getting started ....

You will need   a partner

Give your partner directions on how to get from school to somewhere.
Choose a place your partner will know but don't tell him or her.
You may not use street names.

Example   William chose the Tesco Supermarket.
He told his partner:
> *You go out of the school gate and turn left.*
> *Walk for about 200 m and then turn right.*
> *Walk 4 blocks until you come to some lights.*
> *Turn right.*
> *Walk about 300 m.*
> *Where are you?*

Directions

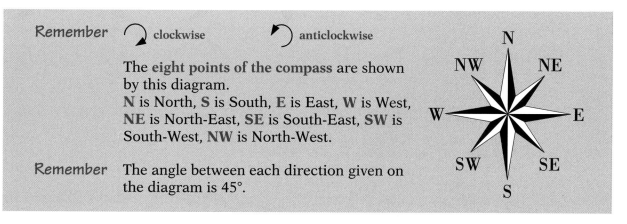

Remember   ⟳ clockwise   ⟲ anticlockwise

The **eight points of the compass** are shown
by this diagram.
N is North, **S** is South, **E** is East, **W** is West,
NE is North-East, **SE** is South-East, **SW** is
South-West, **NW** is North-West.

Remember   The angle between each direction given on
the diagram is 45°.

Example Helen walked from A to B along the path shown.
The instructions for her walk were:

Move forward 20 m.
Turn 90° clockwise.
Move forward 40 m.
Turn 90° anticlockwise.
Move 30 m forward.
Turn 90° clockwise.
Move 25 m forward.
Turn 147° clockwise.
Move 60 m forward.

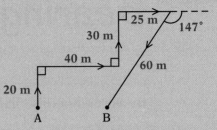

Note: The angle of turn is the angle Helen
actually turns through.

Worked Exam Question

Helen is standing at *H*. She is facing North.
She turns anticlockwise through 1 right angle.
(a)   In what direction is she now facing?   *(1)*

Later, Harry stands at *H*. He faces South.
He turns clockwise through 1½ right angles.
(b)   In what direction will he then be facing?   *(1)*

LONDON

N

H

Answer   (a)   She will be facing **West**.

N
W

(b)   He will be facing **North-West**.

NW
S

Exercise 1   **A**   Write the compass direction for each of these arrows.
The first one is done.

1. ↑   2. ↗   3. ↓   4. ↖   5. ↙   6. ↘
N

B

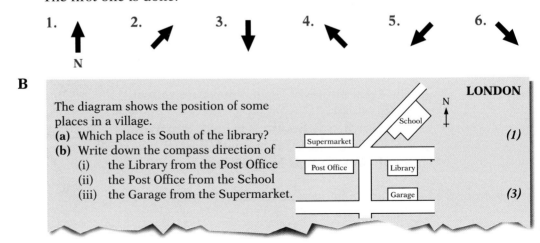

The diagram shows the position of some
places in a village.
(a) Which place is South of the library?   *(1)*
(b) Write down the compass direction of
  (i)   the Library from the Post Office
  (ii)   the Post Office from the School
  (iii)   the Garage from the Supermarket.   *(3)*

LONDON
N
School
Supermarket
Post Office   Library
Garage

C The diagram shows the positions of
  some farms.
  1. Which farm is
    (a) due South of Turner's
    (b) due West of Read's?
  2. Write down the compass direction of
    (a) Turner's from Young's
    (b) Hunt's from Read's
    (c) Long's from Read's
    (d) Hunt's from Smith's.

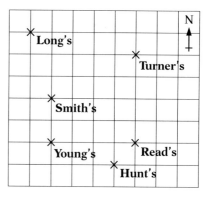

D Paula walks from P to Q along the
  path shown.
  Copy and complete these
  instructions.
    Move forward 30 m
    Turn 90° clockwise

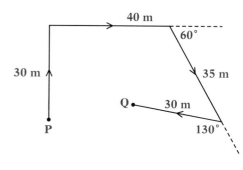

E Copy and complete these instructions
  for getting from S to T. Use compass
  directions.
    Drive 3 km West.
    Drive 2 km South.
    Drive 4 km South-East.

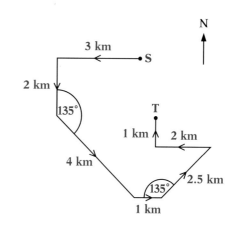

F Yasmin walked from her house
  to Paul's house along the route
  shown.
    Copy these instructions.
    Fill in the missing lines.
    Walk 40 m
  1. ------------------
    Walk 50 m
    Turn 60° anticlockwise
  2. ------------------
  3. ------------------
    Walk 25 m
  4. ------------------
    Walk 20 m.

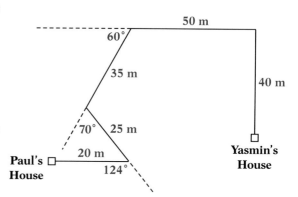

Scales on maps

A **scale** on a map might be given in one of these ways.

1 cm represents 25 km *or* **1 : 2 500 000** *or* **1 cm to 25 km** *or* **1 cm = 25 km**

They all mean the same thing. 1 cm on the map represents 250 000 cm *or* 25 km in real life.

Example   On the map the distance from A to B is 5 cm.
What is the actual distance from A to B?

Answer   Each centimetre represents 25 km.
So 5 cm represents 5 × 25 or 125 km.

Example   Jon wanted to make a scale drawing of this hall.
He wanted 1 cm to represent 4 metres.

12 m
HALL   8 m

Answer   The actual length of the hall is 12 m.
Each 4 m is represented by 1 cm.
So 12 m is represented by 12 ÷ 4 or 3 cm.
The width of the hall is represented by 8 ÷ 4 or 2 cm.

> Divide the actual length by the length that 1 unit on the scale represents.

HALL

Example   Naim sets out on a walk.
He walks 1 mile North from T to U and then 2 miles South-West from U to V.
The scale drawing shows part of the walk.
The scale is 2 cm = 1 mile.
1. Complete the drawing to show the walk from T to V.
2. Join TV. Measure the angle UTV.
3. Measure the length TV.
    How far is Naim from his starting point?

U

T

Answer

1.

> 2cm = 1 mile
> To convert from:
> 1. **cm → miles**
>   ÷ by 2
> 2. **miles → cm**
>   × by 2

2. Angle UTV = 106°.
3. Length TV = 2.8 cm to the nearest 0.1 cm.
    Naim is 2.8 ÷ 2 or 1.4 miles from his starting point.

Exercise 2   **A**   Julian wants to make a scale drawing using a scale where 1 cm represents 8 m.
How long would these **actual** lengths be on his scale drawing?
1. 16 m   2. 12 m   3. 20 m   4. 26 m   5. 14 m

B Gwyneth is making a model of a house.
She is using the scale of **1 : 500**.
This diagram shows the dimensions of two rooms.
On her model, what length will these be
1. the length of the dining room
2. the width of the dining room
3. the length of the lounge?

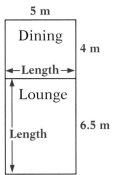

C A scale on a map is to be **4 cm represents 1 m**.
How long, on the map, would an actual distance of 5 m be?

D

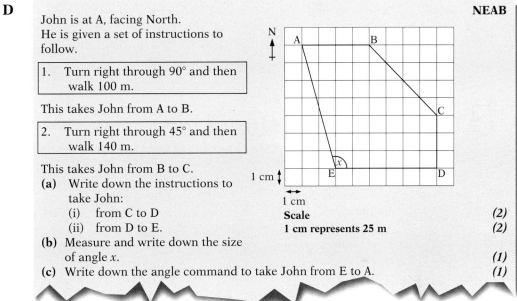

John is at A, facing North.
He is given a set of instructions to
follow.

1. Turn right through 90° and then walk 100 m.

This takes John from A to B.

2. Turn right through 45° and then walk 140 m.

This takes John from B to C.
(a) Write down the instructions to
take John:
  (i) from C to D   *(2)*
  (ii) from D to E.   *(2)*
(b) Measure and write down the size
of angle *x*.   *(1)*
(c) Write down the angle command to take John from E to A.   *(1)*

NEAB

N
A   B

C

1 cm   E   D
1 cm
Scale
1 cm represents 25 m

E This is a sketch of a park.
Use a scale of 1 cm represents 10 m. Make
an accurate scale drawing of the park.
Write down the actual length of side AB of
the park to the nearest metre.

A   B
60 m   80 m
117°   100°
D   70 m   C

F 1. On this map the actual distance
between Village A and Village B is
100 km.
What is the scale of the map?
2. What is the actual distance between
(a) Village A and Village C
(b) Village B and Village C?

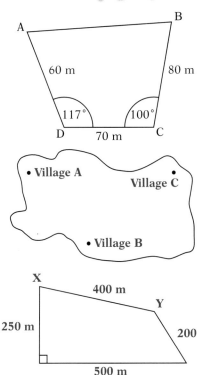

• Village A   • Village C

• Village B

G A surveyor measures the dimensions of a
field, and records them on this diagram.
Using 1 cm grid paper, draw an accurate
scale drawing of the field using a scale of
1 cm to represent 50 m.
Note: You will need to use a compass.

X   400 m
               Y
250 m   200
         500 m

Bearings

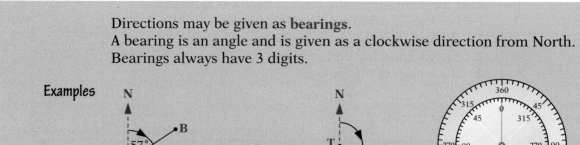

Directions may be given as **bearings**.
A bearing is an angle and is given as a clockwise direction from North.
Bearings always have 3 digits.

Examples

The bearing of
B from A is 057°

The bearing of
S from T is 225°

It is best to use a circular protractor to measure bearings.

Worked Exam Question

WJEC

This diagram is drawn using a scale 1 cm to 1 km. It shows the route taken
by a ship from A to B.

N

B   Scale: 1 cm to 1 km

A

(a) What bearing does the ship take on its journey from A to B?   *(1)*
(b) The ship then sails from B to a point C, 8 km from B on a bearing 120°.
      Show the journey from B to C on the diagram.   *(2)*

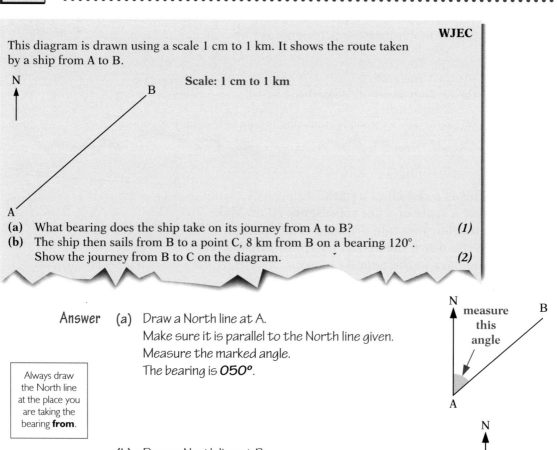

Answer   (a) Draw a North line at A.
                    Make sure it is parallel to the North line given.
                    Measure the marked angle.
                    The bearing is **050°**.

> Always draw
> the North line
> at the place you
> are taking the
> bearing **from**.

            (b) Draw a North line at B.
                    Measure an angle of 120° from this line.
                    1 cm represents 1 km.
                    The line between B and C must be **8 cm** long.

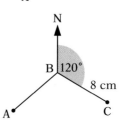

Exercise 3   **A**

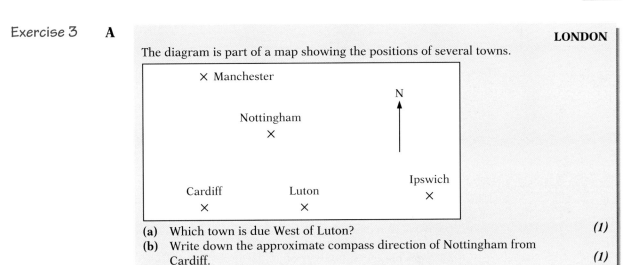

The diagram is part of a map showing the positions of several towns.

(a) Which town is due West of Luton? *(1)*
(b) Write down the approximate compass direction of Nottingham from Cardiff. *(1)*
(c) Measure and write down the bearing of Manchester from Nottingham. *(2)*

B   Copy this diagram.

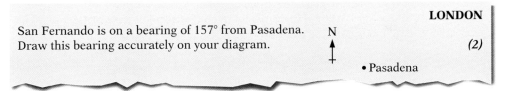

San Fernando is on a bearing of 157° from Pasadena.
Draw this bearing accurately on your diagram. *(2)*

C   Three caravan parks are close together.
     Greenacres is due North of Campalot.
     Campalot is due West of Caravan Bliss.
     Greenacres is North-West of Caravan Bliss.
1. Draw a sketch to show the positions of the three caravan parks.
2. What is the bearing of Caravan Bliss from Campalot?
3. What is the bearing of Caravan Bliss from Greenacres?
4. What is the bearing of Greenacres from Caravan Bliss?

D

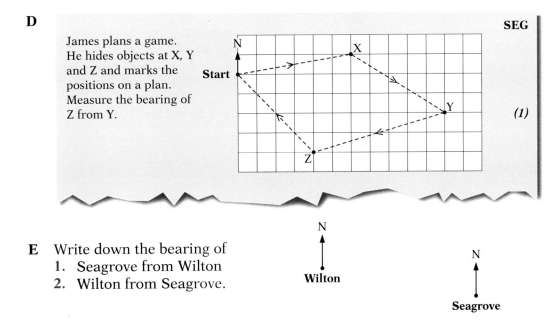

James plans a game.
He hides objects at X, Y and Z and marks the positions on a plan.
Measure the bearing of Z from Y. *(1)*

E   Write down the bearing of
1. Seagrove from Wilton
2. Wilton from Seagrove.

F

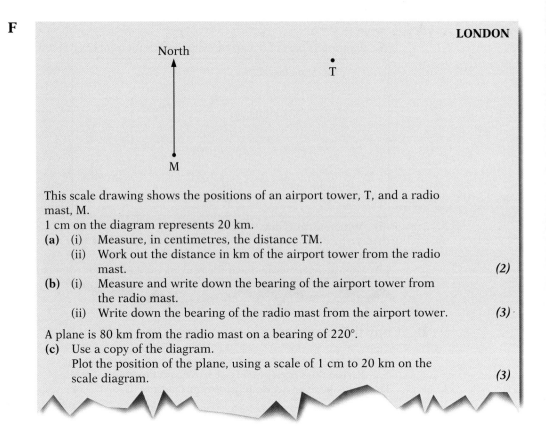

This scale drawing shows the positions of an airport tower, T, and a radio mast, M.
1 cm on the diagram represents 20 km.
(a) (i) Measure, in centimetres, the distance TM.
    (ii) Work out the distance in km of the airport tower from the radio mast. *(2)*
(b) (i) Measure and write down the bearing of the airport tower from the radio mast.
    (ii) Write down the bearing of the radio mast from the airport tower. *(3)*

A plane is 80 km from the radio mast on a bearing of 220°.
(c) Use a copy of the diagram.
Plot the position of the plane, using a scale of 1 cm to 20 km on the scale diagram. *(3)*

G

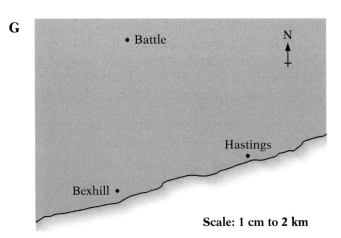

Scale: 1 cm to 2 km

1. A helicopter flies directly from Bexhill to Hastings.
On what bearing does it fly?

2. From Hastings the helicopter flies to Battle.
On what bearing does the helicopter fly?

3. On the map 1 cm represents 2 km.
The helicopter returns to Bexhill from Battle.
Estimate the distance, in miles, between Battle and Bexhill.
Give your answer to an appropriate degree of accuracy.

Finding the position of a point using two bearings

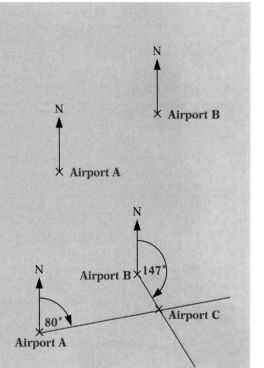

We can find the **position of a point** if we are given its **bearing from two other points**.

Example The diagram shows the position of two airports, A and B.
A third airport, C, is on a bearing of 080° from airport A and 147° from airport B. Mark with a cross, the position of airport C.

Answer
1. Measure and draw an angle of 80° from North at airport A.
2. Measure and draw an angle of 147° from North at airport B.
3. Where these lines meet is the position of airport C. Put a cross here and label it, Airport C.

Exercise 4   **A**   The diagram shows the position of two beacons, A and B.
A helicopter is on a bearing of 320° from Beacon A and a bearing of 030° from Beacon B.
Use a copy of this diagram.
Mark with a cross, the position of the helicopter.

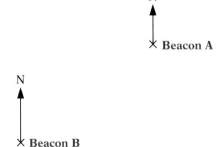

B   The diagram shows the positions of an injured hiker and a rescue unit.
1. Measure and write down the bearing of the rescue unit from the injured hiker.
2. Use a copy of the diagram. On the diagram, mark and label the position of a second rescue unit, U, which is on a bearing of 200° from the injured hiker and a bearing of 280° from the first rescue unit.

C   **MEG**

North

Cove Head

Land

Sea

North

Fish Point

Fish Point and Cove Head are coastguard stations.
They receive a distress signal from a ship S.
Its bearing from Fish Point is 074°.
Its bearing from Cove Head is 206°.
By drawing appropriate lines, find and mark the position S of the ship.   *(3)*

D   The diagram shows the position of a ship, S, in relation to a coastguard station, C.

1. Measure and write down the bearing of the ship from the coastguard station.
2. A second ship is at T, which is on a bearing of 190° from C and a bearing of 280° from S.
   Use a copy of this diagram.
   Mark the position of T on your diagram.

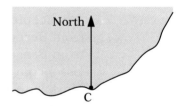

North

C

Scale: 1 cm represents 2km.

North

• S

Homework/Review

A

NEAB

This map shows part of Shropshire.
- **(a)** Which place is about 8 km West of Mortimer? *(1)*
- **(b)** What is the direction of Kinlet from Mortimer? *(1)*
- **(c)** What is the bearing of Cleeton from Mortimer? *(2)*

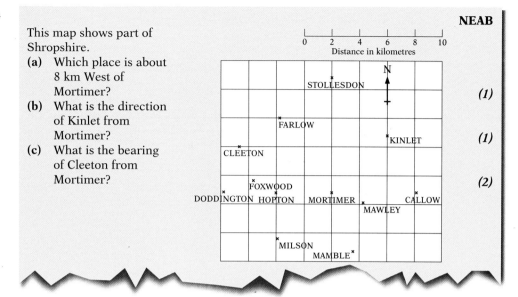

B

NEAB

A ladder is put up against a wall as shown in the sketch.
The bottom of the ladder is 1 m away from the wall.
It reaches 4 m up the wall.
- **(i)** Make a scale drawing to show the position of the ladder.
  Use a scale of 4 centimetres to represent 1 m. *(2)*
- **(ii)** Use your scale drawing to work out the length of the ladder. *(2)*
- **(iii)** Measure and write down the angle between the ladder and the ground. *(1)*

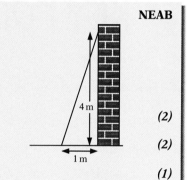

C

MEG

The sketch map shows the positions of Poolbridge (P), Rosegrove (R) and Beacon Point (B).
Beacon Point is 10 km due North of Poolbridge.
Rosegrove is 7 km from Poolbridge on a bearing of 056°.
- **(a)** Construct triangle PBR using a scale of 1 cm to represent 1 km. *(2)*
- **(b)** Use your diagram to find the distance of Rosegrove from Beacon Point. *(1)*
- **(c)** Use your diagram to find the bearing of Rosegrove from Beacon Point. *(2)*

• Beacon Point   N

• Rosegrove

• Poolbridge

D Measure and write down the bearing of
   1. Redding from Leath
   2. Dunhill from Pineacres
   3. Dunhill from Redding
   4. Pineacres from Dunhill
   5. Leath from Pineacres.

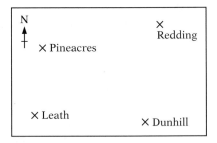

E

The diagram shows the positions of two towns, Appleton, A and Berrytown, B.
Appleton is due north of Berrytown.
Make a copy of the diagram.
Have A and B 8 cm apart.
A third town, Cooksville, is on a bearing of 125° from Appleton.
The bearing of Cooksville from Berrytown is 062°.
Mark with a cross, the position of Cooksville on the diagram.

SEG

(2)

☑ KEY POINTS

☑ ⤵ **clockwise** ⤴ **anticlockwise**

☑ This diagram shows the eight **compass directions**.
N is North, S is South, W is West, E is East. NE is North-East,
SE is South-East, SW is South-West, NW is North-West.

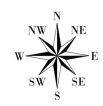

☑ Maps and diagrams often have a **scale**.

> **Examples** 1 cm represents 4 m.
> This tells us that 1 cm on the diagram is an actual distance of 4 m.
>
> 1 : 200 means 1 unit represents 200 units.

☑ To make a **scale drawing**, divide all of the actual distances by the distance that 1 unit on the scale drawing represents.

> **Example** Scale: 1 cm represents 4 m. An actual distance of 20 m will be 20 ÷ 4 or 5cm on the scale drawing.

☑ A **bearing** is used to tell us the direction in degrees of one place from another.
Bearings are always taken in a clockwise direction from North and always have 3 digits.

Examples

The bearing of
B from A is 052°.

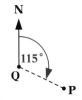

The bearing of
P from Q is 115°.

The bearing of
D from C is 280°.

☑ The **position** of something can be found if we know its bearing from two given points.

◀◀ CHAPTER REVIEW ◀◀

◀◀
Exercise 1
on page 314

A

A map of Whale Island is shown. The grid is divided into 1 km squares.
Captain Whitebeard's treasure is buried on the island.
The position of the treasure can be found using the following instructions.
Mark the point A (2,5)
From A go to (7,5)
Turn clockwise 90° and move forward 1 km.
Turn anticlockwise 90° and move forward 1 km.
Turn anticlockwise 90° and move forward 2 km.
Stop at this point, X.

WJEC

(a) Mark A on the diagram and **clearly mark the path** traced by following the above instructions. *(5)*
(b) Mark X on the diagram.
Write down the coordinates of X. *(1)*

◀◀
Exercises 2 and
3 on pages 316
and 319

B The diagram shows a map of part of Ireland.
1. What is the three figure bearing of Kilkenny from Dublin?
2. The map has been drawn to a scale of 1 cm to 30 km.
   (a) What is the actual distance between Dublin and Kilkenny in kilometres?
   (b) By taking 8 km to be approximately 5 miles, calculate the distance between Kilkenny and Dublin in miles.

• **Dublin**

Kilkenny
•

◀◀
Exercises 2 and
4 on pages 316
and 321

C **You will need 1 cm squared paper**.

WJEC

During the survey of a town the positions of the church (C), the town hall (H) and the library (L) are marked by points on a map. The distances between them are shown on this map.

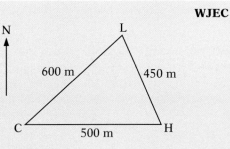

(a) Using 1 cm squared paper, draw an accurate scale drawing of triangle CHL, using a scale of 1 cm to represent 50 m. *(3)*
(b) The position of the police station is to be marked by the letter P on the map. The bearing of P from C is 042°. The bearing of P from H is 300°. By drawing suitable lines, mark the position of P on your diagram. *(3)*

◀◀

Exercises 3 and
4 on pages 319
and 321

D   Use a copy of this diagram.
The diagram is drawn to scale.
It shows the positions of two ships M and N.
(a) What is the bearing of N from M?
(b) A third ship, P, is on a bearing of 110° from
M and a bearing of 170° from N.
Mark the position of ship P accurately on
your diagram.

◀◀

Exercises 2 and 4
on pages 316 and
321

E

SEG

The diagram shows a map of a group of islands.
The map has been drawn to a scale of 1 cm to 5 km.

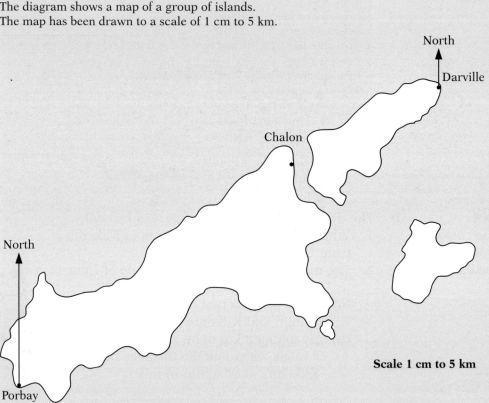

Scale 1 cm to 5 km

(a) A straight road joins Porbay to Chalon.
(i)   Use the map to find the length of this road in kilometres.
(ii) Brian cycles from Porbay to Chalon along this road.
He sets off at 0930 and cycles at an average speed of 18 kilometres per
hour.
At what time does he arrive in Chalon?
(b) A lighthouse is on a bearing of 080° from Porbay and 200° from Darville.
Use a copy of this map.
Mark, with a cross, the position of the lighthouse on the map.

Time and Tables

By the end of this chapter you will be able to:

- use analogue, digital and 24-hour time
- solve problems involving time
- read timetables
- read a table and answer questions about information given in a table.

Getting started ....

	Skin type			
Index	Fair, burns	Fair, tans	Brown skin	Black skin
1/2	Low	Low	Low	Low
3/4	Medium	Low	Low	Low
5	High	Medium	Low	Low
6	Very high	Medium	Medium	Low
7	Very high	High	Medium	Medium
8	Very high	High	Medium	Medium
9	Very high	High	Medium	Medium
10	Very high	High	High	Medium

Low risk: the sun is not likely to harm you. **Medium risk**: avoid direct sunlight for more than 1 to 2 hours. **High risk**: You could burn in 30 to 60 minutes. Try to keep out of direct sunlight, cover up and use a sunscreen of SPF 15+. **Very high risk**: You could burn in 20 to 30 minutes. Stay out of direct sunlight, cover up and use a sunscreen of SPF 15+.

USA/Canada	12p per minute
Australia	22p per minute
Eire	10p per minute
South Africa	38p per minute

(BT weekend rates with above discounts)

Lakes and Mountains

AUSTRIA & LAKES
Lake Wolfgang, Kaprun, Kitzbühel, Söll etc.

Flights from **£99** from **£179**

Date	Board	7 nts	10 nts	11 nts	14 nts
Wed 2, 9 June	Bed & Bkfst	£179	£239	-	£289
	Half Board	£229	£279	-	£349
Sat 5, 12 June	Bed & Bkfst	£179	-	£249	£289
	Half Board	£229	-	£289	£349
Wed 16 June	Bed & Bkfst	£199	£259	-	£309
	Half Board	£249	£299	-	£369
Sat 19 June	Bed & Bkfst	£179	-	£249	£289
	Half Board	£229	-	£289	£349

These tables come from the newspaper.
What information does each give you?

Find some more tables in the newspaper.
Write down what information each gives you.

Time

Remember
60 seconds = 1 minute
60 minutes = 1 hour
24 hours = 1 day

7 days = 1 week
52 weeks = 1 year
365 days = 1 year except a leap
  year has 366 days

Time can be shown as **analogue** or **digital** time.
This is how we read **analogue** time.

Example   twenty to eleven or 20 to 11

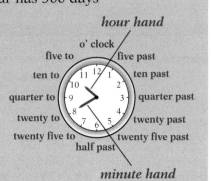

hour hand
o' clock
five to — five past
ten to — ten past
quarter to — quarter past
twenty to — twenty past
twenty five to — twenty five past
half past
minute hand

Examples These show **analogue** and **digital** time.

1.  is **9:35**

2. is **1:45**

Exercise 1 **A** Write down the times shown by these clocks.
The first one is done.

1.
3 o'clock

2.

3.

4.

5.

6.

7.

8.

B Write the times on the clocks in **A** as digital time.

C Draw clock faces to show these digital times.
   1. 2:20   2. 12:30   3. 5:40   4. 7:50   5. 10:35

a.m./p.m. time and 24-hour time

12-hour clock times use **a.m.** and **p.m.** to tell the difference between
times before midday and times after midday.
a.m. is from midnight up to midday.
p.m. is from midday up to midnight.
Midnight is 12 a.m. and midday is 12 p.m.

24-hour clocks number the hours from 0 to 23.
24-hour times always have 4 digits.

Examples 7 a.m. is written as 0700 or 07.00.
2:25 p.m. is written as 1425 or 14.25.

Exercise 2 **A** Write these in 24-hour time.
   1. 7:25 a.m.   2. 11:16 a.m.   3. 3:55 a.m.   4. 1 p.m.
   5. 4:20 p.m.   6. 10:35 p.m.   7. 12:15 a.m.   8. 9:42 p.m.
   9. 35 minutes after midnight.   10. 40 minutes before midday.

B Write these in a.m. or p.m. time.
   1. 0600   2. 0820   3. 1650   4. 1035   5. 1320   6. 2245
   7. 1230   8. 1917   9. 1836   10. 2020   11. 0004   12. 0055

Solving time problems

We often have to **solve time problems** by:

- changing between units of time such as from minutes to hours or minutes to seconds
- adding times
- calculating the length of time taken to do something.

Example How many minutes and seconds in 486 seconds?

Answer There are 60 seconds in 1 minute.
$\frac{486}{60} = 8.1$
There are 8 minutes and 0.1 of a minute.
We must change 0.1 of a minute into seconds.
$0.1 \times 60 = 6$ seconds
so 486 seconds is 8 minutes and 6 seconds.

Note: Some calculators have a key which changes minutes in decimal form into minutes and seconds. (Or hours in decimal form into hours and minutes.) Find out if your calculator has one of these keys. Find out how to use it.

Example Adrian travelled from Cheltenham to Brentwood by car.
1. He left at 11.28 and arrived at 13.21. How many minutes did the journey take?
2. Write 13.21 in a.m. or p.m. time.

Answer 1. From 11.28 to 12.00 there are 32 minutes.
From 12.00 to 13.00 there are 60 minutes.
From 13.00 to 13.21 there are 21 minutes.
$32 + 60 + 21 = 113$
The journey took 113 minutes, or 1 hour and 53 minutes.
2. 13.21 is 1.21 p.m.

Exercise 3   **A**   Use a copy of this.

LONDON

Hamish arrived at the train station at the time shown on the clock.
(a) Write down the time shown.   *(1)*

The train arrived 30 minutes later.
(b) Draw hands on the clock face to show the time when the train arrived.   *(1)*
(c) Write this time as it would be shown on a 24-hour clock.
  (i)   in the morning,
  (ii) in the evening.   *(2)*

B How many hours and minutes are there between
1. 7:10 a.m. and 11:07 a.m.
2. 0832 and 1139
3. 3:48 p.m. and 4:05 p.m.
4. 0946 and 1052
5. 5:53 p.m. and 6:49 p.m.
6. 1435 and 1525
7. 6:40 a.m. and 8:22 a.m.
8. 1643 and 1738
9. 7:52 a.m. and 11:27 a.m.
10. 1957 and 2143?

C Change these to minutes and seconds.
1. 140 seconds   2. 335 seconds   3. 117 seconds   4. 500 seconds

D Change these to hours and minutes.
1. 116 minutes   2. 220 minutes   3. 184 minutes   4. 352 minutes

E Write these in weeks, to the nearest week.
1. 123 days   2. 320 days   3. 438 days   4. 562 days

F Add these times.
1. $2\frac{1}{2}$ hours and 35 minutes
2. $3\frac{1}{4}$ hours and 17 minutes
3. 58 minutes and 63 minutes
4. 1 hour 25 minutes and 58 minutes.

G How many hours and minutes did each of these journeys take?
1. A bus left at 11:38 a.m. and arrived at 1:26 p.m.
2. A car left at 1436 and arrived at 1556.
3. A train left at 2:45 p.m. and arrived at 5:08 p.m.
4. A hiker left at 0824 and arrived at 1116.
5. A cyclist left at 6:42 a.m. and arrived at 10:19 a.m.
6. A coach left at 1057 and arrived at 1608.

H 1. A train left at 1015 and took 3 hours and 36 minutes for the journey.
   At what time did it arrive?
2. A train left Bristol at 0944. It arrived in Newcastle 4 hours and 36 minutes later.
   (a) What time did it arrive?
   (b) Another train left at 0951.
     How much later than the first train did the second train leave?

I
Isobel can swim a length of a pool in 20 seconds.   **LONDON**
She swims 20 lengths.
(a) Work out how long, in seconds, it takes Isobel to swim 20 lengths.   *(1)*
(b) Change your answer to (a) to minutes and seconds.   *(2)*

J Three people go to the gym.
   Siobhan goes for 130 minutes.
   Isobel goes for $2\frac{1}{3}$ hours.
   Usuf goes for 2 hours and 15 minutes.
1. How many minutes does Isobel go for?
2. How many hours and minutes does Siobhan go for?
3. Who went for the longest time?

K Helen catches a coach from Cheltenham to London Heathrow.
The coach leaves Cheltenham at 1640 and arrives at London Heathrow at 1828.
1. What was her time of arrival in 12-hour clock time?
2. How many minutes did the journey take?

L Lamb should be cooked for 65 minutes per kilogram plus 25 minutes.
A leg of lamb weighs 2 kg.
It is placed in the oven at 4:30 p.m.
At what time will it be cooked?

Puzzles

1. Sirah has to be at school at 8:40 a.m.
It takes her 16 minutes to walk to school.
It takes her 15 minutes to eat breakfast.
She does 20 minutes of music practice each morning.
It takes her 24 minutes to get up, have a wash and get dressed.
What time must she get out of bed?

2. How many minutes are there to 6 o'clock if 50 minutes ago it was 6 times as many minutes to 6 o'clock as it is now?

Timetables

Worked Exam Question

Here is a train timetable.
(a) At what time should the train leave Coventry?
(b) How long should it take for the train to travel from Wolverhampton to Milton Keynes?

LONDON

Place	Time of Leaving
Crewe	08:00
Wolverhampton	08:40
Birmingham	09:00
Coventry	09:30
Rugby	09:40
Milton Keynes	10:10
London	10:45

(1)

Read the times carefully. Use a ruler to help.

(2)

Answer (a) 09:30.
(b) The train leaves Wolverhampton at 08:40 and arrives at Milton Keynes at 10:10.
This is **1 hour and 30 minutes** or **90 minutes**.

20 minutes   1 hour   10 minutes
8:40   9:00   10:00 10:10

Exercise 4   **A**   The timetable shows the weekday train times from Derby to London.

Dep	Derby	0756	0902	1002	1102	1202	then every hour until	2002	2108
Arr	London	0930	1046	1148	1242	1348		2150	2238

1. How many minutes does it take the 0902 train to travel from Derby to London?
2. All the trains between the 0902 and the 2002 take approximately the same time to complete the journey.
   Estimate the time at which the 1802 will arrive in London.
3. Nigel wants to leave Derby after half past eleven and be in London before three o'clock in the afternoon.
   List all the possible trains he could catch from Derby.

B

SEG

The times of some early evening television programmes are shown.

BBC 1

5 00   Newsround
5 10   Blue Peter
5 35   Neighbours
6 00   News

(a)   What time does Neighbours start in 24-hour clock time?   *(1)*

(b)   Neighbours is shown twice a day five days a week.
All programmes of Neighbours are the same length.
For how many hours and minutes is Neighbours shown each week?   *(2)*

C

LONDON

The table below shows part of a train timetable.

Mondays to Fridays

London Paddington	1400	1500	1600	1700	1730	1800	1830	1900	2000	2100
Slough	1404	1504	——	——	1734	——	1834	1904	2004	2104
Reading ✈	1427	1525	1610	1710	1755	——	1857	1927	2027	2127
Swindon	1459	1554	1654	1752	1825	——	1934	1959	2059	2200
Bristol Parkway ‡	1527	1620	1720	1819	1852	1919	2002	2027	2127	2228
Newport	1549	1644	1743	1841	1914	1942	2024	2049	2149	2250
Cardiff Central	1606	1701	1800	1858	1931	1959	2041	2106	2206	2312
Bridgend	1626	1721	1820	1918	1951	2019	2101	2126	2226	2332
Port Talbot Parkway	1637	1732	1831	1929	2002	2030	2112	2137	2237	2343
Neath	1645	1740	1839	1937	2010	2038	2120	2145	2245	2351
Swansea	1655	1755	1855	1950	2020	2050	2135	2200	2300	0005
Carmarthen	1744	1904	1954	——	2113	2200	——	——	2348	——
Haverfordwest	1824	1946	——	——	——	2245	——	——	——	——
Milford Haven	1900	2002	——	——	——	2301	——	——	——	——
Fishguard Harbour	——	——	——	——	——	——	——	——	0049	——

(a)   At what time should the latest train leave Newport?   *(1)*

A train arrives in Swindon at 1825.

(b)   At what time should that train have left London?   *(1)*

Only one train goes to Fishguard Harbour.

(c)   At what time should this train leave Cardiff Central?   *(1)*

D A bus timetable is shown.

STRATFORD UPON AVON WOOD STREET	...	**0800**	**0820**	**0935**	**1035**	**1135**	**1235**
Stratford upon Avon Bridge Street	...	0802	0822	0937	1037	1137	1237
Clifford Chambers New Inn	...	0807	0827	0942	1042	1142	1242
Lower Quinton College Arms	...	0818	0836	0951	1051	1151	1251
Mickleton Three Ways	...	...	0845	1000	1100	1200	1300
CHIPPING CAMPDEN NOEL ARMS	**0643**	**0853**	**0853**	...	**1108**	**1208**	...
Broad Campden Bakers Arms	0648	0858	0858	...	1113	1213	...
Blockley Bowling Green	0653	0903	0903	...	1118	1218	...
Weston Sub Edge	...	...	...	1004	...	...	1304
Willersey Pool	...	...	...	1007	...	...	1307
BROADWAY HIGH STREET LYGON ARMS	...	...	...	**1011**	...	...	**1311**

1. David intends to catch a bus from Lower Quinton College Arms to Blockley Bowling Green. He has to be at Blockley Bowling Green at 9:30 a.m. What is the time of the latest bus he can catch?
2. Elise misses the 0800 bus from Stratford upon Avon Wood Street to Chipping Campden and catches the 0820 instead.
   How much shorter time does the journey take?

Other tables

We often have to **read information from a table** and use it to answer questions.

Worked Exam Question

Simon, Petra and their child Cindy book a holiday at the hotel Belaplaya. The holiday is for eleven nights, departing on 6th August 1999. They book a room with a balcony and sea view and decide to have half board.

(a) Calculate the cost of the holiday including insurance. **(7)**

(b) A discount of 10% is given on all costs except the insurance. How much discount is given? **(2)**

SUMMER SUN 1999

WJEC

Hotel name and board	BELAPLAYA Bed & Breakfast				
Number of nights	7	10	11	14	
Adult/child	Adult	Adult	Adult	Adult	Child
Departures on or between					
21 May – 25 May	399	435	445	479	90
26 May – 10 Jun	365	419	435	489	92
11 Jun – 17 Jun	369	429	449	505	94
18 Jun – 24 Jun	369	435	455	515	96
25 Jun – 01 Jul	379	439	459	519	98
02 Jul – 08 Jul	385	445	465	525	100
09 Jul – 16 Jul	385	445	469	529	100
17 Jul – 03 Aug	425	489	515	579	102
04 Aug – 24 Aug	435	495	520	590	105
25 Aug – 07 Sep	419	479	499	555	94
Supplements per adult per night	Balcony £5.50 Balcony & sea view £11.00 Half board £15.50				
Additional costs	Insurance £12.50 per person				

Answer   (a)   From 6th August, 11 nights without any extras cost £520 per adult and £105 per child.

Basic cost	$= 2 \times £520 + £105$
	$= £1145$
Balcony and sea view	$= £11.00 \times 11 \times 2$
	$= £242$
Insurance	$= £12.50 \times 3$
	$= £37.50$
Half Board	$= £15.50 \times 11 \times 2$
	$= £341$
Total cost	$= £1145 + £242 + £37.50 + £341$
	$= \textbf{£1765.50}$

(number of nights, number of adults, number of people, number of nights, number of adults)

(b)   Discount is given on   £1765.50 – £37.50   or   £1728.

$$10\% \text{ of } 1728 = 0.1 \times £1728$$
$$= £172.80$$

The discount is **£172.80**.

Exercise 5   **A**

NEAB

The table below shows the number of Compact Discs (CDs) and the number of Long Playing Records (LPs) that were sold from 1984 to 1992. The figures are in millions.

	1984	1985	1986	1987	1988	1989	1990	1991	1992
Number of CDs (millions)	0	5	10	20	30	35	45	60	70
Number of LPs (millions)	55	55	50	50	45	40	20	15	5

(a) 70 million CDs were sold in 1992.
Write the number 70 million in figures.   *(1)*
(b) In which year did the sales of CDs overtake the sale of LPs?   *(1)*

B

NEAB

This diagram shows some of the tallest buildings in the world and the years when they were built.

(a) How much taller is the Sears Tower than the Great Pyramid?   *(2)*

(b) Which building is about 175 metres high?
(3 feet is approximately 1 metre.)   *(2)*

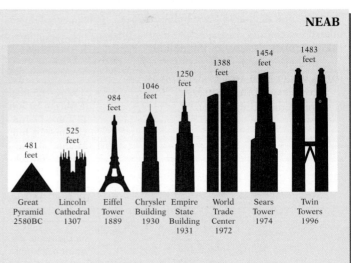

C Use a copy of this.

WJEC

Sian shops at a supermarket and is given the following bill.

(a) Complete the spaces in the above bill. *(3)*

(b) The supermarket gives 1 saver point for every complete £5 spent. How many saver points does Sian get with the above bill? *(1)*

ITEM	COST
1 jar of honey	£1.76
2.5 kilograms of new potatoes at 36p/kg	
2 jars of tea at £1.98 per jar	£3.96
Topside of beef	£11.45
3 packets of Weetabix at £1.54 per packet	
Total	£

D

LONDON

Gino's Pizza Choice	Deep Pan			Thin Crust		
	Regular	**Medium**	**Family**	**Regular**	**Medium**	**Family**
Supreme	£3.30	£5.75	£8.50	£3.10	£5.45	£8.25
Mexican	£3.10	£5.30	£8.00	£2.95	£5.05	£7.70
Vegetable	£2.95	£5.15	£7.40	£2.75	£4.95	£7.15
Seafood	£3.00	£5.20	£7.45	£2.80	£5.00	£7.20

The table shows the cost of some of Gino's pizzas.
(a) Write down the cost of a Deep Pan Regular Vegetable pizza. *(1)*

Alberto spent £5.45 on a pizza.
(b) Which pizza did Alberto buy? *(2)*

E The table shows the costs of posting a letter.

LONDON

First Class	Weight not over	Second Class
26p	60 g	20p
39p	100 g	31p
49p	150 g	38p
60p	200 g	45p
70p	250 g	55p
80p	300 g	64p
92p	350 g	73p
£1.04	400 g	83p
£1.17	450 g	93p
£1.30	500 g	£1.05

First Class	Weight not over	Second Class
£1.60	600 g	£1.25
£2.00	700 g	£1.45
£2.15	750 g	£1.55
£2.30	800 g	
£2.55	900 g	
£2.75	1000 g	
£3.45	1250 g	
£4.15	1500 g	
£4.85	1750 g	
£5.55	2000 g	

A letter weighs 350 g.
(a) Write down the cost of sending the letter by first class post. *(1)*

3 letters each weigh 230 g. They are sent by second class post.
(b) Work out the total cost of sending the 3 letters. *(2)*

One letter weighs 1200 g. Another letter weighs 1 kilogram.
You cannot send a letter which weighs more than 750 g by second class post.
(c) Work out the total cost of sending the 2 letters. *(2)*

F

The table below shows the monthly payments for an insurance scheme.   **LONDON**
The payments depend on the age at which a person starts paying.
There are two rates, Standard Rate
and Discount Rate.
Alison is aged 17. She pays the
Standard Rate.
(a) (i) Write down Alison's
            monthly payment.
      (ii) Work out the total amount
            Alison will pay in a year.
Mr Masili pays at the Discount Rate.
He pays £19.89 each month.
If he were one year older, he would
have to pay £35.19 each month.
(b) How old is Mr Masili?

	Monthly Payments per Person	
Age	Standard Rate in pounds	Discount Rate in pounds
0 – 16	7.20	6.12
17 – 19	12.60	10.71
20 – 39	17.00	14.45
40 – 59	23.40	19.89
60 – 74	41.40	35.19
75 and over	84.80	72.08

(3)

(2)

Homework/Review

A **What would you get if you crossed a bank
book with a maths teacher?**

| 1440 | 10:40 | 6:40 | 8:40 | 1640 | | 1340 | 4:40 | 10:40 | 1840 | 2040 | 8:40 | 1440 | 0440 |

Use a copy of this box.
Write these in 24-hour clock time.
S. 4:40 a.m.   **Y.** 4:40 p.m.   **B.** 6:40 p.m.   **L.** 8:40 p.m.

Write these in 12-hour clock time.
E. 0840   **R.** 1640   **O.** 2240   **N.** 1840

M. A train leaves at 1023. The journey takes 4 hours 17 minutes.
     At what time does the train arrive? Give your answer in 24-hour clock
     time.
P. Mr Chan went shopping at 1008. He shopped for 3 hours 32 minutes.
     At what time did he finish shopping?
     Give your answer in 24-hour clock time.

B

NEAB

In 1996 the Olympic Games
were held in Atlanta USA.
When it is 9 a.m. in Atlanta it
is 2 p.m. on the same day in
England.
Television coverage of one
event in the Olympic Games
begins in England at 6 p.m.
When it is 6 p.m. in England,
what time is it in Atlanta?

Atlanta, USA

9 am

London, England

2 pm

(1)

C

MEG

(a) The table shows the bus times from Rugby to Cambridge.

Rugby	0615	1015	1415	1815
Kettering	0650	1050	1450	1850
Huntingdon	0725	1125	1525	1925
Cambridge	0800	1200	1600	2000

Mrs Adams wants to arrive in Cambridge by 1330.
(i)   What time is the latest bus she can catch from Kettering?   *(1)*
(ii) How long will her bus journey take?   *(1)*

(b) The table shows the bus fares between Rugby, Kettering, Huntingdon and Cambridge.

RUGBY

Key:
S	Single
DR	Day Return

£2.20	£3.50	KETTERING			
£4.10	£5.40	£2.00	£3.00	HUNTINGDON	
£6.00	£6.80	£3.50	£4.00	£2.00	£3.00	CAMBRIDGE
S	DR	S	DR	S	DR

Mr Brown goes on a day trip from Rugby to Huntingdon.
How much does he save by buying a day return instead of two single tickets?   *(1)*

Task

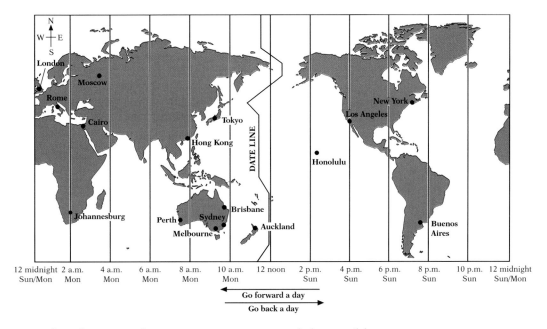

| 12 midnight Sun/Mon | 2 a.m. Mon | 4 a.m. Mon | 6 a.m. Mon | 8 a.m. Mon | 10 a.m. Mon | 12 noon | 2 p.m. Sun | 4 p.m. Sun | 6 p.m. Sun | 8 p.m. Sun | 10 p.m. Sun | 12 midnight Sun/Mon |

← Go forward a day
Go back a day →

This diagram shows time zones around the world.
Work out what time it is in these places when it is 9 p.m. in Britain.

Tokyo   Rome   Los Angeles   New York   Auckland   Sydney   Moscow

Note: If you cross from East to West across the date line you go forward a day.

Example   If it is 7 p.m. on **Sunday** in New York, it will be about 8 a.m. on **Monday** in Hong Kong.

Note: If you cross from West to East across the date line you go back a day.

Example   If it is 2 a.m. on **Tuesday** in Johannesburg it will be 4 p.m. on **Monday** in Los Angeles.

☑ KEY POINTS

☑   60 seconds = 1 minute   24 hours = 1 day   365 days = 1 year
    60 minutes = 1 hour   7 days = 1 week   366 days = 1 leap year
                                 52 weeks = 1 year

☑   Quarter past five or $\frac{1}{4}$ past 5 is **analogue time**.
    5:15 is **digital time**.

☑   **a.m. times** are in the morning, from midnight up to midday.
    p.m. times are in the afternoon and evening, from midday up to midnight.

☑   **24-hour times** always have 4 numbers.
    The hours are numbered from 0 to 23.
    Examples   4:50 p.m. in 24-hour time is 1650.
                 12:05 a.m. in 24-hour time is 0005.

◀◀ CHAPTER REVIEW ◀◀

◀◀
Exercise 2
on page 328

A   1.   Write 4:55 p.m. in 24-hour time.
        2.   Write 2128 in 12-hour clock time.

◀◀
Exercise 3
on page 329

B   The cooking time in a recipe is 25 minutes.
        Alan starts cooking 24 small cakes at 8:45 a.m.
        What time will the cakes be cooked?

◀◀
Exercise 3
on page 329

C

NEAB

In 1954, Roger Bannister was the first man to run a mile in under 4 minutes.
His time was 3 minutes 59.40 seconds.

(i) How much less than 4 minutes was this?
Give your answer in seconds. *(1)*

(ii) In 1985, Steve Cram ran the mile in 3 minutes 46.32 seconds.
How much less than Roger Bannister's time is this? *(1)*

◀◀
Exercises 2,
3, 4 and 5
on pages 328,
329, 332 and
334

D

(a) Write the time 1410 in 12-hour clock time. SEG
A bus timetable for journeys between Doncaster and York is shown.

Doncaster – York

Doncaster			0910	1210	1410	1610	1810	1910
Bentley			0916	1216	1416	1616	1816	1916
Askern			0933	1233	1433	1633	1833	1933
Selby	0820	0920	1020	1320	1520	1720	1920	2020
York	0905	1005	1105	1405	1605	1805	2005	2105

(b) Usaf travels from Doncaster to York on the 1410 bus.
How long does this journey take? *(2)*

◀◀
Exercise 4
on page 332

E Use the timetable given in **D(a)** for this question.

1. Peter wants to arrive in York by 1430.
What is the latest bus he can catch from Bentley?

2. How long will the journey take?

◀◀
Exercise 5
on page 334

F

The length and weight of a puppy are measured every 5 weeks. MEG
The results are shown in the table below.

Age (weeks)	Length (cm)	Weight
0	15	335 g
5	20	650 g
10	27	850 g
15	35	1.1 kg
20	40	1.4 kg
25	44	2.2 kg

(a) How heavy was the puppy at 25 weeks? *(1)*

(b) How old do you think the puppy was when
its length was 30 cm? *(1)*

(c) How much heavier was the puppy at
20 weeks than at 5 weeks? *(2)*

23 Perimeter, Area and Volume

By the end of this chapter you will be able to:

- find the perimeter of a shape
- find the area of a shape by counting squares
- find the area of a square, rectangle or triangle using a formula
- find the perimeter and area of shapes made up of squares, rectangles, triangles or circles
- find the circumference and area of a circle
- find the volume of a solid by counting cubes
- find the volume of a cube or cuboid using a formula.

Getting started ....

You will need   some squared paper

On a 2 × 2 grid there are 5 squares in total.
There are four 1 × 1 squares and one 2 × 2 square.

On a 3 × 3 grid there are 14 squares in total.
  nine 1 × 1 squares
  four 2 × 2 squares
  one 3 × 3 square

How many squares are there on a 4 × 4 grid?
How many squares are there on a 5 × 5 grid?

Fill in this table.
Use your table to find how many squares in total there are in an 8 × 8 grid.

Size of grid	Number of squares					
	1 × 1	2 × 2	3 × 3	4 × 4	5 × 5	Total
3 × 3	9	4	1	—	—	14
4 × 4						
5 × 5						

Perimeter and area

The **perimeter** of a shape is the distance right around the outside of the shape.

Example   The perimeter of this shape is given by
Perimeter = 4 + 3 + 1 + 4 + 5 + 7
        = 24

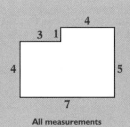

All measurements are in centimetres.

We can find or estimate the **area** of a shape by counting squares.
Area is measured in **mm²**, **cm²**, **m²**, **km²** or **inches²**, **feet²**, **miles²**.

 # Worked Exam Question

· ·

WJEC

The following plan shows the shape of the monkey and zebra cages at
Bryndy Zoo. The grid is divided into one metre squares.

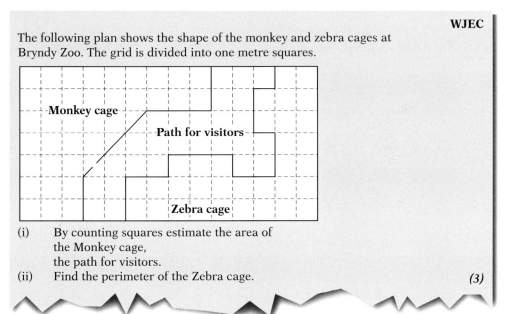

(i)   By counting squares estimate the area of
       the Monkey cage,
       the path for visitors.
(ii)   Find the perimeter of the Zebra cage.   *(3)*

Answer   (i)   It is best to put numbers in
                    the squares as you count
                    them.
                    These are shown in red on
                    the diagram.
                    Two half squares make up
                    square 24.
                    There is a half square, $37\frac{1}{2}$,
                    left at the end.
                    The monkey cage has an
                    area of about **37.5 m²**.

                    The path for visitors has an area of about **27.5 m²**.
            (ii)   The perimeter is the distance around the outside.
                    The perimeter of the zebra cage is **36 m**.

Exercise 1   **A**

LONDON

(a) Find the area, in
     cm², of the
     shape.
(b) Find the
     perimeter, in
     cm, of the shape.

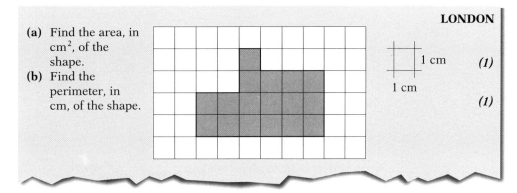

1 cm   *(1)*

1 cm

(1)

B

The diagram shows a pentagon.
Each square on the diagram has an area of 1 cm².
Work out the area of the pentagon.

SEG

(2)

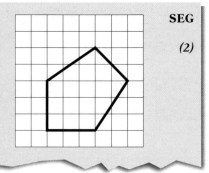

C

The grid is divided into cm squares.
Estimate the area of the shape
shown.

WJEC

(2)

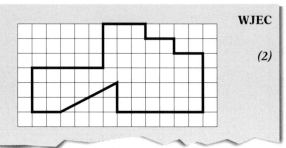

D Use 1 cm grid paper for this question.
Draw a set of axes with *x* and *y*-values from 0 to 8.
   1. On the grid, plot and label the points
       A (1,1),   B (4,4)   C (7,1).
   2. Draw the triangle ABC. Find the area of triangle ABC.

E

The diagram shows a shape.
(a) What are the coordinates
     of P?
(b) Each square on the
     diagram has an area of
     1 cm².
     What is the area of the
     shape?

SEG

(1)

(1)

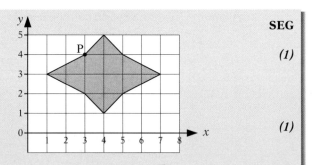

F

The diagram represents the surface of a lake in winter. The lake is shaded   LONDON
on the grid.
(a) Estimate the area, in cm², of the
     diagram that is shaded.

(2)

Each square on the grid represents a
square with sides of length 100 m.
(b) Work out the area, in m², repre-
     sented by one square on the grid.
(c) Estimate the area, in m², of the lake.

(2)
(1)

In summer the area of the lake
decreases by 15%.
(d) Work out the area, in m², of the
     lake in summer.

(2)

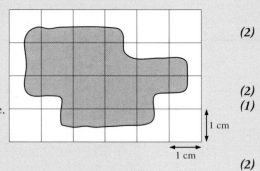

Finding areas of squares, rectangles and triangles

We can use the following formulae to calculate the areas of **squares**, **rectangles** and **triangles**.

Area of a square = length × length or ℓ × ℓ

Area of a rectangle = length × width or ℓ × w

Area of a triangle $= \dfrac{\text{base} \times \text{height}}{2}$ or $\dfrac{b \times h}{2}$

or $\dfrac{1}{2}(b \times h)$

Worked Exam Question

A family buys carpet measuring 12 feet by 12 feet. What is the area of the carpet in square metres?

NEAB

12 feet

12 feet

To convert feet into metres:
multiply by 3 then divide by 10.

Answer   First we must convert 12 feet into metres.

$12 \text{ feet} = \dfrac{12 \times 3}{10}$ metres

$= 3.6$ metres

Area of a square $= \ell \times \ell$

$= 3.6 \times 3.6$

$= \mathbf{12.96 \ m^2}$

Do not forget to put *units* for area with your answer.

Exercise 2   **A**   Work out the perimeter and area of these.

1.

4 m
square

2.
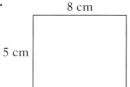
8 cm
5 cm

3.
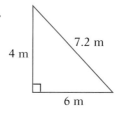
7.2 m
4 m
6 m

4.
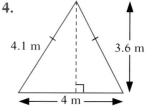
4.1 m
3.6 m
4 m

5.
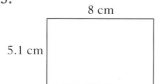
8 cm
5.1 cm

6.

3.6 m
square

7.
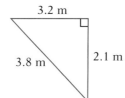
3.2 m
3.8 m
2.1 m

8.
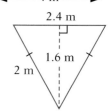
2.4 m
1.6 m
2 m

B

The diagram shows a small gift box in the
form of a triangular prism.
The length of the prism is 6 cm.
The sides of the triangular cross-section are
3 cm, 4 cm, and 5 cm respectively.

Calculate the area of the triangular end, *ADE*,
of the prism.

State clearly the units of your answer.

(2)

WJEC

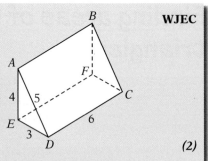

Diagram not drawn to scale

C   The length of a rectangle is 2 cm more than its width.
Calculate the area of the rectangle when the width is
1. 3 cm   2. 4 cm   3. 5 cm   4. 6 cm

D   1.   Write down an expression for the
perimeter of this triangle.
2.   Write down an expression for the
area of this triangle.

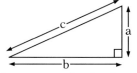

E   Using trial and improvement, find the width of a rectangle if it has a
length 2 cm more than its width and its area is 34 cm².
Give your answer correct to 1 d.p.

Perimeters and areas of composite shapes

Often shapes can be divided up into squares, rectangles and triangles.

Example

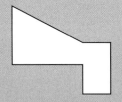

This shape can be
divided into a
triangle, a rectangle
and a square.

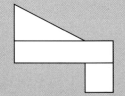

We can find the area of the shape by finding the areas of the triangle,
rectangle and square and adding them together.

Worked Exam Question

(a)   Work out the perimeter of the whole shape
ABCD.

In part **(b)** you must write down the units with
your answers.

(b)   Work out the area of
(i)   the square *EBCD*,
(ii)   the triangle *ABE*.

LONDON
(2)

(5)

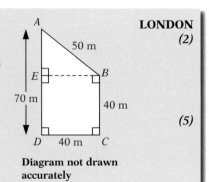

**Diagram not drawn
accurately**

Answer (a) Perimeter $= 70 + 50 + 40 + 40$
$$= 200 \text{ m}$$

(b) (i) area of a square $= \ell \times \ell$
$$= 40 \times 40$$
$$= 1600 \text{ m}^2$$

(ii) To calculate the area of triangle AEB we need to know the height of the triangle, AE.
We find this by subtracting 40 m from 70 m.
$70 - 40 = 30$ m   so AE $= 30$ m.

$$\text{Area of triangle} = \frac{\text{base} \times \text{height}}{2}$$
$$= \frac{40 \times 30}{2}$$
$$= \frac{1200}{2}$$
$$= 600 \text{ m}^2$$

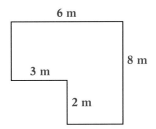

Exercise 3

A This is the floor plan of a room.
Work out the perimeter of the room.

B This shows the end of a building.
It is a rectangle with base 12 m and height 8 m,
on top of which is an equilateral triangle.
Find the perimeter of the shape.

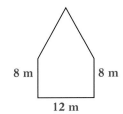

C

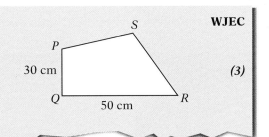

The perimeter of the quadrilateral
PQRS is 150 cm.
PQ = 30 cm, QR = 50 cm and RS = SP.
Find the length of RS.

WJEC

(3)

D 1. Work out the perimeter of the room.
2. Work out the area of the room.

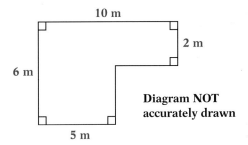

Diagram NOT accurately drawn

E Work out the area of these rooms.

1.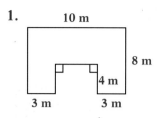

2.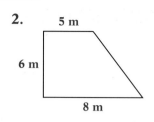

3.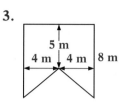

F Katy needs a new carpet for her kitchen.
She measures the floor and draws the plan.
Calculate the total area of the floor.
State the units of your answer.

MEG

(4)

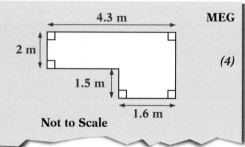

Not to Scale

G Brenda wants to tile her bathroom.
She uses tiles that measure 10 cm by 10 cm.

She tiles this surface.
1. How many tiles does she need?
2. Calculate the area of this surface.
3. Brenda wants to put a wooden strip
   around the perimeter of this surface.
   How many metres of wooden strip will
   she need?

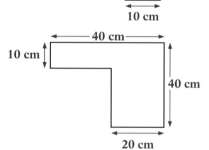

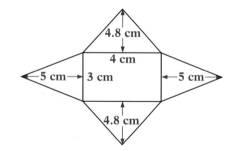

H This is a net for a pyramid.
Using the dimensions shown in the
diagram, calculate the total area of the
five faces of the pyramid.

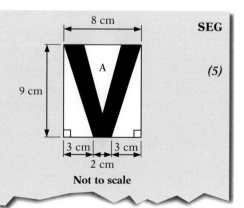

I A letter 'V' is cut from a rectangle measuring
9 cm by 8 cm, as shown.
The area of the triangle marked A is 12 cm².
What is the area of the 'V' shape?

SEG

(5)

Not to scale

Homework/Review 1

A
(a) Write down the co-ordinates of the points
   (i) P,   (ii) Q. *(2)*
Each small square on the grid has a side of 1 cm.
(b) Work out the area of the shaded shape. Write down the units with your answer. *(2)*
(c) Work out the perimeter of the shaded shape. *(2)*

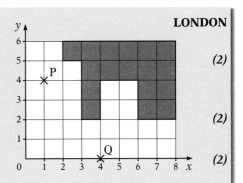

LONDON

B
Two right-angled triangles are put together on a 1 cm grid to make a kite.
(a) What type of angle is the angle marked x? *(1)*
(b) What is the area of the kite? Remember to state the units. *(2)*

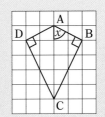

NEAB

C Each square on the grid is 1 cm by 1 cm.
Estimate the area of the oval.
Give the units of your answer.

D Work out the perimeter and area of these shapes.

1. 4.1 cm — square
2. 8 cm, 9.3 cm, 9.6 cm
3. 4.1 m, 5.1 m, 3 m
4. 48 mm, 27 mm

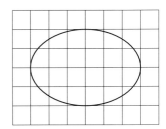

E Work out the area of these shapes.

1. 6 cm, 3 cm, 8 cm, 12 cm
2. 2 m, 5 m, 4 m, 5 m
3. A—7 cm—B, 4 cm, D, 7 cm, C, 6 cm, E

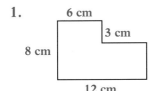

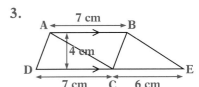

F Work out the perimeter of **E 1** and **E 2**.

Circumference and area of a circle

The perimeter of a circle is called the **circumference**.

> **Circumference of a circle = $\pi \times$ diameter** or **πd**
> or **Circumference of a circle = $2 \times \pi \times$ radius** or **2πr**

> **Area of a circle = $\pi \times$ (radius)^2 or πr^2**

Worked Exam Question

The train on a children's roundabout goes round in a circle
of diameter 6 m.

SEG

(a) **(i)**   Calculate the circumference of the circle.   *(2)*
(ii)   James rides on the train and travels 165 m.
How many complete turns does he go around?   *(1)*

The floor of the roundabout has a radius of 3.5 m.

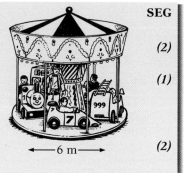

$\longleftarrow$ 6 m $\longrightarrow$ *(2)*

(b) Calculate the area of the floor.

Answer   **(a)** **(i)** Circumference $= \pi \times$ diameter
$\qquad\qquad\qquad = \pi \times 6$
$\qquad\qquad\qquad = \textbf{18.8 m}$ to 1d.p.

> Using the π button,
> $\pi \times 6 = 18.849556$.
> Round this to 1 or 2
> decimal places.

> You can use
> $\pi = 3.14$ or the
> π button on
> your calculator.

(ii) One turn is 18.8 m.
To find how many complete turns James goes around,
we must divide 165 by 18.8.
$165 \div 18.8 = 8.8$ to 1d.p.   So James completed **8** turns.

(b) Area $= \pi \times$ radius^2
$\qquad\quad = \pi \times 3.5 \times 3.5$
$\qquad\quad = \textbf{38.5 m}^2$ to 1d.p.

Example   A different roundabout has an area of 45 m^2.
Calculate the radius of this roundabout.

Answer   To find the radius, follow these steps. Use the balance method to solve.
Area $= \pi \times$ (radius)^2
$\qquad 45 = \pi \times$ (radius)^2

$$\frac{45}{\pi} = \frac{\pi \times (\text{radius})^2}{\pi} \qquad \textbf{Divide both sides by } \pi.$$

$$\frac{45}{\pi} = (\text{radius})^2$$

$$\sqrt{\frac{45}{\pi}} = \sqrt{\text{radius}^2} \qquad \textbf{Take the square root of both sides.}$$

$$\sqrt{\frac{45}{\pi}} = \text{radius}$$

radius = 3.8 to 1d.p.

Use π = 3.14 or use the π button on your calculator.

Exercise 4

A   A circular pool has a radius of 4 m.
  1. Calculate the circumference of the pool.
  2. Calculate the area of the pool.
  3. Another circular pool has an area of 120 m².
      Calculate the radius of this pool.

B
Some oil is spilt. The spilt oil is in the shape of a circle.
The circle has a diameter of 12 centimetres.
  (a) Work out the circumference, in cm, of the spilt oil.
      Give your answer correct to 1 decimal place.
  (b) The diameter of the spilt oil increases by 30%.
      Work out the new diameter, in centimetres, of the spilt oil.

LONDON

(3)

(2)

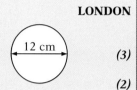

C
A circular flower bed has a diameter of 7.2 metres.
  (a) Work out the radius of the flower bed.
  (b) Calculate the area covered by the flower bed.

MEG
(1)
(3)

D   A circular lake has a diameter of 90 metres.
  1. Mr Pearson is asked to put a fence round the
      lake.
      Fencing comes in 25 m lengths.
      How many lengths must Mr Pearson buy to
      fence the lake?
  2. Calculate the surface area of the lake.
      Remember to state the units.

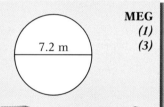

E   A café has circular tables.
      The diameter of each is 102 cm.
  1. Calculate the circumference of each table.
  2. The table mats used each have a radius of
      11 centimetres.
      Work out the area covered by one mat.

F   A circular track has a diameter of 70 metres.
      A horse, Charger, gallops along the diameter AB and back again.
      Another horse, Clem, gallops right around the outside of
      the track once.
      How much further does Clem gallop than Charger?

G   Mia is rolling a wheel along the ground.
      The wheel has a diameter of 90 cm.
      What is the minimum number of complete turns the wheel must make to
      cover a distance of 5 m?

Volume

Volume is the amount of space a solid occupies.
Volume is measured in mm^3 or cm^3 or m^3.

We can find the volume of a solid **by counting cubes**.

Example Each of the small cubes has sides of 1 cm.
The volume of each small cube is $1\ cm^3$.
The solid is made from 20 small cubes.
It has a volume of $20\ cm^3$.

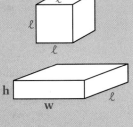

We can find the volume of a cube or cuboid using formulae.

> **Volume of a cube = length × length × length**
> **= length³ or ℓ^3**

> **Volume of a cuboid = length × width × height**
> **= ℓ × w × h**

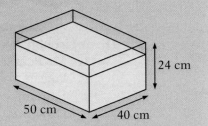

Sometimes we need to know this fact. **1 mℓ = 1 cm³**

Example A rectangular tank has length 50 cm,
width 40 cm and height 24 cm.
It is placed on a horizontal table.
Water is poured into the tank until it is
three quarters full.
1. Calculate the depth of water in the
   tank.
2. Calculate how many litres of water are
   in the tank.

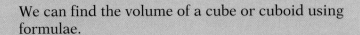

24 cm

50 cm   40 cm

Answer 1. The tank is $\frac{3}{4}$ full.
The depth of the water is $\frac{3}{4}$ of 24 or 18 cm. $\frac{3}{4} \times 24 = 18$
2. Volume of water = ℓ × w × h
   = 50 × 40 × 18
   = 36 000 cm³.
1 mℓ= 1 cm³
So 36 000 cm³ = 36 000 mℓ
To convert this to litres, divide by 1000.   36 000 ÷ 1000 = 36
There are 36 ℓ of water in the tank.

Exercise 5

A The dimensions of a metal container are
30 cm by 10 cm by 40 cm.
1. Calculate the volume of the container,
   stating your units.
2. What volume of water, in ml, would this
   container hold if it was full?

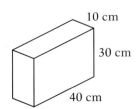

10 cm

30 cm

40 cm

B

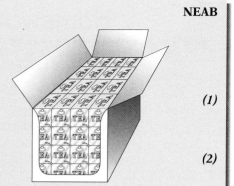

A factory produces packets of tea.
These packets are put into cardboard boxes to
be delivered to shops.
A drawing of one cardboard box is shown.
(a) How many packets of tea are there in
    one cardboard box? *(1)*
(b) Each packet of tea measures 12 cm by
    8 cm by 8 cm.
    Calculate the volume of one packet of
    tea. *(2)*

NEAB

C The sketch shows the cube that Chris made with his
building blocks.
Each block is a cube of volume 1 cm^3
What is the volume of the large cube?

D

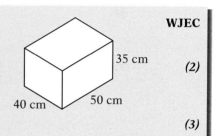

A firm buys coffee powder in boxes 50 cm
long, 40 cm wide and 35 cm high. The boxes
are full.
(a) Calculate the volume of coffee in a box. *(2)*
(b) The firm uses the coffee to fill smaller
    boxes which are cubes of side 10 cm.
    How many smaller boxes can be filled
    from one of the large boxes? *(3)*

WJEC

E

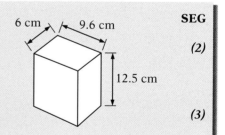

The diagram shows the dimensions of a box
of lawn fertiliser.
(a) Calculate the volume of the box. *(2)*

One box of fertiliser is needed for every
9 m^2 of lawn.
(b) How many boxes are needed to fertilise
    a circular lawn of radius 4 m? *(3)*

SEG

F Tim buys a packet of icing for a birthday cake.
The packet measures 4.5 cm by 6 cm by 10 cm.
1. What is the volume of the icing?
2. The top of the birthday cake is a rectangle
   measuring 20 cm by 24 cm.
   Tim uses the whole packet of icing to ice the
   cake.
   How thick will the icing be when it is rolled
   out to just cover the top of the cake?

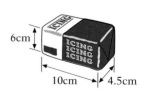

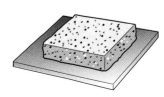

Homework/Review 2

· ·

Use π = 3.14 or use the π button on your calculator.

A

The diagram shows part of a garden, in the form of a square, with a circular pond, of radius 3 m, surrounded by a lawn.

(a) Calculate the circumference of the pond, giving your answer to an appropriate degree of accuracy.

(b) Calculate the area of the lawn.

WJEC

(3)

(3)

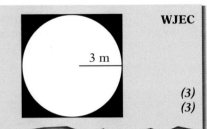

3 m

B

Calculate the area of a semi-circle, radius 20 cm.

SEG
(3)

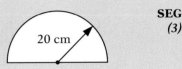

20 cm

Remember, a semi-circle is half of a circle.

C

The penny-farthing is a bicycle with a large front wheel and a small rear wheel.
The radius of the large front wheel is 75 cm.

(a) The front wheel makes one full turn. Calculate the distance that the bicycle moves.

(b) The small rear wheel has a radius of 25 cm. How many full turns will the small wheel make for each full turn of the front wheel?

SEG

(2)

(1)

75cm

D

The stand for the medal winners at an athletics meeting is made up of cubical blocks, as shown in the diagram.
Each block is of side 1 foot.

(a) What is the volume of
   (i) the section marked 3
   (ii) the section marked 2
   (iii) the section marked 1?

(b) Calculate the total volume of the stand.

(c) Work out the area of the front of the whole stand.

MEG

(1)
(1)
(1)
(1)
(2)

E

Mary has some cubes of side 1 centimetre.
She makes this shape with her cubes.

(a) What is the volume of this shape? Remember to state the units. **(2)**

(b) 24 of Mary's cubes just fill this box. What is the height of the box? **(1)**

NEAB

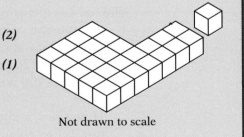

Not drawn to scale

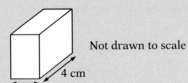

Not drawn to scale

4 cm

2 cm

✓ KEY POINTS

✓ The **perimeter** of a shape is the distance around the outside of the shape.

✓ The **area** of a shape is the amount of space it covers.

✓ We can find the **area of a shape** by counting squares.
Example The area of this shape is 4 cm².

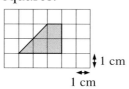

✓ **Area of a square = length × length**

   Area of a rectangle = length × width

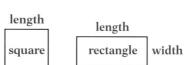

✓ **Area of a triangle = $\frac{1}{2}$ × base × height**

✓ The base and the height must be at right angles to each other.

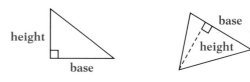

✓ The area of a composite shape can be found by dividing it into squares, rectangles and triangles.

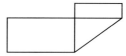

✓ The perimeter of a circle is called the **circumference**

   Circumference of a circle = π × diameter

   $\qquad\qquad\qquad\quad = 2 \times \pi \times \textbf{radius}$

✓ **Area of a circle = π × (radius)²**

✓ **Volume** is a measure of the amount of space a solid occupies.

✓ We can find the **volume** of a solid by **counting cubes**

✓ **Volume of a cube = length × length × length**

✓ **Volume of a cuboid = length × width × height**

Investigation

This rectangle has a perimeter of 32 units.
It is 10 units long and 6 units wide.

Sketch 5 more rectangles which have a perimeter of 32 units.
For all rectangles with a perimeter of 32 units, write down a relationship between the length and the width.

Which rectangle has the greatest area?

◄◄ CHAPTER REVIEW ◄◄

◄◄
Exercise 1
on page 341

A

The diagram shows two shapes.
Each square on the diagram has an area
of 1 cm².
(i)   Find the area of Shape A.
(ii)   Find the perimeter of Shape B.

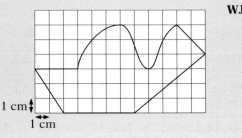

SEG

(1)
(1)

◄◄
Exercise 1
on page 341

B

By counting squares estimate the
area of this shape.

WJEC
(2)

◄◄
Exercises 2, 3
and 4 on pages
343, 345, and
349

C   Find the perimeter and area of these shapes. State the units.

1.

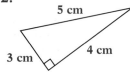

2.

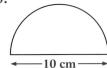

3.

◄◄
Exercise 5
on page 350

D

Jane uses one centimetre cubes to
make a model.
Two views of her model are shown.
(a)   How many cubes has Jane
used?

Jane places her model inside a box.
The box is in the shape of a cube
with sides 3 cm.
(b)   Calculate the volume of space left in the box, stating your units.

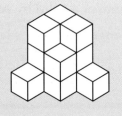

SEG

(1)

(4)

◄◄
Exercise 5
on page 350

E

Water is stored in a tank in the shape of a cuboid with a square base. The
sides of the base are 30 cm long. The depth of the water is 20 cm.
(a)   Work out the volume of the water.

More water is put in the tank. The depth of the
water rises to 21.6 cm.
(b)   Calculate the percentage increase in the
volume of the water in the tank.

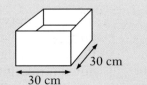

LONDON

(2)

(3)

Index

acute angles 124, 126, 138
adding 110, 122
  decimals 168, 179
  directed numbers 14, 18
  expressions 54, 66
  fractions 40, 41–2, 50
adjacent angles 127, 128, 130, 138
alternate angles 131, 132, 138
analogue time 327–8, 338
angles 124–39
  acute 124, 126, 138
  adjacent 127, 128, 130, 138
  alternate 131, 132, 138
  corresponding 129–30, 132, 138
  drawing 125, 138
  interior 133–4, 135, 138, 292
  measuring 125, 126, 138
  obtuse 124, 126, 138, 185
  opposite 127, 132, 138
  made with parallel lines 129–30,
    131–2, 133–4, 138
  at a point 127, 128, 138
  of polygons 188, 190, 192, 194
  reflex 124, 126, 138
  right 124, 128, 138
  straight 124, 138
  of a triangle 135, 182, 194
area of shapes 56, 63, 341, 343,
  348, 353
average 224–5, 227, 232
axis of symmetry 21–2, 31, 281,
  283, 295

balance method 114, 115, 116, 117,
  122, 253
bar charts 213–14, 232
bearings 318, 321, 322
brackets 16, 18, 58, 116, 122

calculators 37, 68–81, 146–7, 149
changing fractions, decimals and
  percentages 45–6, 50–1
circles 236, 248, 348, 353
class intervals 83, 92, 221
clocks 327–8
collection sheets 84, 85, 92
compass for drawing 236, 248
compass, points of 313, 314
cones 241, 248
congruence 240, 241, 245, 248
consecutive numbers 6, 68
continuous data 82, 92
conversion graphs 258, 265, 267
conversions
  metric 97, 100, 101, 108, 343,
    350
  temperature 64
coordinates of graphs 250–1, 265

corresponding angles 129–30, 132,
  138
crossnumbers 73, 77
cross-section 241, 248
cube numbers 75, 76, 141, 149
cube roots 75, 76, 145, 149
cubes (shape) 241, 248, 350, 353
cuboids 241, 248, 350, 353
cylinders 241, 248

data
  analysing 212–34
  collecting 82–93
  comparing 228–9
  continuous 82, 92
  correlation 304, 311
  discrete 82, 83, 92, 213, 232
  displaying 213–34
  range of 225, 227, 232
  sheets 84, 85, 92
databases 89, 92
decagons 190, 194
decimals 34–7, 45–6
  adding and subtracting 168, 179
  to fractions 45–6, 50
  multiplying and dividing 169, 179
  to percentages 45, 47, 51
  place values 34, 50
  putting in order 34, 50
  rounding 35, 50
denominators 37–8, 39, 42, 50
diameter 236, 248, 348, 353
dice 153, 157, 244
digital time 328, 338
directed numbers 13–14, 18
directions 313–14, 318
discrete data 82, 83, 92, 213, 232
distance/time graphs 261–2, 265
dividing 2, 5, 110, 122, 169, 179
drawing angles 125, 138

enlargement 288, 289–90, 291, 295
equations 110, 123
  with brackets 116, 117, 122
  of a curve 255, 265
  of mirror lines 281, 283, 295
  solving 114, 116–17, 118
  of straight lines 253–4, 255, 265
equilateral triangles 183, 194
equivalent fractions 37–8, 39, 41,
  50
equivalent ratio 270, 271, 278
estimating 11–12, 18, 95
  probability 158, 159, 160, 164
even numbers 140, 149
events 157, 158, 164
expanded form 145, 149
exponent form 145, 149

expressions 54–61, 66
exterior angles 182, 192, 194

factors 140, 141, 142, 149
Fibonacci sequence 198, 201
formulae 62–7, 105, 108, 343, 350
fractions 37–52
  adding 40, 41–2, 50
  using calculators 76
  to decimals 45–6, 50
  equivalent 37–8, 39, 41, 50
  improper 42
  to percentages 45, 47, 51
  simplifying 39
  subtracting 40, 41–2, 50
  using 170–1, 179
frequency diagrams 218, 221, 227,
  229, 232
frequency tables 83, 84, 85, 92
function machines 110–11, 112,
  114, 115, 122

graphs 250–67
  bar-line 214, 232
  conversion 258, 265, 267
  curved 255, 265
  real-life 258, 259, 265
  straight line 253–4, 255, 265
  travel (distance/time) 261–2, 265
  weight/height 259

heptagons 190, 194
hexagons 190, 194, 292
histograms 218

images 281, 290
imperial units 94, 97, 100, 101, 108
improper fractions 42
index notation 146–7, 149
input 110–11, 122
integers 13–14, 18
interest 174, 179
interior angles 133–5, 138, 182,
  190, 194, 292
inverse operations 110
isometric drawing 245–6
isosceles triangles 183, 185, 194

kites 186, 187, 188, 190, 194

likelihood 152, 153, 164
line symmetry 21–2, 31, 187, 194
look and see method 114, 122

maps 270, 272, 316, 322, 326, 337
mean 224–5, 227, 232
measures 94–109
measuring angles 125, 126, 138
median 224, 227, 228–9, 232
metric units 94, 97, 100, 101, 108

mirror lines 21–2, 31, 281, 283, 295
mixed numbers 41–2, 50
modal class 224, 229, 232
mode 224, 227, 228–9, 232
multiples 38, 39, 140, 141, 149
multiplying 5, 8, 110, 122
　decimals 169, 179
　expressions 54
　negative numbers 60
　by 10, 100, 1000 2, 3, 18, 36, 50

negative numbers 13–14, 18, 60
nets of solids 243–4, 248
nth term in a sequence 202, 210
number lines 13, 14, 60
number patterns 197–8, 201, 202,
　210
numbers 1–20
　big 146–7, 149
　directed 13–14, 18, 60
　expected 162, 164
　mixed 41–2, 50
　negative 13–14, 18, 60
　odd and even 140, 149
　positive 13–14, 18
　prime 141, 142, 149
　random 82
　special 140–50
　square 55, 75, 141, 144, 149
　whole 35, 50
numerators 37–8, 39, 42, 50

observation sheets 84, 85, 92
obtuse angles 124, 126, 138, 185
octagons 190, 194
odd numbers 140, 149
opposite angles 127, 132, 138
order of operations 16, 18, 75
order of rotational symmetry 26–7,
　31
outcome 153, 158, 164
output 110–11, 122

parallel lines, angles with 129–30,
　131–2, 133–4, 138, 238, 248
parallelogram 186, 187, 194
Pascal's triangle 140
patterns 197–211, 295
pentagons 190, 194, 292, 342
percentages 44–52, 171, 174–5,
　179
perimeter 55, 340, 341, 344–5, 348,
　353
perpendicular lines 238, 239, 248
pi 348, 349, 353

pictograms 213, 232
pie charts 297–9, 300, 311
place value 2, 18, 34, 50
place value charts 2, 18, 46
planes of symmetry 25, 31
plotting points on graphs 253, 265
polygons 190–6, 292
positive numbers 13–14, 18
powers 145
prime factors 141, 149
prime numbers 141, 142, 149
prisms 25, 26, 241, 243, 245–6, 248
probability 151–166
　calculating 153, 164
　estimating 158, 159, 160, 164
　scales 160–1, 164
proportion 269, 270, 274, 278
protractors 125, 126, 236, 318
pyramids 241, 248

quadrilaterals 186–90, 194, 236,
　248, 284
questionnaires 86, 87, 92

radius 236, 248, 348, 353
random numbers 82
ratio 268, 270, 271, 272, 275, 278
rectangles 56, 186, 187, 194, 236,
　343
reflection 281, 283, 291, 295
reflex angles 124, 126, 138
relative frequency 158–9, 164
rhombus 186, 187, 188, 194
right-angled triangles 183, 194
right angles 124, 128, 138
rotation 284, 291, 295
rotational symmetry 26–7, 28, 31,
　187, 194
rounding 10, 18, 35, 50, 68, 75

samples 87, 92
scale factor 288, 290, 295
scales on maps 272, 316, 318
scales, reading 102–3
scatter graphs 304–5, 311
semi circles 352
sequences 197–8, 201, 202, 210
set squares 238, 239, 248
sharing in a given ratio 275, 278
simplifying 39, 54, 58, 66
　expressions 54, 58, 66
　fractions 39
solids 25–6, 31, 241–9, 350, 353
　see also volume
solving equations 114, 116–17, 118

solving problems 78, 112
special numbers 140–50
special triangles 183, 185, 194
speed 105, 108
spheres 241, 248
square numbers 55, 75, 141, 144,
　149, 206
square roots 75, 79, 145, 149
squares (shapes) 186, 187, 194,
　236, 343, 353
straight line graphs 253–4, 255,
　265
subtracting 5, 110, 122
　decimals 168, 179
　directed numbers 14, 18
　expressions 54, 66
　fractions 40, 41–2, 50
surveys 85, 87, 88
symbols 63, 64, 66, 213
symmetry 21–32
　line 21–32, 187, 194
　planes of 25, 31
　rotational 26–7, 28, 31, 187, 194

tables 308–9, 311, 327, 333–4
tally charts 83, 84, 85, 92
tangent of a circle 236, 248
tangrams 280
terms 54, 66
　lowest 39, 40, 44, 50
　in a sequence 198, 202, 210
tessellations 292, 295
time 327–8
　problems, solving 329
　24-hour 328, 338
　zones 337–8
timetables 331, 332–3
transformations 280–96
translations 287, 291, 295
trapezium 63, 186, 187, 194
travel graphs 261–2, 265
tree diagrams 141, 149
trial and improvement 78, 79
trials 158, 159, 162, 164
triangles 31, 182–6, 190, 194
　angles of 135, 182, 194
　area of 343, 353
　drawing 236–7, 248
　special 183, 194

undoing machines 112, 122

volume 350, 353

whole numbers 35, 50